INTERNATIONAL BIBLIOGRAPHY OF THE HISTORY OF RELIGIONS

BIBLIOGRAPHIE INTERNATIONALE DE L'HISTOIRE DES RELIGIONS

INTERNATIONAL BIBLIOGRAPHY OF THE HISTORY OF RELIGIONS

BIBLIOGRAPHIE INTERNATIONALE DE L'HISTOIRE DES RELIGIONS

1973

COMPILED UNDER THE SUPERVISION OF THE EDITOR IN CHIEF OF NUMEN,
THE JOURNAL OF THE INTERNATIONAL ASSOCIATION FOR THE HISTORY OF RELIGIONS,

DOCTOR C. J. BLEEKER
Emeritus Professor of the History and Phenomenology of Religions, Amsterdam

BY

SALIH H. ALICH

PUBLISHED ON THE RECOMMENDATION OF THE INTERNATIONAL COUNCIL FOR PHILOSOPHY AND HUMANISTIC STUDIES AND WITH THE FINANCIAL SUPPORT OF UNESCO

BY

THE INTERNATIONAL ASSOCIATION FOR THE HISTORY OF RELIGIONS

TUTA SUB AEGIDE PALLAS
EJB

LEIDEN
E. J. BRILL
1979

Publié sur la recommandation du Conseil international de la philosophie et des sciences humaines avec le concours financier de l'Unesco

Subvention Unesco 1975

ISBN 90 04 05881 8

PRINTED IN THE NETHERLANDS

CONTENTS

Preface . . . VII
Abbreviations of Names of Periodicals and Series . . . IX
Unabbreviated Titles of Periodicals . . . XXI

I. GENERAL WORKS

1. Encyclopedias and Dictionaries . . . 1
2. Reference Works . . . 3
3. Psychology of Religion . . . 16
4. Philosophy of Religion . . . 18
5. Sociology of Religion . . . 21
6. Phaenomenology of Religion . . . 24
7. Collections and Miscellanies . . . 30

II. PREHISTORIC AND PRIMITIVE RELIGIONS

1. Prehistoric Religion . . . 37
2. Primitive Religions . . . 38
3. Early European Religion . . . 53

III. RELIGIONS OF ANTIQUITY

1. General and Miscellaneous Works . . . 56
2. Egypt . . . 58
3. Mesopotamia . . . 66
4. Iran . . . 74
5. Asia Minor . . . 76
6. Greek and Roman Religions . . . 79
7. Hellenistic Religions . . . 85

IV. JUDAISM

1. Scriptures . . . 93
2. Qumran (Dead Sea Scrolls) . . . 103
3. Institutions . . . 105
4. Philosophy . . . 110
5. History and General . . . 114

V. CHRISTIANITY

1. Origins . . . 120
2. Patristic Literature . . . 128
3. Apocrypha . . . 139

4. Monasticism 140
5. Churches, Theology 142

VI. ISLAM

1. Pre-Islamic Arabia 153
2. Scriptures, Early Islam 154
3. Theology and Philosophy 157
4. Mysticism 161
5. History and General 164

VII. HINDUISM 184
VIII. BUDDHISM 189
IX. CHINESE RELIGIONS 197
X. JAPANESE RELIGIONS 200
XI. MINOR RELIGIONS 202

Index. 203

PREFACE

During the last few years this compiler has received, either directly or as forwarded to him by the publisher or Professor C. J. Bleeker, a number of written offers by distinguished academic institutions or editorial boards from different countries to exchange their respective periodical publications with this annual bibliography, which is certainly an indication, among others, of the recognized value of the IBHR as a reference work in its field. Strange as it may seem, the fact is that neither the IAHR as such, nor the compiler himself have been in a position to accept such a kind offer. The compiler regrets this all the more since some of the publications offered were valuable indeed, containing articles or book reviews or even abstracts of articles from hundreds of periodicals of great importance to the bibliography, and a regular exchange would no doubt have assisted him considerably in his laborious task. It is greatly to be deplored that such an exchange could not be arranged.

This fact points to a number of serious difficulties surrounding the bibliography and its preparation, about which the readers and even some sponsors, perhaps, may have no clear or adequate picture. As, contrary to what many may believe, the IAHR has never had any research facilities of its own, nor in fact ever been successful in its genuine efforts to organize effectively international research cooperation regarding the bibliography, the compiler himself has always faced on his own the serious problem of finding the proper material to fill a sizable, comprehensive bibliography, international in scope and subject.

With the exception of a small number of current scholarly periodicals, to which the compiler has had to subscribe or which he has otherwise arranged to have constantly at his disposal, and apart from minor research material supplied to him kindly by Professor C. J. Bleeker, or in very few cases by authors or some publishers, the bulk of the material on all the subjects of the bibliography has had to be collected from periodicals or research material, located in different libraries or departments, depending on the subject or even the language; this in itself was often a serious problem, considering the restrictions and regulations found in all such institutions. Even a number of specialized bibliographies in some fields, or bibliographic surveys and *Zeitschriftenschaus*, as found in some scholarly periodicals, could not be used as easily as might be expected, not only because of a different system and arrangement, but also because of the constant necessity to verify the material likely to be useful, and to adapt it for specific use in this bibliography. All this has cost the compiler much time and labor, and has often been a cause of delay in the publication of the bibliography. The UNESCO subvention for the IBHR, while in itself extremely valuable, indeed, and as such duly appreciated, has never in fact been sufficient to cover all the expenses resulting from all the work invested during the preparation and the process of printing of each of the published volumes of the bibliography.

In view of all these mounting difficulties, both financial and technical, the compiler was very pleased to have the privilege of presenting the case of the bibliography at the General Assembly of the International Council for Philosophy and Humanistic Studies (C.I.P.S.H.), held in September 1975 in Dubrovnik, Yugoslavia; there in fact he made the suggestion, in order to ease the work on the bibliography, that a system of a regular exchange of relevant publications be established, at least among the member organizations enjoying financial support from UNESCO. In the ensuing benevolent discussion, with a full understanding on the part of the directors for the problem posed, it was concluded, however, that, since it is unlikely that the publishers, as the real owners of the publications, will be ready to supply a sufficient number of free copies for the purpose of exchange, either the member organizations themselves should appropriate such a stock of free copies, or the C.I.P.S.H. or even UNESCO should subscribe to an adequate number of publications and serve as a kind of "clearing house" for such an exchange among its member organizations.

In this connection it should be noted, though, that there is a basic difference between all the other publications on one hand and the IBHR on the other. While virtually all of the other scholarly publications supported by UNESCO are in fact carried out as an integral part of scholarly activity at different national universities or institutions, private or public, with an agreed international cooperation or division of respective research, the case with the IBHR is entirely different. So far, no national institution, private or public, has been in a position to assume the responsibility for the bibliography and provide means for the five to six months' continuous solid work by the compiler, which is necessary to produce a published volume of the bibliography, and, at the same time be subject to the statutes and regulations of a supra-national organization, such as the IAHR, or to fulfil the conditions for obtaining UNESCO support. When, for instance, after the IAHR Congress in 1960, the Blaisdell Institute in Claremont, California, seemed to be the institution to assume that responsibility, the idea proved not to be workable, because, among other things, the Institute had no up-to-date library of its own and the near-by sizable research library of the associated colleges, focusing mainly on international relations, among other fields, was nontheless inadequate to all the needs of the bibliography in all its sections. Thus the whole burden of the proper research and preparation of the bibliography in its form and full scope, as also of responsibility for it, still rested with the compiler alone. Even later the work of the compiler, due to its special nature and requirements, posed serious difficulties, because, being always a part time activity, it could never be integrated into his regular work, but very often rather clashed with it.

Nevertheless, in spite of all these difficulties, the compiler has been able to carry on his work on the bibliography, primarily because of his own interest in the subject as a special field of historical research and, also, thanks largely to the persistent interest and understanding of, as well as to the good cooperation with, Professor C. J. Bleeker and other sponsors of the IBHR. The result of the compiler's continued efforts are the volumes of the bibliographies, from the one covering the year 1960-1961 to the present one, as they are in their actual shape and form. Any deficiencies or shortcomings found in the bibliography are exclusively those of the compiler, who is himself conscious of all of them, but at the same time hopes that the readers and the sponsors in their judgments will not forget the circumstances under which the bibliography had to be compiled. He also hopes that all these problems may be better solved in the future.

Finally, it should be noted that, in agreement also with the present secretary general of the IAHR, Professor R. J. Z. Werblowsky, and the new editorial board, the IBHR shall remain unchanged in its substance, form and title page, up to the volume covering the bibliography for 1975, the year of the last IAHR Congress in Lancaster, England, with which the compiler had already planned to terminate his work and which he hopes will be published before 1980, the year of the next IAHR Congress.

December 13, 1978
Amersfoort, The Netherlands
375 Utrechtse Weg

Salih H. Alich
71305 Donje Moštre
Yugoslavia

ABBREVIATED TITLES OF PERIODICALS

AAAS: Annales Archéologiques Arabes Syriennes. Revue d'Archéologie et d'Histoire, 21 (1971).
AANL: Atti della Accademia Nazionale dei Lincei, Rendiconti, Classe di Scienze Morali, Storiche e Filologiche, 27.
AARP: Art and Archaeology Research Papers, 3-4.
AAST: Atti della Academia delle Scienze di Torino, 107.
AB: Analecta Bollandiana, 91.
AcAr: Acta Archaeologica (Budapest), 25.
AcAr(D): Acta Archaeologica (København), 44.
Acme: Annali della Facoltà di Lettere e Filosofia dell'Università degli Studi di Milano, 26.
ACUSD: Acta Classica Universitatis Scientiarum Debreceniensis, 9.
AEH: Acta Ethnographica (Budapest), 22.
AEPHEH: Annuaire, Ecole Pratique des Hautes Etudes, IVe section, Sciences Historiques et Philologiques.
AER: The American Ecclesiastical Review, 167.
AES: Archives Européennes de Sociologie, 14.
AESC: Annales, Economies, Sociétés, Civilisations, 28.
AfO: Archiv für Orientforschung, 24.
AFP: Archivum Fratrum Praedicatorum, 43.
AfrSR: African Studies Review, 16.
AHES: Archive for History of Exact Sciences, 10.
AION: Annali dell'Istituto Orientale di Napoli, n.s.23 (33).
AIPHOS: Annuaire de l'Institut de Philologie et d'Histoire Orientales et Slaves, 20.
AJ: Antiquaries Journal, 52.
AJAS: The American Journal of Arabic Studies, 1.
AJHQ: American Jewish Historical Quarterly, 62.
AJPh: American Journal of Philology, 94.
ALUOS: Annual of Leeds University Oriental Society, 7.
ALW: Archiv für Liturgiewissenschaft, 15.
AmAnth: American Anthropologist, 75.
AmIn: América Indígena, 33.
AnAnt: Anales de Antropología (México), 10.
Anadolu. Revue des Etudes d'Archéologie et d'Histoire en Turquie, 15.
ANBr: Annales de Bretagne, 80.
AnCan: L'Année Canonique, 17. (Mélanges offerts à Pierre Andrieu-Guitrancourt).
AnCl: L'Antiquité Classique, 42.
AnthL: Anthropological Linguistics, 15.

AnUSS: Andrews University Seminary Studies, 11.
AOD: Acta Orientalia (København), 35.
AOH: Acta Orientalia Academiae Scientiarum Hungaricae, 27.
Apeiron. A Journal for Ancient Philosophy and Science, 7.
APhQ: American Philosophical Quarterly, 10.
APME: Annali del Pontificio Museo Missionario Etnologico, 37.
ArAnEt: Archivio per l'Antropologia e la Etnologia, 103.
ArAs: Arts Asiatiques, 26-29.
ArchAnz: Archäologischer Anzeiger, 87/4.
Archipel. Etudes interdisciplinaires sur le monde insulindien, 5-6.
ArFi: Archivio di Filosofia (= Demitizzazione e Ideologia).
ArOr: Archiv Orientální, 41.
ArPap: Archiv für Papyrusforschung und Verwandte Gebiete, 22.
ArVöl: Archiv für Völkerkunde (Wien), 27.
AsiSt/EtAs: Asiatische Studien / Etudes Asiatiques, 27.
ASNSP: Annali della Scuola Normale Superiore di Pisa, 3.
ASR: Archives de Sociologie des Religions, XVIII, 34-35.
ASSR: Archives de Sciences Sociales des Religions, 18.
AUAE: Annales de l'Université d'Abidjan, Série F, Ethnosociologie, 3.
AUAL: Annales de l'Université d'Abidjan, Série D: Littérature, Sciences Humaines, 6.
AUBCO: Analele Universitatii Bucureşti, Serie Limbi Clasice şi Orientale, 22.
AuFu: Ausgrabungen und Funde, 18.
AUTM: Annales de l'Université de Toulouse-Le Mirail, 9.
AuÜ: Afrika und Übersee, 56.

BAEO: Boletín de la Asociación Española de Orientalistas, 9.
BAGB: Bulletin de l'Association Guillaume Budé.
BAHR: Bulletin Analytique d'Histoire Romaine, 7.
BAIPU: Bulletin of the Asia Institute, Pahlavi University, 3.
BAMPI: Bollettino d'Arte del Ministero della Pubblica Istruzione, 58.
BASOR: Bulletin of the American Schools of Oriental Research, 209-212.
BCCSP: Bolletino del Centro Camuno di Studi Preistorici, 10.
BCH: Bulletin de Correspondance Hellénique, 97.
BECh: Bibliothèque de l'Ecole des Chartes, Revue d'Erudition, 130.
BEO: Bulletin d'Etudes Orientales, 26.
BGDSL: Beiträge zur Geschichte der Deutschen Sprache und Literatur, 95.
BibAr: The Biblical Archaeologist, 36.
BibOr: Bibbia e Oriente, 15.
BibZ: Biblische Zeitschrift, 17.
BICF: Bulletin of the Iranian Culture Foundation, I/2.
BIES: Bulletin of the Institute of Ethnology, Academia Sinica (Nanking), 36.
BMML: Bulletin des Musées et Monuments Lyonnais, 5.
BMQ: The British Museum Quarterly, 37.
BMWI: Bulletin of the Prince of Wales Museum of Western India, No. 12.
BNfg: Beiträge zur Namenforschung, 8.

BogTr: Bogoslovski Trudy, 9 (1972).
BOS: Bonner Orientalistische Studien, N. S., 27/1 (Studien zum Minderheitenproblem im Islam).
BPhM: Bulletin de Philosophie Médiévale, 15.
BIFAN: Bulletin de l'Institut Fondamental d'Afrique Noire, Série B, 34 (1972), 35.
BIFAO: Bulletin de l'Institut Français d'Archéologie Orientale, 73.
BIFEA: Bulletin de l'Institut Français d'Etudes Andines, 2.
BIHR: Bibliographic Internationale de l'Histoire des Religions. (Voir aussi IBHR!).
Bijdragen. Tijdschrift voor Filosofie en Theologie, 34.
BJES: British Journal of Educational Studies, 21.
BJS: The British Journal of Sociology, 25.
BLE: Bulletin de Littérature Ecclésiastique, 73-74.
BLSMP: Bulletin de la Classe des Lettres et des Sciences Morales et Politiques, Académie Royale de Belgique, 59.
BMBey: Bulletin du Musée de Beyrouth, 24, 26.
BMHBA: Bulletin du Musée Hongrois des Beaux-Arts, 40.
BSEAA: Boletín del Seminario de Estudios de Arte y Arqueología, 39.
BSFE: Bulletin de la Société Française d'Egyptologie, no. 68.
BSHP: Bulletin de la Société de l'Histoire du Protestantisme, 118.
BSOAS: Bulletin of the School of Oriental and African Studies, University of London, 36.
BSSA: Bulletin de la Société Suisse des Americanistes, no. 37.
BSSJ: Bulletin of the Sinological Society of Japan/The Nippon Chugoku-Gakkai-Ho, No. 25.
BTLV: Bijdragen tot de Taal-, Land- en Volkenkunde, 129.
BTS: Bible et Terre Sainte, 147-157.
BulSc: Bulletin des Sciences (Bruxelles), 4.
BurMag: The Burlington Magazine, 115.
BZ: Byzantinische Zeitschrift, 66.

CahTun: Les Cahiers de Tunisie, 21 (81-82).
CAJ: Central Asiatic Journal, 17.
CAS: Contributions to Asian Studies, 3-4.
CBQ: Catholic Biblical Quarterly, 35.
CCC: Citeaux, Commentarii Cisterciences, 24.
CCM: Cahiers de Civilisation Médiévale, 16.
CCRIC: Cahiers du Centre de Recherche sur l'Imaginaire, Circé, no. 3.
CEA: Cahiers d'Etudes Africaines, 13.
CEC: Cahiers d'Etudes Cathares, 24.
CHAr: Cuadernos de Historia y Arqueologia, 23.
CherWal: Les Chercheurs de la Wallonie, 22.
ChrEg: Chronique d'Egypte, 48.
ChStPh: Chinese Studies in Philosophy, 5.
CIS: Cahiers Internationaux de Sociologie, 54.
CivCat: La Civiltà Cattolica.

CJAS: Canadian Journal of African Studies/Revue Canadienne des Etudes Africaines, 7.
CJPh: Canadian Journal of Philosophy, 2-3.
CLOS: Cahiers de Linguistique, d'Orientalisme et de Slavistique, 1-2.
ClPhl: Classical Philology, 68.
ClQuart: The Classical Quarterly, 23.
ClW: The Classical World, 66.
ColCis: Collectanea Cisterciensia, 35.
ColFr: Collectanea Franciscana, 43.
Com.: Comunicaciones (Puebla), 7.
ConAr: Connaissance des Arts, No. 256.
CouRat: Le Courrier Rationaliste, no. 303.
CRA: Cahiers des Religions Africaines, 7.
CRAIBL: Comptes rendus (des séances de l') Académie des Inscriptions et Belles Lettres, 25.
CRFO: Contacts, Revue Française de l'Orthodoxie, 25.
CSSH: Comparative Studies in Society and History, 15.
CUC: Cahiers Universitaires Catholiques, 3-6.
CuEsGa: Cuadernos de Estudios Gallegos, 28.

Daedalus. Journal of the American Academy of Arts and Sciences, 102.
DisAbIn, A: Dissertation Abstracts International, Section A, The Humanities and Social Sciences (Ann Arbor, Mich.), 33.
DR: The Downside Review, 90 (304).
DTT: Dansk Teologisk Tidsskrift, 36.

EastBud: The Eastern Buddhist, 6.
EAZ: Ethnographisch-Archäologische Zeitschrift, 14.
EcRev: The Ecumenical Review, 25.
EdCul: Education et Culture, No. 21.
EgTh: Eglise et Théologie (Ottawa), 4.
EphLit: Ephemerides Liturgicae, 87.
Eranos. Acta Philologica Suecana, 71.
EsBi: Estudios Biblicos, 32.
EsCl: Estudios Clasicos, 16 (66-67).
EsEc: Estudios Eclesiásticos, 48.
EsOr: Estudios Orientales, 8 (23).
EstAg: Estudio Agustiniano, 8.
EtBalk: Etudes Balkaniques, 9.
EtBerg: Les Etudes Bergsoniennes, 10.
EtCl: Les Etudes Classiques, 41.
EtEv: Etudes Evangéliques, 33.
EThL: Ephemerides Theologicae Lovanienses, 49.
EthnSlav: Ethnologia Slavica, 5.
EThR: Etudes Théologiques et Religieuses, 48.
EtPh: Les Etudes Philosophiques.
EvTh: Evangelische Theologie, 33.

EZZ: Ethnologische Zeitschrift Zürich (Bern), 3.

FilMis'l: Filosofska Mis'l(Sofija), 29.
FilNa: Filosofskie Nauki (Moskva), 16.
FolHum: Folia Humanistica, 10.
FZPhTh: Freiburger Zeitschrift für Philosophie und Theologie, 20.

GGA: Göttingische Gelehrte Anzeigen, 225.
GIF: Giornale Italiano di Filologia, nuova ser., 4.
GR: The Germanic Review, 48.
GraecolOr: Graecolatina et Orientalia, 5.
GRBS: Greek, Roman and Byzantine Studies, 14.
GRM: Germanisch-Romanische Monatsschrift, 23.
GTT: Gereformeerd Theologisch Tijdschrift, 73.

HispR: Hispanic Review, 41.
HoR: History of Religions. An International Journal for Comparative Historical Studies, XII, 3-4 – XIII, 1-2.
HSCPh: Harvard Studies in Classical Philology, 77.
HThR: Harvard Theological Review, 66.
HUCA: Hebrew Union College Annual, 43.
HumIs: Humaniora Islamica. An Annual Publication of Islamic Studies and the Humanities. Vol. I.
HumOr: Human Organization, 32.
HUSL: The Hirosima University Studies, Literature Department, 32.

ICI: Informations Catholiques Internationales.
ICSB: Institute of Classical Studies Bulletin, No. 20.
IF: Indogermanische Forschungen. Zeitschrift für Indogermanistik und allgemeine Sprachwissenschaft, 76.
IJMES: International Journal of Middle East Studies, 4.
IIJ: Indo-Iranian Journal, 15.
IJPhR: International Journal for Philosophy of Religion, 4.
IJR: Internationales Jahrbuch für Religionssoziologie, 8.
IKZ: Internationale Kirchliche Zeitschrift, 63.
InfArq: Información Arqueológica, 12.
Interpr: Interpretation. A Journal of Bible and Theology, 27.
IPhC: Indian Philosophy and Culture, 18.
IPhQ: International Philosophical Quarterly, 13.
IrAn: Iranica Antiqua, 10.
IsCul: Islamic Culture, 47.
IslQuart: The Islamic Quarterly, 17.
IslSt: Islamic Studies, 12.
IsMA: Islam and the Modern Age, 4.
ISOANO: Izvestija Sibirskogo Otdelenija Akademii Nauk SSSR, Serija Obščestvennyh Nauk, no. 11.
ISSJ: International Social Science Journal, 25.

IANKO: Izvestija Akademii Nauk Kazahstoj SSR, Serija Obščestvennyh Nauk (Alma Ata), 2.
IBHR: International Bibliography of the History of Religions. (See also BIHR!)
IBLA: Revue de l'Institut des Belles-Lettres Arabes (Tunis), 36.
ITED: Islam Tetkikleri Enstitusu Dergisi, 5.
IThQ: The Irish Theological Quarterly, 40.
ITK: Irodalom-történeti Közlemények (Budapest), 77.
Izvestija: Izvestija Akademii Nauk SSSR, Serija Literatury i Jazyka, 32.

JA: Journal Asiatique, 261.
JAAC: Journal of Aesthetics and Art Criticism, 31.
JAAR: Journal of the American Academy of Religion, 41.
JAAS: Journal of Asian and African Studies, 8.
JACh: Jahrbuch für Antike und Christentum, 15.
JAF: Journal of American Folklore, 86.
JAH: The Journal of African History, 14.
JAL: Journal of Arabic Literature, 4.
JANES: The Journal of the Ancient Near Eastern Society of Columbia University, 5 (= The Gaster Festschrift).
JAOS: Journal of the American Oriental Society, 93.
JAS: The Journal of Asian Studies, 32/3-4 – 33/1-2.
JASB: Journal of the Asiatic Society of Bangladesh, 18.
JBL: Journal of Biblical Literature, 92.
JCS: Journal of Cuneiform Studies, 25.
JDAI: Jahrbuch des Deutschen Archäologischen Instituts, 87.
JEA: The Journal of Egyptian Archaeology, 59.
JEB: Jahrbuch des Evangelischen Bundes, 16.
JES: Journal of Ecumenical Studies, 10.
JESHO: Journal of the Economic and Social History of the Orient, 16.
JFI: Journal of the Folklore Institute, 10.
JHA: Journal for the History of Astronomy, 4.
JHAKU: The Journal of the Historical Association of Komazawa University, no. 20.
JHI: Journal of the History of Ideas, 34.
JHKRAS: Journal of the Hong-Kong Branch of the Royal Asiatic Society, 13.
JHMAS: Journal of the History of Medicine and Allied Sciences (New Haven, Conn., USA), 28.
JHPh: Journal of the History of Philosophy, 11.
JIBS: Journal of Indian and Buddhist Studies, 22.
JIES: The Journal of Indo-European Studies, I.
JIH: Journal of Indian History, 51.
JJE: The Japanese Journal of Ethnology, 38.
JJS: The Jewish Journal of Sociology, 15.
JMVL: Jahrbuch des Museums für Völkerkunde zu Leipzig, 29.
JNES: Journal of Near Eastern Studies, 32.
JoJeS: The Journal of Jewish Studies, 24.
JOR: The Journal of Oriental Research (Madras), 34-35.

JPHS: Journal of the Pakistan Historical Society, 21.
JPS: The Journal of the Polynesian Society, 82.
JQR: The Jewish Quarterly Review, 63/3-4 – 64/1-2.
JR: The Journal of Religion, 53.
JRA: Journal of Religion in Africa, 5.
JRAS: Journal of the Royal Asiatic Society.
JRCI: Journal of the Regional Cultural Institute, 6.
JReS: Journal of Religious Studies (Tokyo), 46-47.
JRH: Journal of Religion and Health, 12.
JRS: The Journal of Roman Studies, 63.
JRTh: The Journal of Religious Thought, 30.
JSFO: Journal de la Société Finno-Ougrienne, 72.
JSJ: Journal for the Study of Judaism, 4.
JSO: Journal de la Société des Océanistes, 29.
JSS: Journal of Semitic Studies, 18.
JSSR: Journal for the Scientific Study of Religion, 12.
JSWASS: Journal of the South West Africa Scientific Society, 27.
JThS: The Journal of Theological Studies, 24.
JUB: Journal of the University of Bombay, 41 (1972).
JYA: Journal of Youth and Adolescence, 2.

KD: Kerygma und Dogma, 19.
Kêmi. Revue de Philologie et d'Archéologie Egyptiennes et Coptes, 21.
Kratylos. Kritisches Berichts- und Rezensionsorgan für indogermanische und allgemeine Sprachwissenschaft, 16.

LingBib: Linguistica Biblica, 21-28.
LitJb: Liturgisches Jahrbuch.
LM: Lutherische Monatshefte, 12.

MAGW: Mitteilungen der Anthropologischen Gesellschaft in Wien, 102.
Maia. Rivista di Letterature Classiche, 25.
Man. The Journal of the Royal Anthropological Institute, 8.
MCV: Mélanges de la Casa de Velazques, 9, (Paris, Boccard).
MDAIK: Mitteilungen des Deutschen Archäologischen Instituts, Abteilung Kairo, 29.
MedWelt: Die Medizinische Welt (Stuttgart), Nr. 7.
MEFRA: Mélanges de l'Ecole Française de Rome, Série: Antiquité, 85.
MEMO: Mirowaja Ekonomika i Meždunarodnye Otnošenija, Moskva.
MKNAW: Mededelingen der Koninklijke Nederlandse Akademie van Wetenschappen, afd. Letterkunde, 36.
MMHUL: Mémoires du Musée Historique de l'Université de Lund, 1971-1972.
MoNi: Monumenta Nipponica, 28.
MonSer: Monumenta Serica, Journal of Oriental Studies, 29, 30.
MSR: Mélanges de Science Religieuse, 30.
MSS: Münchener Studien zur Sprachwissenschaft, 31.
Mundus. A Quarterly Review of German Research, 9.

MusHel: Museum Helveticum, 30.
MUSJ: Mélanges de l'Université Saint Joseph (Beyrouth), 47.
MW: The Muslim World, 63.

Nachrichten der Akademie der Wissenschaften in Göttingen, Philosophisch-historische Klasse, 2-5.
NAK: Nederlands Archief voor Kerkgeschiedenis, nieuwe serie, 53.
NaRel: Nauka i Religija (Moskva), Nos. 1-6.
NAWG: Nachrichten der Akademie der Wissenschaften in Göttingen, Philologisch-historische Klasse.
NeTT: Nederlands Theologisch Tijdschrift, 27.
NKK: Nihonbunka-Kenkyusho-Kiyo (Tokyo), No. 31.
NoTes: Novum Testamentum, 15.
NouCa: Les Nouveaux Cahiers, 8 (No. 31-34).
NRTh: Nouvelle Revue Théologique, 95.
NTA: New Testament Abstracts, 17.
NTS: New Testament Studies, 19.
NZMW: Neue Zeitschrift für Missionswissenschaft.
NZSTh: Neue Zeitschrift für Systematische Theologie und Religionsphilosophie, 15.

OC: Oriens Christianus, 57.
OChP: Orientalia Christiana Periodica, 39.
OERE: Orientations. Essais et Recherches en Education, 13.
OGE: Ons Geestelijk Erf (Antwerpen), 47.
OGN: Oosters Genootschap in Nederland (Leiden).
OJRS: Ohio Journal of Religious Studies, 1.
ÖkRs: Ökumenische Rundschau, 22.
OLP: Orientalia Lovaniensia Periodica, 4.
OLZ: Orientalistische Literaturzeitung, 68.
OM: Oriente Moderno, 53.
OrAn: Oriens Antiquus, 12.
Orient. Report of the Society for Near Eastern Studies in Japan, 8.
OrSu: Orientalia Suecana, 21, 22.
OudhMed: Oudheidkundige Mededelingen uit het Rijksmuseum van Oudheden te Leiden, 52.
ÖZV: Österreichische Zeitschrift für Volkskunde, 27 (76).

PAAJR: Proceedings of the American Academy for Jewish Research, 40.
PalSb: Palestinskij Sbornik, no. 24.
ParPas: La Parola del Passato, 148-149, 151.
PEQ: Palestine Exploration Quarterly, 105.
PesAn: Pesquisas Antropologia, 25.
PhEW: Philosophy East and West, 23.
PhF: The Philosophical Forum, 4.
PhilPer: Philosophische Perspektiven, 5.
PhJ: The Philosophical Journal, 10.

PhLtAnz: Philosophischer Literaturanzeiger, 26.
PhQCS: Philippine Quarterly of Culture and Society, 1.
PhRef: Philosophia Reformata, 38 (dedicated to D. H. Th. Vollenhoven).
PlAnth: Plains Anthropologist, 18.
POF: Prilozi za Orijentalnu Filologiju (Sarajevo), 18-19.
PpAfr: Psychopathologie Africaine, 9.
PPhJ: Pakistan Philosophical Journal, 11.
PRAIGBI: Proceedings of the Royal Anthropological Institute of Great Britain and Ireland.
PrOCh: Proche-Orient Chrétien, 23.
Proteus. Rivista de Filosofia, 4 (11-12).
PUR: Peshawar University Review, I.

RAAO: Revue d'Assyriologie et d'Archéologie Orientale, 67.
RABM: Revista de Archivos, Bibliotecas y Museos, 76.
RACF: Revue Archéologique du Centre de la France, 12.
RAECE: Revue Archéologique de l'Est et du Centre-Est, 24.
RAHAL: Revue des Archéologues et Historiens d'Art de Louvain, 6.
RAN: Revue Archéologique Narbonnaise, 6.
RAQBI: Recherches Amérindiennes au Québec, Bulletin d'Information, 3.
RAr: Revue Archéologique, fasc. 2.
RBPhH: Revue Belge de Philologie et d'Histoire, 51.
RCCM: Rivista di Cultura Classica e Medioevale, 15.
RchSR: Recherches de Science Religieuse, 61.
RDC: Revue de Droit Canonique, 23.
RDCCIF: Recherches et Débats du Centre Catholique des Intellectuels Français, 79.
REAg: Revue des Etudes Augustuniennes, 19.
REArm: Revue des Etudes Armeniennes, 9 (1972).
ReBén: Revue Bénédictine, 83.
REByz: Revue des Etudes Byzantines, 31.
RechGer: Recherches Germaniques, No. 3.
REF: Revista de Etnografie si Folclor, 18.
ReGui: Revista de Guimarães, 83.
REI: Revue des Etudes Islamiques, 41.
REL: Revue des Etudes Latines, 50.
RelEd: Religious Education, 68.
RelSoc: Religion and Society (Bangalore), 19 (1972) – 20.
RelSt: Religious Studies, 9.
ReMet: The Review of Metaphysics, 26-27/1.
RevEg: Revue d'Egyptologie, 25.
RevEsp: Revista de Espiritualidad, 32.
RevRef: La Revue Réformée, 24-26.
RevSR: Revue des Sciences Religieuses, 47.
RFEE: Revue Française de l'Elite Européenne.
RFNS: Rivista di Filosofia Neo-Scolastica, 65.
RFS: Revue Française de Sociologie, 14.

RGE: Revue Géographique de l'Est, 13.
RHA: Revue Hittite et Asianique, 29.
RHCM: Revue d'Histoire et de Civilisation de Maghreb, 10.
RHE: Revue d'Histoire Ecclesiastique, 68.
RhJV: Rheinisches Jahrbuch für Volkskunde, 21.
RHMH: Revue d'Histoire de la Médecine Hébraïque, 101-102.
RHPhR: Revue d'Histoire et de Philosophie Religieuses, 53.
RHR: Revue de l'Histoire des Religions, 183-184.
RHS(=RAM): Revue d'Histoire de la Spiritualité (= Revue d'Ascétique et de Mystique), 49.
RHT: Revue d'Histoire des Textes, 3.
RIC: Répertoire bibliographiques des institutions chrétienne, 6.
RIDA: Revue Internationale des Droits de l'Antiquité, 20.
RIE: Revista de Ideas Esteticas, 31.
RIEI: Revista del Instituto de Estudios Islámicos (Madrid), 17.
RLC: Revue de Littérature Comparée, 47.
RLMF: Revue du Louvre et des Musées de France, 23.
RMM: Revue de Métaphysique et de Morale, 78.
RMPh: Rheinisches Museum für Philologie, 116.
RO: Rocznik Orientalistyczny, 35.
ROMM: Revue de l'Occident Musulman et de la Méditerranée, 13-14.
RPhFE: Revue Philosophique de la France et de l'Etranger, 98.
RPhL: Revue Philosophique de Louvain, 71.
RPhLHA: Revue de Philologie, de Littérature et d'Histoire Ancienne, 47.
RQ: Revue de Qumran, 8 (30).
RQChAK: Römische Quartalschrift für Christliche Altertumskunde und Kirchengeschichte, 68.
RRFC: Rivista Rosminiana di Filosofia e di Cultura, 67.
RSC: Rivista di Studi Classici, 21.
RSF: Rivista di Studi Fenici, 1.
RSJB: Recueils de la Société Jean Bodin, 31.
RSLR: Rivista di Storia e Letteratura Religiosa, 9.
RSO: Rivista degli Studi Orientali, 47 (1972).
RSPhTh: Revue des Sciences Philosophiques et Théologiques, 57.
RThPh: Revue de Théologie et de Philosophie, 23.
RUB: Revue Universitaire du Burundi, 1.
RuSo: Rural Sociology, 38.

Sap: Sapienza. Rivista Internationale di Filosofia e di Teologia, 26.
SBF: Studii Biblici Franciscani Liber Annuus, 23.
SCR: Studies in Comparative Religion, 7.
SEER: The Slavonic and East European Review, 51.
SFQ: Southern Folklore Quarterly, 37.
SGG: Studia Germanica Gandensia, 14.
SIDJCh: Service International de Documentation Judéo-Chrétienne, 6.
SIF: Studi Internazionali di Filosofia, 5.
SJTh: Scottish Journal of Theology, 26.

SMAE: Sbornik Muzeja Antropologii i Etnografii, 29.
SMJ: The Sarawak Museum Journal, 20 (1972).
SoCoR: Social Compass, Revue Internationale des Etudes Socio – Religieuse, 20.
SocRev: The Sociological Review, 21.
Sophia. A Journal for Discussion in Philosophical Theology, 12.
SovAr: Sovetskaja Arheologija.
SovEtn: Sovetskaja Etnografija, 1-6.
StFil: Studia Filozoficzne, 17.
SThV: Studia Theologica Varsaviensia, 11.
StMis: Studia Missionalia, 22 (= "Sacerdoce et prophétie dans le Christianisme et les autres religions").
StN: Studia Neophilologica, 45.
StPh: Studia Philosophica, 32.
StRel: Studies in Religion, 3.
Studia i Prace / Etudes et Travaux, 14.
StuIr: Studia Iranica, 2.
StuIs: Studia Islamica, 37-38.
StuMon: Studia Monastica 15.
StuPap: Studia Papyrologica, 12.
StuRos: Studia Rosenthaliana, 7.
StuTh: Studia Theologica, 27.
STY: Sanat Tarihi Yıllığı, 5.
Sumer. A Journal of Archaeology and History in Iraq, 29.

TF: Tijdschrift voor Filosophie, 35.
Theokratia. Jahrbuch des Institutum Judaicum Delitzschianum, 2 (= Festgabe für Karl Heinrich Rengstorf).
ThG: Theologie und Glaube, 63.
ThLZ: Theologische Literaturzeitung, 98.
ThPh: Theologie und Philosophie, 48.
ThPrQ: Theologisch-Praktische Quartalschrift, 121.
ThQ: Theologische Quartalschrift, 153.
ThRsch: Theologische Rundschau, 38.
ThSt: Theological Studies, 34.
ThT: Theology Today, 30.
ThV: Theologia Viatorum, 11.
ThZ: Theologische Zeitschrift, 29.
TLQ: Temple Law Quarterly, 46.
TNR: Tanzania Notes and Records, 72.
TrvMém: Travaux et Mémoires (Centre de Recherche d'Histoire et Civilisations de Byzance), 5.
TSV: Tijdschrift voor de Studie van de Verlichting, 1.
TThZ: Trierer Theologische Zeitschrift, 82.

VDI: Vestnik Drevnej Istorii, 124-125.
VetChr: Vetera Christianorum, 10.
VeTes: Vetus Testamentum, 23.

VigChr: Vigiliae Christianae, 27.
VitaMon: Vita Monastica, 27.
VMUF: Vestnik Moskovskogo Universiteta, Filosofija, No. 3.
VON: Vestnik Obščestvennyh Nauk (Erevan), no. 8.
VV: Vizantijskij Vremennik, 34.

WI: Die Welt des Islams, 14.
WissWb: Wissenschaft und Weltbild, 26.
WissWeis: Wissenschaft und Weisheit, 36.
WO: Die Welt des Orients. Wissenschaftliche Beiträge zur Kunde des Morgenlandes, 7.
WorldAr: World Archaeology, 5.
WortWahr: Wort und Wahrheit, 28.
WThJ: The Westminster Theological Journal, 35.
WZKS: Wiener Zeitschrift für die Kunde Südasiens und Archiv für indische Philosophie, 17.

ZATW: Zeitschrift für die Alttestamentliche Wissenschaft, 85.
ZÄSA: Zeitschrift für Ägyptische Sprache und Altertumskunde, 99-100.
ZAVA: Zeitschrift für Assyriologie und vorderasiatische Archäologie, 29 (63).
ZDMG: Zeitschrift der Deutschen Morgenländischen Gesellschaft, 123.
ZDPV: Zeitschrift des Deutschen Palästina-Vereins, 89.
ZE: Zeitschrift für Ethnologie, 98.
ZEE: Zeitschrift für Evangelische Ethik, 17.
ZentSt: Zentralasiatische Studien (Wiesbaden), 7.
ZGJ: Zeitschrift für die Geschichte der Juden (Tel-Aviv), 10.
ZKG: Zeitschrift für Kirchengeschichte, 84.
ZKTh: Zeitschrift für Katholische Theologie, 95.
ŽMP: Žurnal Moskovskoj Patriarhii.
ZMRW: Zeitschrift für Missionswissenschaft und Religionswissenschaft, 57.
ZOfg: Zeitschrift für Ostforschung, 22.
ZRGG: Zeitschrift für Religions- und Geistesgeschichte, 25.
ZsBalk: Zeitschrift für Balkanologie, 7.
ZThK: Zeitschrift für Theologie und Kirche, 70.
ZVS: Zeitschrift für vergleichende Sprachforschung (Göttingen), 86.

UNABBREVIATED TITLES OF PERIODICALS

Aegyptus, 53.
Aevum, 47.
Afghanistan, 25-26.
Africa (London), 43.
Africa (Roma), 28.
African Studies, 32.
Africa Quarterly, 12.
Africa-Tervuren, 19.
Das Altertum, 19.
Ambix, 20.
Ampurias, 33-34.
Anadolu/Anatolia, 17.
al-Andalus, 38.
Annales de Bretagne, 80.
L'Année Philologique, 42.
Anthropologica, N.S., 15.
Antike Kunst, 16.
Antike Welt (Zürich), 4.
Antik Tanulmányok, 20.
Antropológica, 34.
Apulum, no. 9 (1971).
Arabica, 20.
Archaeology, 26.
Archeologia (Fr.), 55-60.
Das Argument, 15.
Archeologija (Bulg.), 15.
Ariel, no. 28.
Ars Orientalis, 9.
Art Bulletin, 55.
Asia Major, 18.
Asian Affairs, N.S. 4 (60).
Athenaeum, 51.
Augustiniana, 23.
Augustinianum, 12, 13.
Augustinus, 18.
Aut Aut (Firenze), 134.

Balcanica, 4.
Belleten, 37.
Benedictines, 28.
Berytus, 22.
Biblica (Roma), 54.
Bunka (Sendai), 37.
Bunken Ruimoku, March No.
Byzantinoslavica, 34.
Byzantion, 42.

Cahiers d'Histoire, 18.
Catholica, 27.
Centaurus, 17.
Chinese Culture, 14.
Christus (Paris), 20.
Church History, 42.
Ciencia Tomista, 100.
La Ciudad de Dios, 186.
Comunita (Milano), 27.
Concilium, 81-89.
Conimbriga, 12.
Critique (Paris), 29.
Cultura Turcica, 8-10.
Cultures (Paris), I.
Cultures et Foi, 25.

Dacia, 17.
Diogenes/Diogène, 81-84.
Diotima, 1.
Divinitas, 17.
The Downside Review, 91.

East and West, 23.
Emerita, 41.
Eranos-Jahrbuch, 39-40.
Erasmus, 25.
Erbe und Auftrag, 49.
Esprit, 40-41.
Ethnographia, 84.
L'Ethnographie, N.S., 66-67.
Ethnology, 12.
Ethnomedizin, 1 (1971), 2 (1972).
Ethnomusicology, 17.
Ethnos (Stockholm), 38.
Etudes (Paris).
Etudes de Lettres, 6.
Etyka (Warszawa), no. 12.
Euhemer, 17.
Expedition, 15.

Faith and Thought, 100.
Filosofia (Torino), 24.
Foi et Vie, 72.
Folklore (Calcutta), 14.
Folklore (London), 84.

Gallia, 31.
Germania, 51.
Glotta (Göttingen), 51.
Gnomon (München), 45.
Göttingen Miszellen, H. 5-8.
Gregorianum, 54.
Gregorios Palamas, 56.

Hegel Studien, Beiheft 9.
Helmántica, 24 (75).
Hermes, 101.
Hispania Antiqua, 3.
Historia, 22.
History and Theory, 12.
L'Homme (Paris), 13.
Homo (Göttingen), 24.
Humanitas (Brescia, Italia), 28.

Humanitas (Pittsburg), 9.

Iqbal Review, 14.
Iran (London), 11.
Iraq, 35.
Irian (Djakarta), 2.
Isis, 64.
Der Islam, 50.
Istina (Paris), 17-18.
Izraz (Sarajevo), 17.

Journal des Savants.
Journal of Thought, 8.
Judaica (Zürich), 29.
Judaism (New York), 22.

Kinesis, 5.
Kirjath Sepher, 48.
Kleronomia, 5-6.
Klio, 55.

Latomus, 32.
Laurentianum, 14.
Levant, 5.
Liberté (Montreal), 87-88.
Listy Filologické, 96.

Maison-Dieu, 114-115.
Man in India, 53.
Marg, 26.
Missi (Lyon), No. 1-10.
Mnemosyne, 26.
Moana (Montevideo), 1.
Montalban, 2.
Le Muséon, 86.

Naše Starine, 13 (1972).
Nauka i Religija (Moskva).
Neophilologus, 57.
Nouvelle Ecole, 21-22.
Numen (Leiden), 20.

Objets et Mondes, 13.
Oceania (Sydney), 43/3-4 – 44/1-2.
One in Christ, 9.
Orbis (Louvain), 22.
Orientalia, 42.

El Palacio, 79.
Pensamiento, 29.
La Pensée et les Hommes, 17/4-5.
il Pensiero, 18.
Perficit, 4 (64-65).
Philosophy Today, 17.
Phoenix (N), 19.
Phronesis, 18.
Process Studies, 3.
Proverbium, 22.
Pyrenae, 9.

Les Quatre Fleuves, no. 1.

Reformatio, 22.
Religion, 3.
Renovatio, 8.
Revue Biblique, 80.
Revue Thomiste, 73.
Rivista Biblica, 21.

Salesianum, 35.
Sapientia (La Plata), 28.
Sapienza, 26.
Scando-Slavica, 18.
Sciences Sociales (Moskva).
Scientia (Milano), 108 (9-12).
Sefarad, 33.
Semitica, 22-23.
Sewanee Review, 81.
Sociologus, 23.
Die Sprache, 19.
Staden-Jahrbuch, 20 (1972).
Stimmen der Zeit, 191.
Stromata, 29.
Studia Religioznawcze, no. 8.
Studies in Islam, 10.
Studi Romani, 21.
Studii Clasice, 15.
Studii Teologice, 25 (9-10).
Studium, 69.
Sudhoffs Archiv, 57.
Symposium, 27.
Syria, 49-50.

Tarbiz, 41.
Temenos, 9.
Te Reo (New Zealand), 16.
Terra Ameriga, 9 (29-30).
Theologia (Athinzi), 44.
The Toho Shukyo, no. 42.
T'oung Pao, 59.
Tradition, 13-14.
Tribus, 22.
Turcica, 3.

Universidad (Arg.), 82.
L'Universo (Firenze), 53.

Vav. Revue du Dialogue, 7.
Verbum SVD, 14.
Volkskunde (Antwerpen), 74.
Voprosy Filosofii (Moskva).
Voprosy istorii (Moskva).

Wiener Studien, 7.

I. GENERAL WORKS

1. ENCYCLOPEDIAS AND DICTIONARIES

The Assyrian Dictionary of the Oriental Institute of the University of Chicago. Editorial board: Miguel Civil, Ignace J. Gelb, A. Leo Oppenheim, Erica Reiner. Volume 9: L. (Chicago, Oriental Institute. Glückstadt, J. J. Augustin). 4to. xx, 260 p. (Vol. 8: K, 1971, xx, 618 p.)

Biographisches Lexikon zur Geschichte Südosteuropas. Lfg. 1 und 2/3. (München, R. Oldenbourg-Verlag). 336 S. = Südosteuropäische Arbeiten, 75, 1 und 2/3.

Dictionnaire de Spiritualité Ascétique et Mystique. (Paris, Beauchesne). Tome 8, fasc. LIV-LV.

Eliade, Mircea: "Dictionaries and Encyclopedias", *HoR* XII/3, 288-295. (A review of S. G. F. Brandon, ed., *Dictionary of Comparative Religion*, and A. M. di Nola, ed., *Enciclopedia delle religioni*, vol. 1-3).

Enciclopedia delle religioni. 5 vol. ("Abacuc" – "Tupi-Guarani"). (Firence, Vallechi). quarto. Vol. 1 (1970): 1xxix p., 1734 col. Vol. 2 (1971) xi p., 1794 col. Vol. 3 (1971): xi p., 1894 col. Vol. 4 (1972): xi p., 1954 col. Vol. 5: xi, 1878 col. Illus.

Encyclopaedia of Islam. New Edition. Prepared by a number of leading Orientalists. Under the patronage of the International Union of Academies. Fasc. 61-64: "Irān" – "Istiḥsān and istiṣlāḥ". (Leiden, E. J. Brill). 256 p., 2 sketchmaps (1 fold.), 8 pl.

Encyclopédie de l'Islam. Nouvelle édition. Etablie avec le concours des principaux Orientalistes. Sous le patronage de l'Union Académique Internationale. Livr. 61-64: "Irān" – "Istanbul". (Paris, Editions G.-P. Maisonneuve et Larose. Leiden, E. J. Brill). 256 p., croquis de carte, plan dépl., 8. pl.

Fatás, G. – G. M. Borrás: *Diccionario de términos de arte, elementos de arqueología y numismatica.* (Zaragoza, Anatole). 260 p., 37 pl.

Fohrer, Georg (Hrsg.): *Hebräisches und aramäisches Wörterbuch zum Alten Testament.* (Berlin, 1971). – R: *OLZ* 68, 368-370 (G. Pfeifer).

Friedrich, G.: "Das bisher noch fehlende Begriffslexikon zum Neuen Testament", *NTS* 19/2, 127-152.

Grant, M'chael and John Hazel (ed.): *Who's Who in Classical Mythology.* (London, Weidenfeld and Nicholson). 4to. 446 p., 400 illus. (partly col.), 5 maps, 11 tables.

Handbuch der Religionsgeschichte. Hrsg. von J. P. Asmussen und J. Laessøe in Verbinding mit C. Colpe. Band I. (IBHR, 1971). – R: *Gregorianum* 54, 198-199 (M. Dhavamony). *RHR* 183, 193-194 (J.-P. Roux) *NRTh* 95, 783-784 (J. Scheuer). *ThLZ* 98, 418 (K. Rudolph).

Histoire des Religions. I: *Les Religions Antiques, La Formation des Religions Universelles et des Religion de Salut en Inde et en Extrême Orient.* Publié sous la direction d'Henri-Ch. Puech. (Encyclopédie de la Pleiade). – R: *NRTh* 95, 783-784 (J. Scheuer); *ThLZ* 98, 401-418 (K. Rudolph).

Historia Religionum. Handbook for the History of Religions. Edited by C. J. Bleeker and G. Widengren. Vol. I. Religions of the Past. – R: *NRTh* 95, 781-783 (J. Scheuer). *ThLZ* 98, 401-418 (K. Rudolph).

Lexicon der Ágyptologie. Herausgegeben von Wolfgang Helck und Otto Eberhard. Band I. Lieferung 1 (1972): Allgemeine Abkürzungen – Altes Testament. Lfg. 2 bis 5: Altes Testament – Bildhauer. (Wiesbaden, Otto Harrassowitz). In 4°. xxvii pp., Sp. 1-800, illus.

Lexicon der Arabischen Welt. Ein historisch-politisches Nachschlagewerk von Stephan und Nandy Ronart. (Überarbeitung, Ergänzung und Hinweise: Fritz Hofer, Hans-Jürgen Kornrumpf et al. (Zürich, 1972). – R: *BiOr* 30, 101-102 (S. Balić). (See also a brief review by the editors, *ibid.*, p. 337a).

Lexicon der christilichen Ikonographie. Hrsg. von E. Kirschbaum. I: Allgemeine Ikonographie. A – Ezechiel. (Rom usw., 1968). – R: *OLZ* 68, 362-364 (Hans Bardtke).

Lexicon in Veteris Testamenti Libros. Supplementum. Ediderunt L. Koehler et W. Baumgartner. (Leiden, E. J. Brill). xl, 227 p. (Photomechan. reprint of the original edition, 1958).

Lexicon in Veteris Testamenti Libros. Wörterbuch zum hebräischen Alten Testament in deutscher und englischer Sprache. A Dictionary of the Hebrew Old Testament in English and German. Edidit L. Koehler. *Wörterbuch zum aramäischen Teil des Alten Testaments in deutscher und englischer Sprache. A Dictionary of the Aramaic Parts of the Old Testament in English and German.* Edidit W. Baumgartner. (Leiden, E. J. Brill). lxvi, 1138 p. (Photomech. reprint of the edition, 1958).

Lurker, Manfred: *Wörterbuch biblischer Bilder und Symbole.* (München, Kösel Verlag). 436 S. = Reihe: Biblische Handbibliothek.

Miller, Madeleine S. and J. Lane Miller (ed.): *Black's Bible Dictionary.* In Consultation with Eminent Authorities. Eighth Edition. (London, A. and C. Black). x, 853 p., 18 maps, illus.

Reallexikon der Assyriologie und vorderasiatischen Archäologie. Nach E. Ebeling, B. Meissner, E. Weidner, unter Mitwirkung von P. Calmeyer, A. Moortgat, H. Otten, W. Röllig, W. von Soden, D. J. Wiseman, herausgegeben von D. O. Edzard. Vierter Band, Zweite und Dritte Lieferung: "Handel-Hazazu". (Berlin, W. de Gruyter). S. 81-240.

Rinaldi, G.: "L'*Enciclopedia delle Religioni*", *Bibbia e Oriente* 15/4-5, 209-214.

von Soden, Wolfram: *Akkadisches Handwörterbuch.* Unter Benutzung des lexikalischen Nachlasses von Bruno Meissner (1868-1947). Lieferung 9: 1969, und Lieferung 10: 1971. – R: *BiOr* 30, 57-58 (René Labat).

Storia delle Religioni. 5 volumi. Fondata da Pietro Tacchi Venturi. Diretta da Giuseppe Castellani. 6a ed. interamente rifatta e ampilata. (Torino, Unione Tipografico-Editrice Torinese, 1971). 1: xx, 776 p., 317 illus. 2: xvi, 724 p., 326 illus. 3: xi, 793 p., 343 illus. 4: xv, 895 p., 339 illus. 5: xv, 949 p., 283 illus. 4°. – R: *ThLZ* 98, 401-418 (K. Rudolph). *Anthropos* 68, 311-312 (Karl Hoheisel).

Theologisches Handwörterbuch zum Alten Testament. Herausgegeben von Ernst Jenni, unter Mitarbeit von Claus Westermann. Band I. (München, 1971). – R: *BiOr* 30, 88-89 (Charles T. Fritsch).

Wörterbuch der Mythologie. Herausgegeben von Hans Wilhelm Haussig. 1. Abt.: *Die alten Kulturvölker.* Band 2: *Götter und Mythen im Alten Europa.* (Stuttgart, Ernst Klett Verlag). xxiii, 876 p., illus.

2. REFERENCE WORKS

Afshar, Iraj und Hosein Banī-Ādam: *Ketāb-šenāsī-ye dah-sāle-ye (KŠD) 1333-1342 ketābhā-ye īrān* (Zehn Jahre Bibliographie 1954/55-1964/65 der Bücher Irans). (Teheran, 1346). – R: *OLZ* 68, 61-63 (B. Alavi).

"Afghanistan terre de tous les temps et les temps de l'oubli", *Missi* (Lyon), no. 3, 76-97. (Le bouddhisme, le christianisme et l'islam en Afghanistan).

"Annual Bibliography of Oriental Studies for 1971", *Bunken Ruimoku* (1971), March, 3-377. (In Japanese).

Annual Egyptological Bibliography / Bibliographie Egyptologique Annuelle. Part 23: 1969. Compiled by J. J. Janssen. (Leiden, E. J. Brill). xii, 211 p.

Arab Culture and Society in Change. A Partially Annotated Bibliography of Books and Articles in English, German, French, and Italian. Compiled by the Staff of CEMAM, = *C*entre d'*E*tudes pour le *M*onde *A*rabe *M*oderne, Université St. Joseph, Beirut. (Beirut, Dar el-Mashreq Publishers). xlii, 318 p. = CEMAM, Publications, 1.

van Baaren, Th. P.: "Science of Religion as a Systematic Discipline. Some Introductory Remarks", in: *Religion, Culture and Methodology* (q. v. sub I-7), 35-56. ("References", pp. 54-56).

Balic, Smail: "Necrologie: Gustav Edmund von Grunebaum, 1. 9. 1909-27. 2. 1972. Mensch und Gelehrter" [mit einer Liste seiner Schriften], *BiOr* 30, 307-314. (Die "Auswahlbibliographie" beträgt 181 Titel).

Bardtke, H.: "Zeitschriftenschau: Nouvelle Revue Théologique 103 (Band 93), 1971", *OLZ* 68, 420-421.

Barthélemy, D. und O. Rickenbacher (ed.): *Konkordanz zum hebräischen Sirach mit syrisch-hebräischem Index*. Im Auftrag des Biblischen Instituts der Universität Freiburg/Schweiz herausgegeben. (Göttingen, Vandenhoeck & Ruprecht). vi, 432, 78 S.

Bateni, N. R.: "Kinship terms in Persian", *Anthropological Linguistics* 15, 324-327.

Bausani, Alessandro: *The Persians. From the Earliest Days to the Twentieth Century*. Translated from the Italian by J. B. Donne. (New York, St. Martin's Press). – R: *JAOS* 93, 368-369 (J. A. Bellamy).

Bayer, Oswald: *Was ist das: Theologie. Eine Skizze*. (Stuttgart, Calwer Verlag). 116 S. (Brief note: *BiOr* 30, 123).

Bazin, L.: "Les études turques", *Journal Asiatique* 261, 137-143.

Behrsing, S.: "Zeitschriftenschau: Asiatische Studien (Etudes Asiatiques) 25, 1971", *OLZ* 68, 543-535.

Behrsing, S.: "Zeitschriftenschau: Journal Asiatique 258, 1970", *OLZ* 68, 419-420.

Benoit, A., E. Frézouls, R. Ganghoffer et H. Jouffroy: "Histoire romaine", *BAHR* 7, 1-755. (Ch. 7. Histoire religieuse: paganisme, judaïsme, christianisme).

Bernard, P.: *Fouilles d'ai Khanoum. I: Campagnes 1965, 1966, 1967, 1968*. Rapport Préliminaire publié avec le concours de R. Desparmet, J. C. Gardin, P. Gouin, A. de Lapparent, M. le Berre, G. le Rider, L. Robert, R. Stucki. 1: Texte et Figures. 2: Planches. (Paris, Klincksieck). 4to. xi, 246 p., 48 fig. et 25 p., 143 pl. et cartes. = Mémoires de la Délégation Archéologique Française en Afghanistan, XXI.

Bianchi, Ugo.: "Il dualismo come categoria storico-religiosa", *Rivista di Storia e Letteratura Religiosa* 9/1, 3-16.

"Bibliographie Internationale de Sociologie des Religions./International Bibliography of Sociology of Religion", *SoCoR* 20/1, 85-89.

"Bibliographie von Professor Dr. Endre von Ivanka", *Kairos* 15, Heft 3-4, 319-323.

"Bibliography of the Writings of Father Georges Florovsky", in: *The Heritage of the Early Church, Essays in Honor of G. V. Florovsky* (q. v. sub I-7), 437-451.

Bijlefeld, W. Az: "Introducing Islam: a bibliographical survey", *The Muslim World*, 63, 171-184, 269-279.

Bissoli, C.: "Rivista delle riviste", *Rivista Biblica* 21/1, 3-112.

Blondeau, A. M.: "Les études tibétaines", *Journal Asiatique* 261, 153-174.

Blumenthal, E. und Mitarbeiter: "Zeitschriftenschau: Journal of the American Research Center in Egypt 7, 1968", *OLZ* 68, 418-419.

van Bourgondiën, W.: "Bibliographie internationale de sociologie des religions", *SoCoR* 20/4, 605-608.

du Bourguet, Pierre: "Bibliographie copte. 22 (1972-1973)", *Orientalia* 42, 79*-97*. (228 titres, index).

Bouttier, M.: "Bulletin de Nouveau Testament", *EThR* 48, no. 2, 207-232 (fin).

Brandon, S. G. F.: *Religion in Ancient History. Studies in Ideas, Men and Events.* (London, George Allen & Unwin). xiv, 412 p., illus.

Brock, S. P., C. T. Fritsch and S. Jellicoe: *A Classified Bibliography of the Septuagint.* (Leiden, E. J. Brill). xviii, 217 p. = Arbeiten zur Literatur und Geschichte des Hellenistischen Judentums, VI.

Brockway, D.: "The MacDonald collection of Arabian nights: a bibliography", *MW* 63, 185-205 (cont.)

Cahen, C. et C. Pellat: "Les études arabes et islamiques", *Journal Asiatique* 261, 89-107.

Canard, Marius: *Byzance et les Musulmans du Proche Orient.* Préface de Claude Cahen. (London, Variorum reprints). 536 p. = Collected Studies Series, Variorum reprint CS18.

Canard, Marius: *Miscellanea Orientalia.* Préface de Charles Pellat. (London, Variorum Reprints Publishers). 556 p., 1 portrait. = Variorum Reprints, Collected Studies Series.

Caplice, R. – H. Klengel – C. Saporetti: "Keilschriftbibliographie. 34. 15. VI. 1972 – 15. III. 1973. (Mit Nachträgen aus früheren Jahren)", *Orientalia* 42, 1*-78*. (930 Titel, mit Indices).

Capps, Walter H.: "Geo Widengren on Syncretism: On Parsing Uppsala Methodological Tendencies", *Numen* 20/3, 163-185.

Caquot, A.: "Les études semitiques", *Journal Asiatique* 261, 57-68.

de Certeau, M.: "Lieux de transit. Prophétisme et science religieuse", *Esprit* (Paris), no. 2, 607-625.

Christ, Karl: *Römische Geschichte: Einführung, Quellenkunde, Bibliographie.* (Darmstadt, Wissenschaftliche Buchgesellschaft). 4to. 335 S.

Clark, L. V.: "The Turkic and Mongol Words in William of Rubruck's *Journey*", *JAOS* 93, 181-189.

Coppens, J. et J. Lust: "Elenchus bibliographicus 1973. Scriptura sacra Veteris Testamenti", *EThL* 49, 302-355.

Couchy, L. H. – M. Couchy: "Table alphabétique, analytique et chronologie des noms de personnes et de lieux ainsi que des principales matières que renferme le Bulletin historique et littéraire de la 77e à la 89e année, (1928-1940)", *BSHP* 118, No. 5, 1-472.

Covi, D.: "Breve rassegna bibliografica agostiniana", *Laurentianum* 14/4, 660-665.

Dammann, E.: "Zeitschriftenschau: African Studies 30, 1971", *OLZ* 68, 308-309.

Dammann, Ernst: *Grundriss der Religionsgeschichte.* (Stuttgart, 1972). – R: *Anthropos* 68, 313 (Karl Hoheisel).

Daniélou, J.: "Bulletin d'histoire des origines chrétiennes. I. Judéo-christianisme. II. Justin, Clément, Tertullien. III. Théologie archaïque", *RchSR* 61/2, 233-276.

Daumas, F.: "Après Champollion. Panorama de 150 ans d'égyptologie", *EThR* 48, no. 4, 473-485.

Dehandschutter, B.: "L'état présent des recherches sur la bibliothèque copte gnostique de Nag Hammadi", *Bijdragen* 34/4, 411-416 (en néerlandais).

Deshayes, J.: "Rapport préliminaire sur les septième et huitième campagnes de fouille à Tureng Tepe (1967 et 1969)", *BAIPU* 3, 81-97.

Deshayes, J.: "Rapport préliminaire sur la neuvième campagne de fouille à Tureng Tepe (1971)", *Iran* 11, 141-152.

Dhavamony, M.: "Self-Understanding of World Religions as Religion", *Gregorianum* 54/1, 91-130 (rés. en français).

Dietrich, Abert: "Zeitschriftenschau: al-Mašriq 64, 1970", *OLZ* 68, 218-220.

Dietrich, W.: "Bibliographie Karl Heinrich Rengstorf 1927-1973", *Theokratia* 2, 417-442.

Dobrača, Kasim: "Islamic Studies and Libraries in Yugoslavia", *PUR* I, No. 1, 44-50.

Drijvers, H. J. W.: "Theory Formation in Science of Religion and the Study of the History of Religions", in: *Religion, Culture and Methodology* (q. v. sub I-7), 57-77. ("References", pp. 75-77).

Duplacy, J. et C. M. Martini: "Bulletin de critique textuelle du Nouveau Testament, V. (1re partie)", *Biblica* 54/1, 79-114.

de Durand, G.-M.: "Bulletin de patrologie", *Revue des Sciences Philosophiques et Théologiques* 57/3, 457-480.

Eibl-Eibesfeldt, Irenäus: *Der vorprogrammierte Mensch. Das Ererbte als bestimmender Faktor im menschlichen Verhalten.* (Wien-München-Zürich, Fritz Molden Verlag). 288 p., 125 Abb.

Eissfeldt, O.: "Zeitschriftenschau: Biblische Zeitschrift, N. F., 15, 1971", *OLZ* 68, 102-103.

Eissfeldt, O.: "Zeitschriftenschau: Congress Volume, Rome 1968 Supplements to Vetus Testamentum, XVII", *OLZ* 68, 107-108.

Eissfeldt, O.: "Zeitschriftenschau: Journal of Near Eastern Studies 30, 1971", *OLZ* 316-318.

Eissfeldt, O.: "Zeitschriftenschau: Journal of the American Oriental Society 91 2-3, (91/2-3,) 1971", *OLZ* 68, 215-218.

Eissfeldt, O.: "Zeitschriftenschau: Journal of the American Oriental Society, 91/1, 1971", *OLZ* 68, 109-110.

Eissfeldt, O.: "Zeitschriftenschau: Oriens Antiquus 10, 1971", *OLZ* 68, 621-622.

Eissfeldt, O.: "Zeitschriftenschau: Revue Biblique 76, 1970", *OLZ* 68, 110.

Eissfeldt, O.: "Zeitschriftenschau: The Australian Journal of Biblical Archaeology 1 (1968) – 4 (1971)", *OLZ* 68, 313-314.

Ernst, Y. – G. Kennedy: "Bibliographie de l'année 1971 et complément d'années antérieures", *L'Année Philologique* 42, 1-856.

Fass, J.: "Zeitschriftenschau: Oriens Extremus 17, 1970", *OLZ* 68, 422-423.

Filliozat, J.: "La Sociéte Asiatique: d'hier à demain", *Journal Asiatique* 261, 3-12.

Filliozat, J.: "L'indianisme", *Journal Asiatique* 261, 175-190, bibliographie (5 p.)

Fisher, J.: "Bibliography for the Study of Eskimo Religion", *Anthropologica* 15, No. 2, 231-271.

Flemming, Barbara: *Türkische Handschriften, I.*, und Manfred Götz: *Türkische Handschriften, II.* (Wiesbaden, 1968). – R: *OLZ* 68, 165-173 (J. Blaškovič).

Frank, B.: "Les études japonaises", *Journal Asiatique* 261, 255-295.

Freiman, Aron: *Union Catalog of Hebrew Manuscripts and Their Location.* Vol. 1: Index by Menahim Hayyim Schmelzer. (New York, American Academy for Jewish Research). xxxiv, 280 p.

Freimann, Aron: *Katalog der Judaica und Hebraica*, Stadtbibliothek Frankfurt am Main. Band *Judaica.* Vorwort zur Neuauflage A. Fraenkel. (Graz, 1968). – R: *OLZ* 68, 49-50 (R. Meyer).

Frostin, P.: "Modern Marxist Critique of Religion: A Survey", *Lutheran World* 20, No. 2, 141-154.

Fuks, L. and R. G. Fuks-Mansfeld: *Catalogue of the manuscripts in the Bibliotheca Rosenthaliana, University Library Amsterdam.* (Leiden, E. J. Brill). 4to. xiv, 349 p., 18 pl. = Hebrew and Judaic Manuscripts in Amsterdam Public Collections, I.

Gabrieli, Francesco: "Casual remarks of an Arabist", *Diogenes* 83, 1-11.

Galand, L., P. Galand-Pernet, et C. Lacoste: "Les études berbères", *Journal Asiatique* 261, 109-116.

Genicot, L.: "La religion dans les manuels d'histoire", *Education et Culture*, No. 21, 21-25.

Gese, Hartmut, Maria Höfner, Kurt Rudolph: *Die Religionen Altsyriens, Altarabiens und der Mandäer*, (Stuttgart, 1970). – R: *BiOr* 30, 22-23 (C. J. Bleeker). *JSS* 18, 144-151 (J. Gray).

Gossiaux, P.-P.: "Image des religions noires dans la littérature occidentale classique (1530 à 1730). Introduction", *RUB* 1, no. 3-4, 219-244 (fin).

Groos, Karl: *Die Spiele der Menschheit.* (Hildesheim, Georg Olms Verlag). v, 539 p. = Documenta Semiotica, Serie 3: Semiotik. (Nachdruck der Ausgabe Jena 1899).

Guillaumont, A.: "L'Orient chrétien", *Journal Asiatique* 261, 69-81.

Hahn, R. A.: "Understanding Beliefs: An Essay on the Methodology of the Statement and Analysis of Belief Systems", *CurAnth* 14, No. 3, 207-230.

Hambis, L.: "L'Asie centrale et les études mongoles", *Journal Asiatique* 261, 145-151.

Hammerschmidt, Ernst: *Äthiopische Handschriften vom Tānāsee*, 1. Teil: Reisebericht und Beschreibung der Handschriften in dem Kloster des Heiligen Gabriel auf der Insel Kebran. (Wiesbaden, Franz Steiner Verlag). 4to. 244 S., 26 Tafeln (davon 12 farbig), 1 Karte. = Verzeichnis der Orientalischen Handschriften in Deutschland, XX/1.

Harrington, D. J. and J. W. Dunkly: "Nouveau Testament. Analyses d'articles et de livres", *NTA* 17/2, 131-266.

Harrington, D. J. et J. W. Dunkly: "Nouveau Testament. Analyse d'articles et de livres", *NTA* 18/1, 1-131.

Harrington, D. J. et J. W. Dunkly: "Nouveau Testament. Analyses d'articles et de livres", *NTA* 17/3, 267-456.

Hasler, Juan A.: *Bibliographia Americanistica Brevis.* (Medellín, Colombia, Universidad de Antioquia). 170 p.

Hayes, John L.: "Bibliography of the Works of I. J. Gelb", *Fs Gelb*, 1-8. (174 entries. 87 articles in encyclopedias and encyclopedical dictionaries are indicated, but not listed).

Hazai, G.: "Zeitschriftenschau: International Journal of Middle East Studies, 1, 1970", *OLZ* 68, 109.

Heerma van Voss, M. et al.: *Van Beitel tot Penseel.* Schrift in het oude Nabije Oosten tentoongesteld in het Allard Pierson Museum bij het veertigjarig bestaan van het Vooraziatisch-Egyptisch Genootschap 'Ex Oriente Lux'. (Leiden, E. J. Brill) vi, 41 p.

Hirschberg, Walter: *Religionsethnologie und ethnohistorische Religionsforschung: Eine Gegenüberstellung.* (Wien, Institut für Völkerkunde der Universität Wien, 1972). 132 p. 4to.

Hochegger, Hermann: "Bibliographie Yansi. Bibliographie Yaka", *Cahiers des Religions Africaines* 5, 113-119.

Hoffmann, J. G. H.: "Marxisme-Léninisme et Christianisme", *La Revue Réformée* 25 (no. 94), 65-73.

Hofmann, E.: "Zeitschriftenschau: Münchener Studien zur Sprachwissenschaft 29, 1971", *OLZ* 68, 318.

Hoftijzer, J.: "De ontcijfering van de Deir-'Alla-teksten. Voordracht gehouden voor het Oosters Genootschap in Nederland op 19 januari 1973", *OGN* 5, 111-134.

Höftmann, H.: "Zeitschriftenschau: Anthropos 65, 1970", *OLZ* 68, 528-530.

Hoheisel, Karl: "Religion: ein Legitimationsmechanismus?", *Anthropos* 68, 613-617. (Grundsätzliche Bemerkungen zu A. Gallus: "A Biofunctional Theory of Religion", *Current Anthropology* 13 (1972), 543-568).

Holm, O.: "Bibliografía de Autores Nacionales y Extranjeros, relacionada con temas antropológicos ecuatorianos", *CHAr* 23 (40), 203-232.

Holt, P. M.: *Studies in the History of the Near East.* (London, Frank Cass and Co. Ltd.) x, 261 p., 4 pl.

Hospers, J. H. (ed.): *A Basic Bibliography for the Study of the Semitic Languages,* I. (Leiden, E. J. Brill), xxv, 401 p.

Hultkrantz, Å.: A Definition of Shamanism", *Temenos* 9, 25-37.

Idole. Prähistorische Keramiken aus Ungarn. Ausstellung des Ungarischen Nationalmuseums Budapest im Naturhistorischen Museum Wien vom 11. November 1972 bis 21. Jänner 1973. (Wien, Naturhist. Museum). xii, 51 p., 14 Fig., 31 Taf. = Veröffentlichungen aus dem Naturhistorischen Museum, N. F., 7.

International Bibliography of the History of Religions. / Bibliographie Internationale de l'Histoire des Religions. 1969. Compiled ... by Salih H. Alich. Published on the recommendation of the International Council for Philosophy and Humanistic Studies and with the financial support of UNESCO by the International Association for the History of Religions. (Leiden, E. J. Brill). xvii, 163 p., index.

Janssen, E.: "Zeitschriftenschau: The Jewish Quarterly Review NS 61, 1970/71", *OLZ* 68, 537-539.

de Jong, J. W.: "The Discovery of India by the Greeks", *Asiatische Studien* 27, No. 2, 115-142.

Kaganoff, N. M. and J. E. Endelman: "Judaica Americana", *AJHQ* 62, No. 4, 401-413. (A bibliography of works and articles after 1960).

Kampman, A. A.: "Die Leidener Tontafelsammlung Franz de Liagre Böhl", *Fs de Liagre Böhl* 214-233.

Kaplony-Heckel, Ursula: *Ägyptische Handschriften.* Teil 1. Herausgegeben von Erich Lüddeckens. (Wiesbaden, F. Steiner Verlag, 1971). 4to. xx, 301 S., 8 Taf. = Verzeichnis der Orientalischen Handschriften in Deutschland, 19. – R: *BiOr* 30, 399-400 (Michel Valloggia).

Kirshenblatt-Gimblett, B.: "Toward a Theory of Proverb Meaning", *Proverbium* 22, 821-827.

Kisch, G.: "Jüdisch-Historische Zeitschriften in deutscher Sprache. Ein Ueberblick zum Beginn des zehnten Jahrgangs der Zeitschrift für die Geschichte der Juden", *ZGJ* 10, 1-4.

Köbert, R.: "Arabische Handschriften" [islam-theologischen Inhalts in der Bibliothek des Bibelinstituts, Rom], *Orientalia* 42, 387-392. (17 codices).

Kolmaš, Josef: *Tibetan Manuscripts and Blockprints in the Library of the Oriental Institute Prague.* (Prague, 1969). – R: *OLZ* 68, 618-619 (J. Schubert).

van Koningsveld, P. Sj.: "The Arabic Manuscripts Collection of René Basset (1855-1924)", *BiOr* 30, 370-385, pl. X-XIII. (55 numbers: Or. 14.001 – Or. 14.055, with Indices: a. Authors, b. Titles).

Kornrumpf, Hans-Jürgen unter Mitarbeit von Jutta Kornrumpf: *Osmanische Bibliographie mit besonderer Berücksichtigung der Türkei in Europa.* (Leiden, E. J. Brill). xxiv, 1378 S. = Handbuch der Orientlistik, I. Abteilung: Der Nahe und der Mittlere Osten, Ergänzungsband VIII.

Koskenniemi, Seppo, Asko Parpola, and Simo Parpola: *Materials for the Study of the Indus Script, 1: A Concordance to the Indus Inscriptions.* (Helsinki, Suomalainen Tiedeakatemia). xxviii, 528, 55* p. = Annales Academiae Scientiarum Fennicae, B, 185.

Kristeller, P. O.: *Catalogus translationum et commentariorum: Mediaeval and Renaissance Latin Translations and Commentaries.* Vol. 2. (Washington, D.C., 1971). xv, 440 p. – R: *Gnomon* 45/2, 185-195 (K. Krautter).

Kudsi-Zadeh, A. Albert: *Sayyid Jamāl al-Dīn al-Afghānī. An annotated Bibliography.* (Leiden, 1970). – R: *OLZ* 68, 606-607 (F. Machalski). WI 14, 227 (O. Spies).

Lauwers, J.: "Bibliographie sélectionnée autour du thème de la 'sécularisation' ", *SoCoR* 20/4, 603-604.

Leclant, Jean: "Fouilles et travaux en Egypte et au Soudan, 1971-1972", *Orientalia* 42, 393-440, Tab. III-XXXVI.

Ledoyen, H.: "Bulletin d'histoire bénédictine, t. VIII", *ReBén* 83, no. 1-2 529*-656*; no. 3-4, 657*- 720*.

Libiszowska, M.: "Publications sur la science des religions par le Centre de Perfectionnement des Cadres Laïcs. Esquisse d'une analyse statistique", *Studia Religioznawcze* no. 8, 175-192 (en polonais, rés. en russe, anglais, allem.)

Malamat, A. and H. Reviv: *A Bibliography of the Biblical Period.* (With Emphasis on Publications in Modern Hebrew). Selected and classified. (Jerusalem, Academon). vii, 73 p.

Manik, Liberty: *Batak-Handschriften.* (Wiesbaden, Franz Steiner Verlag). 4to. x, 253 S., 6 Tafeln. = Verzeichnis der Orientalischen Handschriften in Deutschland, 28.

Marco Polo: *Von Venedig nach China. Die grösste Reise des 13. Jahrhunderts.*

Neu herausgegeben und kommentiert von Theodor A. Knust. (Tübingen, Horst Erdmann). 339 p., 31 Abb., 1 Kt.

Margul, Tadeusz: "La vie religieuse, objet essentiel des sciences de la religion", *StFil* 17/2, 153-164 (en polonais).

Matuz, Joseph: "A propos d'une contribution bibliographique pour servir les études ottomanes historiques", *OLZ* 68, 449-451. (With reference to Hans Georg Majer: "Osmanistische Nachträge zum *Index Islamicus* (1906-1965)", *Südostforschungen* XXVII (1968), 242-291).

Mayrhofer, Manfred: *Onomastica Persepolitana. Das altiranische Namengut der Persepolis-Täfelchen.* Unter Mitarbeit von János Harmatta, Walther Hinz, Rüdiger Schmidt und Jutta Seifert. (Wien, Verlag der Oesterreichischen Akademie der Wissenschaften). 358 S., Frontisp. = ÖAW., Philos.-Hist. Klasse, Sitzungsberichte, 286. Band. Veröffentl. der Iranischen Kommission, Band 1.

Meinhold, Peter: "Entwicklung der Religionswissenschaft in der Neuzeit und in der Gegenwart", in: U. Mann (Hrsg.): *Theologie und Religionswissenschaft* (Darmstadt, Wissenschaftliche Buchgesellschaft) 381-412.

Meinhold, Peter: "Entwicklung der Religionswissenschaft im Mittelalter und zur Reformationszeit", in: U. Mann (Hrsg.): *Theologie und Religionswissenschaft* (Darmstadt, Wissenschaftliche Buchgesellschaft) 357-380.

Mensching, Gustav: "Die Hochreligionen Asiens", in: U. Mann (Hrsg.): *Theologie und Religionswissenschaft* (Darmstadt, Wissenschaftliche Buchgesellschaft) 162-188. (I. Der Buddhismus, S. 162-176. II. Der Hinduismus, S. 176-188).

Meslin, M.: *Pour une science des religions.* (Paris, Editions du Seuil). 270 p., index.

Metz, R. – J. Schlick: "Répertoire bibliographiques des institutions chrétiennes", *RIC* 6, 1-515.

Meyer, Gerhard Rudolf: "Zeitschriftenschau: Archiv für Orientforschung 23, 1970", *OLZ* 68, 619-621.

Meyer, Gerhard Rudolf: "Zeitschriftenschau: Archiv für Orientforschung 22, 1968/69", *OLZ* 68, 312-313.

Mitros, Joseph F.: *Religions. A select, classified bibliography.* (New York, Learned Publications; Louvain, Nauwelaerts; Paris, Béatrice-Nauwelaerts). xix, 435 p. = Philosophical Questions Series, 8.

Moereels, L.: "Bulletin bibliographique" (in Dutch), *Ons Geestelijk Erf* 47/1, 64-121.

"Monastica", *Citeaux, Commentarii Cisterciences* 24/1, 71-78.

Monnet Saleh, Janine: *Les antiquités égyptiennes de Zagreb.* Catalogue raisonné des antiquités égyptiennes conservées au Musée Archéologique de Zagreb en Yougoslavie. (Paris-La Haye, Mouton, 1970). 4to. 206 p., ill. – R: *BiOr* 30, 400-402 (B. van de Walle).

Moraldi, L.: "Recenti scoperte archeologiche a letterarie in Palestina", *Rivista Biblica* 21/2, 187-202.

Müller, Walter W.: "Zeitschriftenschau: Archiv Orientální 39, 1971", *OLZ* 68, 309-312.

Müller-Schwefe, Hans-Rudolf: "Praktische Theologie und Religionswissenschaft", in: U. Mann (Hrsg.): *Theologie und Religionswissenschaft* (Darmstadt, Wissenschaftliche Buchgesellschaft) 425-437.

Myszor, W.: "Nag-Hammadi: Texts and Translations", *Studia Theologica Varsaviensia* 11/1, 215-221. (A bibliographic survey).

Nader, A.: "Bilbiographie d'ouvrages en langues européennes concernant la *Kalām*", *BPhM* 15, 191-209.

Nagel, P.: "Zeitschriftenschau: Le Muséon 82, 1969", *OLZ* 68, 539-542.

Neirynck, F. et F. Van Segbroeck: "Elenchus bibliographicus 1973. Scriptura sacra Novi Testamenti", *EThL* 49, 356-414.

Nenola-Kallio, A.: "Report on the Study Conference of the I.A.H.R. on Methodology of the Science of Religion, in Turku, August 27-31, 1973", *Temenos* 9, 15-24.

Nimtz, A., Jr.: "Islam in Tanzania: An Annotated Bibliography", *Tanzania Notes and Records* 72, 51-74.

Nober, Petrus: *Elenchus bibliographicus biblicus.* Vol. 53, pars altera. (Roma, Pontificium Institutum Biblicum). pp. 385-929.

Noja, S.: "Contribution à la bibliographie des Samaritains", *Annali dell'Instituto Orientale di Napoli* 33/1, 98-113.

Norris, R. B.: "Transcendence and the Future: Dialogue with Roger Garaudy", *JES* 10, No. 3, 498-514.

North, R.: "Bibliography of Works in Theology and History", *History and Theory* 12/1, 55-140.

Oelsner, J.: "Zeitschriftenschau: Sumer 24, 1968; 25, 1969", *OLZ* 68, 427-430.

Offenberg, A. K.: "Catalogue of the Hebrew Incunabula in the Bibliotheca Rosenthaliana" (III), *StuRos* 7/1, 128-150, 2 pl. (For I and II see *IBHR* 1971, p. 10).

Oosten, J. G.: "The Examination of Religious Concepts in Religious Anthropology", in: *Religion, Culture and Methodology* (q. v. sub I-7), 99-108.

O'Reilly, P.: "Bibliographie méthodique, analytique et critique de l'île Rapa", *JSO* 29 (39), 169-214.

Otten, H.: "Zeitschriftenschau: Journal of Cuneiform Studies 23, 1970", *OLZ* 68, 218.

Oxtoby, W. G.: "Religion", *University of Toronto Quarterly* 42, 475-488. (A bibliographic survey of mainly English works).

Pani Ermini, L.: "Antichitá cristiane", *Studi Romani* 21/2, 239-244. (A bibliographic survey for 1972).

Paret, Rudi: *The Study of Arabic and Islam at German Universities.* German Orientalists since Theodor Nöldeke. (Wiesbaden, 1968). – R: *OLZ* 68, 274-275 (Johann Fück).

Parrot, André: "Fouilles à Mari 1971/1972", *Archiv für Orientforschung* 24, 186-187, 1 fig.

Parrot, André: "Les fouilles de Mari. Vingtième campagne de fouilles (Printemps 1972)", *Syria* 49, 281-302, 6 pl., 15 fig.

Person, Y.: "Pour une histoire des religions africaines", *ASSR* 18 (36), 91-101 (with English summary).

Petit, P.: "Bulletin de bibliographie catholique", *EThR* 48, no. 2, 197-206.

Pfeifer, G.: "Zeitschriftenschau: Bulletin of the American Schools of Oriental Research, 1970", *OLZ* 68, 103-107.

Polonskaja, L.: "The Religions of the Contemporary East. Ideology and Politics", *MEMO* No. 1, 68-82 (in Russian with English summary).

Popović, A.: "Sur une 'nouvelle' traduction du Coran en serbo-croate", *Arabica* XX/1, 82-84.

"Le Programme général des recherches en science des religions et l'organisation des recherches en Pologne", *Euhemer* 17/4, 3-24 (en polonais).

Ratschow, Carl Heinz: "Systematische Theologie", in: U. Mann (Hrsg.): *Theologie und Religionswissenschaft* (Darmstadt, Wissenschaftliche Buchgesellschaft) 413-424.

Reincke, G.: "Archäologische Bibliographie 1971", Beilage zum *Jahrbuch des Deutschen Archäologischen Instituts*, Band 87, 1972, 1-474 p.

Ries, J. – J. Coppens: "Elenchus bibliographicus, 1973. Historia religionum", *EThL* 49, 288-302.

Ringgren, Helmer: *Religions of the Ancient Near East.* Translated by John Sturdy. (London, S.P.C.K.) x, 198 p.

Rost, L.: "Zeitschriftenschau: Hamizrah Hehadash. The New East. Quarterly of the Israel Oriental Society, Jerusalem, 21, 1971", *OLZ* 68, 414-418.

Rost, L.: "Zeitschriftenschau: Hamizrah Hehadash, 20, 1970", *OLZ* 68, 108-109.

Rouquette, J.: "Les études parues en français dans le domaine biblique", *EThR* 48, No. 1, 81-96.

Royce, J.: "Guide to Notation of Game Observation", *Anthropos* 68, 604-610.

Rudberg, S. Y.: "Aperçu bibliographique 1971-1972. Domaine grec: philosophie, histoire de la religion et des sciences, Nachleben", *Eranos* 71/3-4, 137-143 (in Swedish).

Rudolph, Kurt: "Das Problem der Autonomie und Integrität der Religionswissenschaft", *NeTT* 27/2, 105-131.

Rudolph, Kurt: "*Historia Religionum.* Bemerkungen zu einigen neueren Handbüchern der Religionsgeschichte", *ThLZ* 98/6, 401-418.

Rudolph, K.: "Zeitschriftenschau: History of Religions 11, 1971", *OLZ* 68, 535-537.

Saito, Shiro: *Philippine Ethnography. A critical, Annotated and Selected Bibliography.* (Honolulu, The University Press of Hawai). xxxi, 512 p. in 4°. = East-West Bibliographic Series, 2.

Sapin, J.: "25 ans d'archéologie en Syrie-Palestine (1946-1971) Recherches et perspectives", *EThR* 48/3, 351-369.

Sarma, E. R. Sreekrishna (ed.): *Kauṣītaki-Brāhmaṇa.* I: Text. (Wiesbaden, 1968). = Verzeichnis der Orientalischen Handschriften in Deutschland, 9, 1. – R: *OLZ* 68, 607-612 (A. Parpola).

Sauneron, S.: "Les travaux de l'Institut Français d'Archéologie Orientale en 1972-1973", *BIFAO* 73, 217-263.

Schilling, Werner: "Ökumenische Theologie und Missionswissenschaft", in: U. Mann (Hrsg.): *Theologie und Religionswissenschaft* (Darmstadt, Wissenschaftliche Buchgesellschaft) 438-453.

Schimmel, Annemarie: "Die neue tschechische Koranübersetzung (mit einem Ueberblick über die neuesten tschechischen orientalistischen Arbeiten)", *Die Welt des Orients* 7/1, 154-162.

Schimmel, Annemarie: "Zeitschriftenschau: Studies in Islam 7, 1970", *OLZ* 68, 622.

Schippmann, K.: "Zeitschriftenschau: Archäologische Mitteilungen aus Iran 2, 1969; 3, 1970; 4, 1971", *OLZ* 68, 530-534.

Schmider, Béatrice: *Bibliographie analytique de préhistoire pour le paléolithique supérieur européen.* Publications parues entre 1850 et 1968, conservées à la Bibliothèque du Musée de l'Homme. 2 tomes. 1: Index. 2: Catalogue des publications analysées. (Paris, Centre National de la Recherche Scientifique). 4°. 266 et 277 p.

Schmitt, R.: "Der heutige Stand der altiranischen Namenforschung", *Orbis* 22, no. 1, 248-260.

Schnutenhaus, F., K. F. Müller, A. Strobel, und H.-D. Altendorf: "Die Liturgieforschung in Deutschland", *JLH* 17, 247-263.

Scholer, D. M.: "Bibliographia gnostica: Supplementum III", *NoTes* 15, 327-345.

Seydou, C.: "Panorama de la littérature peule", *BIFAN* 35/1, 176-218.

Skrzypek, M.: "Les métaphores du Siècle de Lumières dans la théorie de la religion selon Lénine", *TSV* I/1, 55-67.

Smith, J. Z.: "When the Bough Breaks", *History of Religions* 12/4, 342-371.

von Soden, W.: "Zeitschriftenschau: Orientalia, N. S., 39, 1970; N. S. 40, 1971", *OLZ* 68, 423-427.

von Soden, W.: "Zeitschriftenschau: Revue d'Assyriologie et d'Archéologie orientale 64, 1970", *OLZ* 68, 221-222.

Soymié, M.: "Les études chinoises", *Journal Asiatique* 261, 209-246, bibliographie.

Spieser, J.-M.: "Inventaires en vue d'un recueil des inscriptions historiques de Byzance. I. Les inscriptions de Thessalonique", *TravMém* 5, 145-180, 10 pl.

Swienko, Henryk: "Matériaux pour la bibliographie de la science des religions. Les publications polonaises dans les années 1966-1971", *Euhemer* XVII, no. 2 (88), 129-138; no. 3 (89), 145-154 (en polonais).

Tamani, G.: "Manoscritti e incunabuli ebraici nella biblioteca dell'Accademia dei Concordi di Rovigo", *AION* 33/2, 207-231, 8 tav.

Thiel, Josef Franz: "Der Nzambi-Name in der Ethonohistorie", *Anthropos* 68, 625-628. (Anmerkungen zu Walter Hirschberg: *Religionsethnologie und ethnohistorische Religionsforschung*, Wien 1972, 132 pp. = Wiener ethnohistorische Blätter, Beiheft 1).

Thils, G. – J. Coppens: "Elenchus bibliographicus, 1973. Generalia", *EThL* 49, No. 2-3, 255-288.

Thomas, M.: "Nouvelles acquisitions latines et françaises du département des manuscrits de la Bibliothèque Nationale pendant les années 1969-1971", *BECh* 130, 493-577.

Thomsen, Peter: *Die Palästina-Literatur.* Eine internationale Bibliographie in systematischer Ordnung mit Autoren- und Sachregister. VII: Die Literatur der Jahre 1940-1945. Lfg. 1 und 2. (Berlin, 1969). – R: *OLZ* 68, 258-259 (G. Wallis).

Trager, Frank N. et al.: *Burma. A Selected and Annotated Bibliography.* (New Haven, Human Relations Area Files Press). xii, 356 p. = Behavior Science Bibliographies.

Tucci, G. – W. Heissig: *Les religions du Tibet et de la Mongolie.* (Traduit de l'allemand par R. Sailley). (Paris, Payot). 517 p., bibliographie (6 p.)

de Veer, A. C. et alii: "Bulletin augustinien pour 1972 et compléments d'années antérieures", *REAg* 19, 305-313.

Veghazi, E. N.: "125 años en el estudio comparado de las religiones", *Stromata* 29, no. 3, 313-323, bibliografia.

Vink, A. J.: "Religious Ethology: Some Methodological Aspects", in: *Religion, Culture and Methodology*, edited by Th. P. van Baaren and H. J. W. Drijvers (q. v. sub I-7), 137-157. ("References", pp. 156-157).

Waardenburg, Jacques (ed.): *Classical Approaches to the Study of Religion. Aims, Methods and Theories of Research.* [An Anthology, edited with an Introduction, biographical notes, and a Bibliography]. Vol. 1: *Introduction and Anthology.* (The Hague-Paris, Mouton). xiv, 742 p. = Religion and Reason, 3. ("Introduction: View of Hundred Years' Study of Religion", pp. 3-78. "Anthology", with introductory and biographical notes, pp. 81-666. "Sources and Acknowledgments", pp. 667-672. "Indexes", pp. 677-742).

Waardenburg, Jacques: "L'organisation des études concernant l'Islam et le Moyen-Orient à l'Université de Californie", *REI* 41/2, 297-305.

Weller, F.: "Zeitschriftenschau: Indo-Iranian Journal 13, 1971", *OLZ* 68, 314-316.

Weller, F.: "Zeitschriftenschau: Harvard Journal of Asiatic Studies 30, 1970; 31, 1971", *OLZ* 68, 212-215.

Weller, F.: "Zeitschriftenschau: Oriens Extremus 16, 1969", *OLZ* 68, 220-221.

Zaidi, S. Mujahid Husain: *Urdu Handschriften.* (Wiesbaden, F. Steiner Verlag). 4to. xx, 104 S., 8 Taf. (davon 2 farbig). = Verzeichnis der Orientalischen Handschriften in Deutschland, 25.

Zoega, Georgius: *Catalogus codicum Copticorum qui in Museo Borgiano Velitris adservantur.* (Romae 1810). Avec une introduction et des notes bibliographiques par Joseph-Marie Sauget. (Hildesheim, Georg Olms Verlag). xliii*, xii, 663 p., 7 tab.

3. PSYCHOLOGY OF RELIGION

Bakan, D.: "Satana nella psiche", *Comunità* 27 (No. 169), 348-398.

Banks, R.: "Religion as Projection: A Re-Appraisal of Freud's Theory", *RelSt* 9/4, 401-426.

Basave, A.: "Estructura y sentido de la filosofia de la religión", *Sapientia* 26, No. 107, 15-30.

Booth, H. J.: "Edwin Diller Starbuck: Pioneer in the Psychology of Religion", *DisAbIn A* 33/12, 7011. (The author's summary of his diss., University of Iowa).

Brown, L. B. (ed.): *Psychology and Religion, Selected Readings.* (Harmondsworth-Baltimore-Ringwood, Penguin Books). = Penguin Education.

Bruno, J.: "Extase, transe et expérimentation", *Critique* 29, No. 312, 417-476.

Crockett, J. D.: "A Factor-Analytic Study of the Religious Beliefs Inventory", *DisAbIn, A* 33/7, 3756-3757. (The author's summary of his diss., Univ. of Minnesota, 1972).

Dumas, A.: *La science de l'âme. Initiation méthodique à l'étude des phénomène supranormaux et aux théories de la métapsychologie.* (Paris, Dervy-Livres). 514 p. = Coll. Les Connaissances Supra-Normales.

Embree, R. A.: "The Religious Association Scale: A Preliminary Validation Study", *JSSR* 12/2, 223-226.

Frazier, A. M.: "The Problem of Psychic Distance in Religious Art", *JAAC* 31, No. 3, 389-393.

Gibbs, D. R., S. A. Mueller, and J. R. Wood: "Doctrinal Orthodoxy, Salience, and the Consequential Dimension", *JSSR* 12, 33-52, bibliography.

Gilman, S. and R. Saeger: "Marx and the Religious: The Gnostic Perspective", *Philosophy Today* 17, 12-21.

Guhl, M.-C.: "Les paradis ou la configuration mythique et archétypale du refuge", *CCRIC*, no. 3, 11-105, bibliographie (3 p.)

Gutmann, D.: "The New Mythologies and Premature Aging in the Youth Culture", *JYA* 2, 139-155, bibliography.

Hamilton, D. G.: "The emergence of religious belief: a psychological sketch", *The Philosophical Journal* 10/1, 27-36.

Hoffman, W. M.: "The Nature of Religious Action", *IJPhR* 4/1, 59-62.

Hoge, D. R. and J. W. Carroll: "Religiosity and Prejudice in Northern and Southern Churches", *JSSR* 12/2, 181-197, bibliohraphy (2 p.)

Kalish, R. A. and D. K. Reynolds: "Phenomenological Reality and Post-Death Contact", *JSSR* 12/2, 209-221.

Laing, R. D.: "Sensibilità religiosa", *Aut Aut* 134, 104-108.

McCurdy, J. D.: "The Face of the Deep", *JAAR* 41, No. 3, 355-370.

Mann, Ulrich: "Religionspsychologie", in: ders. (Hrsg.): *Theologie und Religionswissenschaft* (Darmstadt, Wissenschaftliche Buchgesellschaft) 222-238.

Meissner, W. W.: "Notes on the Psychology of Hope", *Journal of Religion and Health* 12/1, 7-29, bibliography.

Miskel, J. F.: "Religion and Medicine: The Chinese Opium Problem", *Journal of the History of Medicine and Allied Sciences* 28/1, 3-14.

Morris, R. R.: "Anxiety: Freud and Theology", *Journal of Religion and Health* 12/2, 189-201.

Raschke, V.: "Dogmatism and Committed and Consensual Religiosity", *JSSR* 12, No. 3, 339-344, bibliography.

Richardson, J. T.: "Psychological Interpretations of Glossolalia: A Reexamination of Research", *JSSR* 12, 199-207, bibliography.

Shea, J.: "La 'seconde naïveté': manière d'aborder un problème pastoral", *Concilium*, No. 81, 107-116.

Slanikov, I.: "Variations de l'expérience religieuse", *Filosofska Mis'l* 29/5, 64-72 (en bulgare).

Sobosan, J. G.: "Reflections on Kierkegaard and the Dynamics of Love", *AER* 167, No. 4, 226-235.

Straton, G. D.: "The Meaning of Mind Transcendency in a Religious Philosophy of Man", *IJPhR* 4/1, 39-52.

Thouless, R. H.: An Introduction to the Psychology of Religion. Third Edition. (Cambridge University Press, 1971). – R: *JSSR* 12/2, 253-254 (B. Spilka).

Trégaro, L.: "Petit essai sur la superstition", *CouRat* no. 303, 11-46, bibliographie (2 p.)

Vernon, G. M. and W. D. Payne: "Myth-Conceptions about Death", *Journal of Religion and Health* 12/1, 63-76, bibliography.

Wehr, Gerhard: *Wege zur religiöser Erfahrung. Analytische Psychologie im Dienst der Bibelauslegung.* (Olten, Walter-Verlag). x, 136 p.

Wucherer-Huldenfeld, Augustinus: "Sigmund Freud und der Atheismus", *Kairos* 15, Heft 3-4, 311-318.

4. PHILOSOPHY OF RELIGION

Althaus, H.: "Vom *Toten Hunde* Spinoza und Lessings *Atheismus*", *SGG* 14, 161-181.

Antiseri, D.: "La 'mistica' di un 'logico': ovvero la religione in Ludwig Wittgenstein", *Proteus* 4, no. 11-12, 163-170.

Antweiler, A.: "Vom Wesen und Sinn des Menschen und Gottes", *ZMRW* 57/2, 119-128.

Archer, D.: "Philosophical Theology and Anthropology", *Irish Theological Quarterly* 40/1, 69-81.

Attfield, R.: "The God of Religion and the God of Philosophy", *Religious Studies* IX/1, 1-9.

Austin, W. H.: "Religious Commitment and the Logical Status of Doctrines", *RelSt* IX/1, 39-48.

Babolin, A.: "Prospettive e orientamenti di filosofia della religione in Italia, oggi", *RFNS* 65/3, 592-605.

Beierwaltes, Werner: "Wahrheit und Tradition. Eine zeitgemässe Erinnerung", *Kairos* XV/1-2, 3-9.

Brechtken, J.: "Die Religionskritik des frühen Marx und der christliche Glaube", *FZPhTh* 20, 224-238.

Brechtken, J.: "Die Wirklichkeit Gottes in der Philosophie Ludwig Feuerbachs", *TF* 35/1, 87-108.

Burhoe, R. W.: "The Concepts of God and Soul in a Scientific View of Human Purpose", *Zygon* 8/3-4, 412-442.

Bynum, W. F.: "The Anatomical Method, Natural Theology, and the Functions of the Brain", *Isis* 64 (224), 445-468.

Ciafardone, R.: "Le origini teologiche della filosofia wolffiana e il rapporto ragione-esperienza", *Pensiero* 18/1, 54-78.

Cohen, C. B.: "The Logic of Religious Language", *Religious Studies* 9, No. 2, 143-155.

Dupré, W.: "Le problème des vérités intangibles des croyances. Réflexions de philosophie des religions", *Concilium*, No. 83, 71-82.

Ehlen, P.: "Rezeption der Theologie durch sowjetische Philosophen", *ThPh* 48/1, 107-114. (With particular reference to *Filosofskaja Enciklopedija*, Moscow, 1970).

Foard, L. C.: "A Problem in Ludwig Feuerbach's Theory of Religious Language", *RelSt* 9/4, 457-461.

Frison, L.: "Thomas Abbt et la destinée de l'homme. Un singulier apologue de l'absence de Dieu", *RechGer*, No. 3, 3-15.

Gravel, P.: "Hume et le miracle", *Les Etudes Philosophiques* no. 1, 19-41.

Greenfield, S. A.: "A Whiteheadian Perspective of the Problem of Evil: Whitehead's Understanding of Evil and Christian Theodicy", *DisAbIn A* 34/1, 403-404. (The author's summary of his diss., Fordham University, 1973).

Griffin, D.: "Whitehead and Niebuhr on God, Man, and the World", *The Journal of Religion* 53/2, 149-175.

Harris, E. E.: *Salvation from Dispair. A Reappraisal of Spinoza's Philosophy.* (The Hague, Martinus Nijhoff). 270 p., Bibliography.

Hennemann, G.: "Glaube im Sinne des Fürwahrhaltens von Sätzen. Eine sprachlogische Untersuchung", *ZRGG* 25, 304-315.

Hinton, R. T.: "God and the Possibility of Science", *Sophia* 12/1, 25-29.

Holland, J. A. B.: "A System of Classical Atheism", *SJTh* 26/3, 271-294 (with regard to Antony Flew: *God and Philosophy*).

Hubbeling, H. G.: "Theology, Philosophy and Science of Religion and their Logical and Empirical Presuppositions", in: Th. P. van Baaren and H. J. W. Drijvers (ed.): *Religion, Culture and Methodology* (Mouton), 9-33, bibliography.

Hudson, H.: "Wittgenstein and Zen Buddhism", *PhEW* 23/4, 471-478.

Jamke, W.: "Thodizee oder Über die Freiheit des Individuums und das Verhängnis der Welt", *PhilPer* 5, 57-77.

Johnson, C. B.: "Why the Atheist is not a Fool", *International Journal for Philosophy of Religion* 4/1, 53-58.

Kemp, Peter: *Théorie de l'engagement. 1. Pathétique de l'engagement. 2. Poétique de l'engagement.* (Paris, Ed. du Seuil) 319 et 188 p.

King, R. H.: "The Conceivability of God", *Religious Studies* IX/1, 11-22.

Köchler, H.: "Das Gottesproblem im Denken Heideggers", *ZKTh* 95/1, 61-90.

Kurz, O.: "Deus alea ludens", *Filosofia* XXIV/1, 3-12, bibliogr.

Lansing, J. W.: "The 'Natures' of Whitehead's God", *Process Studies* 3, No. 3, 143-152, Bibliography.

Magnus, B.: "Nietzsche's Eternalistic Counter-Myth", *The Review of Metaphysics* 26/4, 604-616.

Nelson, D. F.: "Nietzsche, Zarathustra, and Jesus redivivus: The Unholy Trinity", *The Germanic Review* 48/3, 175-188.

Ogiermann, H.: "Neue Aspekte marxistischer Religionskritik?", *Theologie und Philosophie* 48/1, 1-27.

Oshima, S.: "Barth's Analogia Relationis and Heidegger's Ontological Difference", *JR* 53/2, 176-194.

Pfeil, H.: *Gott und die tragische Welt.* (Aschaffenburg, Paul Pattich Verlag, 1971). 142 S. – R: *PhLtAnz* 26/2, 115-117 G. Kahl-Furtmann).

Picken, S. D. B.: "Kant and Man's Coming of Age", *Scottish Journal of Theology* 26/1, 63-70.

Poulain, J.: *Logique et religion.* L'atomisme logique de L. Wittgenstein et la possibilité des propositions religieuses, suivi de Logic and Religion: A Shortened and Adapted Version. (La Haye-Paris, Mouton). 228 p., index, bibliographie (6 p.)

Reboul, O.: "Le mal dans la philosophie religieuse et politique de Kant", *CJPh* 3/2, 169-175.

Resnick, L.: "God and the Best Possible World", *APhQ* 10/4, 313-317.

von Rintelen, F.-J.: "El pensamiento religioso de la creacion: el mal y el bien", *Folia Humanistica* 10 (117), 687-704.

Schlemmer, A.: "Nietzsche et la Mort de Dieu", *Foi et Vie* 72, no. 5-6, 8-16.

Schlette, Heinz Robert: "Kosmodizee und Theodizee. Ein historischer und hermeneutischer Struktur-Vergleich", *Kairos* 15, Heft 3-4, 188-200.

Schulz, W.: "God of the Philosophers in Modern Metaphysics", *Man and World* 6, No. 4, 353-371.

Sommet, J.: "Univers sans rivage", *Christus* 20, no. 78, 231-241.

Stewart, D.: "Aristotle's Doctrine of the Unmoved Mover", *The Thomist* 37, No. 3, 522-547.

Taureck, B.: "Nihilismus und Christentum. Ein Beitrag zur philosophischen Klärung von Nictzsches Verhältnis zum Christentum", *WissWb* 26/2, 115-133.

Tealdi, C. J.: "Marxismo y religion", *Universidad* 82, 235-250.

Trede, J. H.: "Mythologie und Idee. Die systematische Stellung der 'Volksreligion' in Hegels Jenaer Philosophie der Sittlichkeit (1801-1803)", *Hegel Studien*, Beiheft 9, 167-210.

Ulrich, Ferdinand: "Gnosis und Agape. (Ein Beitrag zum Verhältnis von Philosophie und Religion bei Hegel)", *Kairos* 15, Heft 3-4, 280-310.

Ward, K.: "Explanation and Mystery in Religion", *Religious Studies* IX/1, 23-37.

Weinke, K.: "Ludwig Feuerbachs Religionsphilosophie", *Conceptus* 7, 77-84 (with a summary in English).

Yovel, Y.: "Bible Interpretation as Philosophical Praxis: A Study of Spinoza and Kant", *JHPh* 11/2, 189-212.

5. SOCIOLOGY OF RELIGION

Adam, A.: "Quelques réflexions sur la sociologie musulmane", *ROMM* 13-14, 14-21.

Asuni, T.: "Socio-Medical Problems of Religious Converts", *Psychopathologie Africaine* 9/2, 223-236 (174: rés. en fr.)

Bastide, R.: "Contributions à une sociologie des religions en Amérique Latine", *ASR* 18, No. 35, 139-150.

Belmont, N.: "Fonction de la croyance", *L'Homme* 13, no. 3, 72-81 (with a summary in English).

Büttner, M.: "Neue Strömungen in der Religionsgeographie", *ZMRW* 57, Heft 1, 39-59, Bibliographie (3 S.)

Carter, A. T.: "A Comparative Analysis of Systems of Kinship and Marriage in South Asia", *PRAIGBI* 29-54.

Clanton, G.: "Peter L. Berger and the Reconstruction of the Sociology of Religion", *DisAbIn A* 34/4, 2014. (The author's summary of his diss., Graduate Theological Union, 1973).

Crawford, M. P.: "Retirement: A Rite de passage", *The Sociological Review* 21/3, 447-461.

De Neve, A.: "Secularization in Russian Sociology of Religion", *SoCoR* 20, no. 4, 593-601, with a summary in French.

Desroche, H.: "Sociologies religieuses et discours francophones. Colloque d'Albiez-le-vieux (28 janvier-3 février 1973)", *ASR* 18 (35), 113-138.

Dobbelaere, K. and J. Lauwers: "Definition of Religion. A Sociological Critique", *SoCoR* 20/4, 535-551.

Dux, G.: "Ursprung, Funktion und Gehalt der Religion", *Internationales Jahrbuch für Religionssoziologie* 8, 7-67.

Ellul, J.: *Les Nouveaux Possédés.* (Paris, Arthème Fayard). 286 p.

Ermakov, I. M.: "Quelques pratiques religieuses d'une certaine partie de la jeunesse", *Filosofskie Nauki* 16/3, 102-106.

Fahim, H. M.: "Change in Religion in a Resettled Nubian Community in Upper Egypt", *IJMES* 4/2, 163-177 (with bibliography).

Faulkner, J. E. (ed.): *Religion's Influence in Contemporary Society: Readings in the Sociology of Religion*, 1972. – R: *RuSo* 38/2, 250-251 (R. J. Stellway).

Fossier, R.: "Remarques sur l'étude des 'commotions' sociales aux XIe et XIIe siècles", *Cahiers de Civilisation Médiévale* 16/1, 45-50.

Goodridge, R. M.: "The Secular Practice and the Spirit of Religion", *Social Compass* 20, No. 1, 19-30.

de Graaf, J.: "Die Ethik Schischkins. Ethik als Theorie der Moral in der Sowjetunion", *ZEE* 17/5, 270-284.

Gratzl, K. und R. Senarclens de Grancy: "Materielle und geistige Struktur einer Siedlung am Oberlauf des Amu Darya", *EZZ* 3/1, 54-105.

Grumelli, A.: "Secolarizzazione tra religione e ateismo", *Studium* 69, no. 11-12, 864-876.

Hertz, R.: *Sociologie religieuse et Folklore.* (Paris, PUF, 1970). xx, 205 p. – R: *CIS* 54, 176-180 (M. Matarasso).

Hummel, Gert: "Religionssoziologie und Theologie", in: U. Mann (Hrsg.): *Theologie und Religionswissenschaft* (Darmstadt, Wissenschaftliche Buchgesellschaft) 207-221.

Ivanjan, E. A.: "The social role of the religious propaganda in the Middle Ages", *Voprosy Istorii*, No. 2, 124-137.

Krǎstev, K. N.: "A propos de la nature de la conscience religieuse", *Filosofska Mis'l* 29/1, 122-128 (en bulgare).

Lauwers, J.: "Les théories sociologiques concernant la sécularisation. Typologie et critique", *SoCoR* 20/4, 523-533.

Libiszowska, Maria: "Denomination as a Type of Religious Organization", *Euhemer* XVII/2 (88), 13-21. (in Polish).

McCready, W. – N. McCready: "Socialisation et survivance de la religion", *Concilium*, No. 81, 57-68.

Malamat, Abraham: "Tribal Societies: Biblical Genealogies and African Lineage Systems", *AES* 14, 126-136, 3 tables.

Menu, M.: *Le mythe de la jeunesse.* (Lille, Service de reproduction des thèses, Univ. de Lille III). 525 p., bibliographie. (Thèse, Univ. de Nice, 1970).

Michelat, G. et M. Simon: "Catholiques déclarés et irreligieux communisants: vision du monde et perception du champ politique", *ASR* 18 (35), 57-111 (with English summary).

Mizov, N.: "Le processus de l'élimination de la religion et sa mise en oeuvre", *Voprosy Filosofii* no. 7, 77-82 (en russe).

Müller, G. H.: "Asceticism and Mysticism. A Contribution towards the Sociology of Faith", *IJR* 8, 68-132.

Munters, Q. J.: "La sociologia della religione in Olanda. Alcune linee di sviluppo", *Humanitas* 28/5, 348-368.

Nelsen, H. M.: "Intellectualism and Religious Attendance of Metropolitan Residents", *JSSR* 12/3, 285-296, bibliogr.

Nelson, G. K. and R. A. Clews: "Geographical mobility and religious behaviour", *SocRev* 21/1, 127-135.

Nowaczyk, M.: "Marxism and Religion in the Early Writings of Gramsci", *Euhemer* 17, No. 3, 59-72. (In Polnish).

Okechukwu Odita, E.: "Universal Cults and Intra-Diffusion: Jgbo Jkenga in Cultural Retrospection", *AfrSR* 16/1, 73-82, bibliography.

Orsolić, M.: "La sociologie de la religion d'inspiration marxiste en Yougoslavie", *SoCoR* 20/1, 73-82 (with a summary in English).

Pickering, W. S. F.: "The Persistence of Rites of Passage: Towards an Explanation", *BJS* 25/1, 63-78, Bibliography.

Pospelov, G.: "L'homme et les principes moraux du progres scientifique", *Sciences Sociales* no. 3, 54-69.

Power, D.: "La survivance de la religion. Aperçu théologique", *Concilium*, No. 81, 93-105.

"Religiöse Minderheiten in der UdSSR", *Pogrom* 4 (20), 8-46, Bibliographie (1 p.).

Remy, J. et E. Servais: "Clandestinité et illégitimité: les fonctions de l'occulte et du mystérieux dans la société contemporaine", *Concilium*, No. 81, 69-80.

Rigby, A. — B. S. Turner: "Communes, Hippies et Religion sécularisées. Quelques aspects sociologiques de formes actuelles de réligiosité", *SoCoR* 20/1, 5-18 (with a summary in English).

Roy, A.: "A Marxist View of Liberation", *The Ecumenical Review* 25, No. 2, 202-213.

Samarin, W.: "Religious Motives in Religious Movements", *Internationales Jahrbuch für Religionssoziologie* 8, 163-174.

Scholten, R. G.: "Godsdienstsociologie in Nederlandse theologische en sociaalwetenschappelijke tijdschriften 1965-1971", *NeTT* 27, 71-77.

Schrey, H.-H.: "Neuere Tendenzen der Religionssoziologie", *Theologische Rundschau* 38, 54-63, 99-118.

Sellers, J.: "Theological Belief and Sociological Inquiry: Reckoning with the Tension", *JR* 53/2, 228-238.

Sidler, Nikolaus: *Zur Universalität des Inzesttabu. Eine kritische Untersuchung der These und der Einwände.* (Stuttgart, Ferdinand Enke, 1971). viii, 166 p. = Soziologische Gegenwartsfragen, N.F., 36. – R: *Anthropos* 68, 961-962 (Ferdinand Herrmann).

Smith, A. D.: "Nationalism and Religion. The Role of Religious Reform in the Genesis of Arab and Jewish Nationalism", *ASR* 18 (35), 23-43.

Willaime, J.-P.: "Religion et conflit", *RHPhR* 53/2, 229-245. (A critical review of L. Laeyendecker's book in Dutch under the same title).

Zevaco, P.: "Mythologie indienne et condition ouvrière en Bolivie", *Cultures* 1, no. 2, 91-104, bibliographie.

6. PHAENOMENOLOGY OF RELIGION

Annequin, J.: *Recherches sur l'action magique et ses représentations (Ier et IIe siècles après J.-C.)* (Paris, Les Belles Lettres, CNRS). 240 p., bibliographie (14 p.), index = Annales Littéraires de l'Université de Besançon, 146.

Babajan, F. S.: "Motifs ornementaux de céramique médiévale", *VON* no. 12, 72-81, 2 p. (en arménien, résé en russe).

Barb, A. A.: "Magica varia", *Syria* 49, fasc. 3-4, 343-370, 2 pl.

Baskakov, N. A.: "L'âme dans les anciennes croyances des Turcs de l'Altaï (termes, leur signification et étimologie)", *SovEtn* 5, 108-113 (en russe).

Baumer, I.: "Der Wissenschaftscharakter der Volkskunde insbesondere der religiösen Volkskunde", *ÖZV* 76/1, 9-30.

Beckman, Bjarne: *Die Maus im Altertum.* Vorbereitende Untersuchungen zu einer Herausgabe der hochmittelalterlichen Mäusesagen. (Zürich, Inst. Orell Füssli, 1972). 128 S., 20 Abb. (Darstellung der Rolle der Maus in der Religion und im Volksglauben). – R: *Anthropos* 68, 960 (Ferdinand Herrmann).

Béguin, G.: "Musée Guimet: quatre statues népalaises", *RLMF* 23, no. 6, 387-392.

Benz, Ernst: "Die ewige Jugend in der christlichen Mystik von Meister Eckhart bis Schleiermacher", *Eranos-Jahrbuch* 40, 1-50.

Bertagaev, T. A.: "Le culte de la déesse-mère et du feu chez les Mongols", *SovEtn* no. 6, 120-125 (en russe).

Bichir, G.: "Manifestations de caractère magique et culturel chez les Carpes", *Dacia* 17, 243-256, illus.

Bleeker, C. J.: "Some Remarks on the Religious Significance of Lights", *JANES* 5 (The Gaster Festschrift), 23-34.

Bowker, J.: "Suffering and the Origins of Religion", *Humanitas* 9/1, 111-122.

Boyle, J. A.: "The Hare in Myth and Reality: A Review Article", *Folklore* 84, No. 4, 313-326.

Breydy, Michael: "Der melodische Rhytmus in der Kultdichtung des syro-aramäischen Sprachraumes (von Phönizien bis Chaldäa und Malabar)", *Oriens Christianus* 57, 121-141.

Burns, J. B.: "The Mythology of Death in the Old Testament", *SJTh* 26, No. 3, 327-340.

Buss, R. J.: *The Klabautermann of the Northern Seas. An Analysis of the Protective Spirit of Ships and Sailors in the Context of Popular Belief, Christian Legend, and Indo-European Mythology.* (Berkeley and Los Angeles, University of California Press). 138 p., Bibliography (9 p.) = Folklore Studies, 25.

Chandra, M.: "Studies in the Cult of the mother Goddess in Ancient India", *BMWI* No. 12, 1-47.

Chikovani, M. I.: "Variants of Plot on Pandora in Literature and Folklore of Greece, Georgia, India and Iran", in: *XXIXe Congrès International des Orientalistes. Résumés des Communications*, Sections 1-5. (Paris, Y. Hervouet), pp. 37-38.

Child, Heather and Dorothy Colles: *Christian Symbols, Ancient and Modern.* (London, 1971). – R: *BiOr* 30, 306-307 (J. N. Bakhuizen van den Brink).

Closs, Alois: "Priester, Prophet", *Studia Missionalia* 22, 1-30 Bibliographie (1 p.).

Courtès, P.-C.: "Le mythe et le sacré", *Revue Thomiste* 72/3, 392-407.

Davies, T. W.: *Magic, Divination, and Demonology among the Hebrews and their Neighbors.* – R: *BibZ* 17, 304-305 (Anon.)

Demargne, P.: "Le décor des sarcophages de Xanthos: réalités, mythes, symboles", *CRAIBL*, no. avril-juin, 262-271.

Dioszegi, V. et E. Lot-Falck: "Les tambours chamaniques des Turcs Barabin: étude comparée", *L'Ethnographie* 67, 18-46.

Domenach, J.-M.: "Le requiem structuraliste", *Esprit* (Paris), No. 3, 692-703. (Reflexions on Claude Lévi-Strauss's views in his *Mythologiques* and, especially, his last volume, *L'Homme nu*).

Draževa, R. D.: "Rites en rapport avec la protection de la santé durant les fêtes du solstice d'été chez les slaves orientaux et du Sud", *SovEtn* no. 6, 109-119 (en russe).

Duvernay, J.: "Les voies du chamane", *L'Homme* 13, no. 3, 82-92 (with a summary in English).

Eickelpasch, Rolf: *Mythos und Sozialstruktur.* (Düsseldorf, Bertelsmann Universitätsverlag). 155 S. = Studien zur Sozialwissenschaft 7.

Eilers, Wilhelm: *Semiramis. Entstehung und Nachhall einer altorientalischen Sage.* (IBHR, 1971, S. 23). – R: *Syria* 49, 452-454 (M. Lambert). *JNES* 32, 260-261 (L. D. Levine). *RAAO* 67, 94 (J. Nougayrol).

Fédry, J.: "Langage et ethnographie. Une étude de J. S. Mbiti sur l'eschatologie en Afrique", *RchSR* 61/1, 139-151 (with a summary in English. For Mbiti's work see *IBHR*, 1971, p. 120).

Foubert, J.: "Mystique plotinienne. Mystique bergsonienne", *Les Etudes Bergsoniennes* 10, 7-71.

Gallardo, M. D.: "La mitologia en le pintura del Museo del Prado", *Estudios Clasicos* 16, no. 66-67, 205-217.

Gaulier, S.: "Aspects iconographiques des croyances eschatologiques dans le bassin du Tarim d'après deux documents Pelliot", *ArAs* 28, 165-178, 6 pl.

Gese, Hartmut: "Der bewachte Lebensbaum und die Heroen. Zwei mythologische Ergänzungen zur Urgeschichte der Quelle J", *Festschrift Elliger* (q.v. sub I-7), 87-94.

Girard, R.: "Vers une définition systématique du sacré", *Liberté*, no. 87-88, 58-74.

Goetz, J.: "Ethnologie du sacerdoce", *Studia Missionalia* 22, 31-65.

Grambo, R.: "Sleeps as a Means of Ecstasy and Divination", *AEH* 22, no. 3-4, 417-425.

Grisward, J. H.: "Trois perspectives médiévales", *Nouvelle Ecole*, No. 21-22, 80-89 (d'après la méthode de Dumézil).

Hara, M.: "The King as a Husband of the Earth (mahi-pati)", *asiSt/EtAs* 27, No. 2, 97-114.

Hart III, G. L.: "Woman and the Sacred in Ancient Tamilnad", *The Journal of Asian Studies* 32/2, 233-250.

Haug, Walter: "Die Tristansage und das persische Epos Wîs und Râmîn", *GRM* 23, 404-423.

Hebga, M. et alii: *Croyance et guérison.* (Paris, Taoundé). 152 p.

de Heusch, L.: "Le sorcier, le père Tempels et les jumeaux mal venus", in: *La Notion de personne en Afrique Noire.* Colloques internationales du CNRS, 11-17 Octobre 1971. (Paris, CNRS), no. 544, 231-242, bibliographie.

Hooykaas, C.: *Bagus Umbara. Prince of Koripan. The Story of a Prince of Bali and a Princess of Java.* (London, 1968). – R: *OLZ* 68, 613-614 (Gertrud Pätsch).

Ionova, Ju. V.: "Les rites funeraires des Coréens", *SMAE* 29, 80-94 (en russe).

Jesi, F.: "La festa e la macchina mitologica", *Comunità* 27, no. 169, 317-347.

Kamenetzky, C.: "Herder und der Mythos des Nordens", *Revue de Littérature Comparée* 47/1, 23-41.

Kartomi, M. J.: "Music and Trance in Central Java", *Ethnomusicology* 17, No. 2, 163-208.

Kerns, T. A.: "The Mystical Experience and Veridicality: A History of the Argument from Unanimity", *Kinesis* 5/2, 111-133.

Kirk, G. S.: *Myth, its Meaning and Functions in Ancient and Other Cultures.* (London, Cambridge University Press). xii, 290 p. = Sather Classical Lectures, 40. (Reprint).

Kirk, G. S.: "On Defining Myths", in: *Exegesis and Argument, Studies in Greek Philosophy Presented to Gregory Vlastos* (Assen, Van Gorcum) 61-69.

Klímová, Dagmar: "Beitrag zur Problematik der Entwicklung der folkloristischen Motive Schlafkraut und Lebenskraut der Schlangen", *Fs de Liagre Böhl* (q. v. sub I-7), 243-252.

Köngas Maranda, E.: "Five Interpretations of a Melanesian Myth", *JAF* 86 (No. 339), 3-13.

Krstić, Nevena: "Zajednički motivi u *Hiljadu i jednoj noći* i u Vukovoj zbirci narodnih pripovedaka i pesama" (The related motifs in the *Arabian Nights* and in the Collection of folk tales and poems by Vuk St. Karadžić), *POF* 18-19, 121-204. (In Serbo-Croatian, with English summary, pp. 201-204).

Kvastad, N. B.: "Philosophical Problems of Mysticism", *International Philosophical Quarterly* 13/2, 191-207.

La Barre, W.: *The Ghost Dance: Origins of Religion,* (Garden City, N.Y., Doubleday, 1970), xvi, 677 p. – R: *AmAnth* 75, 489-491 (S. P. Dunn).

Leertouwer, L.: "Inquiry into Religious Behaviour. A Theoretical Reconnaissance", in: *Religion, Culture and Methodology* (q. v. sub I-7), 79-98. ("References", pp. 96-98).

Ligeti, L.: "Le sacrifice offert aux ancêtres dans l'*Histoire secrète*", *AOH* 27/2, 145-161.

Lörincz, L.: "Die mongolische Mythologie", *Acta Orientalia* (Budapest) 27, No. 1, 103-126.

Maillard, M.: "Essai sur la vie matérielle dans l'oasis de Tourfan pendant le haut Moyen Age", *ArAs* 29 (no. spécial), 1-187, 105 pl., bibliographie. (Religions: Bouddhisme, Manichéisme, Nestorianisme, Islam).

Mainberger, G.: "Glaubensformeln in der Philosphie? Die mythologische Funktion des Bejahens und Verneinens", *LingBib* No. 27-28, 14-24. (With a summary in English).

Mande, P. B.: "Dakkalwars and their Myths", *Folklore* (Calcutta) 14, No. 2, 69-76.

Mareuil, A.: "Réflexions sur le rôle de l'enseignement littéraire pour la découverte des mythes", *OERE* 13 (48), 85-118.

Martin, F. D.: *Art and the Religious Experience: The "Language" of the Sacred.* (Lewisburg, Bucknell University Press, 1972). 288 p. – R: *Process Studies* 3, No. 3, 230-235 (J. L. Smith).

Meinardus, Otto: "The equestrian deliverer in eastern iconography", *Oriens Christianus* 57, 142-155, 3 pl.

Meletinsky, E.: "Les théories mythologiques du XXe siècle", *Sciences Sociales*, no. 3, 109-124.

Meletinsky, E. M.: "Typological Analysis of the Palaeo-Asiatic Raven Myths", *AEH* 22, 107-155.

Mode, Heinz: *Fabeltiere und Dämonen. Die phantastische Welt der Mischwesen.* (Leipzig, Edition Verlag). 280 S., zahlr. Abb. (teils farbig).

Mugler, C.: "Sur quelques points de contact entre la magie et les sciences appliquées des anciens", *RPhLHA* 47/1, 31-37.

Mulder, D. C.: "Mogelijkheden en grenzen van een fenomenologie der religies" (Possibilities and limits of a phenomenology of religion), *GThT* 73, 30-40.

Müller, Werner: "Raum und Zeit in Sprachen und Kalendern Nordamerikas und Alteuropas", *Anthropos* 68, 156-180, 8 Abb., 2 Taf. (with English summary and bibliography).

Nakamura, H.: "Faith and Reason in Early Buddhism and Christianity", *Journal of Ecumenical Studies* 10/1, 30-50. (With summaries in French, German, Spanish and Italian).

Nowotny, Karl A.: *Beiträge zur Geschichte des Weltbildes. Farben und Weltrichtungen.* (Horn/Wien, F. Berger & Söhne, 1970, 1970). 263 S., illus. = Veröffentlichungen des Instituts für Völkerkunde der Universität Wien, 17. – R: *Anthropos* 68, 959-960 (Ferdinand Herrmann).

Oakes, R. A.: "Noumena, Phenomena, and God", *IJPhR* 4/1, 31-38.

Ogibenin, B. L.: *Structure d'un mythe védique. Le mythe cosmogonique dans le Rgveda.* (traduit du russe par Catherine Brodsky-Campbell). (The Hague, Martinus Nijhoff). 170 p. = Approaches to Semiotics, 30.

Pairault, C.: "Sacrifices africains et sacrifices judéo-chrétiens", *AUAL* 6, 319-328.

Panoff, M.: "Lévi-Strauss tel qu'en lui-même", *Esprit* (Paris) No. 3, 704-710. (Analysis of Lévi-Strauss's *L'Homme nu*, vol. 4 of his *Mythologiques*).

Perczak, E.: "Les courants principaux dans la recherche de la mythologie lunaire", *SThV* 11/1, 241-254 (in Polnish).

Petit-Klinkenberg, D.: "Mythe et expérience mystique selon Lucien Lévy-Bruhl", *RPhL* 71, no. 9, 114-125 (with a summary in English).

Pichon, J. C.: "Vie et mort des structures mythiques", *Liberté* (Montreal), No. 87-88, 17-51.

Pollak-Eltz, A.: "María Lionza, Mito y Culto Venezolano", *Montalban* 2, 509-576.

Putscher, Marielene: *Pneuma, Spiritus, Geist. Vorstellungen vom Lebensantrieb in ihren geschichtlichen Wandlungen.* (Wiesbaden, Franz Steiner Verlag). xi, 278 p., 21 Taf.

Ramsaran, J. A.: *English and Hindi Religious Poetry. An Analogical Study.* (Leiden, E. J. Brill). x, 199 p. = Supplements to Numen (Studies in the Histories of Religions), 22.

Reno, St. J.: "Myth in Profile", *Temenos* 9, 38-54.

Richard, J.-G.: "Rome: mythe, histoire et héritage", *Nouvelle Ecole*, No. 21-22, 96-101. (Etude d'après la méthode de Dumézil).

Rivière, J.-C.: "Pour une lecture de Dumézil. Introduction à son oeuvre", *Nouvelle Ecole*, No. 21-22, 115-120.

Röhr, H.: "Buddha und Jesus in ihren Gleichnissen", *NZSTh* 15, Heft 1, 65-86.

Röhr, H.: "Buddhismus und Christentum. Untersuchung zur Typologie zweier Weltreligionen", *ZRGG* 25/4, 289-303.

Rombach, H.: "Die Religionsphänomenologie. Ansatz und Wirkung von M. Scheler bis H. Kessler", *ThPh* 48/4, 477-493.

Rosen, L. N.: "Contagion and Cataclysm: A Theoretical Approach to the Study of Ritual Pollution Beliefs", *African Studies* 32/4, 229-246.

Sabourin, Leopold: *Priesthood. A Comparative Study.* (Leiden, E. J. Brill). 279 p. = Studies in the History of Religions (Supplements to *Numen*), XXV.

Sadjadi, Z.: "Mithra et Crhist dans l'oeuvre de Khaghani", in: *XXIXe Congrès International des Orientalistes. Résumés des Communications*, Sections 1-5. (Paris, Y. Hervouet) 6, p. 117.

Schilling, R.: "Georges Dumézil: une grande aventure", *Nouvelle Ecole*, No. 21-22, 103-108.

von Schmidt, W. A.: "Mythologie und Uroffenbarung bei Herder und Friedrich Schlegel", *ZRGG* 25/1, 32-45.

Schröder, Dominik: *Aus der Volksdichtung der Monguor*, 2. Teil: *In den Tagen der Urzeit. Ein Mythus vom Licht und vom Leben.* Aufgenommen und übersetzt. (Wiesbaden, Harrassowitz, 1970). 168 p., 10 Abb., 2 Taf. = Asiatische Forschungen, 31. – R: *Anthropos* 68, 328-331 (A. Róna-Tas).

Schwarz, P.: *Die neue Eva. Der Sündenfall in Volksglaube und Volkserzählung.* (Göppingen, Verlag Alfred Kümmerle). viii, 250 S. = Göppinger Arbeiten zur Germanistik, 77.

Shapiro, S.: "Patterns of Religious Reformations", *CSSH* 15/2, 143-157 (in Buddhism, Hinduism, Islam, and Christianity).

von Sicard, Harald: "Zur Frage der ostafrikanischen 'Dilemma-Märchen' ", *Anthropos* 68, 294-296 (Bibliographie).

Simionescu, P.: "Réminiscences mythologiques. Significations d'un ancien culte de l'eau", *REF* 18/6, 465-476 (en roumain, rés. en fr.)

Smith, P.: "La nature des mythes", *Diogène*, No. 82, 91-108.

Spaemann, R.: "Mystique et Aufklärung", *Concilium*, No. 85, 81-92.

Srinivasan, D.: "The Myth of the Panis in the Rig Veda", *JAOS* 93/1, 44-57.

Stillman, Y. K.: "The Three Magic Objects: A Yemenite Follitale", *Fabula* 14, Heft 3, 228-236.

Sukeo, H.: "The Myth of Visiting the Land of the Dead", *The Japanese Journal of Ethnology* 38/1, 1-18. (In Japanese with English Summary).

Top, S.: "La relation entre le brigand et le diable dans la légende populaire et dans la littérature apparentée", *Volkskunde* 74 (24), 303-318 (en néerlandais).

Turner, V.: "The Center out There: Pilgrim's Goal", *History of Religions* XII, No. 3, 191-230.

Vidal de Brandt, M. M.: "La iconografia del grifo en la Península Ibérica", *Pyrenae* 9, 7-151, 4 pl.

Višnevskaja, O. A.: *La culture des Saks du bas Syr-Daria du VIIe au Ve s. avant n. e.* (Moskva, Izdatel'stvo "Nauka"). 159 p. (En russe).

Vorbichler, Anton: "Die Bedeutung der religiösen Grundkulturen für die christliche Verkündigung", *Verbum SVD* 14, 122-131.

Waardenburg, J. D. J.: "Religionen der Gegenwart im Blickfeld phänomenologischer Forschung", *NZSTh* 15, 304-325.

Waardenburg, J. D. J.: "Research on Meaning in Religion", in: *Religion, Culture and Methodology*, edited by Th. P. van Baaren and H. J. W. Drijvers (q. v. sub I-7), 109-136.

Waida, M.: "Symbolism of 'Descent' in Tibetan Sacred Kingship and Some East Asian Parallels", *Numen* 20/1, 60-78.

Wainwright, W. J.: "Mysticism and Sense Perception", *Religious Studies* 9, No. 3, 257-278.

Weinfeld, M.: "Rider of the Clouds and Gatherer of the Clouds, Divine Imagary, East and West", in: *XXIXe Congrès International des Orientalistes. Résumés des Communications*, Sections 1-5. (Paris, Y. Hervouet), p. 55.

Welte, B.: "Religiöse Sprache", *ALW* 15, 7-21.

Zinn, G. A., Jr.: "Mandala Symbolism and Use in the Mysticism of Hugh of St. Victor", *History of Religions* 12/4, 317-341.

7. COLLECTIONS AND MISCELLANIES

[Abegg, W.:] *Artes Minores. Dank an Werner Abegg.* Herausgegeben von Michael Stettler und Machtild Lemberg. (Bern, Verlag Stämpfli). 262 S., 183 Abb. (davon 9 farbig).

Actas del II Coloquio Hispano-Tunecino de Estudios Históricos (Madrid/Barcelona, mayo de 1972). (Madrid, Instituto Hispano-Arabe de Cultura). 308 p.

Actes de la XVIIe Rencontre Assyriologique Internationale, Université Libre de Bruxelles, 30 juin-4 juillet 1969. (Ham-sur Heure, Comité Belge de Recherches en Mésopotamie, 1970). 197 p. — R: *Orientalia* 42, 528-530 (Luigi Cagni).

Altheim, Franz und Ruth Stiehl: *Geschichte Mittelasiens im Altertum. Mit Beiträgen von* J. Harmatta (u. a.) (Berlin, 1970). — R: *OLZ* 68, 494-497 (O. Klíma).

Arberry, A. J. (ed.): *Religion in the Middle East. Three Religions in Concord and Conflict.* I: *Judaism and Christianity*, ed. by E. I. J. Rosenthal and M. A. C. Warren. II: *Islam*, ed. by C. F. Beckingham. (London, 1969). — R: *OLZ* 68, 565-570 (Hans Bardtke).

Archäologische Mitteilungen aus Iran, Neue Folge, Band 4/1971. — R: *BiOr* 30, 472-474 (Prudence Oliver Harper).

van Baaren, Th. P. and H. J. W. Drijvers (Ed.): *Religion, Culture and Methodology. Papers of the Groningen Working-group for the Study of Fundamental Problems and Methods of Science of Religion.* (The Hague-Paris, Mouton). 171 p. = Religion and Reason, 8.

Başgöz, Ilhan and Andreas Tietze: *Bilmece: A Corpus of Turkish Riddles.* (Berkeley and Los Angeles, University of California Press). 1063 p. = Folklore Studies, 22.

Biezais, Haralds (ed.): *The Myth of the State.* Based on Papers read at the Symposium on the Myth of the State held at Åbo on the 6th-8th September 1971. (Stockholm, Almquist & Wiksell, 1972). 188 p. = Scripta Instituti Donneriani Aboensis VI. — R: *BiOr* 30, 505-507 (C. J. Bleeker).

Biobaku, S. O. (ed.): *Sources of Yoruba History.* (Oxford, Clarendon Press). xi, 268 p., 14 fig., 4 pl. = Oxford Studies in African Affairs.

Blue, L.: "Practical Ecumenism: Jews, Christians and Moslems in Europe", *Journal of Ecum. Studies* 10/1, 17-29.

[Brandon, S. G. F.:] *Man and his Salvation. Studies in Memory of S. G. F. Brandon.* Edited by Eric J. Sharpe and John R. Hinnells. (Manchester, Manchester University Press).

Brentjes, B.: *Drei Jahrtausende Armenien.* (Leipzig, Koehler & Amelang). 240 S., 30 Abbildungen im Text, 115 Abb. a. Taf., 4 Farbatf.

Brentjes, B.: "Konferenzbericht" [: 1. Die Materialien der Konferenz von 1971: *Biruni i gumanitarnye Nauki*, (Taschkent, 1972), aufgeführt (14 Beiträge), (und) 2. Der Kongress von 1972 in Taschkent über "Biruni und die Naturwissenschaften", mit Angabe der 18 Vorträge], *BiOr* 30, 315-316.

Brugman, J., M. David, F. R. Kraus, P. W. Pestman, and M. H. van der Valk: *Essays on Oriental Laws of Succession.* (Leiden, 1969). — R: *OLZ* 68, 136-137 (R. Haase). *ArOr* 41, 378-379 (J. Klíma).

[Cerfaux, L.:] *L'Evangile de Luc. Problèmes littéraires et théologiques. Mémorial Lucien Cerfaux.* (Gembloux, J. Duculot).

[David, M.:] *Symbolae iuridicae et historicae Martino David dedicatae.* Tomus alter: *Iura Orientis Antiqui.* Edid.: J. A. Ankum, R. Feenstra, W. F. Leemans. – R: *JNES* 32, 259-260 J. A. Brinkman). *ArOr* 41, 166-167 (J. Klíma). *BiOr* 30, 194-196 (D. O. Edzard).

Deuel, Leo: *Das Abenteuer Archäologie. Berühmte Ausgrabungsberichte aus dem Nahen Osten.* (München, C. H. Beck'sche Verlagsbuchhandlung). 336 p., 40 Abb., 1 Karte.

[Dupont-Sommer, A.:] *Hommages à André Dupont-Sommer.* (Paris, Adrien Maisonneuve, 1971). – R: *Euhemer* XVII/2 (88), 111-115 (Witold Tyloch).

[Elliger, K.:] *Wort und Geschichte. Festschrift für Karl Elliger zum 71. Geburtstag.* (Kevelaer, Butzon & Bercker/Neukirchen/Vluyn, Neukirchener Verlag). 215 S. = Alter Orient und Altes Testament, 18.

Enchora. Zeitschrift für Demotistik und Koptologie, 2. Herausgegeben von E. Lüddeckens, H.-J. Thissen und K.-Th. Zauzich. (Wiesbaden, 1972). – R: *BiOr* 30, 244-245 (Richard Holton Pierce).

[Evans-Pritchard, E. E.:] *The Translation of Culture. Essays to E. E. Evans-Pritchard.* Edited by T. O. Beidelman. (London, Tavistock Publ.) ix, 440 p. = Social Science Paperbacks, 117. (First published in 1971).

[Florovsky, G. V.:] *The Heritage of the Early Church. Essays in Honor of the Very Reverend Georges Vasilievich Florovsky.* Edited by D. Neiman and M. Schatkin. (Roma, Pontificium Institutum Studiorum Orientalium). 473 p., bilbiographie (15 p.), 1 pl. = Orientalia Christiana Analecta, 195.

Forge, Anthony (ed.): *Primitive Art and Society.* (London, Oxford University Press). xxii, 286 p., illus.

von Gabain, A.: *Das Leben im uigurischen Königreich von Qočo (850-1250).* 2 Bände. 1: Textband. 2: Tafelband. (Wiesbaden, Otto Harrassowitz). Bd. 1: 251 p. Bd. 2: 57 Bl. mit 235 Abb. = Veröffentlichungen der Societas Uralo-Altaica, 6.

[Gelb, I. J.:] "Approaches to the Study of the Ancient Near East: A Volume of Studies Offered to Ignace Jay Gelb on the Occasion of his Sixty-Fifth Birthday, October 14, 1972. (Edited by G. Buccellati)", *Orientalia* 42, 1-338, portr. (Abbr.: *Fs Gelb*).

[Glueck, N.:] *Essays in Honor of Nelson Glueck. Near Eastern Archaeology in the Twentieth Century,* ed. by J. A. Sanders. (New York, 1970). – R: *OLZ* 68, 587-588 (Otto Eissfeldt).

[Gordon, C. H.:] *Orient and Occident. Essays presented to Cyrus H. Gordon on the Occasion of his Sixty-fifth Birthday.* Edited by Harry A. Hoffner, Jr. (Kevelaer, Butzon & Bercker/Neukirchen-Vluyn, Neukirchener Verlag). ix, 286 p., frontisp. (portr.), 36 fig., 3 pl. = Alter Orient und Altes Testament, Veröffentlichungen zur Kultur und Geschichte des Alten Orients und des Alten Testaments, Band 22.

Haberland, Elke (ed.): *Leo Frobenius. An Anthology.* Foreword by Léopold Sedar-Senghor. (Wiesbaden, F. Steiner). xiv, 233 p., 55 fig., 24 pl. = Studien zur Kulturkunde, 32.

Harner, Michael J. (ed.): *Hallucinogens and Shamanism.* (London, Oxford University Press). xv, 200 p., illus.

Heissig, W.: *Serta Tibeto-Mongolica. Festschrift für Walther Heissig.* (Wiesbaden, Otto Harrassowitz). ??? p.

de Heusch, Luc: *Pourquoi l'épouser? et autres essais.* (Paris, Gallimard, 1971). 331 p. = Bibliothèque des Sciences Humaines. – R: *Anthropos* 68, 630-631 (Albert Doutreloux).

Hintze, F.: "Otto Eissfeldt, *1. September 1887 in Northeim/Hann., † 23. April 1973 in Halle/Saale", *OLZ* 68, [325-326].

Honko, L.: "The Finnish Society for the Study of Comparative Religion in 1963-1973", *Temenos* 9, 5-14.

Hügli, A., P. Magnenat, et L. Boros: "Der Tod. La Mort. (Symposium de la Société Suisse de Philosophie à Lausanne le 27 février 1972)", *Studia Philosophica* 32, 1-55.

Ikbal Ali Shah, The Sirdar (ed.): *The Spirit of the East.* An Anthology of the Scriptures of the East, with an explanatory Introduction. (London, The Octagon Press). 277 p.

Die Jagd bei den altaischen Völkern. Vorträge der VIII. Permanent International Altaistic Conference vom 30. 8. bis 4. 9. 1965 in Schloss Auel. (Wiesbaden, 1968). – R: *OLZ* 68, 59-61 (U. Johansen).

[Kahle, P.:] *In Memoriam Paul Kahle*, hrsg. von M. Black und G. Fohrer. (Berlin, 1968). – R: *OLZ* 68, 264-267 (Johann Fück).

Kratz, U.: *Indonesische Märchen.* Herausgegeben und aus dem Indonesischen übertragen. (Düsseldorf-Köln, Diederichs). 292 S. = Die Märchen der Weltliteratur.

Kusunoki, Masahiro: "In memoriam of Prof. Teruji Ishizu", *Numen* 20, 161-162.

[Langosch, K.:] *Literatur und Sprache im europäischen Mittelalter. Festschrift für Karl Langosch zum 70. Geburtstag.* Herausgegeben von A. Önnerfors, J. Rathofer und F. Wagner. (Darmstadt, Wissenschaftliche Buchgesellschaft). viii, 525 S., Front. (portr.).

Leemans, W. F.: *L'égyptologie Conrade Leemans et sa correspondance. Contribution à l'histoire d'une science.* Publié à l'occasion du cent-cinquantième anniversaire du déchiffrement des hiéroglyphes et du centenaire des Congrès des Orientalistes. (Leiden, E. J. Brill). viii, 105 p.

[Leroi-Gourhan, A.:] *L'Homme hier et aujourd'hui. Recueil d'études en hommage à André Leroi-Gourhan.* (Paris, Ed. Cujas).

[de Liagre Böhl, F. M. Th.:] *Symbolae Biblicae et Mesopotamicae Francisco Mario Theodoro de Liagre Böhl dedicatae.* Ediderunt M. A. Beek, A. A. Kampman, C. Nijland, J. Ryckmans. (Leiden, E. J. Brill). 4to. viii, 416 p., portrait, 15 fig. 10 pl. = Nederlands Instituut voor het Nabije Oosten. Studia Francisci Scholten Memoriae Dicata, IV. (Abbr.: Festschrift/Fs. de Liagre Böhl!).

Lohner, Edgar (Hrsg.): *Studien zum West-östlichen Divan Goethes.* (Darmstadt, Wissenschaftliche Buchgesellschaft). xvii, 324 S. = Wege der Forschung, Band 287.

Maas, Paul: *Kleine Schriften.* Herausgegeben von Wolfgang Buchwald. (München, C. H. Beck'sche Verlagsbuchhandlung). xii, 705 S., Porträt.

Mann, Ulrich (Hrsg.): *Theologie und Religionswissenschaft. Der gegenwärtige Stand ihrer Forschungsergebnisse und Aufgaben im Hinblick auf ihr gegenseitiges Verhältnis.* (Darmstadt, Wissenschaftliche Buchgesellschaft). xiv, 481 S.

Mason, Philip (ed.): *India and Ceylon: Unity and Diversity. A Symposium.* (London, 1967). – R: *OLZ* 68, 185-190 (Heinz Bechert).

Moriarty, F. L.: *The Word in the world. Essays in Honor of Frederick L. Moriarty, S. J.* Edited by R. J. Clifford and G. W. MacRae. (Cambridge, Mass., Weston College Press).

Parsons, Robert T. (ed.): *Windows on Africa. A Symposium.* (Leiden, 1971). – R: *OLZ* 68, 97-99 (E. Dammann).

Paulme, Denise (ed.): *Classes et associations d'âge en Afrique de l'Ouest.* (Paris, Librairie Plon, 1971) 354 p., illus. = Recherches en Sciences Humaines, 35. – R: *Anthropos* 68, 652-654 (Jacques Binet).

Pennington, B.: "Association for Cistercian Studies", *Citeaux, Commentarii Cisterciences* 24/1, 53-61.

Pennington, B.: "Third Cistercian Studies Conference sponsored by the Institute for Cistercian Studies, Western Michigan University, Kalamazoo, Michigan, April 29-May 2 1973", *CCC* 24/2, 180-187.

[Pericot, L.:] *Estudios dedicados al Prof. Dr. Luis Pericot.* (Barcelona, Universidad, Instituto de Arqueologia y Prehistoria). xxxvi, 441 p. = Publicaciones eventuales, 23.

Presler, Henry H.: "Patronage for Public Religious Institutions in India", *Numen* 20, Nr. 2, 116-124.

Pritchard, James B. (ed.): *The Ancient Near East. Supplementary Texts and Pictures Relating to the Old Testament.* (Princeton, 1969). – R: *OLZ* 68, 473-474 (O. Eissfeldt).

Proceedings of the Twelfth International Congress of Papyrology. Edited by Deborah H. Samuel. (Toronto, 1970). – R: *BiOr* 30, 238-240 (T. Reekmans).

Proceedings of the Twenty-Sixth International Congress of Orientalists, New Delhi, January 4-10, 1964. 4 vols. (with vol. 3 in two parts). (New Delhi, 1966-1970). – R: *OLZ* 68, 238-246 (G. Hazai).

Pye, Michael and Robert Morgan (ed.): *The Cardinal Meaning. Essays in Comparative Hermeneutics: Buddhism and Christianity.* (The Hague and Paris, Mouton). 202 p. = Religion and Reason, 6.

[Rengstorf, K. H.:] *Festgabe für Karl Heinrich Rengstorf zum 70. Geburtstag.* (= *Theokratia. Jahrbuch des Institutum Judaicum Delitzschianum*, Vol. 2. Leiden, E. J. Brill). viii, 444 S., Porträt, 13 Taf.

[Renou, L.:] *Mélanges d'Indianisme à la Mémoire de Louis Renou.* (Paris, 1968). – R: *OLZ* 68, 67-75 (Friedrich Weller).

Resch, A. (Ed.): *Der kosmische Mensch.* (Paderborn, Verlag Schöningh). = Imago Mundi, 4.

Robe, S. L.: *Index of Mexican Folktales.* (Los Angeles, University of California Press). 276 p. = Folklore Studies, 26.

Robinson, J. D.: " 'La parole issue du silence'. Symposium sur les spiritualités des religions à travers le monde", *Concilium* No. 89, 109-117.

Robinson, James M. (ed.): *Religion and the Humanizing of Man.* (Waterloo/Ontario, Can., The Council on the Study of Religion). iv, 226 p.

Schmidt, L.: "Rudolf Kriss 70 Jahre. Eine Bibliographie seiner Veröffentlichungen von 1926 bis 1972", *ÖZV* 76/1, 1-8.

Shelton, John C.: *Papyri from the Michigan Collection.* (Toronto, 1971). – R: *BiOr* 30, 240-243 (E. Van 't Dack).

Sources Orientales, VIII: Génies, Anges et Démons. Egypte, Babylone, Israël, Islam, Peuples Altaïques, Inde-Birmanie, Asie du Sud-Est, Tibet, Chine. (Paris, 1971). – R: *OLZ* 68, 127 (G. Mensching).

Speth, William W.: " 'Leaders of Modern Anthropology': Robert H. Lowie", *Anthropos* 68, 296-299. (An extensive review of Robert F. Murphy: *Robert H. Lowie*, New York, Columbia University Press, ix, 179 p. = Leaders of Modern Anthropology Series).

Sprung, Mervyn (ed.): *The Problem of Two Truths in Buddhism and Vedānta.* Edited and Introduced. (Dordrecht, D. Reidel Publishing Company). viii, 125 p.

[Stählin, G.:] *Verborum Veritas. Festschrift für Gustav Stählin zum 70. Geburtstag.* (Wuppertal, 1970). – R: *ZRGG* 25, 88-90 (G. Hummel).

[Stinespring, W. F.:] *The Use of the Old Testament in the New and Other Essays. Studies in Honor of William Franklin Stinespring.* (Durham, N.C., 1972). – R: *JSJ* 4, 72-74 (A. S. van der Woude).

[de Strijcker, E.:] *ZETESIS. Door collegas en vrienden aangeboden aan Prof. Dr. Emile De Strijcker.* (Antwerpen/Utrecht, De Nederlandsche Boekhandel).

Temming, Rolf L. (ed.): *Seemanns-Sagen und Schiffermärchen.* Gesammelt von Heinrich Smidt. (Frankfurt a.M., Fischer). 189 p. = Fischer Taschenbuch, 1377.

Thomas, D. Winton (ed.): *Archaeology and Old Testament Study.* Jubilee Volume of the Society for Old Testament Study, 1917-1967. (Oxford, 1967). – R: *OLZ* 68, 471-473 (G. Wallis).

[Vlastos, G.:] *Exegesis and Argument. Studies in Greek Philosophy Presented to Gregory Vlastos.* Edited by E. N. Lee, A. P. D. Mourelatos and R. M. Rorty. (Assen, Van Gorcum). xviii, 452 p., portr.

Wallis, Gerhard: "In Memoriam Otto Eissfeldt, 1. September 1887 – 23. April 1973", *BiOr* 30, 347-348, Plaat IX.

Wiessner, Gernot (ed.): *Erkenntnisse und Meinungen, I.* (Wiesbaden, Otto Harrassowitz). iii, 238 S., 9 Abb. = Göttinger Orientforschungen, 1, Reihe: Syriaca, Band 3.

[Wilson, J. A.:] *Studies in Honor of John A. Wilson, September 12, 1969.* (Chicago, Ill., 1969). – R: *OLZ* 68, 570-574 (Elke Freier).

II PREHISTORIC AND PRIMITIVE RELIGIONS

1. PREHISTORIC RELIGION

Abásolo, J. A.: "Nuevas urnas 'en forma de casa' procedentes de Poza de la Sal (Burgos)", *BSEAA* 39, 434-443.

Almagro Gorbea, M. J.: *Los ídolos del Bronce I Hispano*. (Madrid, C. S. l. C.) 354 p., 57 pl. = Bibliotheca praehistorica Hispana, 12.

Anati, E.: "La stele di Triora (Liguria)", *BCCSP* 10, 101-126, 10 fig., bibliografia (1 p., with French and English summaries).

Arnal, J.: "Note sur la chronologie des statues-menhirs anthropomorphes en France", *RAN* 6, 263-265.

Behrens, H.: "Götterthron oder Altar? Neuartige Gegenstände der mitteldeutschen neolitischen Bernburger Kultur", *AuFu* 18/1, 19-22, 1 fig., 1 pl.

Cauvin, Jacques: *Religions neolithiques de Syro-Palestine, Documents.* (Paris, Maisonneuve). 140 p., 34 fig. = Publications du Centre de Recherches d'Ecologie et de Préhistoire, I.

Duchesne-Guillemin, J.: "On the Complaint of the Ox-Soul", *JIES* 1, No. 1, 101-104.

Engel, F. A.: "La Gorge de Huarangal: Ebauche d'une monographie de géographie humaine préhistorique", *BIFEA* 2/2, 1-26.

Feustel, R.: "Zum Problem der Evolution und Revolution in urgeschichtlicher Zeit" (mit Diskussionsbeiträgen von J. Herrmann, P. Donat, A. Häusler, H. Qitta, G. Guhr, W. Padberg, H. Behrens, I. Sellnow, B. Gramsch, H. Grünert und F. Schlette), *EAZ* 14/1, 55-133.

Gimbutas, M.: "Old Europe c. 7000 – 3500 B.C.: The Earliest European Civilization before the infiltration of the Indo-European Peoples", *JIES* I/1, 1-20.

Gómez-Tabanera, J. M.: "Sobre el denominado 'idolo prehistórico de Llamoso", *CuEsGa* 28 (84), 41-51.

Jankuhn, H.: *Vorgeschichtliche Heiligtümer und Opferplätze in Mittel- und Nordeuropa*. Bericht über ein Symposium in Reinhausen bei Göttingen vom 14. bis 16. Oktober 1966. (Göttingen, 1970). – R: *Germania* 51/2, 646-650 (R. A. Maier).

Maher, J. P.: "The Linguistic Paleontology of some Pre-Christian Burial Terms in Slavic Lexicon", *JIES* 1/1, 105-110.

Maringer, Johannes: "Das Wasser in Kult und Glauben der vorgeschichtlichen Menschen", *Anthropos* 68, 705-776. (Summarium in English. "Bibliographie", S. 761-776).

Masimov, I. S.: "Fouilles d'un sanctuaire de l'âge du bronze dans l'agglomération d'Altyn-Dépé (Turkmenistan)", *SovAr* no. 2, 139-145 (rés. en français).

Rao: S. R.: *Lothal and the Indus Civilization*. With a Foreword by Sir Mortimer Wheeler. (Bombay, Asia Publishing House). 4°. xix, 215 p., 44 fig., 125 pl.

Soutou, A.: "Les trois statues-menhirs des Ardaliès (Saint – Izaire, Aveyron)", *RAN* 6, 255-261.

Starr, Chester G.: *Early Man. Prehistory and the Civilizations of the Ancient Near East*. (New York, Oxford University Press). 206 p., illus.

Veiga Ferreira, O.: "Acerca das placas-idolos com mãos encontradas em Portugal e o culto da fecundidade", in: *Estudios dedicados al Prof. Dr. L. Pericot* (q.v.sub I-7), 233-240.

2. PRIMITIVE RELIGIONS

Abela de la Rivière, MarieThérèse: "Dioliba, village modèle. Un essai d'amélioration de l'habitat rural au Mali", *Anthropos* 68, 192-234, cartes, diagrs., tabl., English summary, bibliographie. ("Les observations ont maintes fois montré comment le village est dépendent, non seulement de l'environnement physique" ..., "mais aussi du système de production et de la vie sociale et religieuse dont la disposition des quartiers et des maisons est souvent le reflet et l'expression symbolique", p. 193).

Adler, A.: "Les Jumeaux sont rois", *L'Homme* 13, no. 1-2, 167-192.

Alsdorf-Bollee, A. et R. Chaudenson: "Deux contes populaires seychellos: texte, traduction et notes", *Te Reo* 16, 60-86.

Anton, Ferdinand: *Die Frauen der Azteken-Maya-Inka-Kultur*. (Berlin, W. Kohlhammer). 88 p. in quarto, 114 Taf.

Arinze, Francis A.: *Sacrifice in Ibo Religion*. Edited by J. S. Boston. (Ibadan, University Press, 1970). vii, 129 p., 4 pl. – R: *Anthropos* 68, 661-664 (Guglielmo Guariglia).

Aschwanden, H.: "Symbolik der Schlange im traditionellen Mwari-Kult der Karanga", *EZZ* 3/2, 7-19.

Aufenanger, H.: "Krankheiten und Heilmittel im Bismarck Gebirge und am Wahgi-Fluss im Hochland von Neu-Guinea", *Ethnomedizin* II/3-4, 329-360.

Aufenanger, H.: "The Dinggan, Spirit of Desease in the Central Highlands of New Guinea", *Ethnomedizin* I/3-4, 373-396.

Awolalu, J. Omosade: "Yoruba Sacrificial Practice", *Journal of Religion in Africa* 5, No. 2, 81-93.

Barnes, R. H.: "The Rainbow in the Representations of inhabitants of the Flores Area of Indonesia", *Anthropos* 68, 611-613, bibliography (3 ref.)

Bascom, William: *The Yoruba of Southwestern Nigeria.* (New York, Rinehart and Winston, 1969). xxii, 118 p., 31 pl., map. = Case Studies in Cultural Anthropology. – R: *Anthropos* 68, 656 (Walther F. E. Resch).

Becher, H.: "Die Haartracht der Yanonámi-Indianer Nordwestbrasiliens als Ausdrucksmittel religiöser Vorstellungen", *Kosmetologie* (Karlsruhe), 2-3.

Beck, J. C.: " 'Dream Messages' from the Dead", *Journal of the Folklore Institute* 10, 173-186.

Becquelin, P.: "Distribution de quelques éléments iconographiques des stèles mayas de Copan, Honduras", in: *L'Homme hier et aujourd'hui. Recueil d'études en hommage à André Leroi-Gourhan* (Paris, Cujas), pp. 253-262, bibliographie.

Benz, E. and K. W. Luckert: "The Road of Life: Report of a Visit by a Navaho Seer", *Ethnomedizin* II/3-4, 405-416.

Benzi, Marino: *Les derniers adorateurs du peyotl. Croyances, coutumes et mythes des indiens Huichol.* (Paris, Gallimard, 1972). 446 p., 52 illus., 4 cartes.

Bergsma, H. M.: "Tiv *Kuraiyol*, Body Protectors", *Africa* 43/2, 147-152 (with bibliography and a summary in French).

Berndt, R. M.: *Australian aboriginal religion.* Fasc. 1: introduction, the Southeastern Region. Fasc. 2: The Northeastern Region and North Australia. Fasc. 3: North Australia (cont.) Fasc. 4: Central Australia, Conclusion. (Leiden, E. J. Brill). 4to. *1*: ix, 44 p., 45 pl., 2 fold. maps. *2*: viii, 42 p., 41 pl., 2 fold. maps. *3*: viii, 28 p., 40 pl. *4*: viii, 37 p., 39 pl., fold. map. = Iconography of Religions, 5.

de Bianchi, M. Rivera: "Mitología de los pueblos del Chaco, según visión de los autores de los siglos XVII y XVIII", *AmIn* 33, no. 3, 695-734.

Bidou, P.: "Représentations de l'espace dans la mythologie tatuyo (Indiens Tucano)", *JSAm* 61, 45-105, bibliographie.

Biebuyck, Daniel: *Lega Culture. Art. Initiation, and Moral Philosophy among a Central African People.* (Berkeley, Uni- of California Press). xxiii, 268 p., 111 pl.

Bischofberger, Otto: *The Generation Classes of the Zanaki* (Tanzania). (Fribourg, University Press, 1972). 112 p., 12 pl., 1 diagr., 2 maps. = Studia Ethnographica Friburgensia, 1. – R: Anthropos 68, 669 (Léon de Sousberghe).

Blackman, M. B.: "Totems to Tombstones: Culture Change as Viewed through the Haida Mortuary Complex, 1877-1971", *Ethnology* 12/1, 47-56.

Blixen, Olaf: "Tradiçiones pascuenses. II. Ure o hei y los tres espiritus vengadores. Tuapoi, La vieja del Brazo Largo, La niña de la Roto", *Moana* I/6, 1-11.

Boccassino, R.: "Il culto dei defunti praticato dagli Acioli dell'Uganda", *APME* 37, 9-62, 50 photos.

Bolton, Ralph: "*Tawanku*: Intercouple Bonds in a Qolla Village (Peru)", *Anthropos* 68, 145-155 (with bibliography).

Bonnafé, P.: "Une grande Fête de la vie et de la mort: le miyali, cérémonie funéraire d'un seigneur du ciel kukuya (Congo-Brazzaville)", *L'Homme* 13, 97-166.

Bradbury, R. E.: *Benin Studies*. Edited with an Introduction by Peter Morton-Williams. Foreword by Daryll Forde. (London, Oxford University Press). xxi, 293 p., 9 fig., 4 pl., 1 map.

Brain, James L.: "Ancestors as Elders in Africa: Further Thoughts", *Africa* 43, No. 2, 122-133, bibliography.

Brain, James L.: "Tales from Uluguru in Eastern Tanzania", *Anthropos* 68, 113-136. (Introduction, 6 tales in original texts and parallel English translations, and bibliography).

Brand, Roger: "Notes sur des poteries rituelles au Sud-Dahomey", *Anthropos* 68, 559-568, 3 fig., carte, summarium en anglais.

Bromley, M.: "Ethnic Groups in Irian Jaya", *Irian* 2, No. 3, 1-37.

Bureau, R.: " 'Connais-tu la mort?'. Les trois nuits rituelles du Bwiti Fang", *AUAL* 6, 231-303, 12 fig. (dont deux cartes).

Burridge, Kenelm: *Encountering Aborigines. A Case Study: Anthropology and the Australian Aboriginal*. (Sydney, Pergamon Press). xi, 260 p. = Pergamon Frontiers of Anthropology Series.

Buxton, Jean: *Religion and Healing in Mandari*. (Oxford, Clarendon Press). xiv, 443 p., 14 fig., 7 pl., 2 maps.

Carneiro Da Cunha, M.: "Logique du mythe et de l'action. Le mouvement messianique canela de 1963", *L'Homme* 13/4, 5-37, bibliographie (3 p.)

Ceyssens, R.: "Les masques en bois des Kete du Sud, région du Kasaï occidental, République du Zaïre" (1), *Africa – Tervuren* 19/4, 85-96.

Comhaire-Sylvain, S.: *Qui mange avec une femme. Contes zaïrois et haïtiens*. (Bandundu, Centre d'Etudes Ethnologiques). xv, 310 p. Quarto. = CEEBA, Publications, Série II, 6.

Coppel, W. G.: "About the Cook Islands. Their Nomenclature and a Systematic Statement of Early European Contacts", *JSO* 29, 23-56.

Corzannet, F.: *Mythes et coutumes religieuses des tsiganes*. (Paris, Payot). 227 p.

Coupez, A. et Th. Kamanzi: *Littérature de cour au Rwanda*. (Oxford, Clarendon Press, 1970). xi, 237 p., 2ct. = Oxford Library of African Literature. – R: *Anthropos* 68, 339-340 (Léon de Sousberghe).

Cowan, H. K. J.: "La légende de Samudra (texte malais avec introduction, commentaire et traduction abrégée)", *Archipel* 5, 253-286.

Crumrine, N. R.: "La tierra te devorará: un análisis estructural de los mitos de los indígenas mayo", *AmIn* 33/4, 1119-1150.

Dammann, E.: "Alte Berichte aus dem Ovamboland von Martti Rautanen", *JSWASS* 27, 31-47.

Dammann, Ernst: " 'Primitive' Religionen der Gegenwart", in: U. Mann (Hrag.): *Theologie und Religionswissenschaft* (Darmstadt, Wissenschaftliche Buchgesellschaft) 189-206.

Della Capanna, G. P.: "Rilievi antropologici e etnografici sui Quijos (Ecuador)", *ArAnEt* 103, 133-221.

Della Capanna, G. P.: "Rilievi antropologici e etnografici sui Salasacas andini di altopiano (Ecuador)", *ArAnEt* 103, 253-293.

Deluz, A.: "Réflexions sur la fonction politique chez des islamisés et des animistes: Malinké, Sia, Guro de Côte d'Ivoire", *L'Homme* 13, 83-96.

Deng, Francis Mading: *The Dinka and Their Songs.* (Oxford, Clarendon Press). viii, 301 p. = Oxford Library of African Literature.

Devish, R.: "Le problème de la sacralisation et de la désacralisation dans une religion traditionnelle. Essai d'une approche théorique", *CJAS* 7/1, 77-95.

Diouf, Niokhobaye: "Chronique du royaume du Sine; suivie de notes sur les traditions orales et les sources écrites concernant le royaume du Sine" par Charles Becker et Victor Martin, *BIFAN* 34/4, 702-777.

Downes, R. M.: *Tiv Religion.* (Ibadan, 1971). – R: *JRA* 5, 67-68 G. Parrinder).

Dräger, L.: "Häuptlingstum und religiöse Autorität bei den Zentral-Algonkin", *JMVL* 29, 29-56.

Eibl-Eibesfeldt, Irenäus: "Die Waruwádu (Yuwana), ein kürzlich entdeckter, noch unerforschter Indianerstamm Venezuelas", *Anthropos* 68, 137-144, 6 Taf. (Summarium in Englisch, Bibliographie).

Eibl-Eibesfeldt, I.: "!Ko-Buschleute (Kalahari). Trancetanz", *Homo* 24, Heft 3-4, 245-252.

Elenga, L.: "Etude sur le serment boondo", *Cahiers des Religions Africaines* 7, no. 14, 287-296.

Engl, E.: "L'apparizione del Sole all'Inca Pachacutec Yupanqui", *Terra Ameriga* 9 (29-30), 69-73, bibliographie.

Erdheim, Mario: *Prestige und Kulturwandel. Eine Studie zum Verhältnis subjektiver und objektiver Faktoren des kulturellen Wandels zur Klassengesellschaft bei den Azteken.* (Wiesbaden, Focus-Verlag). 122 p. = Kulturanthropologische Studien zur Geschichte, 2.

Espinoza Soriano, W.: "Los grupos étnicos en la Cuenca del Chuquimayo, siglos XV y XVI", *BIFEA* 2, no. 3, 19-73.

Etienne, P.: "L'individu et le temps chez les baoulè", *Cahiers d'Etudes Africaines* 13/4, 631-648.

Evans-Pritchard, E. E.: *Nuer Religion* (Oxford, 1970). – R: *BTLV* 129, 155-156 (J. G. Oosten).

Evans-Pritchard, E. E.: "Some Zande Texts on Vengeance for Death", *Africa* 43, No. 3, 236-243.

Fabrega, Horacio, Jr. and Daniel B. Silver: *Illness and Shamanistic Curing in Zinacantan. An Ethnomedical Analysis.* (Stanford, Calif., Stanford University Press). xv, 285 p., 6 fig., 16 tab.

Feachem, R.: "The Religious Belief and Ritual of the Raiapu Enga", *Oceania* 43, No. 4, 259-285, bibliography.

Feer, M.: "*The Skunk and the Smallpox*: Mythology and Historical Reality", *PlAnth* 18 (59), 33-39, bibliography (1 p.)

Felbermayer, F.: "Zwei Erzählungen der Osterinsulaner", *Tribus* 22, 79-90.

Fichte, Hubert: "Abó. Anmerkungen zu den rituellen Pflanzen der afrobrasilianischen Religionsgruppe", *Ethnomedizin* 2, 361-403.

Figge, Horst H.: *Geisterkult, Besessenheit und Magie in der Umbanda-Religion Brasiliens.* (Freiburg und München, Karl Alber Verlag). 340 S., 55 Abb.

Figge, H. H.: "Schriftverkehr mit Geistern. Eine Untersuchung von Umbanda-Zetteln", *Staden-Jahrbuch* 20, 91-102.

Figge, Horst H.: "Umbanda: Eine brasilianische Religion", *Numen* 20, Nr. 2, 81-103. Bibliographie.

Figge, H. H.: "Zur Wirkweise magischer Praktiken", *Ethnomedizin* II, Heft 1-2, 113-132.

Fischer, E. und H. Shah: "Tatauieren in Kutch, Arbeitsweise und Muster der Harijan und Rabari in den Gemeinden Rapar und Anjar", *EZZ* 3/2, 105-129.

Fischer, H. J.: "Conversion reconsidered: some historical aspects of religious conversion in black Africa", *Africa* 43/1, 27-40. (Against the views of Robin Morton in his article published *ibid.*, 41, 85-108. Cf. *IBHR*, 1971, p. 40).

Flasche, Rainer: *Geschichte und Typologie afrikanischer Religiosität Brasiliens.* (Marburg an der Lahn, Univ.-Bibliothek). iii, 302 p. = Marburger Studien zur Afrika und Asienkunde, Serie A. 1.

Forno, Mario: "I timidi Piaroa poeti dell'inferno verde", *L'Universo* 53, 1-36, illus.

Forno, M.: "Racconti e canti del gruppo Ghivaro (Ecuador e Perù)", *APME* 37, 561-591.

Franklin, K. J.: "A Ritual Pandanus Language of New Guinea", *Oceania* 43/1 66-76.

Friedberg, C.: "Repérage et découpage du temps chez les Bunaq du centre de Timor" (avec deux contes Bunaq traduits par L. Berthe), *Archipel* 6, 119-144.

Frobenius, L.: "African Hunters: Bushmen and Hunting Spirits", *Studien zur Kulturkunde* 32, 119-124.

Frobenius, L.: "The Religion of the Yoruba", *Studien zur Kulturkunde* 32, 160-191.

Galvin, A. D.: "Kenyah Imen Birds and Beasts", *The Sarawak Museum Journal* 20 (40-41), 53-62.

Gass, P.: "Croyances, magie et superstitions des Bagwe ou Basukuma établis au sud du lac Victoria-Nyanza", *APME* 37, 385-459.

Gass, P., P. Girodon et P. Bourget: "Le Bugwe, Le Buzinza, Le Roi de Mwanza et de Babinza. Us et coutumes de Bagwe", *APME* 37, 325-383.

Del Gaudio, G.: "Le varie forme della schiavitù in uso tra le popolazioni del Sudan occidentale e della guinea superiore", *APME* 37, 63-324, bibliografia (7 p.)

Gerhardt, L.: "Abriss der nominalen Klassen im Koro, North – Central State, Nigeria", *AuÜ* 56/4, 245-266.

Gloria, H.: "The Legend of Lapulapu: An Interpretation", *PhQCS* I/3, 200-208.

Goody, Jack: *The Myth of the Bagre*. (Oxford, Clarendon Press). xii, 381 p., 9 pl. = Oxford Library of African Literature. – R: *JRA* 5, 235-236 (E. Dammann).

Gossiaux, P.-P.: "Note sur un type de masque Lubahemba", *RUB* 1, no. 3-4, 255-260, 1 photo.

Gravand, H.: "Le symbolisme Sérèr", *Psychopathologie Africaine* 9, no. 2, 237-265 (183-184, summary in English).

Guiart, J.: "Prescriptions matrimoniales négatives aux Nouvelles-Hébrides", *JSO* 29 (41), 339-368.

Haaf, E.: "Aus dem Leben der Meta-Frauen (Kameroun). Menstruation, Schwangerschaft und Geburt", *Ethnomedizin* I/1, 83-100.

Harjula, B.: *God and the Sun in Meru Thought*. (Helsinki, 1969). – R: *OLZ* 68, 413-414 (E. Dammann).

Harrisson, T.: "Dancing Out 'The Journey of the Dead' ", *The Sarawak Museum Journal* 20 (40-41), 173-178.

Hartmann, Günther: *Litjoko. Puppen der Karaja, Brasilien*. (Berlin, Museum für Völkerkunde). 133 p., 69 Abb., 74 Skizzen. = Veröffentlichungen des Museums für Völkerkunde Berlin, N.F., 23.

Hartmann, Horst: *Die Plains- und Prärieindianer Nordamerikas*. (Berlin, Museum für Völkerkunde). 422 p., 150 Abb., 16 Farbtaf., 4 Zeichn., 4 Kt. = Veröffentlichungen des Museums für Völkerkunde Berlin, N.F., 22. Abt. Amerikanische Naturvölker, II.

Hartog, J. and G. Resner: "Malay Folk Treatment Concepts and Practices with Special Reference to Mental Disorders", *Ethnomedizin* I/3-4, 353-372.

Harwood, A.: *Witchcraft, Sorcery and Social Categories among the Safwa* (London, 1970). – R: *BTLV* 129, 152-155 (W. Thoden van Velzen-Van Wetering).

Hayano, D. M.: "Sorcery Death, Proximity, and the Perception of Out-groups: The Tauna Awa of New Guinea", *Ethnology* 12, 179-191, bibliography.

Heath, D. B.: "New Patrons for Old: Changing Patrón-Client Relationships in the Bolivian Yungas", *Ethnology* 12/1, 75-98.

Heinen, H. D. – J. Lavandero: "Computación del tiempo en dos subtribus Warao", *Antropológica* 34, 3-24.

Heintz, B.: *Besessenheitsphänomene im mittleren Bantu-Gebiet.* (Wiesbaden, 1970). – R: *JRA* 5, 54-55 (J. K. Parrett).

Helfrich, Klaus: *Menschenopfer und Tötungsrituale im Kult der Maya.* (Berlin, Gebr. Mann Verlag). Quarto. 212 p., 39 Taf., 1 Kt. = Monumenta Americana, 9.

Henderson, Richard N.: *The King in Every Man. Evolutionary Trends in Onitsha Ibo Society and Culture.* (New Haven, Yale University Press, 1972). vii, 576 p., 48 fig. – R: *Anthropos* 68, 656-659 (Guglielmo Guariglia).

Héritier-Izard, F.: "La paix et la pluie. Rapports d'autorité et rapport au sacré chez les Samo", *L'Homme* 13/3, 121-138.

Hermanns, Matthias: *Die religiös-magische Weltanschauung der Primitivstämme Indiens.* Band 3: *Die Oraon.* (Wiesbaden, F. Steiner Verlag). x, 420 S., 32 Taf., 49 Bildern, 1 Karte.

Heun, E.: "Nahrungsenthaltung bei Indianer-Stämmen Südamerikas", *ZMRW* 57, Heft 4, 268-284.

Hochegger, Hermann: *Femme, pourquoi pleures-tu? Mythes buma.* (Bandundu, Centre d'Etudes Ethnologiques, 1972). vi, 214 p., carte. = CEEBA, série II, vol. 5. – R: *Anthropos* 68, 665-666 (A. Retel-Laurentin).

Hochenegg, H.: "Das Zauberbüchlein eines Oberinntaler Bauern aus dem Beginn des zwanzigsten Jahrhunderts", *ÖZV* 27/4, 286-302.

Hohnschopp, Henning: *Untersuchung zum Para-Mikronesien-Problem, unter besonderer Berücksichtigung der Wuvulu- und Aua-Kultur.* (München, Klaus Renner Verlag). vii, 215 p., 24 Taf., 1 Karte. = Arbeiten aus dem Institut für Völkerkunde der Universität zu Göttingen, 7.

Horcasitas, F.: "Cambio y evolución en la antroponimia náhuatl", *Anales de Antropología* 10, 265-283.

Huber, Hugo: "L'existence humaine en face du monde sacré. Rites domestiques chez les Nyende du Dahomey", *Anthropos* 68, 377-441, 5 pl., fig., carte, summarium en anglais, bibliographie. (Sommaire: Introduction, I. Les autels, II. Les rites).

Hultkranz, Å.: *Prairie and Plains Indians*. (Leiden, E. J. Brill). 4to. x, 46 p., 5 fig., 48 pl. = Iconography of Religions, X, fasc. 2.

Hultkranz, Å.: "The Hare Indians: Notes on their Traditional Culture and Religion, Past and Present", *Ethnos* 38, 113-152.

Humphrey, C.: "Some Ritual Techniques in the Bull-cult of the Buriat-Mongols', *PRAIGBI* 15-28.

Hurbon, Laënnec: *Dieu dans le Vaudou haïtien*. Préface de Geneviève Calame-Griaule. (Paris, Payot, 1972). 269 p. = Bibliothèque Scientifique. – R: *Anthropos* 68, 345-347(Jacques Binet).

Ilogu, Edmund: "Worship in Ibo Traditional Religion", *Numen* 20, 229-238.

Isaacman, A.: "Madzi-Manga, Mhondoro and the Use of Oral Traditions: A Chapter in Barue Religious and Political History", *JAH* 14, 395-409.

Jageneau, R.: 'Résultats de l'enquête sur les légendes dans le domaine linguistique néerlandais. XXXVI le canton de Borgloon", *Volkskunde* 74/1, 49-68.

Johnston, T. F.: "A Social Explanation of Tsonga Song-Texts Making Reference to Food and Drink", *EZZ* 3/2, 21-35.

Johnston, T. F.: 'Dagga Use Among the Shangana-Tsonga of Mozambique and the Northern Transvaal", *ZE* 98/2, 277-286.

de Jonge, K.: "Etat matromonial, mobilité conjugale et fécondite chez les Nyakyusa: une étude sociodémographique dans une région rurale en Tanzanie", *CEA* 13/4, 711-721.

Judenko, Konstanty: "Bronislaw Malinowski o magii', *Euhemer* XVII/2 (88), 63-75. (In Polish).

Kaoze, S.: "Proverbes tabwa", présentés par Geneviève Nagant, *Cahiers d'Etudes Africaines* 13/4, 744-768.

Kasprús, Aloys: *The Tribes of the Middle Ramu and the Upper Keram Rivers*. (St. Augustin bein Bonn, Anthropos-Institut). ix, 193 p., 4 pl., 2 maps. = Studia Instituti Anthropos, 17.

Kayombo, ka Chinyeka: *Vihandyeka vya mana. Sayings of Wisdom*. (Wien, Institut für Völkerkunde der Universität). 80 p., 2 fig., 1 map. = Acta Ethnologica et Linguistica, 30. Series Africana, 8.

Kibicho, S. G.: "The Kikuyu Conception of God. Its Continuity into the Christian Era, and the Question it Raises for the Christian Idea of Revelation", *DisAbIn A* 33/12, 7014 (The author's summary of his diss., Vanderbilt University, 1972).

Kiefer, Th. M.: "Parrang Sabbil: Ritual Suicide among the Tausug of Jolo", *BTLV* 129/1, 108-123.

Kilson, M.: *Kpele Lala. Ga Religious Songs and Symbols.* (Cambridge Mass., 1971). – R: *JRA* 5, 62-63 (G. Parrinder).

Kilson, M.: "Twin Beliefs and Ceremony on Ga Culture", *Journal of Religion in Africa* 5/3, 171-197.

Kil-Sung, Ch.: "The Initiation in Korean Shamanism", *JJE* 38, No. 2, 108-119. (In Japanese, with English summary).

Kim, N. V.: "La destinée d'une manuscrit", *Sovetskaja Etnografija*, No. 2, 107-112 (en russe, résumé en anglais).

Kimpianga, K. M.: "Purification and Millenarianism in Zaire. A Case Study in the Socio-Medical and Magico-Religious Practice of the Kongo of Zaire", *CRA* 7 (14), 227-245, French summary.

Kirtley, B. F. and S. H. Elbert: "Animal Tales from Rennell and Bellona", *JPS* 82/3, 241-265.

Kjelström, Rolf: *Eskimo marriage. An account of traditional Eskimo courtship and marriage.* Translation by Donald Burton. (Stockholm, Nordiska Museet). 267 p., 31 fig., 4 pl., 2 maps.

Kronenfeld, D. B.: "Fanti Kinship: The Structure of Terminology and Behavior", *AmAnth* 75/5, 1577-1595.

Kuper, H.: "Costume and Cosmology: The Animal Symbolism of the Ncwala", *Man* 8, No. 4, 613-630.

Ladiges, P. M.: "Der Feuerlauf auf La Réunion und eine Sammlung anderer Zeugnisse", *Ethnomedizin* II/3-4, 255-296.

de La Fuente, N. R.: "Nuevos restos de la vialidad incaica en la provincia de La Rioja, Rep. Argentina", *Ampurias* 33-34, 339-346.

Lagercrantz, Sture: "Counting by Means of Tally Sticks or Cuts on the Body in Africa", *Anthropos* 68, 569-588, 13 fig., map, bibliography (5 p.)

Lane, E.: "Kigeri II Meets that Peculiar Lady, Nyirabiyore: A Study in Prophecies", *History of Religions* 13/2, 129-148.

Lee, J. Y.: "Concerning the Origin and Formation of Korean Shamanism", *Numen* 20, Nr. 2, 135-159.

Lee, J. Y.: "The Seasonal Rituals of Korean Shamanism", *History of Religions* XII, No. 3, 271-287.

Lehmann, H. et A. Ichon: "Les 'sarcophages' de pierre de San Andrés Sajcabajá", *Objets et Mondes* 13/1, 35-46.

Leininger, M.: "Witchcraft Practices and Psychocultural Therapy with Urban U. S. Families", *HumOr* 32/1, 73-83.

Litvak, J.: "Los patrones de cambio de estadio en el valle de Xochicalco, México", *AnAnt* 10, 93-110.

Loving, R.: "Awa Kinship Terminology and its Use", *Ethnology* 12/4, 429-436.

Lukas, Renate: *Nicht-islamische Ethnien im südlichen Tschadraum.* (Wiesbaden, Franz Steiner Verlag). viii, 565 p., 8 Taf., 4 Kt. = Arbeiten aus dem Seminar für Völkerkunde der Johann Wolfgang Goethe-Universität Frankfurt a. M.)

Lukesch, Anton: "Kontaktaufnahme mit Urwaldindianern (Brasilien). Die Asurini im Xingu-Gebiet", *Anthropos* 68, 801-814, 1 Taf., 1 Karte. (Summarium in English, Bibliographie).

Lumbwe Mudindaámbi, NG. W.: *Pourquoi le coq ne chante plus? Mythes mbala.* (Bandundu, Zaïre, Centre d'Etudes Ethnologiques Bandundu). ix, 207 p. in 4°. = CEEBA Publications, Mémoires et Monographies, 8.

Lunardi, E.: "Il 'Signore – volto di sole' e il 'Serpente Piumato' ", *Terra Ameriga* 9 (29-30), 33-56, bibliogr.

Luomala, K.: "Moving and Moveable Images in Easter Island Custom and Myth", *JPS* 82/1, 28-46.

MacEwen, A. M.: "Kinship and Mobility on the Argentine Pampa", *Ethnology* 12, No. 2, 135-151.

McKenny, M. G.: "The Social Structure of the Nyakyusa: A Re-evaluation", *Africa* 43, 91-107.

McKnight, D.: "Sexual Symbolism of Food among the Wik-Mungkan", *Man* 8/2, 194-209.

Makarius, L.: "Une interprétation de l'Incwala swazi. Etude du symbolisme dans la pensée et les rites d'un peuple africain", *AESC* 28/6, 1403-1421 bibliographie.

Mario, F.: "Racconti e canti del gruppo Ghivaro (Ecuador e Perù)", *APME* 37, 561-591.

Masamba, M. M.: "Le problème de la sorcellerie (Point de vue d'un chrétien)", *CRA* 7 (14), 247-269.

Mayer, R.: "Un millier de légendes aux îles Wallis et Fatuna", *JSO* 29, 69-100.

Mazzoleni, Gilberto: *I buffoni sacri d'America. Studio a lungo termine di una istituzione socio-culturale del Sud-Ovest* (Roma, Bulzoni Editore). 160 p. 6 mappe. = Quaderni di SMSR 7.

Medina, A.: "Notas etnográficas sobre los Mames de Chiapas, México", *Anales de Antropologia* 10, 141-220.

Meggers, Betty J.: *Amazonia. Man and Culture in an Counterfeit Paradise.* Foreword by Walter Goldschmidt. (Chicago, Aldine, 1971). ix, 182 p., 17 pl., 19 fig., 5 tab. – R: *Anthropos* 68, 674-677 (Hans Becher).

Meggitt, M. J.: "The Sun and the Shakers: A Millenarian Cult and its Transformation in the New Guinea Highlands", *Oceania* 44, 1-37, 109-126.

Metuh, E. E.: "The Supreme God in Igbo Life and Worship", *Journal of Religion in Africa* 5/1, 1-11.

Middleton, J.: "Secrecy in Lugbara Religion", *History of Religions* 12/4, 299-316.

Miller, E. K.: *Mexican Folk Narrative from the Los Angeles Area.* (Austin, University of Texas Press). 388 p., Bibliography (14 p.) = American Folklore Society, Memoir Series, vol. 56.

Mitrani, Ph.: "Contribution à l'étude des formes religieuses et culturelles chez les Yaruro de l'Apure", *Antropológica* 34, 25-67.

Montoya, Sanchez Javier: *Antología de creencias, mitos, teogonías, leyendas y tradiciones de algunos grupos aborígines colombianos.* Selección, presentación y notas. (Bogotá, Bedout). 236 p.

Moos, G.-D.: "Gewebte Götterbilder aus dem Alten Peru", *Antike Welt* 4 (Sonderheft), 45-49, 13 Photos (12 farb.)

Münzel, Mark: *Erzählungen der Kamayurá, Alto Xingú-Brasilien.* Deutsche Übersetzung und Kommentar. (Wiesbaden, Franz Steiner Verlag). vii, 368 p., 12 Abb. = Studien zur Kulturkunde, 30.

Murray, J.: "The Kikuyu Spirit Churches", *Journal of Religion in Africa* 5, No. 3, 198-234.

Muzungu, B.: "Le problème des sources de la religion traditionnelle du Rwanda et du Burundi", *RUB 1*, no. 3-4, 203-217.

Nebel, P. A.: "Dinka-Folklore", *Archiv für Völkerkunde* 27, 69-144.

Neumann, F. J.: "Paper: A Sacred Material in Aztec Ritual", *History of Religions* 13/2, 149-159.

Newbery, S. J.: "Los pilagá: su religión y sus mitos de origen", *América Indígena* 33/3, 757-770, with a summary in English.

Niangoran-Bouah, G.: "Symboles institutionnels chez les Akan", *L'Homme* 13, no. 1-2, 207-232, 10 pl.

Noggler, Albert: *Vierhundert Jahre Araukanermission.* 75 Jahre Missionsarbeit der bayerischen Kapuziner. (Schöneck, Administration der NZMW). xxvi, 505 p., 1 Taf., 4 Kt. = NZMW, Supplementa, 20.

Noguera, E.: "Las funciones del momoztli", *Anales de Anrtropología* 10, 111-122.

van Nunen, B. O.: "The Community of Kugapa. A Report on Research Conducted in 1957-1958 among a Group of Moni in the Central Highlands of Irian Jaya", *Irian* 2/2, 1-100.

Ochoa, L.: "El culto fálico y la fertilidad en Tlatilco, México", *Anales de Antropología* 10, 123-139.

Ohnuki-Tierney, E.: "Sakhalin Ainu Time Reckoning", *Man* 8/2, 285-299.

Ohnuki-Tierney, E.: "The Shamanism of the Ainu of the Northwest Coast of Southern Sakhalin", *Ethnology* 12/1, 15-29.

Omoyajowo, J. A.: "Human Destiny, Personal Rites and Sacrifices in African Traditional Religion. (A Means of Ultimate Transformation)", *JRTh* 30/1, 5-15, bibliography.

Orbell, M.: "Two versions of the Maori story of Te Tahi o te Rangi", *JPS* 82, No. 2, 127-140.

Otterbein, Ch. S. and K. F.: "Believers and Beaters: A Case Study of Supernatural Beliefs and Child Rearing in the Bahama Islands", *AmAnth* 75/5, 1670-1681.

Park, J.: "A Consideration of the Tikopia Sacred Tale", *The Journal of the Polynesian Society* 82/2, 154-175, bibliography.

Paul, S.: "Kranksein und Kulturwandel in Kenya. Abajusii beantworten medizinische Fragen", *Ethnomedizin* I/1, 11-42.

Pereira, P. A. H.: "Os espíritos maus dos Nanbikuára", *Pesquisas Antropologia* 25, 1-33.

Plack, Arno (Ed.): *Der Mythos vom Agressionstrieb.* (München, List Verlag). 399 p.

Platvoet, J. G.: "Glissements dans une religion de l'Afrique occidentale. Aveux de sorcellerie et origine des dieux 'bourreaux' dans la religion des Ashanti", *Bijdragen* 34/1, 15-39 (in Dutch, with a summary in English).

Pleuss, P.: "Zwei Goldstatuetten aus dem Schatz von Frias", *Antike Welt* 4 (Sonderheft), 50-56.

Pollak-Eltz, Angelina: *Cultos afroamericanos.* (Caracas, Universidad Católica Andres Bello, Facultad de Humanidades y Educación). 258 p.

Poppe, N.: "Der mongolische schamanistische Ausdruck udqa", *JSFO* 72, 309-317.

Posern-Zielińska, Miroslawa: *Peyotism, A Religion of North American Indians* (*IBHR*, 1972). – R: *Euhemer* XVII/2 (88), 94-96 (Bohdan Kohutnicki). (In Polish).

Pouillon, J.: "A quelque chose malheur est bon", *L'Homme* 13, no. 3, 93-100.

Poushinsky, J. M. and N. W. Poushinsky: "Superstition and Technological Change: An Illustration", *JAF* 86 (341), 289-293.

Price, R.: "Avenging Spirits and the Structure of Saramaka Lineages", *BTLV* 129, 86-107.

Raats, P. J.: "Mandarangan: A Bagobo Spirit of Sky and Heat", *PhQCS* I/2, 95-119.

Rahmann, R., M. N. Maceda, and R. M. Lopez: "Field Work among the Negritos of Northern Negros: An Additional Report", *PhQCS* I/3, 149-166.

Ramírez, G.: "Análisis filosófico de la mitología Chibcha", *Franciscanum* 15 (45), 257-350, bibliografia.

Ranger, T.: "Territorial Cults in the History of Central Africa", *JAH* 14, No. 4, 581-597.

Rašev, R.: "Monument protobulgare de culte de Madara", *Arheologija* 15/2, 29-38 (en bulgare, rés. en français. Représentation d'un mort avec l'image symbolique (oiseau) de son âme qui se détache de son corps; motif proprement turc).

Raum, O. F.: *The Social Functions of Avoidances and Taboos among the Zulu.* (Berlin, Walter de Gruyter). 576 p. in 4°, 35 fig., 15 pl. = Monographien zur Völkerkunde, 6.

Ray, B.: " 'Performative Utterances' in African Rituals", *History of Religions* 13, No. 1, 16-35.

Revunenkova, E. V.: "Les sceptres magiques des Bataks de Sumatra", *SMAE* 29, 183-200 (en russe).

Richards, A.: "Iban Augury", *The Sarawak Museum Journal* 20 (40-41), 63-82.

Richards, J. V. O.: "The *Sande* and some of the Forces that Inspired its Creation or Adoption with some References to the *Poro*", *JAAS* 8, 69-77.

Riché, P.: "La magie à l'époque carolingienne", *CRAIBL*, no. janvier-mars, 127-138.

Rosen, L. N.: "Contagion and Cataclysm: A Theoretical Approach to the Study of Ritual Pollution Beliefs", *African Studies* 32/4, 229-246.

van Roy, Hubert: "Les *Bambwíiti*, peuplade préhistorique du Kwango (Rép. du Zaïre)", *Anthropos* 68, 815-880, 4 cartes, bibliographie (3 p.)

Ruelland, Suzanne: *La fille sans mains. Analyse de dix-neuf versions africaines du conte.* (Paris, Société d'Etudes Linguistiques et Anthropologiques). 209 p. = Bibliothèque de la SELAF, 39-40.

Sawyerr, H. A. E.: *God: Ancestor or Creator? Aspects of Traditional Belief in Ghana, Nigeria and Sierra Leone* (London, 1970). – R: *JRA* 5, 57-58 (J. Thrower).

Sbrzesny, H.: "!Ko-Buschleute (Kalahari). Der Eland-Tanz. Kinder spielen das Mädchen-Initiationsritual", *Homo* 24, 233-244.

Schefold, Reimar: "Religiöse Vorstellungen auf Siberut, Mentawai (Indonesien)", *Anthropos* 68, 93-112, 1 Tafel mit 5 Photos, English summary, p. 111, "Bibliographie", p. 112. (Inhalt: 1. Seelen, 2. *badjou*, 3. Mittler, 4. Geister und Ahnen, 5. Religiöse Vorstellungen und soziale Struktur, 6. Mythen, 7. Tabus, 8. Krankenheilung, 9. Religiöse Vorstellungen und alltägliches Verhalten, 10. Religiöse Feste).

Schindler, H.: "Warum kann man den Itutari mit dem Gwaruma erschlagen?", *Zeitschrift für Ethnologie* 98/2, 246-276.

Schlegel, Alice: *Male Dominance and Female Autonomy. Domestic Authority in Matrilineal Societies*. With a Foreword by Raoul Naroll. (New Haven, 1972). xv, 206 p. – R: *Anthropos* 68, 633-634.

Schlosser, Katesa (ed.): *Zauberei im Zululand*. Manuskripte des Blitz-Zauberers Laduma Madela. Illustrationen von Laduma Madela, Muziwezixwala Tabete und Jabulani Ntuli. (Kiel, Schmidt & Klaunig, 1972). xxviii, 467 p., illus. = Arbeiten aus dem Museum für Völkerkunde der Universität Kiel, 4. – R: *Anthropos* 68, 340-341 (Georg Höltker).

Schmidt, S.: "Die Mantis religiosa in den Glaubensvorstellungen der Khoesan-Völker", *ZE* 98/1, 102-127.

Schmidt, S.: "Volkserzählungen der Buschmänner, Khoe-Khoen und Dama", *JSWASS* 27, 57-71.

Schmidt, W.: "Ekstase, Zauber, Überwelt. Umbanda, Macumba und Spiritismus in Brasilien", *LM* XII/2, 86-91.

von Schuler-Schömig, Immina: *Figurengefässe aus Oaxaca, Mexico*, 1970, und Dieter Eisleb: *Westmexikanische Keramik*, 1971. (beide: Berlin, Museum für Völkerkunde). – R: *Anthropos* 68, 344-345 (Bodo Spranz).

Simpson, C. A.: "Tahiti, George Pritchard et le 'mythe' du 'royaume missionnaire' ", *JSO* 29, 57-68.

de Sousberghe, Léon: "Union structurale et Alliance en Afrique Centrale", *Anthropos* 68, 1-92, 491-536. (English summary: pp. 1-2, "Bibliographie": pp. 2-5).

Specker, Johann: "Algunos aspectos de aculturación religiosa en la región Puebla-Tlaxcala", *Comunicaciones* 7, 105-107.

Spencer, Paul: *Nomads in Alliance. Symbiosis and growth among the Rendille and Samburu of Kenya*. (London, Oxford University Press). x, 230 p., 10 tab., 12 charts, 3 maps.

Spoehr, Alexander: *Zamboanga and Sulu. An Archeological Approach to Ethnic Diversity*. With Reports on Faunal Remains by Alan C. Ziegler and Danielle Fellows. (Pittsburgh, Dept. of Anthropology, Univ. of Pittsburgh). 298 p., 182 fig., 13 tab. = Ethnology Monographs, 1.

Sterly, Joachim: *Krankheiten und Krankenbehandlung bei den Chimbu im zentralen Hochland von Neuguinea*. (Hammburg, Klaus Renner Verlag). 289 p., 20 abb. = Beiträge zur Ethnomedizin, Ethnobotanik und Ethnosoziologie, 2.

Stewart, K.: "Mortuary Practices of the Mohave Indians", *El Palacio* 79/4, 2-12.

Stewart, K. M.: "Witchcraft among the Mohave Indians", *Ethnology* 12/3, 315-324, bibliography (9 references).

Susnik, B.: "L'Homme et le surnaturel (Gran Chaco)", *BSSA* no. 37, 35-47, bibliographie (with English summary).

Suzuki, P. T. et al.: "Feasts Among Niasans of the Batu Islands, Indonesia", *Anthropos* 68, 597-603, map, bibliography.

Swanson, G.E.: "The Search for a Guardian Spirit: A Process of Empowerment in Simpler Societies" *Ethnology* 12/3, 359-378, bibliography (4 p.)

Świderski, Stanislaw: "Die sakrale Verzierung der Tempel in den synkretischen Sekten in Gabun", *MAGW* 102, 105-113, 6 Taf., 1 Kt.

Świderski, Stanislaw: "Notes biographiques sur les fondateurs et les guides spirituels des sectes syncrétiques au Gabon", *Anthropologica* 15, 37-87.

Thiel, Josef Franz: "Geschichtliche Überlieferungen der Yansi (Zaïre)", *Anthropos* 68, 236-291, 2 Karten. (Summarium in English und Bibliographie, S. 290-291).

Thompson, J. Eric S.: *The Civilisation of the Mayas.* (Chicago, Field Museum Press). 97 p., 14 fig., 15 pl. = Field Museum of Natural History, Popular Series, Anthropology, 25.

Todorov, T.: "Le discours de la magie" *L'Homme* 13, no. 4, 38-65.

Torelli, P.: "Notes ethnologiques sur les Banya-Mwenge du Toro (Uganda)", *APME* 37, 461-559.

Torres, Laborde Alfonso: *Mito y cultura entre los Barasana, un grupo indígena tukano del Vaupés.* (Bogota, Universidad de los Andes, Departamento de Antropologia, 1969); 182 p., 99 fig., 1 mapa. – R: *Anthropos* 68, 350 (Wilhelm Saake).

Ubald, T. P.: "Notes ethnologiques sur les Banya-Mwenge du Toro (Uganda)", *APME* 37, 461-559.

Verstraelen, E.: "Analysis of Ibanag", *PhQCS* I/3, 175-199 (concluded).

Vincent, S.: "Structure du rituel: La tente tremblante et le concept de mista. pe.w", *RAQBI* 3, no. 1-2, 69-83, bibliogr.

Vogler, P.: "Structuralisme et théologie. La divinité chez les Mosi", *AUBE* 3, 231-335, bibliographie (3 p.)

Vogt, E. Z.: "Gods and Politics in Zinacantan and Chamula", *Ethnology* 12, No. 2, 99-114, bibliography.

Vorbichler, Anton: "Religiöse Vorstellungen und ihre Bedeutung für die religiöse Praxis bei den Bantu-Völkern", *Verbum SVD* 14, 273-279.

Vredenbregt, J.: "Dabus in West Java", *BTLV* 129, 302-320.

Wachtel, Nathan: *La vision des vaincus. Les Indiens du Pérou devant la conquête espagnole 1530-1570.* (Paris, Gallimard, 1971). 395 p. = Bibliothèque des Histoires.

Watanabo, Hitoshi: *The Ainu Ecosystem. Environment and Group Structure.* (Seattle, University of Washington Press). ix, 170 p., 8 fig., 2 maps. 4°. = The American Ethnological Society, Monogr., 54.

von Wedemeyer, I.: "Coca, Rauschmittel im alten Perú", *Ethnomedizin* I/1, 101-112.

von Wedemeyer, I.: "Mais, Rausch- und Heilmittel im akten Perú", *Ethnomedizin* II/1-2, 99-112.

Weidkuhn, Peter: "Die Rechtfertigung des Mannes aus der Frau bei Ituri-Pygmäen", *Anthropos* 68, 442-455, Bibliographie.

Werner, R.: "Nose Flute Blowers of the Malayan Aborigines (Orang Asli)", *Anthropos* 68, 181-191, map, 3 fig., 1 pl. (with bibliography). (Symbolic importance and metaphysical aspects of the nose).

Wilbert, Johannes: *Survivors of Eldorado. Four Indian Cultures of South America.* (New York, Prager, 1972). xi, 212 p., 32 pl., 2 maps. – R: *Anthropos* 68, 348-350 (Angelina Pollak-Eltz).

Williams, P. V. A.: "Myths, Symbols and the Concept of Immortality among some American Societies", *Folklore* 84/4, 327-338.

Wymeersch, P.: "le problème du mal chez le muntu. (Considerations sur la mort et la protection contre les maléfices chez les Luwa, Bemba et Suku)", *Africa* 28/4, 575-582 (with summaries in Italian and English).

Zimmermann, Francis: *La parenté*. (Vendôme, Presses Universitaires de France, 1972). 94 p. = Dossiers Logos, 46. – R: *Anthropos* 68, 632 (Léon de Sousberghe).

Zimmermann, G.: "Kosmos und Götter bei den Azteken", *Zeitschrift für Ethnologie* 98/2, 216-229.

Zolla, Elémire: *The Writer and the Shaman. A Morphology of the American Indian*. Transl. by Raymond Rosenthal. (New York, Harcourt Brace). viii, 312 p.

Zuidema, R. T.: "Kinship and Ancestorcult in Three Peruvian Communities. Hernandes Principe's Account of 1622", *BIFEA* 2/1, 16-33.

Zwernemann, J.: "Masken und Figuren der Dogon im Linden – Museum: Versuch einer Interpretation", *Tribus* 22, 55-78.

3. EARLY EUROPEAN RELIGION

Banti, Luisa: *The Etruscan Cities and their Culture*. Translation by E. Bizarri. (London, B. T. Batsford Ltd.). vi, 322 p., 96 pl., 13 maps.

Bloch, Raymond: *Die Etrusker*, übersetzt von W. Zschietzschmann. (Stuttgart, 1970). – R: *OLZ* 68, 333-336 (B. Barschel).

Bogaers, J. E. and M. Gysseling: "Nehalennia, Gimio en Ganuenta", *OudhMed* 52, 86-92, 1 pl. (mit deutscher Zusammenfassung).

Bogaers, J. E. and M. Gysseling: "Over de naam van de godin Nehalennia", *OudhMed* 52, 79-85, 1 pl. (mit deutscher Zusammenfassung).

Callmer, J.: "A Contribution to the Knowledge of the Burial Customs in Southern Scandinavia at the Beginning of the Second Milennium B.C.", *MMHUL* (1971-1972), 17-31.

Dennis, George: *Die Städte und Begräbnisplätze Etruriens*. Mit einem Vorwort zur Neuausgabe von Otto-Wilhelm von Vacano. (Darmstadt, Wissenschaftliche Buchgesellschaft). xx, 29, 62 S., 106 Abb., 1 Karte. = Reprografischer Nachdruck der von N N. W. Meissner übersetzten Ausgabe, Leipzig 1852.

Dubuisson, D.: "Les talismans du roi Cormac et les trois fonctions", *Revue Historique*, no. 508, 289-294.

Eloy, L.: "Symbole solaire découvert à Marche-les Dames et considérations sur quelques cas de céramique funéraire à symbole astral du début de la romanisation", *CherWal* 22, 291-302.

d'Encarnação, J.: "Banda, uma importante divindade indígena", *Conimbriga* 12, 199-214.

Gäters, A.: "Literaturbericht: Zu Forschungen über die Götter der alten Letten" [von H. Biezais], *ZOfg* 22/4, 717-722.

Georgiev, V. I.: "Die Herkunft der etruskischen mythologischen Namen", *Beiträge zur Namenforschung* 8/2, 139-148.

Gröteke, F.: *Etruskerland: Geschichte, Kunst, Kultur. Studienführer zu den Grabungsstätten und Museen*. (Stuttgart, Hans E. Günther Verlag). 447 S., 71 Abb., 28 Karten und Pläne.

Hatt, J.-J.: "Claude et le dieu Lug", *RAECE* 24, no. 3-4, 465-469.

Hazanov, A. M.: "Le sacerdoce scythe", *SovEtn* no. 6, 41-50 (en russe, rés. en anglais).

Henkel, O. V.: "De hond van Nehalennia", *Nederlands Theologisch Tijdschrift* 27/3, 201-209.

Höfler, O.: *Verwandlungskulte, Volkssagen und Mythen*. (Wien, Österreichische Akademie der Wissenschaften). 290 S. = ÖAW Philos.-hist. Klasse, 279, Heft 2.

Hummel, S.: "Zentralasien und die Etruskerfrage. Anmerkungen", *Rivista degli Studi Orientali* 48, 251-257.

Nicolaescu-Plopşor, D. et W. Wolski: "Une contribution de l'anthropologie historique concernant le problème des permanences dans les pratiques rituelles funéraires", *Apulum* 9, 735-752 (en roumain, rés. en fr.)

Nicoulitsé, I. T.: "Rites funéraire des Gètes aux IVe et IIIe ss. av. J.-C.", *SovAr* no. 2, 27-44 (en russe, rés. en fran.)

Oppermann, M.: "Zu einigen Weihdenkmälern mit der Darstellung des thrakischen Reitergottes aus der SR Rumänien und der VR Bulgarien", *Klio* 55, 197-214, 22 photos.

Pigott, Stuart: *Ancient Europe from the Beginnings of Agriculture to Classical*

Antiquity. A survey. (Edinburgh, The University Press). xxiv, 341 p., 51 pl., illus.

Rassadin, V. I.: "Le culte de l'ours chez les Tofalars", *ISOANO* no. 11, 122-125 (en russe).

Richard, L.: "Au dossier de *Brigantia*", *Société d'Emulation des Côtes-du-Nord* 101, 20-29.

Rosenfeld, H.: "*Phol ende Wuodan vuorum zi holza.* Baldermythe oder Fohlenzauber?", *BGDSL* 95/1-3, 1-12.

Sanquer, R.: "La grande statuette de bronze de Kerguilly-en-Dineault (Finistère)", *Gallia* 31/1, 61-80.

Schlumberger, E.: "Nos vrais ancêtres les Celtes", *Connaisance des Arts*, No. 256, 80-89.

Schwartz, S. P.: *Poetry and Law in Germanic Myth.* (Los Angeles, University of California Press). 61 p., Bibliography. = Folklore Studies, 27.

Stjernquist, B.: "Das Opfermoor in Hassle Bösarp, Schweden", *Acta Archaeologica* (Køb.) 44, 19-62.

Strömberg, M.: "Das Ganggrab in Ingelstorp", *MMHUL* (1971-1972) 39-106.

Stuart, P.: "A New Temple of Nehalennia", *OudhMed* 52, 76-78, 4 plates.

Taillandier, M.-N.: "Un nouveau dieu-cavalier en Auvergne. De la disparition et de la redécouverte d'une sculpture galloromaine", *RACF* 12 (no. 45-46), 11-20.

Taniguchi, Y.: "La sépulture et la représentation des morts chez les Germains", *HUSL* 32/2, 140-161 (en japonais).

Wellard, J.: *The Search for the Etruscans.* (London, Thomas Nelson & Sons). 223 p., illus.

III. RELIGIONS OF ANTIQUITY

1. GENERAL AND MISCELLANEOUS WORKS

Amad, Gladys: *Le baiser rituel, un geste méconnu.* (Beyrouth, Dar el-Machreq). 125 p., 77 illus. on 38 pl., bibliographie (7 p.)

The Cambridge Ancient History. Third edition. Volume II, Part 1: *History of the Middle East and the Aegean Region c. 1800-1380 B.C.* Edited by I. E. S. Edwards, The Late C. J. Gadd, N. G. L. Hammond, E. Sollberger. (Cambridge, At the University Press). xxiii, 868 p. – R: *BiOr* 30, 390-391 (Josef Klíma).

Carter, T. H.: "The Arab-Iranian Gulf, the Cultural Crossroad of the Ancient Near East", *Archaeology* 26, 16-23.

Cogan, M.: "Tyre and Tiglath-Pileser III. Chronological Notes", *JCS* 25, 96-99.

Couroyer, B.: "Origine des Phéniciens", *Revue Biblique* 80, no. 2, 264-276.

Courtois, J. C.: "Le sanctuaire du dieu au lingot d'Enkomi-Alasia (Chypre) et les lieux de culte contemporains en Méditerranée orientale", *CRAIBL*, no. avril-juin, 223-246.

Dunayevsky, I. and A. Kempinski, "The Megiddo Temples", *ZDPV* 89/2, 161-187, 4 pl.

Fantar, M.: "Le Dieu Dagan. Les sources", *Cah Tun* 21 (81-82), 7-31.

Ferron, J.: "La nature du Dieu Ṣid d'après les découvertes récentes d'Antas", in: *XXIXe Congrès International des Orientalistes. Résumés des Communications*, Sections 1-5. (Paris, Y. Hervouet), pp. 26-27.

Finkelstein, Jacob J.: "The Goring Ox. Some Historical Perspectives on Deodands, Forfeitures, Wrongful Death and the Western Notion of Sovereignty", *TLQ* 46, 169-290.

Garcia de la Fuente, O.: "La observación de las aves en Roma", *Helmantica* 24 (No. 73), 135-157.

Garelli, Paul: *Le Proche-Orient Asiatique des origines aux invasions des peuples de la mer.* (Paris, 1969). – R: *OLZ* 68, 31-34 (H. Klengel).

Green, A. R. W.: "The Role of Human Sacrifice in the Ancient Near East", *DisAbIn A* 34/4, 1799. (The author's summary of his diss., University of Michigan, 1973).

Groenewegen-Frankfort, H. A.: *Arrest and Movement*, (New York, 1972). – R: *BiOr* 30, 18-19 (Ingrid Gamer-Wallert).

Haldar, Alfred: *Who were the Amorites?* (Leiden, 1971). – R: *BiOr* 30, 84-85 (C. H. J. de Geus).

Helck, W.: *Betrachtungen zur Grossen Göttin und den ihr verbundenen Gottheiten.* (IBHR, 1971, S. 48). – R: *ThLZ* 98, 663-668 (O. Kaiser). *BiOr* 30, 19-22 (W. A. Ward).

Herrmann, W.: "ttrt-hr", *Die Welt des Orients* 7/1, 135-136.

Homès-Fredericq, Denyse: "Quelques aspects spécifiques des fouilles de Nimrud", *AIPHOS* 20, 273-284, 4 pl.

Horn, S. H.: "The Crown of the King of the Ammonites", *AnUSS* 11, No. 2, 170-180, 4 plates.

Jantzen, Ulf: *Ägyptische und orientalische Bronzen aus dem Heraison von Samos.* (Bonn, Rudolf Habelt Verlag). 4to. viii, 108 S., 85 Taf. = Deutsches Archäologisches Institut, Samos, Band VIII. – R: *BiOr* 30, 198-200 (George M. A. Hanfmann).

Keilschriftforschung und alte Geschichte Vorderasiens. 4. Abschn.: *Orientalische Geschichte von Kyros bis Mohammed.* Lfg. 2. Mit Beiträgen von A. Dietrich, G. Widengren, F. M. Heichelheim. (Leiden, 1966). – R: *OLZ* 68, 461-464 (Joachim Oelsner).

Lipiński, E.: "Beth-Schemesch und der Tempel der Herrin der Grabkammer in den Amarna-Briefen", *VeTes* 23/4, 443-445.

McCarter, P. K. and R. B. Coote: "The Spatula Inscription from Byblos", *BASOR* No. 212, 16-22.

Mac Dermot, Violet: *The Cult of the Seer in the Ancient Middle East.* A Contribution to Current Research on Hallucinations drawn from Coptic and other Texts. (London, 1971). – R: *BiOr* 30, 202-203 (Tito Orlandi).

Mallet, J.: *Tell el-Far'ah (Région de Naplouse). L'installation du Moyen Bronze antérieure au rempart.* (Paris, Gabalda). 149 p., 28 p. (fig. et cartes), 35 pl. = Cahiers de la Revue Biblique, 14.

Mazar, A.: "A Philistine Temple at Tell Qasile", *The Biblical Archaeologist* 36/2, 42-48.

Richter, G. M. A.: "Der Zusammenhang zwischen ägyptischer und griechischer Kunst", *Das Altertum* 19/2, 74-88.

Salditt-Trappmann, R.: *Tempel der ägyptischen Götter in Griechenland und an der Westküste Kleinasiens,* (Leiden, 1970). – R: *Gnomon* 45/5, 521-524 (L. Castiglione).

von Soden, W.: "Sprache, Denken und Begriffsbildung im Alten Orient", *Akademie der Wissenschaften und der Literatur, Abhandlungen der Geistes- und Sozialwissenschaftlicher Klasse*, Heft 6, 5-41.

Vattioni, F.: "Appunti sulle iscrizioni siriache antiche", *Augustinianum* 13, no. 1, 131-140.

Weinfeld, M.: "Covenant Terminology in the Ancient Near East and its Influence on the West", *JAOS* 93, 190-199.

Will, Edouard: *Le monde grec et l'Orient.* Tome 1: *Le Ve siècle (510-403).* (Paris, Presses Universitaires de France, 1972). 709 p., 6 plans, carte. = Peuples et Civilisations, 2. — R: *Etudes Classiques* 41, 261-262 (A. Wankenne).

Yoyotte, Jean: "Les inscriptions hiéroglyphiques égyptiennes et la statue de Darius", *CRAIBL* 256-259.

Zaccagnini, Carlo: *Lo scambio dei doni nel Vicino Oriente durante i secoli XV-XIII.* (Roma, Centro per le Antichità e la storia dell'Arte del Vicino Oriente). xii, 224 p. = Orientis Antiqui Collectio, 11.

2. EGYPT

Aggebracht, Arne: *Schlachtungsbräuche im alten Aegypten und ihre Wiedergabe in Flachbild bis zum Ende des mittleren Reiches.* (Inaugural-Dissertation, München). v, 301 S., 14 Taf.

Aldred, Cyril: *Akhenaten and Nefertiti.* (New York, The Brooklyn Museum/The Viking Press). 231 p., 232 fig.

Allam, S.: "De la divinité dans le droit pharaonique", *Bulletin de la Société Française d'Egyptologie* 68, 17-30.

Altermüller, B.: "Zum Synkretismus in den Sargtexten", *Göttinger Miszellen* 7, 7-10.

Anus, P. et R. Sa'ad: "Habitations de prêtres dans le temple d'Amon de Karnak", *Kêmi* 21, 217-238, 3 pl., 6 dépl.

Assmann, J.: *Der König als Sonnenpriester*, (Glückstadt, 1970). — R: *ChrEg* 48 (96), 287-292 (P. Derchain).

Aubert, Jacques-F.: "Sculptures inédites de la période amarnienne", *Orientalia* 42, 479-488, XXXVII-XXXIX.

Badawy, A. M.: "Aberrations about Akthenaton", *ZÄSA* 99/2, 65-72.

Bakry, H. S. K.: "The Discovery of a Temple of Merenptah at Ōn", *Aegyptus* 53, 3-21, 9 pl., 2 tab.

Baqués Estapé, L.: "Catálogo inventario de las piezas egipcias del Museo Episcopal de Vic', *Ampurias* 33-34, 209-250.

Baqués Estapé, L.: "Galería de personajes en las piezas egipcias de los museos catalanes y Museo Balear", *InfArq* 12, 135-144.

Barta, W.: "Bemerkungen zu einem alten Götterhymnus", *Revue d'Egyptologie* 25, 84-91.

Barta, W.: "Bemerkungen zu Rekonstruktion des abydenischen Kultbildrituals" (von H. Altenmüller), *MDAIK* 29/2, 163-166.

Barta, Winfried: *Das Gespräch eines Mannes mit seinem BA* (Papyrus Berlin 3024). – R: *BiOr* 30, 44-45 (Ronald J. Williams).

Barta, Winfried: *Untersuchungen zum Götterkreis der Neunheit.* (München-Berlin, Deutscher Kunstverlag). 252 S. = Münchener ägyptologische Studien, 28.

Barta, Winfried: "Zur Urgestalt des Gottes Kentechthai", *ZÄSA* 99/2, 76-81.

Basta, M.: *The Most Principal Monuments in the Pyramids Area at Giza.* Drawings by S. Ahmed. (Cairo, Bibliothèque du Musée Egyptien). 52 p., 20 pl.

Bell, L.: "In the Tombs of the High Priests of Amun", *Expedition* 15, No. 2, 17-27.

Björkman, Gun: *Kings at Karnak. A Study of the Treatment of the Monuments of Royal Predecessors in the Early New Kingdom.* (Uppsala, 1971). – R: *BiOr* 30, 222-223 (Robert Hari).

Blankenberg-van Delden, C.: *The Large commemorative Scarabs of Amenhotep III.* (Leiden, 1969). – R: *OLZ* 68, 345-346 (E. Hornung).

Bleeker, C. J.: "Der religiöse Gehalt einiger Hathor-Lieder", *ZÄSA* 99/2, 82-88.

Bleeker, C. J.: *Hathor and Thoth, Two Key Figures of the Ancient Egyptian Religion.* (Leiden, E. J. Brill), x, 171 p. = Studies in the History of Religions (Supplements to Numen), XXVI.

Bleeker, C. J.: "Man and his salvation in the ancient Egyptian religion", in: *Man and his Salvation, Studies in Memory of S. G. F. Brandon* (Manchester) 65-74.

Bogoslovskij, E.: "Monuments et documents de Der-el-Medina conservés dans les musées d'URSS. Index", *VDI* no. 3, 80-86.

Bogoslovskij, E.: "Objets et documents de Der-el-Medina, gardés dans les musées d'URSS, VI", *VDI* no. 2, 70-102, 6 pl.

Bogoslovski, E.: "The Two Best Egyptian Statuettes in the Collection of the Museum of Fine Arts, Moscow", *Studia i Prace* 14/7, 21-40.

Bonneau, D.: "Note papyrologique III", *Revue d'Egyptologie* 25, 257-261.

Borghouts, J. F.: "The Evil Eye of Apopis", *JEA* 59, 114-150, 1 pl.

Borghouts, J. F.: *The Magical Texts of Papyrus Leiden I 348.* (Leiden, 1971). – R: *BiOr* 30, 203-206 (David Lorton).

Bosse-Griffiths, K.: "The Great Enchantress in the Little Golden Shrine of Tut'ankhamūn", *JEA* 59, 100-108, 2 pl.

Bresciani, Edda: *Letteratura e Poesia dell'Antico Egitto*, (Torino, 1969). – R: *BiOr* 30, 28-31 (A. Rosenvasser).

Brierbrier, M. L.: "Here, Wife of the High Priest Paiankh", *JNES* 32/3, 311.

Broekhuis, J.: *De Godin Renenwetet* (Assen, 1971). – R.: *Vox Theologica* 43, 330-331 (M. Heerma van Voss).

Carter, Howard: *Das Grab des Tut-Ench-Amun*. (Wiesbaden, F. A. Brockhaus). 255 S., 65 fig., 17 col. pl.

Cazemier, L. J.: "Die Baw der alten Hauptstädte", *Festschrift de Liagre Böhl* (q. v. sub 1-7), 71-80.

Couroyer, B.: "Pount et la terre du Dieu", *Revue Biblique* 80, 53-74.

Couroyer, B.: "Sapin vrai et sapin nouveau", *Orientalia* 42, 339-356.

David, A Rosalie: *Religious Ritual at Abydos (c. 1300 B. C.)* (Warminster, Aris & Phillips). 353 p., 57 plans, 7 phot. = Modern Agyptology Series.

Derchain, Philippe: *Hathor quadrifrons. Recherches sur la syntaxe d'un mythe égyptien*. (Leiden, 1972). – R: *BiOr* 30, 209-211 (Erich Winter).

Doresse, M.: "Le dieu voilé dans sa châsse et la fête du début de la décade", *RevEg* 25, 92-135, 2 pl. (Suite; à suivre).

Edel, Elmar: *Die Felsengräber der Qubbet el Hawa bei Assuan*. II. Abt.: Die althieratischen Topfaufschriften. I. Bd.: Die Topfaufschriften aus den Grabungsjahren 1960, 1961, 1962, 1963 und 1965. 2. Teil: Text (Fortsetzung). (Wiesbaden, 1970). – R: *OLZ* 68, 341-345 (W. Barta).

Faulkner, R. O.: *The Ancient Egyptian Coffin Texts*. Volume I: *Spells 1-354*. (Warminster, Aris & Phillips). xiii, 285 p.

Fecht, G.: "Ägyptische Zweifel am Sinn des Opfers. Admonitions 5, 7-9", *ZÄSA* 100, Heft 1, 6-16.

Ferron, J.: "Horus l'enfant sur les stèles votives de Carthage", *IBLA* 36, no. 131, 79-96, 5 fig.

Fischer, Henry: *Dendara in the Third Millenium B.C.* (New York, 1968). – R: *BiOr* 30, 227-231 (François Daumas).

Fischer, H. G.: "An Eleventh Dynasty Couple Holding the Sign of Life", *ZÄSA* 100, No. 1, 16-28, 1 pl.

Fóti, L.: "Amulettes en forme de porc dans la Collection Egyptienne", *BMHBA* 40, 3-8, 97-101.

George, B.: "Stand der Untersuchungen über den Synkretismus im Totenbuch (Ausgabe Neville)", *Göttinger Miszellen* 7, 11-13.

George, Beate: *Zu den altägyptischen Vorstellungen vom Schatten als Seele*, (Bonn, 1970). – R: *BiOr* 30, 45-47 (A. Barucq).

Ghalioungui, Paul: *The House of Life (Per Ankh). Magic and Medical Science in Ancient Egypt*. (Amsterdam, B. M. Israël). 198 p., 26 pl.

Giveon, Raphhaël: *Les bédouins Shosou des documents égyptiens*, (Leiden, 1971). – R: *BiOr* 30, 33-35 (A. Barucq).

Goedicke, Hans: *Re-used Blocks from the Pyramid of Amenemhet I at Lisht*, (New York, 1971). – R: *BiOr* 30, 32-33 (Winfried Barta).

Goyon, Jean-Claude: *Rituels Funéraires de l'Ancienne Egypte. Le Rituel de l'Embaumement. Le Rituel de l'Ouverture de la Bouche. Les Livres des Respirations.* (Paris, 1972). – R: *BiOr* 30, 219-221 (Erhart Graefe).

Graefe, E.: "Einige Bemerkungen zur Angabe der *st*3t-Grösse auf der weissen Kapelle Sesostris I", *JEA* 59, 72-76.

Graefe, E.: "Index der im Katalog beschriebenen und im Tafelband abgebildeten Stelen zu Peter Munro, *Die spätägyptischen Totenstelen*: Ägyptologische Forschungen, 25, Glückstadt 1973", *Göttinger Miszellen*, H. 5, 47-57.

Grieshammer, Reinhard: *Das Jenseitsgericht in den Sargtexten.* (Wiesbaden, 1970). – R: *OLZ* 68, 346-348 (L. Kákosy).

Griffiths, J. G.: "Triune Conceptions of Deity in Ancient Egypt", *ZÄSA* 100, Heft 1, 28-32.

Guilmot, M.: "Lettre à une épouse défunte (Pap. Leiden I, 371)", *ZÄSA* 99/2, 94-103, bibliographie.

Haikal, Fayza Mohamed Hussein: *Two Hieratic Funerary Papyri of Nesmin.* Part two. Translation and commentary. (Bruxelles, 1972). – R: *BiOr* 30, 398-399 (L. Kákosy).

Hassan, A.: "Drei Stelen aus Elkab", *MDAIK* 29/1, 5-7, 1 Taf.

Hayes, William C.: *A Papyrus of the Late Middle Kingdom in the Brooklyn Museum* (Papyrus Brooklyn 35.1446). (New York, 1972). – R: *BiOr* 30, 207-209 (O. D. Berlev).

Heerma van Voss, M.: "Drie Egyptische Goden", *Festschrift de Liagre Böhl* (q. v. sub 1-7), 185-187.

Helck, Wolfgang: *Das Bier im Alten Ägypten*, Berlin, 1971. (IBHR 1971, p. 53). – R: *BiOr* 30, 40-42 (Wolfhart Westendorf).

Helck, Wolfgang: *Der Text der 'Lehre Amenemhets I. für seinen Sohn*, (Wiesbaden, 1969), und ders.: *Die Prophezeiung des Nfr.tj.* (Wiesbaden, 1970). – R: *BiOr* 30, 28 (Ronald J. Williams).

Helck, W.: "Die Handwerker- und Priesterphylen des Alten Reiches in Aegypten", *Die Welt des Orients* 7/1, 1-8.

Helck, Wolfgang: *Die Lehre des Dw3-Htjj.* Textzusammenstellung. (Wiesbaden, 1970). – R: *BiOr* 30, 218 (Dieter Mueller).

Helck, W.: "Zur Opferliste Amenophis' IV (JEA 57, 70 ff.)", *JEA* 59, 95-99.

Hodžas, S. I.: "Les scarabées égyptiens de la fin du Moyen Empire conservés au musée Pouchkine et au musée de l'Ermitage", *VDI* no. 3, 56-79, 4 pl.

Hofmann, Inge: *Studien zum meroitischen Königtum.* (Bruxelles, 1971). – R: *BiOr* 30, 236-238 (Helen Jacquet Gordon).

Hornung, E.: *Das Grab des Haremhab im Tal der Könige.* Unter Mitarbeit von F. Teichmann. (Bern, 1971). – R: *BiOr* 30, 232-236 (J. Zandee).

Hornung, Erik: *Der Eine und die Vielen. Ägyptische Gottesvorstellungen.* Darmstadt, 1971. (*IBHR* 1971, p. 53). – R: *BiOr* 30, 42-44 (L. Kákosy).

Hornung, E.: "Die *Kammern* des Thot-Heiligtumes", *ZÄSA* 100, Heft 1, 33-35, 1 Tafel.

Huard, Paul et Jean Leclant: *Problèmes archéologiques entre le Nil et le Sahara.* (Le Caire, 1972). – R: *BiOr* 30, 405-407. Taf. XIX-XX (Inge Hofmann).

Jacobsohn, H.: "Das göttliche Wort und der göttliche Stein im alten Ägypten", *Eranos-Jahrbuch* 39, 217-241.

James, T. G. H.: *Hieroglyphic Texts from Egyptian Stelae* etc. Part 9. (London, 1970). – R: *BiOr* 30, 214-216 (Henri Wild).

Jelgersma, H. C.: "Een hypothese over Echnaton en de negerkunst', *Phoenix* 19/1, 231-240.

Kakosy, L.: "Fragmente eines unpublizierten magischen Textes", in: *XXIXe Congrès International des Orientalistes. Résumés des Communications*, Sections 1-5. (Paris, Y. Hervouet), p. 24.

Kákosy, L.: "Totenbuchstudien", *Göttinger Miszellen* 7, 34.

Kayser, Hans: *Die ägyptischen Altertümer im Roemer-Pelizaeus-Museum in Hildesheim.* (Hildesheim, H. A. Gerstenberg Verlag). 4to. 172 S., 12 Farbtaf., 120 Abb. = Pelizaeus-Museum zu Hildesheim, Wissenschaftliche Veröffentlichungen, 8.

Kemp, B. J.: "The Osiris Temple at Abydos. A postscript to MDAIK 23 (1968) 138-155", *Göttinger Miszellen* 8, 23-25.

Kitchen, K. A.: *Ramesside Inscriptions, Historical and Biographical.* I, fasc. 4. (Oxford, B. H. Blackwell), pp. 97-128.

Kitchen, K. A.: *Ramesside Inscriptions, Historical and Biographical.* I, fasc. 3. (Oxford, B. H. Blackwell). pp. i, 65-96.

Kitchen, K. A.: *Ramesside Inscriptions, Historical and Biographical.* Vol. I, Fasc. 2; II, 6. (Oxford, 1971). – R: *BiOr* 30, 212-214 (W. Helck).

Kitchen, K. A.: *Ramesside Inscriptions, Historical and Biographical.* Vol. V, Fasc. 2 and 3. (Oxford, 1972). – R: *BiOr* 30, 397-398 (W. A. Helck).

Kitchen, K. A.: *The Third Intermediate Period in Egypt (1100-650 B.C.).* (Warminster, England, Aris & Phillips). xvii, 525 p., 10 fig., 24 tables.

Kuhlmann, K. P.: "Eine Beschreibung der Grabdekoration mit der Aufforderung zu kopieren und zum Hinterlassen von Besucherinschriften aus saitischer Zeit", *MDAIK* 29/2, 205-213.

Leek, F. Filce: *The Human Remains from the Tomb of Tut'Ankhamun.* (Oxford, 1972). – R: *BiOr* 30, 402-403 (Lennart Diener).

Lesko, L. H.: *The Ancient Egyptian Book of Two Ways.* (Berkeley and Los Angeles, 1972). – R: *ChrEg* 48 (96), 284-287 (P. Barguet).

Lichtheim,Mariam (ed.): *Ancient Egyptian Literature. A Book of Readings.* Vol. I: *The Old and Middle Kingdoms.* (Berkeley and Los Angeles, University of California Press). xxi, 245 p.

Lüddeckens, E.: "Ägyptische Tempelmythen", *ZRGG* 25/3, 261-266. (Betrachtungen zu E. A. E. Reymond: *The Mythical Origin of the Egyptian Temple*, Manchester, 1969).

Malaise, M.: "La pierre *nmḥf* et son identification avec le défunt dans le Livre des Morts", *ChrEg* 48 (95), 26-35.

Maragioglio, Vito – Celeste Rinaldi: "Note complementari sulla tomba di Neferu-Ptaḥ", *Orientalia* 42, 357-369.

Martin, G. T.: "Excavations in the Sacred Animal Necropolis at North Saqqâra, 1971-2: Preliminary Report", *JEA* 59, 5-15, 17 pl.

Medinet Habu, Vol. VIII. The Eastern High Gate, with Translation of Texts, by the Epigraphic Survey, (Chicago, 1970). – R: *BiOr* 30, 38-40 (B. van de Walle).

Meeks, D.: "Le nom du dauphin et le poisson de Mendès", *RevEg* 25, 209-216. (= *H3t-mḥjt!*)

Mendelssohn, K.: "Pyramid technology", *Bibliotheca Orientalis* 30, 349-355, 4 Figures.

Morenz, Siegfried: "Ägypten", in: U. Mann (Hrsg.): *Theologie und Religionswissenschaft* (Darmstadt, Wissenschaftliche Buchgesellschaft) 47-64.

Morenz, Siegfried: *Egyptian Religion*. Translated by Ann E. Keep. (London, Methuen). xvi, 379 p. = Methuen's Handbooks of Archaeology.

Morenz, Siegfried: *Bóg i czlowiek w starożytnym Egipcie*. (Gott und Mensch im alten Ägypten. Polnische Übersetzung von Mieczyslaw Szczudlowski. Warszawa, PIW, 1972). 169 p. – R: *Euhemer* XVII/2 (88), 103-105 (Wladyslaw Palubicki).

Moursi, Mohamed I.: *Die Hohenpriester des Sonnengottes von der Frühzeit bis zum Ende des Neuen Reiches*. (München, 1972). – R: *BiOr* 30, 404-405 (David Lorton).

Niccacci, A.: "Testi dell'antico Egitto sulla 'religione del povero' e alcune concezioni bibliche", *Rivista Biblica* 21, no 4, 413-427.

Peterson, B. E. J.: *Zeichnungen aus einer Totenstadt. Bildostraka aus Theben-West, ihre Fundplätze, Themata und Zweckbereiche mitsamt einem Katalog der Gayer-Anderson-Sammlung in Stockholm.* (Stockholm, The Museum of Mediterranean and Near Eastern Antiquities). 144 p., 80 Taf., Bibliographie (11 p.)

Posener, G.: "Le chapitre IV d'Aménémopé", *ZÄSA* 99/2, 129-135.

Radwan, A.: "Amenophis III, dargestellt und angerufen als Osiris (*wnn-nfrw*)", *MDAIK* 29/1, 71-76, 1 Taf.

Redford, D. B.: "An Interim Report on the Second Season of Work at the Temple of Osiris, Ruler of Eternity, Karnak", *JEA* 59, 16-30, 5 pl.

Reymond, E. A. E. and J. W. B. Barns: *Embalmers' Archives from Hawara.* (Oxford, Griffith Institute). 4to. xvii, 170 p., 16 pl. = Catalogue of Demotic Papyri in the Ashmolean Museum, Oxford.

Ricke, Herbert: *Der Harmachistempel des Chefren in Giseh.* – Siegfried Schott: *Ägyptische Quellen zum Plan des Sphinxtempels.* (Cairo-Wiesbaden, 1970). – R: *OLZ* 68, 128-131 (W. Wolf).

Rosenvasser, A.: "La religion égyptienne dans Hérodote: La vrai signification du passage II, 50 (in fine): 'Les Egyptiens ne rendent non plus aucun culte à des héros' (Trad. Legrand)", in: *XXIXe Congrès International des Orientalistes. Résumés des Communications,* Sections 1-5, (Paris, Y. Hervouet), pp. 21-22.

Sadek, A.-A. F.: "A Stela of Purification from the Tomb of Kha'emhat at Thebes", *MDAIK* 29/1, 63-69, 3 pl.

Saleh, Abdel-Aziz: "An Open Question on Intermediaries in the Incense Trade during Pharaonic Times", *Orientalia* 42, 370-382.

Samson, Julia: *Amarna, City of Akhenaten and Nefertiti.* Key Pieces from the Petrie Collection. With an Introduction by H. S. Smith. (London, 1972). – R: *BiOr* 30, 231 (Bengt J. Peterson).

Samuel, A. E., W. K. Hasting, A. K. Bowman, R. S. Bagnall: *Death and Taxes, Ostraka in the Royal Ontario Museum,* I. (Amsterdam, Hakkert, 1971). – R: *BiOr* 30, 216-218 (Guy Wagner).

Sauneron, Serge: *Le Papyrus Magique illustré de Brooklyn (Brooklyn Museum 47.218.156).* (New York, 1970). – R: *OLZ* 68, 29-31 (J. F. Borghouts).

Schiff Giorgini, Michela – Clément Robichon – Jean Leclant: *Soleb II, Les Nécropoles.* (Florence, 1971). – R: *BiOr* 30, 35-38 (Ph. Derchain).

Schneider, H. D.: "Gleanings in the Egyptian Collection at Leiden" (I), *OudhMed* 52, 8-21, 2 pl.

Siegler, Karl Georg: *Kalabsha. Architektur und Baugeschichte des Tempels.* (Berlin, 1970). – R: *BiOr* 30, 225-227 (Alexander M. Badawy).

Simpson, William Kelly (ed.): *The Literature of Ancient Egypt. An Anthology of Stories, Instructions, and Poetry.* New Edition. With Translations by R. O. Faulkner, E. F. Wente, Jr., and W. K. Simpson. (New Haven, Yale University Press). viii, 350 p.

Śliwa, J.: "The God Nkiro-mnt", *ZDMG* 123, Heft 1, 6-8, 1 pl.

Störk, L.: "Gab es in Ägypten den rituellen Königsmord?", *Göttinger Miszellen,* Heft 5, 31-32.

Tawfik, S.: "Aton Studies", *MDAIK* 29/1, 77-86, 2 pl.

Thausing, Gertrud und Hans Goedicke: *Nofretari. Eine Dokumentation der Wandgemälde ihres Grabes.* (Graz, 1971). – R: *OLZ* 68, 574-576 (S. Wenig).

Théodoridès, A.: "Les Egyptiens anciens: 'citoyens' ou 'sujets de Pharaon'?", *RIDA* 20, 51-112.

Trigger, Bruce G.: *The Meroitic Funerary Inscriptions from Arminna West*, with comments and indexes by André Heyler, (New Haven, 1970). – R: *BiOr* 30, 31-32 (Inge Hofmann).

Vandersleyen, C.: *Les guerres d'Amosis, fondateur de la XVIIIe Dynastie.* (Bruxelles, 1971). – R: *BiOr* 30, 223-225 (Donald B. Redford).

Vandier d'Abbadie, J.: *Catalogue des objets de toilette égyptiens.* (Paris, 1972). – R: *BiOr* 30, 218-219 (Birgit Nolte).

te Velde, H.: "Egyptologisch veldwerk van de Universiteit van Pennsylvania te Dra Aboe'l Naga", *Phoenix* 19/1, 219-230.

Vergote, J.: *De godsdienst van de Egyptenaren.* (Roermond, 1971). – R: *BiOr* 30, 393-396 (J. Zandee). *BTLV* 129, 151 (M. Heerma van Voss).

Vernus, P.: "La stèle C3 du Louvre", *RevEg* 25, 217-234, 1 pl.

Vila, A.: "Un rituel d'envoûtement au Moyen Empire égyptien", in: *L'Homme, hier et aujourd'hui. Recueil d'études en hommage à André Leroy-Gourhan* (Paris, Cujas), pp. 625-639.

Weinstein, J. M.: "Foundation Deposits in Ancient Egypt", *DisabIn A* 34/4, 1802. (The author's summary of his diss., University of Pennsylvania, 1973).

Wessetzky, V.: "Die ägyptische Tempelbibliothek. Der Schlüssel der Lösung liegt doch in der Bibliothek des Osymandyas?", *ZÄSA* 100/1, 54-59.

vanWijngaarden, W.D.: "Zes oud-egyptische stèles van provinciale herkomst", *OudhMed* 52, 1-7, 2 pl.

Wildung, D.: "Göttlichkeitsstufen des Pharao", *OLZ* 68, 549-565. (A review article on Labib Habachi: *Features of the Deification of Ramesses II*, Glückstadt, 1969).

Wildung, D.: "Un aspect amonien du roi d'Egypte", in: *XXIXe Congrès International des Orientalistes. Résumés des Communications*, Sections 1-5. (Paris, Y. Hervouet), p. 24.

Wilson, John A.: *Herodotus in Egypt.* (Leiden, 1970). – R: *OLZ* 68, 246-250 (M. Kaiser).

Winter, E.: "Arensnuphis, sein Name und seine Herkunft", *RevEg* 25, 235-250.

Wortmann, D.: *Neue magische Texte*, (Bonn, 1968). – R: *BiOr* 30, 206-207 (P. J. Sijpestijn).

Wright, R. M.: *Kalabsha. The Preserving of the Temple.* (Berlin, 1972). – R: *BiOr* 30, 403-404 (Alexander M. Badawy).

3. MESOPOTAMIA

Ali, F. A.: "Ishtar and Tammuz: the Origin of their Beliefs in Mesopotamian Civilization", *Sumer* 29/1-2, 35-70 (in Arabic).

Alster, Bendt: "An Aspect of 'Enmerkar and the Lord of Aratta' ", *RAAO* 67, no. 2, 101-110.

Alster, Bendt: *Dumuzi's Dream: Aspects of Oral Poetry in a Sumerian Myth.* (Copenhagen, Akademisk Forlag, 1972). 162 p., 22 pl. – R: *Orientalia* 42, 525-526 (R. Caplice). *RAAO* 67, 90-92 (J. Nougayrol).

Amiet, P.: "Mari, après quarante ans d'exploration", *RFEE* no. 268, 23.

Arnaud, D.: "Un document juridique concernant les oblats", *RAAO* 67, no. 2, 147-156.

Aro, Jussi – Jean Nougayrol: "Trois nouveaux recueils d'haruspicine ancienne", *RAAO* 67, 41-56.

Baer, André: "Neuf cylindres-sceaux inédits de la collection privée L. Buffet", *RAAO* 67, 63-71, 9 fig.

Bayliss, M.: "The Cult of Dead Kin in Assyria and Babylonia", *Iraq* 35, No. 2, 115-125.

Beljawski, W. A.: *Vavilon legendarnyj i Vavilon instoričeskij* (= Das legendäre Babylon und das historische Babylon), (Moskva, 1971). – R: *BiOr* 30, 247-249 (Josef Klíma).

Berger, P.-R.: *Die neubabylonischen Königsinschriften. Königsinschriften des ausgehenden babylonischen Reiches (626-539 v. Chr.)* Teil I. (Kevelaer, Butzon & Bercker/Neukirchen-Vluyn, Neukirchener Verlag des Erziehungsvereins). 349 S., 1 Taf. = Alter Orient und Altes Testament. Veröffentlichungen zur Kultur und Geschichte des Alten Orients, 4/1.

Biggs, R. D.: "Pre-Sargonic Riddles from Lagash", *Journal of Near Eastern Studies* 32, 26-33, 3 fig.

Borger, R.: "Die Weihe eines Enlil-Priesters", *Bibliotheca Orientalis* 30, 163-176, Taf. I-IV. (Text in Umschrift, Übersetzung und Kommentar).

Borger, Rykle: *Handbuch der Keilschriftliteratur.* I: *Repertorium der sumerischen und akkadischen Texte.* (Berlin, 1967). – R: *OLZ* 68, 576-580 (J. Oelsner).

Borger, R.: "Keilschrifttexte verschiedenen Inhalts", *Festschrift de Liagre Böhl* 38-55.

Borger, R.: "Tonmännchen und Puppen", *BiOr* 30, 176-183, Taf. V-VII. (Text in Umschrift, Übersetzung und Kommentar).

Börker-Klähn, J.: "Eine Bronzestatue aus Assur?", *ZAVA* 63/2, 272-287.

Bottéro, Jean: [Compte-rendu des conférences:] "Antiquités assyro-babyloniennes", *AEPHEH* 1972, 93-131.

Brinkman, J. A.: "Additional Texts from the Reigns of Shalmaneser III and Shamshi-Adad V", *JNES* 32, 40-46, 4 fig.

Brinkman, J. A.: "Comments on the Nassouhi Kinglist and the Assyrian Kinglist Tradition", *Orientalia* 42 (Fs Gelb), 306-319.

Brinkman, J. A.: "Sennacherib's Babylonian Problem: An Interpretation", *JCS* 25, 89-95.

Cagni, L.: *Das Erra-Epos. Keilschrifttext.* (Rom, 1970). – R: *BiOr* 30, 433 (R. Frankena)

Calmeyer, P.: *Reliefbronzen in babylonischem Stil: Eine westiranische Werkstatt des 10. Jahrhunderts v. Chr.* (München, Verlag der Bayerischen Akademie der Wissenschaften). 251 S., 144 Abb., 8 Taf., 3 Tab. = BAW, Phil.-Hist. Klasse, Abh. N. F., 73.

Caplice, R.: "E.MUN in Mesopotamian Literature", *Orientalia* 42 (Fs Gelb), 299-305.

Caplice, R.: "Further Namburbi Notes", *Orientalia* 42, 508-517, Tab. XL. (Texts, translations, and commentaries).

Cassin, Elena: *La splendeur divine. Introduction à l'étude de la mentalité mésopotamienne.* (Paris-La Haye, 1968). – R: *OLZ* 68, 351-354 (B. Bruška).

Castellino, G. R.: *Two Šulgi Hymns(BC).* (Roma, Instituto di Studi del Vicino Oriente, Università di Roma). 322 p., 20 fig., 23 pl. = Studi Semitici, 42.

Cocquerillat, D.: "Recherches sur le verger du temple campagnard de l'Akitu ($KIRI_6$ hallat)", *WO* 7/1, 96-134.

van Compernolle, René: "L'inscription de Salmanasar III, IM 55644, du Musée de Bagdad, la chronologie des rois de Tyr et la date de la fondation de Carthage (806/5 avant notre ère)", *AIPHOS* 20, 467-479.

Crawford, H. E. W.: "Mesopotamia's invisible exports in the third millenium B.C.", *world Archaeology* 5/2, 232-241.

Cuneiform Texts from Babylonian Tablets in the British Museum. Part 48: *Old-Babylonian Legal Documents* by J. J. Finkelstein. (London, 1968). – R: *OLZ* 68, 464-468 (H. M. Kümmel).

Dalley, Stephanie: "Old Babylonian Greetings Formulae and the Iltani Archive from Rimah", *JCS* 25, 79-88.

David, Martin: "Kritik an einem Rechtsspruch aus Larsa", *Festschrift de Liagre Böhl* (q. v. sub I-7), 94-99.

van Dijk, J.: "Une incantation accompagnant la naissance de l'homme", *Orientalia* 42, 502-507.

van Dijk, Jan: "Un rituel de purification des armes et de l'armée", *Festschrift de Liagre Böhl* (q. v. sub I-7), 107-117.

Dossin, G.: "Amurru, dieu cananéen", *Festschrift de Liagre Böhl* (q. v. sub I-7), 93-98.

Dossin, Georges: "L'Euphrate au secours des parturientes", *AIPHOS* 20, 213-221.

van Driel, G.: "On 'Standard' and 'Triomphal' Inscriptions", *Festschrift de Liagre Böhl* 99-106.

van Driel, G.: *The Cult of Aššur.* (Assen, Royal Vangorcum, 1969). – R: *BiOr* 30, 433-436 (Walter Farber).

During Caspers, E. C. L.: "Dilmun and the Date-Tree", *East and West* 23, no. 1-2, 75-78, 2 pl.

Edzard, D. O.: *Altbabylonische Rechts- und Wirtschaftsurkunden aus Tell ed-Dēr bei Sippar*, (Wiesbaden, 1971). – R: *BiOr* 30, 63-66 (R. R. Jestin).

Edzard, Dietz Otto: *Altbabylonische Rechts- und Wirtschaftsurkunden aus Tell ed-Dēr im Iraq Museum, Baghdad*, (München, 1970). – R: *BiOr* 30, 61-63 (F. R. Kraus).

Edzard, D. O.: "Puzriš – Dagān-Silluš – Dagān", *ZAVA* 63/2, 288-294.

Edzard, Dietz Otto: "Zwei Inschriften am Felsen von Sar-i-Pūl-i-Zohāb: Anubanini 1 und 2", *AfO* 24, 73-77.

Eichler, B. L.: Indenture at Nuzi: *The Personal Tidennūtu Contract and its Mesopotamian Analogues.* (New Haven, Yale University Press). xiii, 163 p. = Yale Near Eastern Researches, 5.

Ellis, R. S.: *Foundation Deposits in Ancient Mesopotamia*, (New Haven, Yale University). – R: *ArOr* 41, 376-377 (P. Charvát).

Fales, F. M.: "Remarks on the Neirab Texts", *Oriens Antiquus* 12, 131-142.

Farber, Walter: "Die Erbschaft der Rībatum", *Die Welt des Orients* 7/1, 18-24.

Farber-Flügge, Gertrud: *Der Mythos "Inanna und Enki" unter besonderer Berücksichtigung der Listederme.* (Rome, Biblical Institute Press). xv, 256 S., 1 Abb. = Studia Pohl, 10.

Ferrara, A. J.: *Nanna-Suen's Journey to Nippur.* (Rome, Biblical Institute Press). ix, 190 p., 11 fig., 1 pl. = Studia Pohl, Ser. Maior 2.

Finet, André: *Le Code de Hammurapi. Introduction, traduction et annotation.* (Paris, Les Editions du Cerf). 155 p., 2 cartes. = Littératures Anciennes du Proche-Orient, 6.

Finet, André: "Hamu-rapi et l'épouse vertueuse. A propos des §§ 133 et 142-143 du Code", *Fs de Liagre Böhl* (q. v. sub I-7), 137-143.

Frankena, R.: "Einige Bemerkungen zu den Hauptpersonen der Lagaba Tafeln", *Fs de Liagre Böhl* 149-160.

Freydank, Helmut: "Vorstellungen und Kenntnisse vom Kosmos in der Keilschriftlichen Überlieferung", *Das Altertum* 19, 67-74, 3 Abb.

Géza, K.: "L'évolution de la poèsie épique en Mésopotamie", *Ethnographia* 84/3, 274-300 (en hongrois, rés. en allem., russe).

Gragg, Gene: "The Fable of the Heron and the Turtle", *Archiv für Orientforschung* 24, 51-72, 5 fig.

Habib, G.: "Deities of Hatra", *Sumer* 29/1-2, 157 (in Arabic).

Hallo, W. W.: *Sumerian Archival Texts.* (Leiden, Nederlands Instituut voor het Nabije Oosten). 4to. 8 p., 67 pl. = Tabulae Cuneiformes a F. M. Th. de Liagre Böhl collectae Leidae conservatae III (= TLB III). – R: *BiOr* 30, 430-432 (Hartmut Waetzoldt).

Hallo, W. W.: "The Seals of Aššur – remanni", *Festschrift de Liagre Böhl* (q. v. sub I-7), 180-184.

Hallo, W. W., – J. J. A. van Dijk: *The Exaltation of Inanna.* – R: *Oriens Antiquus* 12, 70-74 (L. Cagni).

Heimpel, Wolfgang: "Der Tod der Göttin Baba von Lagaš. Eine Beobachtung zum sumerischen Götterglauben", in: *Festschrift für Hermann Heimpel*, Dritter Band, (Göttingen, Vandenhoeck & Ruprecht, 1972), 661-667.

Hirsch, H.: "Zum Fluss-Ordal in Elam", *RAAO* 67, 75-77.

Hruška, Blahoslav: "Die innere Struktur der Reformtexte Urukaginas von Lagaš", *ArOr* 41, 4-13, 104-132.

Hruška, Blahoslav: "Einige Überlegungen zum Erraepos", *BiOr* 30, 3-7. (Erörterung einer "Reihe von Fragen und Problemen, zu denen das Buch [*L'Epopea di Erra*, Roma, 1969] von L. Cagni anregt").

Hvidberg-Hansen, O.: "Ba'al-malagē in the Treaty between Asarhaddon and the King of Tyre", in: *XXIXe Congrès International des Orientalistes.* Résumés des Communications, Sections 1-5. (Paris, Y. Hervouet), p. 29.

Hvidberg-Hansen, O.: "Ba'-al-Malagē dans le traité entre Asarhaddon et le roi de Tyr", *AOD* 35, 57-81.

Jacobsen, Thorkild: "Notes on Nintur", *Orientalia* 42 (Fs Gelb), 274-298.

Jacobsen, Thorkild: *Toward the Image of Tammuz and Other Essays on Mesopotamian History and Culture*, (Harvard University Press, 1970), – R: *BiOr* 30, 66-70 (H. Waetzoldt).

Jawad, Abdul-Jalil: *The advent of the Era of Township in Northern Mesopotamia.* (Leiden, 1965). – R: *OLZ* 68, 250-255 (Rolf Hachmann).

Jestin, R. R.: "Les noms de profession en NU-", *Festschrift de Liagre Böhl* (q. v. sub I-7), 211-213.

Kienast, B.: "Der Weg zur Einheit Babyloniens unter staatsrechtlichen Aspekten", *Orientalia* 42, 489-501.

Kienast, B.: "Weisheit des Apada von Eridu", *Festschrift de Liagre Böhl* (q. v. sub I-7), 234-239.

Klengel, Horst: *Altbabylonische Rechts- und Wirtschaftsurkunden.* (Berlin, Akademie-Verlag). 12 S., 50 Taf. = Vorderasiatische Schriftdenkmäler der Staatlichen Museen zu Berlin, N. F., Heft II.

Klima, Josef: "Ein Nachlass von Türen aus Nippur", *Festschrift de Liagre Böhl* (q. v. sub I-7), 240-242.

Köcher, Franz: *Die babylonisch-assyrsiche Medizin in Texten und Untersuchungen IV: Keilschrifttexte aus Assur 4, Babylon, Nippur, Sippar, Uruk und unbekannter Herkunft. (IBHR,* 1971). – Nota bibliographica: *Orientalia* 42, 469-470 (R. Caplice).

Komoróczy, Géza: "Arbeit und Streik der Götter. Neues Licht auf das Gesellschaftsbild der sumerisch-akkadischen Mythologie", *Antik Tanulmányok* 20, 1-28. (In Hungarian).

Kraus, F. R.: *Briefe aus dem Istanbuler Museum*, (Leiden 1972). – R: *BiOr* 30, 60-61 (Wolfram von Soden).

Kraus, F. R.: *Sumerer und Akkader: Ein Problem der altmesopotamischen Geschichte*, (Amsterdam, 1970). – R: *Orientalia* 42, 526-527 (R. Caplice). *BiOr* 30, 245-247 (Josef Klíma).

Kraus, F. R.: *Vom mesopotamischen Menschen der altbabylonischen Zeit und seiner Welt.* Eine Reihe Vorlesungen. (Amsterdam, North-Holland Publ. Co.) 149 p. = Mededelingen der Koninklijke Nederlandse Akademie van Wetenschappen, Afd. Letterkunde, N.R., Deel 36, No. 6 (pp. ii, 199-345).

Krecher J.: "Neue sumerische Rechtsurkunden des 3. Jahrtausends", *ZAVA* 63, Heft 2, 145-271.

Kümmel, H. M.: "Bemerkungen zu den altorientalischen Berichten von der Menschenschöpfung", *WO* 7/1, 25-38.

Kutscher, Raphael: "Imittu Postponed and Replaced: A New Document", *BiOr* 30, 363-366 (Wadsworth Atheneum 16.92).

Labat, René: "Un prince éclairé: Assurbanipal", *CRAIBL* 1972, 670-676.

Lambert, W. G.: "A New Fragment from a List of Antediluvian Kings and Marduk's Chariot", *Fs de Liagre Böhl* (q. v. sub I-7), 271-280.

Lambert, W.,G.: "Studies in Nergal": Egbert von Weiher: *Der babylonische Gott Nergal.* (Kevelaer, Butzon und Bercker, 1971), *BiOr* 30, 355-363.

Lambert, W. G. – A. R. Millard: *Atra-ḫasīs. The Babylonian Story of the Flood.* With the Sumerian Flood Story by M. Civil. – R: *JAOS* 93, 75-76 (H. Nash Wolfe). *JNES* 32, 342-344 (J. Renger).

Lambert, W. G. and A. R. Millard: *Catalogue of the Cuneiform Tablets in the Kouyunjik Collection of the British Museum.* Second Supplement. (London, 1968). – R: *OLZ* 68, 34-36 (R. Borger).

Leemans, W.,F.: "Quelques remarques à propos d'un texte concernant l'administration vieux-babylonienne", *Fs de Liagre Böhl* 281-292.

Leichty, E.: *The Omen Series* šumma izbu, (Locust Valley, N.Y., 1970). – R: *JAOS* 93, 585-587 (W. Heimpel).

Levine, Louis D.: "The Second Campaign of Sennacherib", *JNES* 32, 312-317, 1 fig.

Lyczkowska, Krystyna: "La prière d'Antiochus Ier Sôter au dieu Nabu", *Euhemer* 17/3 (89), 83-86.

McCarter, P. K.: "Rib-Adda's Appeal to Aziru (EA 162, 1-21)", *Oriens Antiquus* 12, 15-18.

Malamat, Abraham: *A Collection of Mari Documents in Akkadian Transliteration and Hebrew Translation.* Third, enlarged edition. (Jerusalem, Academon). 69 p., 1 map.

Malamat, Abraham: *Mari and the Bible. A Collection of Studies.* (Jerusalem, Hebrew University). viii, 162 p., 3 maps. (In English and Hebrew).

Margueron, Jean-Claude: "Deux *kudurru* de Larsa, I. Etude iconographique", *RAAO* 66, 147-161, 6 fig.

de Meyer, Léon, Hermann Gasche et Roland Paepe: *Tell ed-Der I: Rapport préliminaire sur la première campagne (février 1970)* (Louvain, 1971). – R: *BiOr* 30, 72-73 (M. N. van Loon).

Millard, A. R.: "Adad-Nirari III, Aram, and Arpad", *Palestine Exploration Quarterly* 105, 161-164.

Millard, A. R.: "Some Esarhaddon Fragments Relating to the Restoration of Babylon", *AfO* 24, 117-119, pl. 13-14.

Millard, A. R. – H. Tadmor: "Adad-Nirari III in Syria, Another Stele Fragment and the Dates of his Campaigns", *Iraq* 35, 57-64, 1 fig., 1 pl.

Mittmann, Siegfried: "Das südliche Ostjordanland im Lichte eines neuassyrischen Keilschriftbriefes aus Nimrūd", *ZDPV* 89, 15-25.

Moorey, P. R. S. – O. R. Gurney: "Ancient Near Eastern Seals at Charterhouse", *Iraq* 35, 71-81, 2 pl.

Moortgat-Correns, Ursula: *Die Bildwerke vom Djebelet el Beda in ihrer räumlichen und zeitlichen Umwelt,* (Berlin, 1972). – R: *BiOr* 30, 70-72 (Hartmut Schmökel).

Moriarty, F. L.: "Antecedents of Israelite Prophecy in the Ancient Near East", *Studia Missionalia* 22, 255-277.

Naster, Paul: "*sullūlu* dans Gilgamesh XI, 31", *Festschrift de Liagre Böhl* (q. v. sub I-7), 295-298.

Nougayrol, Jean: "Einführende Bemerkungen zur babylonischen Religion", in: U. Mann (Hrsg.): *Theologie und Religionswissenschaft* (Darmstadt, Wissenschaftliche Buchgesellschaft) 28-46.

Nougayrol, Jean: "Textes religieux" (II), *RAAO* 66, 141-145. (= AO 7682 et BM 97877).

Oberhuber, Karl: "Sumer", in: U. Mann (Hrsg.): *Theologie und Religionswissenschaft* (Darmstadt, Wissenschaftliche Buchgesellschaft) 3-27.

Oppenheim, A. Leo: "A New Subdivision of the Shekel in the Arsacide Period", *Orientalia* 42 (Fs Gelb), 324-327.

Oppenheim, A. Leo: *Letters from Mesopotamia.* Official, Business, and Private Letters on Clay Tablets from Two Millenia, translated and with an Introduction. (Chicago, 1967). – R: *OLZ* 68, 36-39 (Hans Martin Kümmel).

Parrot, A.: "Les fouilles de Mari. Vingtième campagne printemps 1972", *AAAS* 23, no. 1-2, 9-24, 10 pl.

Petschow, Herbert: "Zur mittelbabylonischen 'Buchhaltungstechnik' und zur Tempelwirtschaft der NIN.DINGIR-Priesterinnen", *Fs de Liagre Böhl* (q.v. sub I-7), 298-307.

Pettinato, Giovanni: *Das altorientalische Menschenbild und die sumerischen und akkadischen Schöpfungsmythen.* (*IBHR*, 1971, p. 62). – R: *JAOS* 93, 581-585 (J. S. Cooper).

Pomponio, F.: " 'Löwenstab' e 'Doppellöwenkeule'. Studio su due simboli dell' iconografia mesopotamica. Oriens Antiquus 12, no. 3, 183-208. (With reference to U. Seidl: "Die babylonischen Kudurru-Reliefs", *Baghdader Mitteilungen* 4 (1968)).

Postgate, J. N.: "Neo-Assyrian Royal Grants and Decrees: Addenda and Corrigenda", *Orientalia* 42, 441-444.

Rabinovič, E. G.: "Kolodec Šamaša" (The well of Šamaš), *VDI* 124/2, 103-106 (in Russian, with a summary in English).

Rapaport, I.: *A New Interpretation of §§ 6-8 of the Code of Hammurabi* – R: *JRAS* (1972, publ. 1973), 58-60 (G. R. Driver).

Raschid, F.: "Eine religiöse Bewegung in prähistorischer Zeit und ihre Wirkung auf die sumerische Kunst", *Sumer* 29/1-2, 23-30, 1 pl.

Reiner, Erica: "Inscription from a Royal Elamite Tomb", *Archiv für Orientforschung* 24, 87-102, 2 fig., 2 tables, pl. 11-12.

Reisman, D.: "Iddin-Dagan's Sacred Marriage Hymn", *JCS* 25/4, 185-202.

Rosengarten, Yvonne: *Trois aspects de la pensée religieuse sumérienne*, (*IBHR*, 1971). – R: *Orientalia* 42, 468-469 (J. L. Zubizarreta).

al-Salihi, Wathiq: "Hercules-Nergal at Hatra", *Iraq* 33, 113-115, 2 pl. 35, 65-68, 4 pl., 1 fig. (See also under: Segal, J. B.).

Salonen, Armas: *Die Fussbekleidung der alten Mesopotamier nach sumerisch-akkadischen Quellen. Eine lexikalische und kulturgeschichtliche Untersuchung.* (Helsinki, 1969). – R: *OLZ* 68, 137-139 (H. Freydank).

Saporetti, C.: "Nota sulla lettura di tre stele di Assur", *AION* 23 (33), 277-282.

Saporetti, C.: *Onomastica medio-assira* (SP6). – R: *Archiv für Orientforschung* 24, 141-142 (E. Weidner). *BiOr* 30, 58-60 (A. R. Millard).

Sasson, Jack M.: "Bibliographical Notices on Some Royal Ladies from Mari", *JCS* 25, 59-78.

Schramm, W.: *Einleitung in die assyrischen Königsinschriften*. Zweiter Teil: 934-722 v. Chr. (Leiden, E. J. Brill). xi, 141 S. = Handbuch der Orientalistik, Erste Abteilung, Ergänzungsband V, 1. Abschnitt.

Segal, J. B.: "Additional Note on Hercules-Nergal", *Iraq* 35, 68-69. (See also under' al-Salihi, W.)

Sjöberg, Åke W.: "A Hymn to the Goddess Sadarnuna", *JAOS* 93, 352-353.

Sjöberg, Åke W.: "Der Vater und sein missratener Sohn", *JCS* 25, 105-169.

Sjöberg, Å. W.: "Die göttliche Abstammung der sumerisch – babylonischen Herrscher", *Orientalia Suecana* 21, 87-112.

Sjöberg, Å. W.: "Hymn to Numušda with a Prayer for Siniqīšam of Larsa and a Hymn to Ninurta", *OrSu* 22, 107-121.

Sjöberg, Å. W.: "Miscellaneous Sumerian Hymns", *ZA VA* 29 (63), 1-55, 6 fig.

Sjöberg, Åke W.: "Nungal in the Ekur", *Archiv für Orientforschung* 24, 19-46, 8 fig., pl. 4-10.

Sjöberg, Åke W.: "Two Prayers for King Samsuiluna of Babylon", *JAOS* 93, 544-547.

Sollberger, Edmond: *The Business and Administrative Correspondence under the Kings of Ur.* (Locust Valley, N.Y., 1966). – R: *OLZ* 68, 132-136 (J. Renger).

Spycket, A.: "Le culte du dieu-lune à Tell Keisan", *Revue Biblique* 80, no. 3, 384-395, 1 pl.

Veenhof, K. R.: "An Old Babylonian Deed of Purchase of Land in the De Liagre Böhl Collection", *Fs de Liagre Böhl* 359-379.

Walters, S. D.: "The year Names of Sumu-el", *RAAO* 77, no. 1, 21-40.

Wilcke, C.: *Das Lugalbandaepos.* – R: *Erasmus* 25, 114-118 (A. Salonen). *OrAn* 12, 165-171(G. Pettinato). *ZDMG* 123, 379-382 (J. Bauer). *OLZ* 68, 580-586 (H. Sauren).

Wilcke, C.: "Der Anfang von 'Inanna und Sukalletuda", *Archiv für Orientforschung* 24, 86.

Wilcke, C.: "Der Titel u_5 giš-gi-kù-ta in zwei sumerischen Literaturkatalogen", *AfO* 24, 50.

Wilcke, Claus: "Sumerische literarische Texte in Manchester und Liverpool", *AfO* 24, 1-17, Taf. I-III.

Wilcke, Claus: "Zur ersten Tafel von an-gim-dím-ma", *Archiv für Orientforschung* 24, 18.

Wilcke, Claus: "Zur Rekonstruktion von Sulgi E", *Archiv für Orientforschung* 24, 18.

Wilhelm, G.: "Ein Brief der Amarna-Zeit aus Kâmid el-Lôz (KL 72:600)", *ZAVA* 63, 69-75, facs.

Xella, Paolo: "L' 'inganno' di Ea nel mito di Adapa", *Oriens Antiquus* 12, no. 4, 257-266.

Yaron, R.: *The Laws of Eshnunna.* – R: *JRAS* (1972, publ. 1973), 57-58 (G. R. Driver).

4. IRAN

Akataev, S. N.: "le culte des ancêtres chez les Kazakhs dans le passé et le zoroastrisme", *IANKO* 2, 43-49 (en russe, rés. en kazakh).

Amiet, Pierre: "La civilisation du desert du Lut", *Archeologia* 60, 20-27.

Bauer, J.: *Symbolik des Parsismus.* Tafelband. Unter Benutzung der Vorarbeiten von Eleonore Kohlhagen von Tessin bearbeitet. (Stuttgart, Hiersemann). 146 S., 100 Abb., 1 Karte. = Symbolik der Religionen, XVIII. Tafelband zu Band VIII des Textwerkes.

Belenizkii, A. M.: *Monumentalnoe iskusstvo Pendžikenta: Živopis, skulptura.* (Monumental art of Pendžikent: painting and sculpture). (Moskva, Iskusstvo). 56 p., 25 fig., 76 illus. (partly col.) = Pamjatniki Drevnego Iskusstva.

vanden Berghe, Louis: *De iconografische Betekenis van het sassanidisch Rotsrelief van Sarab-i Qandil (Iran).* (Bruxelles, Koninklijke Academie voor Wetenschappen, Letteren en Schone Kunsten van België). 46 p., 22 pl. = Mededelingen, Klasse der Letteren, Jaargang XXXV, Nr. 1.

Bogoljubov, M. N.: "Aramaic inscriptions on ritual objects from Persepolis" (in Russian), *Izvestija Akademii Nauk SSSR, Serija Literatury i Jazyka* 32/2, 172-177. (A review of R. A. Bowman, *Aramaic Ritual Texts from Persepolis*, Chicago, The Univ. of Chicago Press, 1970).

Bowman, R. A.: *Aramaic Ritual Texts from Persepolis*, (Chicago, Oriental Institute Publications, 91). – *JRAS* 63-64 (A. R. Millard).

Cameron, George G.: "The Persian Satrapies and Related Matters", *JNES* 32, 47-56.

Chaumont, M.-L.: "Conquêtes sassanides et propagande nazdéenne (IIIe s.)", *Historia* 22/4, 664-710, bibliographie.

Dandamaev, M. A.: "Royal estate workers in Iran (End of VI – first half of V century B.C.)", *VDI* 125/3, 3-26 (in Russian, with an English summary).

Gaube, H.: *Arabosasanidische Numismatik.* (Braunschweig, Klinkhardt & Biermann). vi, 171 p., 24 Taf., 1 Tab., 1 Karte. 4°. Handbücher der mittelasiatischen Numismatik, 2.

Ghirshman, Roman: "Les tribus perses et leur formation tripartite", *CRAIBL* 210-221, carte.

Ghirshman, Roman: *Tchoga Zanbil* (Dur-Untash), II. *Temenos, Temples, Palais, Tombes*, (Mémoires de la Délegation Archéologique en Iran, t. 40, Mission de Susiane). – R: *AfO* 24, 133-138 (E. Heinrich).

Göbl, R.: *Der sāsānidische Siegelkanon.* (Braunschweig, Klinkhardt & Biermann), x, 72 p., 42 Taf. = Handbücher der mittelasiatischen Numismatik, 4.

Hallock, Richard T.: "The Persepolis Fortification Archive", *Orientalia* 42 (Fs Gelb), 321-323.

Harmatta, J.: "Altiranische Funde und Forschungen", *Die Sprache* 19, 68-79. (Bemerkungen über W. Hinz: *Altiranische Funde und Forschungen.* Mit Beiträgen von R. Borger und G. Gropp).

Hartman, Sven S.: "Iran" (Meinem Lehrer und Freund Geo Widengren zugeeignet), in: U. Mann (Hrsg.): *Theologie und Religionswissenschaft* (Darmstadt, Wissenschaftliche Buchgesellschaft) 106-123.

Hinz, W.: *Altiranische Funde und Forschungen.* Mit Beiträgen von R. Borger und G. Gropp. – R: *ZAVA* 63, 134-137 (P. Calmeyer). (Vide supra sub: Harmatta, J.)

Hinz, W.: *Neue Wege im Altpersischen.* (Wiesbaden, O. Harrassowitz). 174 S., 8 Taf. = Göttinger Orientforschungen, Reihe III: Iranica, 1.

Hlopin, I. H.: "Les sept 'Karšvar' de l'Avesta", *Klio* 55, 79-86.

Humbach, H.: "Al-Biruni und die Sieben Strome des Awesta", *Bulletin of the Iranian Culture Foundation* 1, No. 2, 47-52.

Humbach, Helmut: "Beobachtungen zur Überlieferungsgeschichte des Awesta", *Münchener Studien zur Sprachwissenschaft*, Heft 31.

Kellens, J.: "Les frauuašis dans l'art sassanide", *Iranica Antiqua* 10, 133-138.

Kuz'mina, E. E.: "Le sommet de hampe aux cavaliers provenant de Daghestan (et la question de l'extension de l'equitation et du culte de cheval au Caucas et en Iran)", *SovAr* 2, 178-190, 1 fig. (In Russian, with a summary in French).

Mayrhofer, M.: *Aus der Namenwelt Alt-Irans.* (*IBHR*, 1971, S. 65). R: *Archiv Orientální* 41, 379-380 (O. Klima).

de Meyer, Léon: "Epart sukkalmah?", *Festschrift de Liagre Böhl*, (q. v. sub I-7), 293-294.

Naveh, Joseph and Shaul Shaked: "Ritual Texts or Treasury Documents?", *Orientalia* 42, 445-457. (Critical remarks on R. A. Bowman: *Aramaic Ritual Texts from Persepolis*, Chicago, 1970).

Schippmann, K.: *Die iranischen Feuerheiligtümer.* (Berlin, W. de Gruyter, 1971). – R: *Syria* 49, 257-258 (D. Schlumberger).

Schlerath, Bernfried: *Awesta-Wörterbuch.* Vorarbeiten, I. Index locorum zur Sekundärliteratur des Awesta. (Wiesbaden, 1968). – R: *OLZ* 68, 173-175 (Hanns-Peter Schmidt).

in der Smitten, Wilhelm Th.: "Beobachtungen zur Lexicographie und Grammatik der achämenidischen Königsinschriften", *BiOr* 30, 366-367.

in der Smitten, Wilhelm Th.: "Xerxes und die Daeva", *BiOr* 30, 368-369. (Text in Umschrift und Übersetzung, und Interpretation).

Snesarev, G. P.: "Trois légendes khwarezmiennes à la lumière des notions démonologiques" (en russe), *SovEtn* 1, 48-59.

Sundermann, Werner: *Mittelpersische und parthische kosmogonische und Parabeltexte der Manichäer.* Nebst einigen Bemerkungen zu Archiven der Parabeltexte von Friedmar Geissler. (Berlin, Akademie-Verlag). 4to. 148 S., 156 Faksimiles auf 33 Tafeln. = Berliner Turfantexte, IV. Schriften zur Geschichte und Kultur des Alten Orients, 8.

Vanden Berghe, L.: "Pusht-i Kûh, Luristan", *Iran* (London) 11, 207-209, 2 pl. (Survey of Excavations in Iran 1971-1972).

Vasilescu, E.: "La religion de l'Iran antique", *Studii Teologice* 25, no. 9-10, 683-675.

Widengren, Geo: *Der Feudalismus im Alten Iran.* – R: *Archiv Orientáení* 41, 168-171 (O. Klima).

5. ASIA MINOR

Archi, Alfonso, Paolo Emilio Pecorella, Mirjo Salvini: *Gaziantep e la sua regione. Uno studio storico e topografico degli insediamenti preclassici.* (Roma. 1971). – R: *BiOr* 30, 259-260 (C. H. J. de Geus).

Balkan, Kemal: *Inandik'ta 1966 Yılında Bulunan Eski Hitit Çağına Ait Bir Bağiş Belgesi.* (Ankara, Türk Tarih Kurumu Basımevi). xii, 103 p., illus. = Anadolu Medeniyetlerini Araştırma Vakfı Yayınları, 1. (Titel: Eine Schenkungsurkunde aus der althethitischen Zeit, gefunden in Inandik 1966).

Burney, C. and D. M. Lang: *The People of the Hills. Ancient Ararat and Caucasus.* – R: *JAOS* 93, 578-579 (K. S. Rubinson). *JRAS* 68-69 (S. Lloyd). *AJ* 52, 372-373 (J. Mellaart).

Carruba, Onofrio: *Das Palaische, Grammatik, Lexikon.* (Wiesbaden, 1970). – R: *BiOr* 30, 440-443 (E. Laroche).

Christmann-Franck, L.: "Le rituel des funérailles royales hittites", *RHA* 29, 61-111.

Cornelius, Fr.: *Geschichte der Hethiter.* Mit besonderer Berücksichtigung der geographischen Verhältnisse und der Rechtsgeschichte. (Darmstatt, Wissenschaftliche Buchgesellschaft). xviii, 382 S., 48 Abb., 2 Ktn. – R: *BiOr* 30, 437 (Richard Haase).

Del Monte, G. F.: "La porta nei rituali di Boğazköy", *Oriens Antiquus* 12, no. 2, 107-129.

Gaster, Theodore H.: "A Hang-up for Hang-ups. The Second Amulet Plaque from Arslan Tash", *BASOR* 209, 18-26.

Greenfield, Jonas C.: "Un rite religieux araméen et ses parallèles", *Revue Biblique* 80/1, 46-52.

Grothus, Jost: *Die Rechtsordnung der Hethiter.* (Wiesbaden, Otto Harrassowitz). xv, 87 S.

Güterbock, Hans: *Keilschrifttexte aus Boghazköi,* Heft 18. (Hethitische Briefe, Inventare und verwandte Texte). (Berlin, 1971). – R: *BiOr* 30, 73-75 (Bernhard Rosenkranz).

Güterbock, Hans G.: "Hattušili II Once More", *JCS* 25, 100-104.

Güterbock, Hans G.: "Hittite Hieroglyphic Seal Impressions from Korucutepe", *JNES* 32, 135-147, 6 fig.

Güterbock, Hans G.: "Ivory in Hittite Texts", *Anadolu* 15, 1-7.

Haas, V.: *Der Kult von Nerik. Ein Beitrag zur hethitischen Religionsgeschichte (SP 4).* – R: *JAOS* 93, 65-67 (C. Carter). *BSOAS* 36, 128 (J. D. Hawkins). *BiOr* 30, 75-77 (Gabriella Szabó).

Herdner, A.: "Une prière à Baal des Ugaritains en danger", *CRAIBL* 25 (no. avr.), 693-708.

Jirku, Anton: "Neue Götter und Dämonen aus Ugarit", *Archiv Orientální* 41, 97-103.

Kammenhuber, A.: *Materialien zu einem hethitischen Thesaurus.* Lieferung 1-2. (Heidelberg, Carl Winter). iv, 200 Bl.

Kapelrud, Arvid S.: *The Violent Goddess. Anat in the Ras Shamra Texts.* (Oslo, 1969). – R: *OLZ* 68, 46-47 (G. Wallis).

Kathcart, Kevin J.: *Nahum in the Light of Northwest Semitic.* (Rome, Biblical Institute Press). 171 p. = Biblica et Orientalia, 26.

Klengel, Horst: *Hethitische Rituale und Festbeschreibungen.* (Berlin, Akademie-Verlag). x S., 50 Taf. = Keilschrifturkunden aus Boghazköi, Heft 44.

Klengel, Horst: *Keilschrifturkunden aus Boghazköi.* Heft XLIV. (Berlin, Akademie-Verlag). 10 S., 50 Bl. = Akademie der Wissenschaften der DDR, Zentralinstitut für alte Geschichte und Archäologie.

Klíma, Josef: "L'Empire hittite, ses origines, son développement, sa destruction", in: *Les Grandes Empires* (Recueil de la Société Jean Bodin l'Histoire Comparative des Institutions, 31, Bruxelles 1973), 135-147.

Kühne, Cord und Heinrich Otten: *Der Sausgamuwa – Vertrag.* (Wiesbaden, 1971). – R: *BiOr* 30, 439-440 (Horst Klengel).

Kümmel, Hans Martin: "Die Religion der Hethiter", in: U. Mann (Hrsg.): *Theologie und Religionswissenschaft* (Darmstadt, Wissenschaftliche Buchgesellschaft) 65-85.

Laroche, Emmanuel: "Les hiéroglyphes d'Altıntepe", *Anadolu* 15, 55-61.

Laroche, Emmanuel: *Les Noms des Hittites*, (Paris, 1966). – R: *BiOr* 30, 252-257 (Philo H. J. Houwink ten Cate).

Maróth, M.: "Bemerkungen zum ugaritischen Text Krt", *Acta Orientalia* (Budapest) 27, 301-307.

Matouš, Lubor: "Beiträge zum Eherecht der anatolischen Bevölkerung im 2. Jahrtausend v.u.Z.", *ArOr* 41, 309-318.

Means Starr, O.: "A Search for the Identity of Yamm, 'Prince Sea', of the Canaanite Baal and Anath Cycle", *Folklore* 84, 224-237.

del Monte, G. F.: "Il terrore dei morti", *Annali dell'Instituto Orientale di Napoli* 33, no 3, 373-385.

del Monte, G. F.: "La porta nei rituali di Boğazköy", *Oriens Antiquus* 12, 107-129.

de Moor, J. C.: "*Rapi'u* de Heiland en de Refaïm", *GTT* 73, 129-146.

de Moor, J. C.: *The Saesonal Pattern in the Ugaritic Myth of Ba'lu*, according to the Version of Ilimilku, (*IBHR*, 1971, p. 68). – R: *WO* 7/1, 173-175 (R. Degen).

Neu, F.: *Ein althethitisches Gewitterritual* (StBoT 12). – R: *IF* 76, 271-272 (G. Neumann).

North, R.: "Ugarit Grid, Strata, and Find-Localizations", *ZDPV* 89/2, 113-160, 1 tab.

Otten, Heinrich: "Das Ritual der Allī aus Arzawa" *ZAVA* 63, 76-82.

Otten, H.: *Ein hethitisches Festritual* (KBo XIX 128) (StBoT 13). – R: *IF* 76, 272-274 (G. Neumann). *Mundus* 9, 135-136 (K. Hecker).

Otten, H.: *Eine althethitische Erzählung um die Stadt Zalpa.* (Wiesbaden, Otto Harrassowitz). xiii, 91 S., 4 Taf. = Studien zu den Boğazköy-Texten, herausgegeben von der Kommission für den Alten Orient der Akademie der Wissenschaften und der Literatur, 17.

Otten, H.: *Keilschrifttexte aus Boghazköi*, Heft 21. (Insbesonders Texte aus Gebäude A). (Berlin, Gebr. Mann). xvi S., 53 Taf. = Wissenschaftliche Veröffentlichungen der Deutschen Orient-Gesellschaft, 89.

Otten, Heinrich: *Materialien zum hethitischen Lexikon* (StBoT 15). – R: *Mundus* 9, 135-136 (K. Hecker). *Kratylos* 16, 161-164 (V. Haas).

Otten, Heinrich und Christel Ruster-Werner: *Keilschrifttexte aus Boghazköi*, zwanzigstes Heft (insbes. Texte aus Gebäude A), (Berlin, 1971). – R: *BiOr* 30, 252 (E. Laroche).

Otten, H. – V. Souček: *Ein althethitisches Ritual für das Königspaar* (StBoT 8). – R: *VDI* 125/3, 198-207 (V. G. Ardzinba).

Piotrovskij, B. B.: *Il Regno di Van-Urartu.* Traduzione di M. Salvini. (Roma, 1966). – R: *OLZ* 68, 468-471 (J. A. H. Potratz).

Riemschneider, K.: *Babylonische Geburtsomina in hethitischer Übersetzung* (StBoT 9). – R: *IF* 76, 265-267 (G. Neumann).

Röllig, Wolfgang: "Die Religion Altsyriens", in: U. Mann (Hrsg.): *Theologie und Religionswissenschaft* (Darmstadt, Wissenschaftliche Buchgesellschaft) 86-105.

von Schuler, Einar: *Die Kaskaër. Ein Beitrag zur Ethnographie des alten Kleinasien.* (Berlin, 1965). – R: *BiOr* 30, 77-79 (Philo H. J. Houwink ten Cate).

Soyez, B.: "Le Bétyle dans le culte de l'Astarté phénicienne", *MUSJ* 47, 147-169, 4 pl.

Szabó, Gabriella: *Ein hethitisches Entsühnungsritual für das Königspaar Tutḫaliịa und Nikalmati* (THeth 1). – R: *ZVS* 86, 322-323 (G.N.); *OrAn* 12, 171-177 (G. F. del Monte). *BiOr* 30, 438-439 (Hans Martin Kümmel).

Werner, Rudolf: "Ein Kultlieferungstext aus Bogazköy", *Festschrift de Liagre Böhl* (q. v. sub I-7), 393-395.

Willemaers, N.: "Contribution iconographique à l'histoire du rituel hittite", *RAHAL* 6, 7-18, 5 fig.

Willemaers, N.: "Une identification contestée d'Ištar-Šaušga", *Le Muséon* 86, no. 3-4, 467-473, 1 pl.

Xella, Paolo: *Il mito di šhr e šlm. Saggio sulla mitologia ugaritica.* (Roma, Instituto di Studi del Vicino Oriente, Università di Roma). 166 p. = Studi Semitici, 44.

6. GREEK AND ROMAN RELIGIONS

Adam, J.-P.: "Le temple de Héra II à Paestum", *Revue Archéologique*, no. 2, 219-236.

Alfonsi, L.: "Sull'*Aspis* e sulle 'sentenze' latine", *Aegyptus* 53, 71-74.

Aujolat, N.: "Les *katachthonioi daimones* et la destinée des âmes humaines après la mort d'après le *Commentaire sur les Vers d'Or des Pythagoriciens* de Hiéroclès", *AUTM* 9/5, 25-47.

Bammer, A.: "Neue Forschungen am Altar des Artemisions von Ephesos", *ArchAnz* 87, Heft 4, 714-728, 24 Abb.

den Boer, W.: "Aspects of Religion in Classical Greece", *HSCPh* 77, 1-21. (With reference to G. Murra and A. J. Toynbee).

den Boer, W.: "Heerserscultus en ex-voto's in het Romeinse keizerrijk", *Mededelin-*

gen der Koninklijke Nederlandse Akademie van Wetenschappen, Afdeling Letterkunde, Nieuwe reeks, Deel 36, nr. 4, 99-115.

Boucher, S.: *Bronzes romains figurés du Musée des Beaux-Arts de Lyon*. (Lyon, Ed. de Boccard). 209 p. (Publié avec concours de CNRS).

Bouzek, J.: "Two Cycladic Idols", *Listy Fololologické* 96/4, 189-190, 2 pl.

Braham, A.: "A Reappraisal of 'The Introduction of the Cult of Cybele at Rome' by Mantegna", *BurMag* 115 (844), 457-463.

Brommer, F.: *Der Gott, Vulkan auf provinzialrömischen Reliefs*. (Köln, Böhlau). vii, 55 S., 55 Taf.

Budde, L.: "Julian-Helios Sarapis und Helena-Isis", *Archäologischer Anzeiger* 87/4, 630-642, mit 31 Abbildungen.

Burnand, Y.: "Fragments d'inscriptions latines inédites de Lyon au Musée de la Civilisation Gallo-Romaine", *BMML* 5/3, 139-155.

Cacoullos, A. R.: "The Doctrine of Eros in Plato", *Diotima* 1, 81-99.

Calame, C.: "Essai d'analyse sémantique de rituels grecs", *Etudes de Lettres* VI, no. 1, 50-82.

Cébeillac, M.: "Octavia, épouse de Gamala, et la *Bona Dea*", *MEFRA* 85, no. 2, 517-553, 1 photo.

Cook, B. F.: "The Tympanum of the Fourth-Century Temple of Artemis at Ephesus", *BMQ* 37/3-4, 137-140, 2 pl.

Detienne, M.: "L'Olivier: un mythe politico-religieux", in: M. I. Finley: *Problèmes de la terre en Grèce ancienne*, (Paris-La Haye, Mouton), pp. 293-306. (Published under the same title in *RHR* 178, 1970, 5-23).

Devauges, J. B.: "Le fanum de Crain (Yonne). Fouille de sauvetage", *RAECE* 24, no. 92, 169-213.

Deyts, S.: "La religion gallo-romaine en Bourgogne", *Archeologia* 57, 21-27.

Dirat, M.: *L'Hybris dans la Tragédie grecque*. (Lille, Service de Reproduction des Thèses, Univ. de Lille III). 2 tomes (= 919 p., bibliographie, indiex). (Thèse, Univ. de Toulouse-Le Mirail, 1972).

Drew-Bear, T. and W. D. Lebek: "An Oracle of Apollo at Miletus", *GRBS* 14, no. 1, 65-73.

Dubarle, D.: "Le poème de Parménide, doctrine du savoir et premier état d'une doctrine de l'être", *RSPhTh* 57, 3-34, 397-432 (with a summary in English).

Engemann, J.: "Untersuchungen zur Sepulkralsymbolik der späteren römischen Kaiserzeit", *JACh* (Supplementband) 2, 1-94, 59 Taf.

Fasciano, D.: "Le numen chez Ovide", *RCCM* 15/3, 257-296.

Festugière, A. J.: "Tragédie et tombes sacrées", *RHR* 184/1, 3-24.

Fishwick, D.: "The Severi and the Provincial Cult of the Three Gauls", *Historia* 22/4, 627-649.

Gagé, J.: "La Némésis de Camille et les superstitions étrousques de la *Porta Rauducsulana*: à propos des origines de la *Porta Triumphalis*", *REL* 50, 111-138.

Gagé, J.: "Une consultation d'haruspices: sur les tabous étrusques de la statue dite d'Horatius Coclès", *Latomus* 32/1, 3-22.

Giangrande, G.: "Emendation d'une crux dans l'hymne à Zeus de Cléanthès", *AnCl* 42, no. 1, 181-184.

Gigante, M.: "Per la critica esegetica degli Oracoli di Hierapolis", *ParPas* no. 151, 275-276.

Guarducci, M.: " 'Chi è Dio?'. L'oracolo di Apollo Klarios e un' epigrafe di Enoanda", *AANL* 27, no. 7-12, 335-347.

Guillén, J.: "Los sacerdotes romanos" *Helmantica* 24 (no. 73), 5-76.

Guiraud, H.: "Quelques divinités guerrières sur des pierres gravées trouvées en Gaule", *AUTM* 9/5, 115-137, 1 pl.

Guittard, C.: "Le calendrier romain des origines au milieu du Ve siècle avant J.-C.", *BAGB* no. 2, 203-219.

Huxley, G.: "Fulgentius on the Cretan Hecatomphonia", *Classical Philology* 68, No. 2, 124-127.

Jacques, F.: "Inscriptions latines de Bourges", *Gallia* 31, no. 2, 297-312, (21 stèles, avec figures).

Jeanneret, R.: *Recherches sur l'hymne et la prière chez Virgile*. Essai d'application de la méthode tagmémique à des textes littéraires de l'Antiquité. (Bruxelles, Aimav/Paris, Didier). 246 p., 5 tabl.

Jürs, Fritz, Reimar Müller und Ernst Günther Schmidt: *Griechische Atomisten. Texte und Kommentare zum materialistischen Denken der Antike*. (Leipzig, Verlag Philipp Reclam jun.). 12mo. 704 S. = Reclam Universal Bibliothek, 409.

Kleywegt, A. J.: "Varro über die Penaten und die 'grossen Götter' ", *Mededelingen der Koninklijke Nederlandse Akademie van Wetenschappen, Afdeling Letterkunde*, Nieuwe reeks, Deel 35, nr. 7, 247-290.

Lafrance, Y.: "Amour et violance dans la dialectique platonicienne", *Dialogue* 12/2, 288-308.

Langdon, M. K.: "The Sanctuary of Zeus Ombrios on Mount Hymettos", *Dis-*

AbIn, A 33/7, 3517. (The author's summary of his Diss., University of Pennsylvania, 1972).

Langholf, V.: *Die Gebete des Euripides und die zeitliche Folge der Tragödien.* (Göttingen, 1971). – R: *Gnomon* 45/2, 134-139 (S. Jäkel).

Lausberg, M.: "Iupiter in manibus (Ov. am. 2, 1, 15)", *Museum Helveticum* XXX/2, 122-125.

Lesky, A.: "Zu einem ephesischen Graffito", *Wiener Studien* 7, 240-243. (With reference to W. Jobst: "Griechische Wandinschriften aus dem Hanghaus II in Ephesos", *ib.* 6, 235-245, 2. pl.)

Lesnickaja, M. M.: "Une tête d'Asclépius (Esculape) trouvée à Olbia", *VDI* no. 3, 87-92 (en russe, rés. anglais).

Lévêque, P.: "Continuités et innovations dans la religion grecque de la première moitié du Ier millénaire", *ParPas* 148-149, 23-50.

Lossky, B.: "Les figures des dieux pour la tenture des *Mois arabesques.* Identification", *RLM* 23/3, 169-172.

McDermott, W. C.: „Flavius Silva and Salvius Liberalis", *The Classical World* 66, No. 6, 335-351.

Marchetti, P.: "La marche du calendrier romain de 203 à 190 (années varr. 551-564), *AnCl* 42/2, 473-496.

Martin. P. M.: "Contribution de Denys d'Halicarnasse à la connaissance du 'ver sacrum' ", *Latomus* 32/1, 23-38.

Mawet, F.: "*Algea didomi,* formule de la langue des dieux chez Homère", *RBPhH* 51, no. 1, 5-12.

Maxwell-Stuart, P. G.: "Myrtle and the Eleusinian Mysteries", *Wiener Studien* 6 (1972), 145-161.

Montanari, F.: "Eros venerato ed Eros non venerato (Eur., *Hipp.* 525-544)", *ASNSP* 3, no. 1, 43-47.

Morgan, G.: "Villa Publica and Magna Mater. Two Notes on Manubial Building at the Close of the Second Century B.C.", *Klio* 55, 215-245.

Morocho Gayo, G.: "El mito de la edad de oro en Hesiodo", *Perficit* 4, no. 64-65, 65-100.

Moskovszky, E.: "Larentia and the God. Archaeological Aspects of an Ancient Roman Legend", *AcAr* 25, 241-264, bibliography (3 p.)

Musgrave Calder III, William und Jacob Stern: *Pindaros und Bakchylides.* (Darmstadt, 1970). – R: *BiOr* 30, 279-280 (E. J. Jonkers).

Noyes, R., Jr.: "Seneca on Death", *JRH* 12, No. 3, 223-240, with bibliography.

Oksala, T.: *Religion und Mythologie bei Horaz. Eine literarhistorische Untersu-*

chung. (Helsinki, Dissertation). 233 p., Bibliographie (4 p.) = Commentationes Humanarum Literarum, 51.

Orban, M.: " 'Dieu a besoin des hommes' ou la leçon du *Dyscolos*", *Les Etudes Classiques* 41/2, 145-162.

Oroz, J.: "En torno al estoicismo", *Augustinus* 18 (no. 70), 171-180.

Orr, D. G.: "Roman Domestic Religion: A Study of the Roman Household Deities and their Shrines at Pompeii and Herculaneum", *DisAbIn, A* 33/11, 6260. (The author's summary of his diss., University of Maryland, 1972).

Panyagua, E. R.: "Catálogo de representaciones de Orfeo en el arte antiguo" (3), *Helmántica* 24 (75), 87-152, fig. 17-44.

Peschlow-Bindokat, A.: "Demeter und Persephone in der attischen Kunst des 6. bis 4. Jahrhunderts v. Chr.", *JDAI* 87, 60-157.

Petersmann, H.: "Zu einem altrömischen Opferritual (Cato, *De agricultura* c. 141)", *RMPh* 116, 238-255.

Petzold, Karl-Ernst: *Studien zur Methode des Polybios und ihrer historischen Auswertung*. (München, 1969). – R: *BiOr* 30, 280-282 (W. den Boer).

Pigeaud, J.: "Quel Dieu est Epicure? Quelques remarques sur Lucrèce, V, 1 à 54", *REL* 50, 139-162.

Pighi, G. B.: "Ennio e Tutilina", *Atti della Academia delle Scienze di Torino* 107/1, 277-280.

Pöschl, V.: "Die Dionysosode des Horaz (c. 2, 19)", *Hermes* 101, Heft 2, 208-230.

Pötscher, Walter: " 'Schicksalswägungen' ", *Kairos* 15, Heft 1-2, 60-68.

Rawson, E.: "Scipio, Laelius, Furius and the Ancestral Religion", *JRS* 63, 161-174.

Robert, L.: "De Cilicie à Messine et à Plymouth, avec deux inscriptions grecques errantes", *Journal des Savants* no. 3, 161-211.

Rougemont, G.: "La hiéroménie des Pythia et les 'trèves sacrées' d'Eleusis, de Delphes et d'Olympie", *BCH* 97/1, 75-106.

Roulleau, D.: "Autour de *Tempus* et de *Fortuna*", *Latomus* 32, No. 4, 720-736.

Sanquer, R.: "Une nouvelle lecture de l'inscription à Neptune trouvée à Douarnenez (Finistère) et l'industrie du garum armoricain", *Annales de Bretagne* 80/1, 215-236.

Santini, C.: "Toni e strutture nella rappresentazione delle divinità nei *Fasti*", *GIF* 4/1, 41-62.

Saunders, T. J.: "Penology and Eschatology in Plato's Timaeus and Laws",

Saunders, T. J.: "Penology and Eschatology in Plato's Timaeus and Laws", *ClQuart* 23, No. 2, 232-244.

Savino, E.: "I concetti di colpa e di cosmo nel teatro di Sofocle", *Acme* 26, no. 3, 359-383.

Schefold, K.: "Das Diesseitige des griechischen Jenseitsglaubens", *ZÄSA* 100, Heft 1, 43-49.

Schiff, F.: "Athena Parthenos, die vision des Phidias", *Antike Kunst* XVI, Heft 1, 57-59, 2 Taf.

Schilling, R.: "Georges Dumézil et la religion romaine", *Nouvelle Ecole*, No. 21-22, 91-96.

Schmidt, V.: "Dans la chambre d'or de Vulcain (à propos de Virg. *En.* 8, 370sqq)", *Mnemosyne* 26, 350-375.

Simon, S. J.: "The Greater Official Priests of Rome under the Flavian-Antonine Emperors", *DisAbIn A* 34/4, 1800. (The author's summary of his diss., Loyola University of Chicago, 1973).

Simpson, W. K.: "The Terrace of the Great God at Abydos: the Offering Chapels of Dynasties 12 and 13", in: *XXIXe Congrès International des Orientalistes. Résumés des Communications*, Section 1-5. (Paris, Y. Hervouet), pp. 22-23.

Sinnige, T. G.: "Cosmic Religion in Aristotle", *GRBS* 14, No. 1, 15-34.

Smith, David R.: "The Hieropoioi on Kos", *Numen* 20/1, 38-47.

Sokolowski, F.: "On the New Pergamene *Lex Sacra*", *GRBS* 14, No. 4, 407-413. (Based on the text published by Chr. Habicht: *Die Inschriften des Asklepeions*, 1969).

Sokol'skij, N. I.: "Le culte d'Aphrodite à Cepi de la fin du VIe au Ve s. av. n. E.", *VDI* no. 4, 88-92 (with and English summary).

Speyer, Wolfgang: "Religionen des griechisch-römischen Bereiches", in: U. Mann (Hrsg.): *Theologie und Religionswissenschaft* (Darmstadt, Wissenschaftliche Buchgesellschaft) 124-143.

Stepniowski, W.: "La conception de l'immortalité dans les écrits de M.T. Cicéron", *Euhemer* 17/4 (90), 103-110. (En polon.)

Thaniel, G.: "Le scepticisme et le refus de croyance touchant l'au-delà dans la Rome du Ier siècle avant J.-C.", *AnCl* 42, no. 1, 155-166.

Thompson, G. R.: "Elagabalus: Priest-Emperor of Rome", *DisAbIn, A* 33/11, 6260-6261. (The author's summary of his diss., University of Kansas, 1972).

Tóth, I.: "Ornamenta Iovis Dolicheni", *ACUSD* 9, 105-109.

Valgiglio, E.: "Tra scetticismo filosofico e tradizionalismo religioso (C. Aurelio Cotta in Cicerone e Cecilio Natale in Minucio Felice)", *RSC* 21/2, 234-255.

Vernant, J.-P. – P. Vidal-Naquet: *Mythe et tragédie en Grèce ancienne*. (Paris,

François Maspero, 1972). 354 p. – R: *Voprosy Filosofii* 10, 167-169 (I. D. Rožanskij).

Vidal-Naquet, P.: "Valeurs religieuses et mythiques de la terre et du sacrifice dans l'Odyssée", in: M. I. Finley, ed.: *Problèmes de la terre en Grèce ancienne*, (Paris – La Haye, Mouton), pp. 269-292.

de Vries, G. J.: "Mystery Terminology in Aristophanes and Plato", *Mnemosyne* 26, No. 1, 1-8.

Walla, M.: *Der Vogel Phoenix in der antiken Literatur und der Dichtung des Laktanz.* (Wien, 1969). – R: *Gnomon* 45/2, 208-210 (J. Fontaine).

Waters, Kenneth H.: *Herodotus on Tyrants and Despots. A Study in Objectivity.* (Wiesbaden, 1971). – R: *BiOr* 30, 97-98 (A. B. Breebaart).

Woodard, W. S.: "Prolegomena to the Religion of Knossos", *DisAbIn A* 34/4, 1802. (The author's summary of his diss., University of Pennsylvania, 1973).

Young, D. C.: *Pindar Isthmian 7, Myth and Exempla.* (Leiden, E. J. Brill, 1971). 51 p. – R: *Gnomon* 45/2, 197-199 (W. J. Slater).

Zellweger, S.: "Ein frühes Palladion", *Antike Kunst* 16/2, 139-142, 1 Tafel.

Ziegler, J.: *Zur religiösen Haltung der Gegenkaiser im 4. Jh. n. Chr.* (Kallmünz, 1970). – R: *Gnomon* 45/4, 389-393 (P. Petit).

7. HELLENISTIC RELIGIONS

Aland, B.: "Die Apophasis Megale und die simonianische Gnosis. Bemerkungen zu J. Frickel, die Apophasis Megale in Hippolyts Refutatio (VI 9-18). Eine Paraphrase zur Apophasis Simons", *ThPh* 48/3, 410-418.

Alexandre, Egly: "Une Ecole d'Art Bactrienne: Khalchayan", *BiOr* 30, 186-192.

Aubet, M. E.: "Dos marfiles con representación de esfinge de la necrópolis púnica de Ibiza", *RSF* I, 59-68.

Balil, A.: "Algunos trofeos alusivos a Hispania en el mundo romanao", *Conimbriga* 12, 219-222.

Balil, A.: "Sobre las relaciones entre los pueblos orientales y el mundo griego", *ReGui* 83, 77-104.

Balil, A. y R. Martín Valls: "Una representación dionisíaca de Becilla de Valderaduey", *BSEAA* 39, 426-431.

Bethge, H. G.: "*Nebront.* Die zweite Schrift aus Nag-Hammadi-Codex VI", *ThLZ* 98/2, 98-105.

Bisi, A. M.: "Le terrecotte figurate di tipo grecopunico di Ibiza. I. Museo del Cau Ferrat a Sitges", *RSF* 1, 69-89.

Blázquez, J. M.: "Terracotas púnicas de Ibiza", *RSF* 1, 207-214.

van den Braden, A.: "Il sacrificio umano presso i Punici", *Bibbia e Oriente* 15/4-5, 197-208.

Brestou, P.: "The Monosexuality: The Gnostic Ideal", *Kleronomia* 5, No. 1, 1-27 (in Greek, with English summary).

Breton, S.: "Actualité du néoplatonisme", *Revue de Théologie et de Philosophie* 23/2, 184-200.

van den Broek, R.: "The Shape of Edem According to Justin the Gnostic", *Vigiliae Christianae* 27/1, 35-45.

Browne, Gerlad M.: *Documentary Papyri from the Michigan Collection.* (Toronto, 1970). – R: *BiOr* 30, 419-424 (Fritz Uebel).

Brunner, F.: "Le premier traité de la cinquième 'Ennéade': 'Des trois hypostases principielles", *RThPh* 23, No. 2, 135-172.

Burton, A.: *Diodorus Siculus.* Book I. *A Commentary.* (Leiden, E. J. Brill, 1972). xxvi, 301 p., front. = Etudes Préliminaires aux Religions Orientales dans l'Empire Romain, 29. – R: *BiOr* 30, 481-484(Michel Malaise).

de Capitani, F.: "Studi recenti sul manicheismo", *Rivista di Filosofia Neo-scolastica* 65/1, 97-118.

Castiglione, L.: "Footprints of the Gods in India and in the Hellenistic World: Influence or Parallelism?", *AAAS* 21, no. 1-2, 25-37, 2 pl., bibliographie.

Colpe, C.: "Heidnische, jüdische, und christliche Überlieferung in den Schriften aus Nag Hammadi" (I), *JACh* 15, 5-18.

Deckers, J. G.: "Die Wandmalerei des tetrarchischen Lagerheiligtums im Ammon-Tempel von Luxor", *RQChAK* 68, 1-34, Taf. 1-12.

Dörrie, H.: "La doctrine de l'âme dans le néoplatonisme de Plotin a Proclus", *RThPh* 23/2, 116-134, bibliographie.

Dragojlović, D.: "Les sources des Slaves du Sud pour l'histoire du mouvement paulicien en Asie Mineure et dans les Balkans", in: *XXIXe Congrès Intern. des Orientalistes, Résumés des Communications*, Sections 1-5, (Paris, Y. Hervouet), p. 41.

Dunand, F.: *Le culte d'Isis dans le bassin oriental de la Méditerranée.* 3 vol. I. *Le culte d'Isis et les Ptolémées.* II. *Le culte d'Isis en Grèce.* III. *Le culte d'Isis en Asie mineure. Le clergé et rituel des sanctuaires isiaques. Prosopographie du clergé isiaque.* (Leiden, E. J. Brill). Vol. 1: xxxii, 249 p., front., 10 fig., 45 pl., 2 cartes. Vol. 2: xii, 223 p., 7 fig., 45 pl., 3 cartes. Vol. 3: xii, 400 p., 3 fig., 23 pl., 2 cartes. = Etudes Préliminaires aux Religions Orientales dans l'Empire Romain, 26.

Dunand, M.: "La piscine du trône d'Astarté dans le temple d'Echmoun à Sidon", *BMBey* 24, 19-25, 3 pl.

Dunant, Christiane: *Le sanctuaire de Baalshamin à Palmyre*, vol. III, *Les inscriptions. Mission archéologique suisse en Syrie, 1954-1966.* (Institut suisse de Rome, 1971). – R: *BiOr* 30, 260-262 (Comte du Mesnil du Buisson).

Fauth, W.: "Seth-Typhon, Onoel und der eselköpfige Sabaoth. Zur Theriomorphie der ophitisch-barbelognostischen Archonten", *Oriens Christianus* 57, 79-120.

Fischer, K. M.: "Der Gedanke unserer grossen Kraft (noēma). Die vierte Schrift aus Nag-Hammadi Codex VI. Eingeleitet und uübersetzt vom Berliner Arbeitskreis für Koptisch-gnostische Schriften", *ThLZ* 98/3, 169-175.

Fleischer, R.: *Artemis von Ephesos und verwandte Kultstatuen aus Anatolien und Syrien.* (Leiden, E. J. Brill). xviii, 450 S., Frontispiz, 2 Abb., 171 Taf. = Etudes Préliminaires aux Religions Orientales dans l'Empire Romain, 35.

Foerster, Werner: *Gnosis. A Selection of Gnostic Texts.* English Translation edited by R. Mcl. Wilson, I. Patristic evidence. (Oxford, 1972). – R: *BiOr* 30, 307 (G. Quispel).

Forni, G.: "El culto de Augusto en el compromiso oficial y en el sentimiento oriental", *BSEAA* 39, 105-113.

Forte, Antonio: "Deuz études sur le manichéisme chinois", *T'oung Pao* 59, 220-253.

Fouquet, A.: "Quelques représentations d'Osiris-Canope au musée du Louvre", *BIFAO* 73, 61-69, 7 pl.

Frickel, J.: "Eine neue kritische Textausgabe der *Apophasis Megale* (Hippolyt, Ref. 6, 9-18)?", *Wiener Studien* 6 (1972), 162-184.

von Funk, W. P.: " 'Authentikos Logos'. Die dritte Schrift aus Nag-Hammadi-Codex VI", *ThLZ* 98/4, 251-259.

Gager, J. G.: *Moses in Greco-Roman Paganism*, 1972. – R: *Biblica* 54, No. 2, 281-283 (E. Des Places).

Gawlikowski, Michal: *Le Temple Palmyrénien. Etude d'épigraphie et de topographie historique.* (Warszawa, Editions Scientifiques de Pologne). 4to. 125 p., 12 fig., 5 plans. = Palmyre, VI.

Gawlikowski, M.: "Liturges et custodes sur quelques inscriptions palmyréniennes", *Semitica* 23, 113-124.

Gersch, S. E.: *Kinèsis akinètos. A Study of Spiritual Motion in the Philosophy of Proclus.* (Leiden, E. J. Brill). viii, 143 p. = Philosophia Antiqua, 26.

Gibbons, J. A.: "A Commentary on The Second Logos of the Great Seth", *DisAbIn A* 33/12, 7013. (The author's summary of his diss., Yale University, 1972).

Haardt, Robert: *Die Gnosis.* Wesen und Zeugnisse. (Salzburg, 1967). – R: *OLZ* 68, 22-25 (M. Krause).

Hadot, P.: "L'être et l'étant dans le néoplatonisme", *Revue de Théologie et de Philosophie* 23/2, 101-115, bibliographie.

Hajdenova, V.: "Un nouveau monument dédié à Mithra de Novae", *Archeologija* 15/4, 45-50 (en bulgare, rés. en français).

Heidenreich, R.: "Der Tempel bei Garni in Armenien", *Antike Welt* 4, Heft 3, 2-9.

Henrichs, A.: "Mani and the Babylonian Baptists: A Historical Confrontation", *HSCPh* 77, 23-59.

Henry, P. et H.-R. Schwyzer (Ed.): *Plotini Opera*, t. III: *Enneas VI.* (Paris, Desclée de Brouwer; Leiden, E. J. Brill). xlviii, 464 p. = Museum Lessianum, Series Philosophica, 35.

Herbert, Kevin: *Greek and Latin Inscriptions in the Brooklyn Museum.* (Brooklyn, N. Y., 1972). – R: *BiOr* 30, 275 (E. J. Jonkers).

Himmelmann, N.: *Typologische Untersuchungen an römischen Sarkophagreliefs des 3. und 4. Jahrhunderts n. Chr.* (Mainz, Verlag Philipp von Zabern). xi, 66 p., 60 Taf.

Holleman, A. W. J.: "An Enigmatic Function of the *flamen dialis* (Ovid, *Fast.*, 2.282) and the Augustan Reform", *Numen* 20, 222-228.

Hornbostel, W.: *Sarapis. Studien zur Überlieferungsgeschichte, den Erscheinungsformen und wandlungen der Gestalt eines Gottes.* (Leiden, E. J. Brill). xix, 482 S., Frontis., 3 fig., 220 Taf., 2 Karten. = Etudes Préliminaires aux Religions Orientales dans l'Empire Romain, 32.

Iversen, E.: "The Inscriptions from the Obelisks of Benevento", *AOD* 35, 15-28 (translation and commentary).

Kaoukabani, B.: "Les monuments de Wadi Cana", *BMBey* 24, 27-37, 13 pl.

Kaoukabani, B.: "Rapport préliminaire sur les fouilles de Kharayeb 1969-1970", *BMBey* 26, 41-59, 19 pl.

Kater-Sibbes, G. J. F.: *A preliminary catalogue of Sarapis monuments.* (Leiden, E. J. Brill). xl, 230 p., frontis., 33 pl., 12 maps. = Etudes Préliminaires aux Religions Orientales dans l'Empire Romain, 36.

Keizer, L. S.: "The Eighth Reveals the Ninth: Tractate 6 of Nag Hammadi Codex VI", *DisAbIn A* 34/4, 2016. (The author's summary of his diss., Graduate Theological Union, 1973).

Krause, Martin – Pahor Labib: *Gnostische und hermetische Schriften aus Codex II und Codex VI.* (IBHR, 1971, S. 75). – R: *Orientalia* 42, 530-534 (H. Quecke).

Kübel, Paul: *Schuld und Schicksal bei Origenes, Gnostikern und Platonikern.* (Stuttgart, Calwer Verlag). 128 p. = Calwer Theologische Monographien, 1.

Lapidge, M.: "ἀρχαί and στοιχεῖα: A Problem in Stoic Cosmology", *Phronesis* 18, 240-278.

Lecerf, J.: "Au sujet des Frères de la Pureté (Lettre) à Déodat Roché", *CEC* 24 (no. 59), 32-33.

Leclant, J. – G. Clerc: *Inventaire bibliographique des Isiaca* (Ibis). (Répertoire analytique des travaux relatifs à la diffusion des cultes isiaque 1940-1969) A – D. (Leiden, 1972). – R: *Listy Filologické* 96/3, 179-180 (L. Vidman).

Lemerle, P.: "L'histoire des Pauliciens d'Asie Mineure d'après les sources grecques", *Travaux et Mémoires* 5, 1-144, 2 pl., 1 carte.

Luck, G.: "Virgil and the Mystery Religions", *AJPh* 94/2, 147-166.

Maehler, Herwig: *Urkunden römischer Zeit*, (Berlin, 1968). – R: *BiOr* 30, 243-244 (E. Boswinkel).

Mantero, T.: "I rapporti tra il de mysteriis di Giamblico e gli Oracoli Caldei", *Maia* 25/2, 156-160.

Mariner, S.: "Pax Augusta: historia de una leyenda", *Hispania Antiqua* 3, 319-329.

Matthews, J. F.: "Symmachus and the Oriental Cults", *The Journal of Roman Studies* 63, 175-195.

Merkelbach, R.: "Die Tazza Farnese, die Gestirne der Nilflut und Erastosthenes", *ZÄSA* 99/2, 116-127, Taf. V.

du Mesnil du Buisson, R.: *Etudes sur les dieux phéniciens hérités par l'Empire romain*. (Leiden, E. J. Brill, 1970). – R: *OLZ* 68, 474-475 (O. Eissfeldt). *JNES* 32, 265-266 (M. Astour).

du Mesnil du Buisson, Cte R.: *Nouvelles études sur les dieux et les mythes de Canaan*. (Leiden, E. J. Brill). xxiv, 274 p., 133 fig., 19 pl. = Etudes Préliminaires aux Religions Orientales dans l'Empire Romain, 33.

Moeller, W. O.: *The Mithraic Origin of the Rotas-Sator square*. (Leiden, E. J. Brill). ix, 53 p., frontis., 6 pl. = Etudes Préliminaires aux Religions Orientales dans l'Empire Romain, 38.

Monnot, G.: "Quelques textes de 'Abd al-Jabbâr sur le manichéisme", *RHR* 183, No. 1, 3-9 (with bibliographic references).

Muhitdinov, H. Ju.: "Les statuettes d'une divinité féminine au miroir provenant de Saksonokhout", *SovEtn* 5, 99-107.

Nag Hammadi Codices. The Facsimile Edition. Published under the Auspices of the Department of Antiquities of the Arab Republic of Egypt in Conjunction with the United Nations Educational, Scientific and Cultural Organization. Codices 11, 12 and 13. Editorial board: James M. Robinson (Secretary), Shafik Farid, Gérard Garitte, and others. (Leiden, E. J. Brill). xviii, 120 p.

Nagel, Peter: *Das Wesen der Archonten aus Codex II der gnostischen Bibliothek von Nag Hammadi*, (Halle, 1970). – Nota bibliographica: *Orientalia* 42, 472-473 (H. Quecke).

Nag Hammadi Codices. Facsimile Edition. Published under the Auspices of the Department of Antiquities of the Arab Republic of Egypt in Conjunction with the UNESCO. Codex VI. (Leiden, 1972). – R: *BiOr* 30, 428-430 (R. Haardt).

Naudon, P.: *La tradition et la connaissance primordiale dans la spiritualité de l'Occident. Les silènes de Rabelais*. (Paris, Devy-Livres). 279 p., bibliographie (9 p.) = Coll. Histoire et Tradition.

Orlandi, T.: "Due nuove collane dedicate ai testi gnostici copti di Nag Hammadi", *RSO* 47, 47-53.

Padró, J.: "Un escarabeo de ámbar procedente de las excavaciones de Rhode (Roses)", *Ampurias* 33-34, 293-296.

Parássoglou, G. M.: "On Priests and Their Affairs in Roman Egypt", *Studia Papyrologica* 12/1, 7-21.

Perkins, A.: *The Art of Dura-Europos.* (Oxford, Clarendon Press; London, Oxford University Press). xiii, 130 p., 7 fig., 52 fig. on 32 pl.

Petolescu, C.: "Les cultes orientaux dans la Dacie Inférieure", *Apulum* no. 9, 643-658, 1 carte.

Petolescu, C. C.: "Un relief votif dédié à la triade égyptienne", *Studii Clasice* 15, 159-161, 1 pl.

Pritchard, J. B.: "Les fouilles de Sarepta font revivre l'antique ville phénicienne", *BTS* no. 157, 4-14, illus.

Quispel, G.: "From Mythos to Logos", *Eranos-Jahrbuch* 39, 323-340.

Quispel, Gilles: "Gnosis und hellenistische Mysterienreligionen", in: U. Mann (Hrsg.): *Theologie und Religionswissenschaft* (Darmstadt, Wissenschaftliche Buchgesellschaft) 318-331.

Quispel, G.: "The Birth of the Child. Some Gnostic and Jewish Aspects", *Eranos-Jahrbuch* 40, 285-309.

Quispel, Gilles: *Gnostic Studies.* (Leiden, Nederlands Instituut voor het Nabije Oosten). 2 pts. (= xii, 600 p.) = Publications de l'Institut Historique et Archéologique Néerlandais de Stamboul, vol. XXXIV.

Renard, M.: "Recherches récentes sur la pénétration et la diffusion des cultes égyptiens en Italie", *BLSMP* 59/1, 16-18.

Riaz, Muhammad, "Studies in the History of the Sabeans", *JPHS* 21, 233-240.

Ries, J.: "Tôchme-Sôtme, le dialogue gnostique du salut dans les textes manichéens coptes de Médînet Mâdi", in: *XXIXe Congrès International des Orientalistes. Résumés des Communications,* Sections 1-5. (Paris, Y. Hervouet), p. 47.

Rinaldi, G.: "Il 'pianoro da Madaba a Dibon' ", *Bibbia e Oriente* 15, no. 4-5, 215-220, 2 tav.

Rist, J. M.: "The One of Plotinus and the God of Aristotle", *The Review of Metaphysics* 27/1, 75-87.

Rondeau, M.-J.: "Transcendance 'grecque' et transcendance chrétienne", *Les quatre fleuves*, no. 1, 41-56.

Rudolph, K.: "Gnosis und Gnostizismus. Ein Forschungsbericht", *Theologische Rundschau* 38, 1-25 (Schluss).

San Nicolo, Mariano: *Ägyptisches Vereinswesen zur Zeit der Ptolemäer und Rö-*

mer. Erster Teil: *Die Vereinsarten*. Zweiter Teil: *Vereinswesen und Vereinsrecht*. (München, C. H. Beck'sche Verlagsbuchhandlung, 1972). 256 und 231 S. (Second edition revised by J. Herrmann). R: *BiOr* 30, 418-419 (Alan K. Bowman).

Schachermeyr, Fritz: *Alexander der Grosse. Das Problem seiner Persönlichkeit und seines Wirkens*. (Wien, Österreichische Akademie der Wissenschaften). 724 S., 24 Taf., 12 Karten. = ÖAW, Philosophisch-historische Klasse, Sitzungsberichte, 285.

Schlumberger, D.: "La cour hexagonale du sanctuaire de Jupiter à Baalbek", *BMBey* 24, 3-9.

Schuhl, P. M.: "Descente métaphysique et ascension de l'âme dans la philosphie de Plotin", *SIF* 5, 71-84.

Schwarz, W.: "A Study in Pre-Christian Symbolism: Philo, *De somniis* I. 216-218, and Plutarch *De Iside et Osiride* 4 and 77", *ICSB* No. 20, 104-117.

Sed, N.: "Le livre Bahir et les sources gnostiques (le problème des 72 langues)", in: *XXIXe Congrès International des Orientalistes. Résumés des Communications*, Section 1-5. (Paris, Y. Hervouet), pp. 53-54.

Seibert, Jakob: *Untersuchungen zur Geschichte Ptolemaios' I*. (München, 1969). – R: *BiOr* 30, 407-418 (G. Wirth).

Sfameni Gasparro, Giulia: *I culti orientali in Sicilia*. (Leiden, E. J. Brill). xv, 338 p., front., 122 tav., 2 carte. = Etudes Préliminaires aux Religions Orientales dans l'Empire Romain, 31.

Sieber, J. H.: "An Introduction to the Tractate Zostrianos from Nag Hammadi", *NoTes* 15, 233-240.

Simonetti, M.: "Note sull'interpretazione gnostica dell'Antico Testamento", *Vetera Christianorum* 10/1, 103-126.

von Soden, Heiko: *Untersuchungen zur Homologie in den griechischen Papyri Ägyptens bis Diokletian*. (Köln-Wien, Böhlau Verlag). x, 150 S. = Graezistische Abhandlungen, 5.

Solomonik, E. I.: "La vie religieuse dans les villes nordiques du Pont dans l'antiquité tardive. (D'après des documents épigraphiques", *VDI* No. 1, 55-77 (with a summary in English).

Springer, J. L.: "Plotinus: filosoof en mysticus", *Nederlands Theologisch Tijdschrift* 27/3, 210-223.

Stucky, R. A.: "Prêtres syriens. I. Palmyre", *Syria* 50/1-2, 163-180.

Swarney, Paul R.: *The Ptolemaic and Roman Idios Logos*, (Toronto, 1970). – R: *BiOr* 30, 55-56 (G. Poethke).

Szirmai, K.: "Die Bildtypen auf den Denkmälern des Kaiserkults in Aquincum und ihr Ursprung", *ACUSD* 9, 83-89.

Tardieu, Michel: "Les Trois Stèles de Seth. Un écrit gnostique retrouvé à Nag Hammadi. Introduction et traduction", *RSPhTh* 57, 545-575.

Tardieu, M.: "Pour un phénix gnostique", *Revue de l'Histoire des Religions* 183, no. 2, 117-142.

Thausing, Gertrud: "Altägyptische Gedanken in der Gnosis", *Kairos* 15, Heft 1-2, 116-122.

Thomov, T.: "Les appellations de 'Bogomiles' et 'Bulgares' et leurs variantes et équivalents en Orient et en Occident", *EtBalk* 9/1, 77-99.

Tran Tam Tinh, V. et Y. Labreque: *Isis lactans. Corpus des monuments greco-romains d'Isis allaitant Harpocrate.* (Leiden, E. J. Brill). 225 p., 78 pl., carte. = Etudes Préliminaires aux Religion Orientales dans l'Empire Romain, 37.

Tröger, K.-W.: "Die sechste und siebte Schrift and Nag-Hammadi-Codex VI", *ThLZ* 93, Heft 7, 495-503.

Trouillard, J.: "Le merveilleux dans la vie et la pensée de Proclos, RPhFE. 98, no. 4, 439-452.

Trouillard, J: 'Le Parménide de Platon et son interprétation néoplatonicienne", *RThPh* 23/2, 83-100, bibliographie.

Wagner, G. et J. Quaegebeur: "Une dédicace grecque au dieu egyptien Mestasytmis de la part de son synode (Fayoum-époque romaine)", *BIFAO* 73, 41-60, 1 pl.

Waldmann, H.: *Die kommagenischen Kultregformen unter König Mithridates I. Kallinikos und seinem Sohne Antiochos I.* (Leiden, E. J. Brill). xxii, 257 p., 2 fold. tab., 40 pl., appendix. = Etudes Préliminaires aux Religions Orientales dans l'Empire Romain, 34.

Wolski, W. et I. Berciu: "Contribution au problème des tombes romaines à dispositif pour les libations funéraires", *Latomus* 32/2, 370-379, 5 pl.

Wright, G. R. H.: "An Early Ptolemaic Temple in the Cyrenaica. (Some Literary and Religious Evidence)", *MDAIK* 29/1, 87-96, 1 pl.

Yamauchi, E. M.: *Pre-Christian Gnosticism: A Survey of the Proposed Evidences.* (Grand Rapids, Mich., W. B. Eerdmans). xi, 208 p.

IV. JUDAISM

1. SCRIPTURES

Airoldi, N.: "La funzione giuridica dei cosidetti 'racconti storici' del II° discorso di Mosè al popolo (Dt 5, 9s)", *Augustinianum* 13/1, 75-92.

Ambanelli, I.: "Il significato dell'espressione *da'at' ĕlōhim* nel profeta Osea", *Rivista Biblica* 21/2, 119-145.

Amsler, S.: "Les prophètes et la politique", *Revue de Théologie et de Philosophie*, No. 1, 14-31.

Auvray, P.: *Isaïe 1-39*. (Paris, Librairie Lecoffre, 1972). 338 p. = Sources Bibliques. – R: *BiOr* 30, 462-463 (Hubertus Vogt).

Baars, W. (ed.): *New Syro-Hexaplaric Texts*. Edited, commented upon and compared with the Septuagint. (Leiden, 1968). – R: *BiOr* 30, 467-468 (R. Degen).

Bader, G.: "Das Gebet Jonas. Eine Meditation", *ZThK* 70/2, 162-205.

Baltzer, Dieter: *Ezechiel und Deuterojesaja. Berührungen in der Heilserwartung der beiden grossen Exilspropheten*. (Berlin, 1971). – R: *BiOr* 30, 87-88 (Herbert Haag).

Bardtke, Hans: "Erwägungen zu Psalm 1 und Psalm 2", *Festschrift de Liagre Böhl* (q. v. sub I-7), 1-18.

Baruch, J. Z.: "Le rapport entre le péché et la maladie dans l'Ancien Testament", *RHMH*, no. 101, 5-9.

Beauchamp, P.: "Quelques faits d'écriture dans la poésie biblique", *RchSR* 61, No. 1, 127-138.

Becker, J.: "Einige Hyperbata im Alten Testament", *Biblische Zeitschrift* 17, Heft 2, 257-263.

Bee, R. E.: "The Use of Statistical Methods in Old Testament Studies", *Vetus Testamentum* 23/3, 257-272.

Beek, M. A.: "Das Mit-Leiden Gottes", *Festschrift de Liagre Böhl* (q. v. sub I-7), 23-30.

Bernhardt, K. H.: "Problematik und Probleme der alttestamentlichen Einleitungswissenschaft", *ThLZ* 98/7, 481-496.

Bernini, G.: "I profeti neel'Antico Testamento", *Studia Missionalia* 22, 279-308.

Beuken, W. A. M.: "Jes 50, 10-11: Eine kultische Paränese zur dritten Ebedprophetie", *ZATW* 85/2, 168-182.

Black, M.: *Apocalypsis Henochi Graece*. A. M. Denis: *Fragmenta Pseudepigraphorum quae supersunt Graeca una cum Historicorum et Auctorum Iudaeorum Hellenistarum fragmentis*. (Leiden 1970). – R: *BiOr* 30, 471-472 (E. J. Jonkers).

Blau, J.: "Sind uns Reste arabischer Bibelübersetzungen aus vorislamischer Zeit erhalten geblieben?", *Le Muséon* 86, 67-72.

de Boer, P. A. H.: "Jeremias 45, verse 5", *Festschrift de Liagre Böhl* (q. v. sub I-7), 31-37

de Boer, P. A. H.: "The Son of God in the Old Testament", in: *Syntax and Meaning. Studies in Hebrew Syntax and Biblical Exegesis* (Leiden, E. J. Brill) 188-207.

Bonnard, P.-E. -C. Kannengiesser: "Jérémie (prophète)", *Dictionnaire de Spritualité Ascétique et Mystique*, t. 8, fasc. 54-55, col. 877-901.

Breech, E.: "These Fragments 1 Have Shored against My Ruins: The Form and Function of 4 Ezra", *JBL* 92, 267-274.

Bright, J.: "The Apodictic Prohibition: Some Observations", *Journal of Biblical Literature* 92, 185-204.

Brock, S. P.: "An Unrecognised Occurrence of the Month Name Ziw (2 Sam. XXI 6)", *VeTes* 23/1, 100-103. (The Hebrew original to read *bymy zw* instead of *ḥymy qṣyr!*).

Brockington, L. H.: *The Hebrew Text of the Old Testament. The Readings Adopted by the Translators of the New English Bible*. (London, The Delegates of the Oxford University Press and the Syndics of the Cambridge University Press). 269 p.

Bulman, J. M.: "The Identification of Darius the Mede", *The Westminster Theological Journal* 35/3, 247-267.

Bunge, J. G.: "Der 'Gott der Festungen' und der 'Liebling der Frauen'. Zur Identifizierung der Götter in Dan. 11, 36-39", *JSJ* 4, 169-182.

Cassuto, U.: *Biblical and Oriental Studies*. Volume 1: *Bible*. Translated from the Hebrew and Italian by I. Abrahams. (Jerusalem, The Magnes Press/Hebrew University). 309 p. = Publications of the Perry Foundation for biblical Research.

Cathcart, K. J.: *Nahum in the Light of Nortwest Semitic*. (Rom, Biblical Institute Press). 171 p. = Biblica et Orientalia, 26.

Cathcart, Kevin J.: "Treaty Curses and the Book of Nahum", *CBQ* 35, 179-187.

Cazelles, H.: "Langages bibliques et Parole de Dieu dans l'Ancien Testament", *Les Quatre Fleuves* no. 1, 21-30.

Chambers, W. V.: "The Confessions of Jeremiah: A Study in Prophetic Ambivalence", *DisAbIn A* 34/4, 2013. (The author's summary of his diss., Vanderbilt University, 1972).

Charlesworth, J. H.: *The Odes of Solomon.* Edited with Translation and Notes. (Oxford, Clarendon Press). xv, 167 p., bibliography (20 p.)

Claburn, W. E.: "The Fiscal Basis of Josiah's Reforms", *JBL* 92/1, 11-22.

Clifford, Richard J.: *The Cosmic Mountain in Canaan and the Old Testament.* (Cambridge, Mass., Harvard University Press). 221 p. = Harvard Semitic Monographs, 4. – R: *ZATW* 85, 386-387 (Anon.) *CBQ* 35, 369-370 (K. J. Cathcart). *JBL* 92, 443-444 (D. L. Petersen).

Coats, G. W.: "Moses in Midian", *JBL* 92/1, 3-10.

Craigie, P. G.: "Helel, Athtar and Phaethon (Jes 14, 12-15)", *ZATW* 85, 223-225.

Delcor, M.: "Homonymie et interprétation de l'Ancien Testament", *Journal of Semitic Studies* 18/1, 40-54.

Delcor, M.: *Le Livre de Daniel.* (Paris, Gabalda, 1971). 296 p. = Sources Bibliques. – R: *VeTes* 23/1, 113-117 (A. Caquot). *BiOr* 30, 263-266 (Hans Bardtke).

Delcor, M.: *Le Testament d'Abraham.* Introduction, traduction du texte grec et commentaire de la recension grecque longue. Suivi de la traduction des Testaments d'Abraham, d'Isaac et de Jacob d'après les versions orientales. (Leiden, E. J. Brill). x, 282 p. = St. in Vet. Test. Pseudep., II.

Despina, M.: "La Haggadah de Pesah de la gueniza du Caire", *SIDJC* VI/1, 47-52.

Dirksen, P. B.: *The Transmission of the Text in the Peshitta Manuscripts of the Book of Judges.* (Leiden, 1972). – R: *BiOr* 30, 469-470 (R. Degen).

Ehrman, A.: "A Note on Micah VI 14", *Vetus Testamentum* 23/1, 103-105.

Eissfeldt, Otto: *Kleine Schriften.* IV. Band. Hrsg. von R. Sellheim und F. Maas. (Tübingen, 1968). – R: *OLZ* 68, 40-42 (G. Wallis).

Emerton, J. A.: "Notes on Two Proposed Emendations in the Book of Judges (11, 24 and 16, 28)", *ZATW* 85/2, 220-223.

Fannon, P.: "Emerging Secularity in the Old Testament", *Irish Theological Quarterly* 40/1, 20-37.

Fendler, M.: "Zur Sozialkritik des Amos. Versuch einer wirtschafts- und sozialgeschichtlichen Interpretation alttestamentlicher Texte", *Evangelische Theologie* 33/1, 32-53.

Fohrer, Georg: *Studien zur alttestamentlichen Theologie und Geschichte* (1949-1966). (Berlin, 1969). – R: *OLZ* 68, 46 (O. Eissfeldt).

Gerleman, G.: "Die Wurzel *šlm*", *ZATW* 85. 1-14. (With English and French Summaries).

Gilbert, M.: *La critique des dieux dans le Livre de la Sagesse* (Sg 13-15). (Rome,

Biblical Institute Press). xix, 323 p., 3 tabl. = Analecta Biblica, 53. – R: *RThL* 4/3, 361-363 (P. M. Bogaert).

Goldberg, A.: "Der Vortrag des Ma'asse Merkawa. Eine Vermutung zur frühen Merkawamystik", *Judaica* 29/1, 4-24.

Grimm, D.: "Erwägungen zu Hosea 12, 12 'in Gilgal opfern sie Stiere' ", *ZATW* 85/3, 339-347.

Grossfeld, B.: "A critical note on Judg 4, 21", *ZATW* 85/3, 348-351.

Haag, E.: "Ez 37 und der Glaube an die Auferstehung der Toten", *Trierer Theologische Zeitschrift* 82/2, 78-92.

Hanson, P. D.: "Zachariah 9 and the Recapitulation of an Ancient Ritual Pattern", *JBL* 92/1, 37-59.

Hasel, G. F.: "Semantic Values of Derivatives of the Hebrew Root *š'r*", *AnUSS* 11, No. 2, 152-169.

Heintz, Jean Georges: "Langage prophétique et 'style de cour' selon *Archives Royales de Mari X* et l'Ancien Testament", *Semitica* 22, 5-12.

Hermisson, H.-J.: "Zukunftserwartung und Gegenwartskritik in der Verkündigung Jesajas", *Evangelische Theologie* 33/1, 54-77.

Horwitz, W. J.: "Another Interpretation of Jonah I 12", *Vetus Testamentum* 23, No. 3, 370-372.

Horwitz, W. J.: "Were There Twelve Horite Tribes?", *Catholic Biblical Quarterly* 35/1, 69-71.

Humphreys, W. L.: "A Life-Style for Diaspora: A Study of the Tales of Esther and Daniel", *JBL* 92, 211-23.

van Iersel, B.: "A propos de l'alternance de tendances sécularisantes et sacralisantes dans l'Ecriture", *Concilium*, No. 81, 81-91.

Izco Ilundain, J.A.: "El conocimiento de Dios entre los Gentiles según el Antiguo Testamento", *EthL* 49, 36-75.

Jacobs, L.: "The Talmudic *Sugya* as a Literary Unit: An Analysis of Baba Ḳamma 2a-3b", *JoJeS* 24/2, 119-126.

Jellicoe, S.: "Some reflections on the χαίγε recension", *Vetus Testamentum* 23, No. 1, 15-24.

Jones, B. W.: "Ideas of History in the Book of Daniel", *DisAbIn, A* 33/7, 3758. (The author's summary of his diss., Graduate Theological Union, 1972).

Kaiser, Otto: "Altes Testament – Vorexilische Literatur", in: U. Mann (Hrsg.): *Theologie und Religionswissenschaft* (Darmstadt, Wissenschaftliche Buchgesellschaft) 241-268.

Kaiser, O.: *Der Prophet Jesaja*, übersetzt und erklärt. Kap. 13-39. (Göttingen,

Vandenhoeck und Ruprecht). xi, 327 S. = Das Alte Testament Deutsch. Neues Göttinger Bibelwerk, 18.

Kaiser, O.: "Wirklichkeit, Möglichkeit und Vorurteil. Ein Beitrag zum Verständnis des Buches Jona", *EvTh* 33/1, 91-103.

van der Kam, J.: "The Theophany of Enoch I 3b-7, 9", *Vetus Testamentum* 23, No. 2, 129-150.

Kamhi, D. J.: "The Root *ḥlq* in the Bible", *Vetus Testamentum* 23, No. 2, 235-239.

Kearney, P. J.: "The Role of the Gibeonites in the Deuteronomic History", *CBQ* 35/1, 1-19.

Keel, Othmar: "Das Vergraben der 'fremden Götter' in Genesis XXXV 4b", *Vetus Testamentum* 23, 305-336, 8 Abb.

Keel, Othmar: *Die Welt der altorientalischen Bildsymbolik und das Alte Testament. Am Beispiel der Psalmen.* (Zürich, 1972). – R: *EThL* 49, 180-181 (J. Lust).

Keller, C.-A.: "Die Eigenart der Prophetie Habakuks", *ZATW* 85, No. 2, 156-167. (Summaries in English and French).

Kikawada, I. M.: "The Irrigation of the Garden of Eden", in: *XXIXe Congrès Intern. des Orientalistes, Résumés des Communications*, Sections 1-5, (Paris, Y. Hervouet), p. 51.

Koch, K.: "Die Herkunft der proto-Theodotion-Übersetzung des Danielbuches", *Vetus Testamentum* 23, 362-365.

van Koningsveld, P. Sj.: "New quotations from Hafs al-Quti's translation of the Psalms", *BiOr* 30, 315. (3 Arabic verses with the related Latin lines).

Kutsch, E.: "Das sogenannte 'Bundesblut' in Ex. XXIV 8 und Sach. IX 11", *Vetus Testamentum* 23/1, 25-30.

Kutsch, E.: "Hiob: leidender Gerechter, leidender Mensch", *Kerygma und Dogma* 19/3, 197-214.

Lapp, Paul W.: *Biblical Archaeology and History*. (New York, 1969). – R: *OLZ* 68, 39-40 (Otto Eissfeldt).

Larès, M.: "Arnold J. Toynbee et la religion de l'Ancien Testament", *RHR* 184, no. 2, 159-208.

van Leeuwen, C.: "De oudtestamentische profeten in het onderzoek van het laatste tien jaar", *NeTT* 27, 289-319 (in Dutch: The Old Testament Prophets in the Research of the Last Ten Years).

Di Lella, Alexander A.: *The Hebrew Text of Sirach. A Text-critical and Historical Study*. (The Hague, 1966). – R: *OLZ* 68, 148-149 (R. Meyer).

Lipiński, E.: "Eshmun, 'Healer' ", *AION* 33, no. 2, 161-183.

Lipiński, E.: "La colombe du Ps. LXVIII 14", *Vetus Testamentum* 23, 365-368.

Lipiński, E.: "Le *šʾr yšwb* d'Isaïe VII 3" *Vetus Testamentum* 23/2, 245-246.

Lipiński, E.: "Obadiah 20", *Vetus Testamentum* 23, No. 3, 368-370.

Lipiński, E.: "On the Comparison in Isaiah LV 10", *Vetus Testamentum* 23/2, 246-247.

Long, B. O.: "2 Kings III and Genres of Prophetic Narrative", *Vetus Testamentum* 23, No. 3, 337-348.

Long, Burke O.: *The Problem of Etiological Narrative in the Old Testament.* (Berlin, 1968). – R: *OLZ* 68, 139-141 (G. Wallis).

Lowe, A. D.: "Ben Sira: Some Notes on Examining the Hebrew Manuscripts", in: *XXIXe Congrès Intern. des Orientalistes, Résumés des Communications*, Sections 1-5, (Paris, Y. Hervouet), pp. 51-52.

Loza, J.: "Exode XXXII et la rédaction JE", *Vetus Testamentum* 23/1, 31-55.

Luciani, F.: "Camminare davanti a Dio", *Aevum* 47, 287-297,.

Lundbom, J. R.: "Jeremiah: A Study in Ancient Hebrew Rhetoric", *DisAbIn A* 34/4, 2016-2017. (The author's summary of his dissertation, Graduate Theological Union, 1973).

Lys, D.: *L'Eoclésiaste ou que vaut la vie?* (Lille, Service de reproduction des thèses, Université de Lille III). 416 p., bibliographie (9 p.)

Lys, D.: "Par le temps qui court. Ec 3/1-8", *Etudes Théologiques et Religieuses* 48/3, 299-316.

McEvenue, Sean E.: *The Narrative Style of the Priestly Writer.* (Rome, Biblical Institute Press, 1971). xi, 218 p. = Analecta Biblica, 50. R: *BiOr* 30, 455-459 (Hermann Schulz).

Macintosh, A. A.: "Psalm XCI 4 and the Root shr", *Vetus Testamentum* 23, No. 1, 56-62.

Malamat, A.: "Charismatic Leadership in the Book of Judges", in: *XXIXe Congrès Intern. des Orientalistes, Résumés des Communications*, Sections 1-5, (Paris, Y. Hervouet), p. 30.

Ménard, J.-E. (éd.): *Exégèse biblique et judaisme.* (Leiden, E. J. Brill). 255 p.

Metzger, B. M.: *La Haggada enluminée. I. Étude iconographique et stylistique des manuscripts enluminés et décorés de la Haggada du XIIIe au XVIe siècle.* Avec une préface par R. Crozet. (Leiden, E. J. Brill). In-4°. xxx, 518 p., 83 pl. = Etudes sur le judaïsme médiévale, II.

Michel, D.: "Nur ich bin Jahwe. Erwägungen zur sogenannten Selbstvorstellungsformel", *ThV* 11, 145-156.

Monsengwo Pasinya, L.: *La notion de 'nomos' dans le Pentateugue grec.* (Rome, Biblical Institute Press). 246 p. = Analecta Biblica, 52.

Morag, S. (ed.): *The Book of Daniel with Saadia's translation. A Babylonian-Yemenite manuscript*. Published in facsimile with an introduction. (Leiden, E. J. Brill). vii, 8 p. (English text), xi, 57 p. (Hebrew t.), 82 facs.

Murdoch, B.: "The River that Stopped Flowing: Folklore and Biblical Typology in the Apocryphal Lives of Adam and Eve", *SFQ* 37/1, 37-51.

Neiman, D.: "The Polemic Language of the Genesis Cosmology", in: *The Heritage of the Early Church, Essays in Honor of G. V. Florovsky* (q. v. sub I-7), 47-63.

Neumann, P. K. D.: "Das Wort, das geschehen ist... Zum Problem der Wortempfangsterminologie in Jer. I – XXV", *VeTes* 23, 171-217.

Neusner, J.: "In Praise of the Talmud", *Tradition* 13/3, 16-35.

Neusner, J. (ed.): *The modern study of the Mishnah*. (Leiden, E. J. Brill). xxviii, 283 p. = Studia Post-Biblica, XXIII.

Newsome, J. D., Jr.: "The Chronicler's View of Prophecy", *DisAbIn A* 34/4, 2019. (The athor's summary of his diss., Vanderbilt University, 1973).

Nicholson, E. W.: *Preaching to the Exiles: A Study of the Prose Tradition in the Book of Jeremiah*, (Oxford, 1970). – R: *GGA* 225, 1-14 (H. Weippert).

Nickelsburg, G. W. E., Jr.: "Narrative Traditions in the Paralipomena of Jeremiah and 2 Baruch", *CBQ* 35, 60-68.

de Nicola, A.: "Il monte Hermon", *Bibbia e Oriente* 15/3, 109-122.

Nielsen, E.: "Creation and the Fall of Man: A Cross-Disciplinary Investigation", *HUCA* 43, 1-22.

North, R.: "The Hivites", *Biblica* 54, no. 1, 43-62.

Ouellette, J.: "The Shaking of the Thresholds in Amos 9: 1", *HUCA* 43, 23-27.

Paper, H. H.: "Another Judeo-Persian Pentateuch Translation, Ms HUC 2193", *HUGA* 43, 207-251.

Paper, Herbert H.: "Ecclesiastes in Judeo-Persian", *Orientalia* 42 (Fs Gelb), 328-337. (Original text on pp. 330-337).

Pearce, R. A.: "Shiloh and Jer. VII 12, 14 and 15", *Vetus Testamentum* 23/1, 105-108.

Peter, M.: "Qui a béni Abraham d'après Gen. 14, 18", in: *XXIXe Congrès Intern. des Orientalistes, Résumés des Communications*, Sections 1-5, (Paris, Y. Hervouet), pp. 52-53.

Preuss, H. D.: *Verspottung fremder Religionen im Alten Testament* (Stuttgart, 1971). – R: *ZRGG* 25, 180-183 (G. Wanke).

Rabin, C.: "Hebrew baddīm 'Power' ", *Journal of Semitic Studies* 18/1, 57-58.

von Rad, Gerhard: *Gesammelte Studien zum Alten Testament*. Band II. Herausgegeben von Rudolf Smend. (München, Chr. Kaiser Verlag). 328 p. = Theologische

Bücherei. Neudrucke und Berichte aus dem 20. Jahrhundert. Altes Testament, Band 48.

Radday, Y. T.: "Chiasm in Joshua, Judges and Others", *Linguistica Biblica*, No. 27-28, 6-13.

Ralston, W. H., Jr.: "That Old Serpent (For C.T.H.)", *Sewanee Review* 81, No. 3, 389-428.

Ridenhour, T. E.: "The Old Testament and the Patriarchal Traditions", *DisAbIn, A* 33/11, 6443. (The author's summary of his diss., Duke University, 1972).

Robinson, J.: *The First Book of Kings*. Commentary. The Cambridge Bible Commentary. (Cambridge, 1972). – R.N. Whybray: *The Book of Proverbs*. Commentary. The Cambridge Bible Commentary. (Cambridge, 1972). – J. C. Dancy with Contributions by W. J. Fuerst and R. J. Hammer: *The Shorter Books of the Apocryphal: Tobit, Judith, Rest of Esther, Baruch, Letter oof Jeremiah, additions to Daniel and Prayer of Manasseh*. The Cambridge Bible Commentary. (Cambridge, 1972). – R: *BiOr* 30, 459-462 (Hans Bardtke).

Rosenstiehl, Jean-Marc: *L'Apocalypse d'Elie*. Introduction, traduction et notes. (Paris, Geuther, 1972). 151 p. – R: *Le Muséon* 86, 239-241 (A. M. Denis). *BiOr* 30, 463-464 (J. T. Nelis).

Rudolph, W.: *Joel – Amos – Obadja – Jona*. (Gütersloh, 1971). – R: *BiOr* 30, 266-269 (Gerhard F. Hasel).

Sacchi, P.: "Metodi e problemi di filologia veterotestamentaria", *ParPas* no. 151, 237-270.

Sasson, J. M.: "A Further Cuneiform Parallel to the Song of Songs?", *ZATW* 85/3, 359-360.

Sawyer, J. F. A.: "Joshua 10: 12-14 and the Solar Eclipse of 30 September 1131 B.C.", *PEQ* 104, 139-146.

Schiltknecht, H. R.: "Konflikt und Versöhnung in der biblischen Erzählung von Jakob und Esau", *Reformatio* 22/10, 522-531.

Schmid, Herbert: "Altes Testament – Exilische und nachexilische Literatur", in: U. Mann (Hrsg.): *Theologie und Religionswissenschaft* (Darmstadt, Wissenschaftliche Buchgesellschaft) 269-285.

Schoneveld, J.: "Het breken van de staf des broods" (Lev. 26, 26), *NeTT* 27, 132-145.

Schoors, A.: *I am God your Saviour. A form-critical study of the main genres in Is. xl-lv*. (Leiden, E. J. Brill). x, 343 p., 6 tables. = Vetus Testamentum, Supplements, XXIV.

Schulz, Hermann: *Das Buch Nahum: Eine redaktionskritische Untersuchung*. (Berlin, W. de Gruyter). viii, 163 S. = Beiheft zur *ZATW*, 129.

Schunck, K.-D.: "Der fünfte Thronname des Messias (Jes. IX 5-6) *Vetus Testamentum* 23/1, 108-110.

Schüngel-Straumann, H.: "Zur Gattung und Theologie des 139. Psalms", *Biblische Zeitschrift* 17/1, 39-51.

Schuttermayr, G.: " 'Schöpfung aus dem Nichts' in 2 Makk 7,28? Zum Verhältnis von Position und Bedeutung", *BibZ* 17/2, 203-228.

Seebass, H.: "Elia und Ahab auf dem Karmel", *ZThK* 70/2, 121-136.

Seebass, H.: "Micha ben Jimla", *Kerygma und Dogma* 19/2, 109-124.

van Selms, A.: "Isaiah 28, 9-13: An Attempt to Give a New Interpretation", *ZATW* 85/3, 332-339.

Seybold, K.: "Elia am Gottesberg. Vorstellungen prophetischen Wirkens nach 1. Könige 19", *EvTh* 33/1, 3-18.

Sharpe, J. L. III: "The Second Adam in the Apolypse of Moses", *CBQ* 35, NO. 1, 35-46.

Slingerland, H. D.: "The Testaments of the Twelve Patriarchs: A History of Research with Attendant Conclusions", *DisAbIn* 34/3, 13355-1356. (The author's summary of his diss., Union Theological Seminary, New York City, 1973).

in der Smitten, Wilhelm Th.: *Esra: Quellen, Überlieferung und Geschichte*. (Assen, van Gorcum). xi, 169 p. = Studia Semitica Neerlandica, 15.

in der Smitten, Wilhelm Th.: "Genesis 34 – Ausdruck der Volksmeinung", *BiOr* XXX, No. 1-2, 7-9.

in der Smitten, Wilhelm Th.: "Marginalien zur Restvorstellung im AT", *BiOr* XXX, No. 1-2, 9-10.

Sperber, A. (ed.): *The Bible in Aramaic*. Based on Old Manuscripts and Printed Texts. Vol. IV B: *The Tergum and the Hebrew Bible*. (Leiden, E. J. Brill). xv, 417 p.

Steck, O. H.: "Rettung und Verstockung. Exegetische Bemerkungen zu Jesaja 7, 3-9", *EvTh* 33/1, 77-90.

Stone, M. E.: "Some Observations on the Armenian Version of the Paralipomena of Jeremiah", *CBQ* 35, 47-59.

Stuart, S.S., Jr.: "The Exodus Tradition in Late Jewish and Early Christian Literature: A General Survey of the Literature and a Particular Analysis of the Wisdom of Solomon, II Esdras and the Epistle to the Hebrews", *DisAbIn A* 34/4, 2023 (The author's summary of his diss., Vanderbilt University, 1973).

Tournay, R.: "Note sur le Psaume XXII 17", *Vetus Testamentum* 23/1, 111-112.

de Vaux, Roland: *Bible et Orient*. (Paris, 1967). – R: *OLZ* 68, 43-45 (G. Wallis).

de Vaux, R.: *The Bible and the Ancient Near East*. – R: *AnUSS* 11, 195-197 (S. H. Horn). *JR* 53, 382-384 (J. Blenkinsopp).

de Vries, S. J.: "David's Victory over the Philistine an Saga and as Legend", *JBL* 92, No. 1, 23-36.

Wakeman, M. K.: *God's battle with the monster. A study in biblical imagery.* (Leiden, E. J. Brill). viii, 151 p., 2 fig.

Walters (= Katz), Peter: *The Text of the Septuagint, its Corruptions and their Emendation.* Edited by D. W. Gooding. (Cambridge, University Press). xx, 419 p.

Weil, G. E.: "La Massorah", *REJ* 131, 5-104.

Weippert, Helga: *Die Prosareden des Jeremiabuches.* (Berlin, Walter de Gruyter). viii, 256 p. = Beihefte zur *ZATW*, 132.

Welten, P.: "Naboths Weinberg (1. Könige 21)", *EvTh* 33/1, 18-32.

Westermann, Claus: *Genesis.* Lieferung 8. (Neukirchen-Vluyn, Neukirchener Verlag). S. 561-640. = BKAT I, 8.

Westermann, Claus: *Genesis.* Lfg. 4. (Neukirchen-Vluyn, 1970). – R: *OLZ* 68, 590-591 (G. Wallis).

White, H. C.: "The Divine Oath in Genesis", *Journal of Biblical Literature* 92, No. 2, 165-179.

Wijngaards, J. N. M.: *The Dramatization of Salvific History in the Deuteronomic Schools.* (Leiden, 1969). – R: *OLZ* 68, 588-590 (G. Wallis).

Willi-Plein, I.: "ḥn, Ein Uebersetzungsproblem. Gedanken zu Sach. XII 10", *Vetus Testamentum* 23/1, 90-99.

Willis, J. T.: "The Function of Comprehensive Anticipatory Redactional Joints in I Samuel 16-18", *ZATW* 85/3, 294-314.

Wilms, F.-E.: "Die Frage nach dem historischen Mose. Der Stand der Mose-Forschung", *ThQ* 153/4, 353-363.

Wilson, R. R.: "Genealogy and History in the Old Testament: A Study of the Form and the Function of the Old Testament Genealogies in their Near Eastern Context", *DisAbIn, A* 33/7, 3769. (The author's summary of his diss., Yale University, 1972).

Wiseman, D.J. (ed.): *Peoples of Old Testament Times.* Edited ... for the Society for Old Testament Study. (Oxford, Clarendon Press). xxi, 402 p., 6 fig., 8 pl.

Wolff, H. W.: *Gesammelte Studien zum Alten Testament.* 2. erweiterte Auflage. (München, Kaiser Verlag). 458 S. = Theologische Bücherei, 22. – R: *BiOr* 30, 448 (C. van Leeuwen).

van der Woude, A. S.: "Micah IV 1-5: An Instance of the Pseudo-Prophets quoting Isaiah", *Fs de Liagre Böhl* (q. v. sub I-7), 396-402.

Würthwein, Ernst: *Der Text des Alten Testaments. Einführung in die Biblia Hebraica.* 4. erweiterte Auflage. (Stuttgart, Würtembergische Bibelanstalt). iv, 230 S., 48 Taf.

Zandee, J.: "Das Alte Testament im Urteil des Gnostizismus", *Festschrift de Liagre Böhl* (q. v. sub I-7), 403-411.

Zimmerli, Walther: *Ezechiel, I und II.* (Neukirchen-Vluyn, 1958-1969). – R: *OLZ* 68, 142-143 (W. Kessler).

2. QUMRAN (DEAD SEA SCROLLS)

Abraham, A. T.: "The Baptismal Initiation of the Qumran Community", *DisAbIn A* 34/6, 3521. (The author's summary of his diss., Princeton Theological Seminary, 1973).

Adam, A.: *Antike Berichte über die Essener.* 2. neubearbeitete und erweiterte Auflage von Christoph Burchard. (Berlin, W. de Gruyter, 1972). – R: *BiOr* 30, 471 (A. Marx et R. Stehly/partie arabe/).

Allegro, John M.: with the collaboration of Arnold A. Anderson: *Aumrân Cave 4. I (4 Q 158-4 Q 186).* (Oxford, 1968). – R: *OLZ* 68, 42-43 (O. Eissfeldt).

d'Arès, J.: *Les Esséniens et le judaïsme à travers les manuscrits de la mer Morte.* (Paris, Institut d'Herméneutique). 30 f. multigr. = Conférences des Lundis de l'Institut d'herméneutique.

Baillet, M.: "Les manuscrits de la grotte 7 de Qumran et le Nouveau Testament", in: *XXIXe Congrès International des Orientalistes. Résumés des Communications*, Sections 1-5. (Paris, Y. Hervouet), p. 37.

Benoit, P.: "Nouvelle note sur les fragments grecs de la grotte 7 de Qumran", *Revue Biblique* 80/1, 5-12.

Berger, K.: "Der Streit des guten und des bösen Engels um die Seele. Beobachtungen zu 4Q Amr^{b} und Judas 9", *JSJ* 4, 1-18.

Dequeker, L.: "The 'Saints of the Most High' in Qumran and Daniel", In: *Syntax and Meaning* (Leiden, E. J. Brill) 108-187.

Dupont-Sommer, A.: "Observations nouvelles sur l'expression 'suspendu vivant sur le bois' dans le *Commentaire de Nahum* (4 Q pNah II 8), à la lumière du *Rouleau du Temple* (11 Q Tempel Scroll LXIV 6-13)", *CRAIBL* 25 (no. avr.), 709-720.

Fitzmyer, Joseph A.: *The Genesis Apocryphon of Qumran Cave I. A Commentary.* Second revised Edition. (Rome, 1971). – R: *BiOr* 30, 89-91 (Hans Bardtke).

Garcia de la Fuente, O.: "La búsqueda de Dios en los escritos de Qumrán", *Estudios Biblicos* 32/1, 25-42.

Hoenig, S. B.: "Qumran Fantasies. A rejoinder to Dr. Driver's Mythology of Qumran", *JQR* 63, 247-267, 292-316.

Horgan, M. P.: "A Lament ober Jerusalem (4 Q 179)", *Journal of Semitic Studies* 18, No. 2, 222-234.

Laperrousaz, E. M.: "Le mère du Messie et la mère de l'Aspic dans les Hôdâyôt de Qumran. Quelques brèves remarques sur la structure de 1 QH III, 1-18", in:

XXIXe Congrès International des Orientalistes. Résumés des Communications, Sections 1-5. (Paris, Y. Hervouet). p. 29.

Le Moyne, J.: *Les Sadducéens.* (Paris, Gabalda, 1972). 464 p. = Etudes Bibliques. – R: *Revue de Qumran* 8 (30), 271-275 (I. Rabinowitz).

Levine, B. A.: "Damascus Document IX, 17-22: A New Translation and Comments", *RQ* VIII (30), 195-196.

Milik, J. T.: "A propos de 11 Q Jub", *Biblica* 54/1, 77-78.

Morrow, F. J., Jr.: "11 Q. Targum Job and the Massoretic Text", *Revue de Qumran* VIII (30), 253-256.

Muraoka, T.: " 'Essene' in the Septuagint", *Revue de Qumran* VIII (30), 267-268.

Nebe, G.-W.: "'*br* in 4 Q 186", *Revue de Qumran* VIII (30), 265-266.

Nebe, G.–W.: "Der Gebrauch der sogenannten *nota accusativi 'eth* in Damaskuschrift XV, 5-9 und 12", *RQ* VIII (30), 257-263.

Neusner, J.: " 'By the Testimony of Two Witnesses', in the Damascus Document IX, 17-22 and in Pharisaic-Rabbinic Law", *RQ* VIII (30), 197-217.

Noack, B.: "Note sur de prétendus fragments du Nouveaux Testament à Qumran", *DTT* 36/2, 152-155 (en danois).

O'Callaghan, J.: "El ordenador, 7 Q 5 y Homero", *StuPap* 12/2, 73-79.

O'Callaghan, J.: "Les papyrus de la grotte 7 de Qumrân", *Nouvelle Revue Théologique* 95/2, 188-195.

O'Callaghan, J.: "Notas sobre 7 Q tomadas en el 'Rockefeller Museum' de Jerusalem", *Biblica* 53/4, 517-533, 2 pl.

Otzen, B.: " 'Belial' dans l'Ancien Testament et dans le judaïsme tardiff" *Dansk Teologisk Tidsskrift* 36/1, 1-24 (in Danish).

Pardee, D.: "A Restudy of the Commentary on Psalm 37 from Qumran Cave y (*Discoveries in the Judean Desert of Jordan*, vol. V no. 171)", *RQ* VIII (30), 163-194.

van der Ploeg, J. P. M.: "Fragments d'un Psautier de Qumrân", *Festschrift de Liagre Böhl* (q. v. sub I-7), 308-309.

van der Ploeg, J. P. M.: "Les Manuscrits du Déser de Juda. Encore quelques publications", *BiOr* 30, 183-186.

Rabinowitz, I.: "*Pĕsher/pattārōn*, Its Biblical Meaning and Its Significance in the Qumran Literature", *RQ* VIII (30), 219-232.

Sanders, J. A.: "Palestinian Manuscripts 1947-1972", *Journal of Jewish Studies* 24, No. 1, 74-83.

Sanders, J. A.: "The Dead Sea Scrolls. A Quarter Century of Study", *BibAr* 36, No. 4, 110-148.

Skehan, P. W.: "A Liturgical Complex in 11a QPsa", *Catholic Biblical Quarterly* 35/2, 195-205.

Starkova, K. B.: "Monuments littéraires de la communauté de Qumrân", *Palestinskij Sbornik* no. 24, 3-136, bibliographie (7 p.)

Tyloch, Witold: "Le florilège de la IVe grotte de Qumran", *Euhemer* XVII/3 (89), 87-94 (en polonais).

Urbán, A. C.: "Observaciones sobre ciertos papiros de la cueva 7 de Qumran", *RQ* VIII (30), 233-251.

de Vaux, R.: *Archaeology and the Dead Sea Scrolls*. (London, Oxford University Press). xv, 142 p., 42 pl. = The Schweich Lectures of the British Academy 1959. (Revised Edition in English Translation).

White, W., Jr.: "Notes on the Papyrus Fragments from Cave 7 at Qumran", *WThJ* 35, No. 2, 221-226.

3. INSTITUTIONS

Abel, E. L.: "The Nature of the Patriarchal God '*El Šadday*' ", *Numen* 20, 48-59.

Abramowitz, M.: "The Sanctification of the Moon: Ancient Rite of Rebellion", *Judaism* 22/1, 45-52.

Albeck, Chanoch: *Einführung in die Mischna*, (Berlin, 1971). – R: *BiOr* 30, 92-93 (Charles T. Fritsch).

Alonso Díaz, J.: "El alcance de la 'prohibidión de las imágines' en el Decálogo mosaico", *EsEc* 48 (186), 315-326.

Bastomsky, S. J.: "The Talmudic View of Epicureanism", *Apeiron* 7, No. 1, 17-19, bibliographical notes.

Berman, S. J.: "The Extended Notion of the Sabbath", *Judaism* 22/3, 342-352.

Bianchi, H.: "Tsedeka-Justice", *Bijdragen. Tijdschrift voor Filosofie en Theologie* 34/3, 306-318, bibliography.

Bleich, J. D.: "Establishing Criteria of Death", *Tradition* 13, No. 3, 90-113.

Boertien, Maas: *Nazir – Nasiräer*. (Berlin, 1971). – R: *BiOr* 30, 272-273 (Otto Böcher).

Budd, P. J.: "Priestly Instruction in Pre-Exilic Israel", *Vetus Testamentum* 23/1, 1-14.

Bunte, Wolfgang: *Kelim-Gefässe*. (Berlin, W. de Gruyter, 1972). vi, 557 S. = Die Mischna, Text, Übersetzung und ausführliche Erklärung, VI, 1. – R: *BiOr* 30, 470-471 (Otto Böcher).

Carr, G. L.: "The Claims of the Chronicler for the Origin of the Israelite Priesthood", *DisAbIn A* 33/12, 7012. (The author's summary of his diss., Boston University Graduate School, 1973).

Cody, A.: *A History of the Old Testament Priesthood* (Rome, 1969). – R: *JSS* 18/2, 282-285 (E. W. Nicholson).

Cody, A.: "Priesthood in the Old Testament", *Studia Missionalian* 22, 309-329.

Donaldson, J.: "The Title Rabbi in the Gospels. Some Reflections on the Evidence of the Synoptics", *JQR* 63, 287-291.

Dupuy, B.-D.: "La joie de la Tora", *Vav, Revue du Dialogue* 7, no. 3, 27-37.

Eissfeldt, Otto: "Monopol-Ansprüche des Heiligtums von Silo", *OLZ* 68, 327-333.

Elon, M.: *Ha-Mishpat ha-Ivri – Jewish Law: History, Sources, Principles.* (Jerusalem, The Magnes Press). 1594 p. (in Hebrew).

Freudenstein, E. G.: "A Swift Witness", *Tradition* 13/3, 114-123.

Gamoran, H.: "Talmudic Controlls on the Purchase of Futures", *JQR* 64/1, 48-66.

Gil, M.: "The Term *aqōlīthōs* in Medieval Jewish Deeds", *JNES* 32/3, 318-320.

Görg, Manfred: *Das Zelt der Begegnung. Untersuchung zur Gestalte der sakralen Zelttraditionen Altisraels.* (Bonn, 1967). – R: *OLZ* 68, 475-476 (O. Eissfeldt).

Greenberg, S.: "Reactions to the Rabbinical Assembly Maḥzor", *Judaism* 22, No. 4, 440-454.

Gross, H.: "Institution und Charisma im Alten Testament", *Trierer Theologische Zeitschrift* 82/2, 65-77.

Grossfeld, B.: "Targum Onkelos and Rabbinic Interpretation to Genesis 2: 1,2", *JoJeS* 24/2, 176-178.

Haran, M.: "The Beginnings of the Israelite Priesthood", in: *XXIXe Congrès International des Orientalistes, Résumés des Communications*, Sections 1-5, (Paris, Y. Hervouet), p. 27.

Hasel, Gerhard F.: *The Remnant. The History and Theology of the Remnant Idea from Genesis to Isaiah.* (Andrew University Press, 1972). – R: *BiOr* 30, 453-454 (P. J. Cools).

Hennig, J.: "Die Liturgie und das Judentum", *ALW* 15, 268-279.

Hennig, J.: "Liturgiereform im jüdischen Bereich heute", *Liturgisches Jahrbuch*, Heft 2, 127-136.

Ishida, T.: "The Leaders of the Tribal Leagues 'Israel' in the Pre-Monarchic Period", *Revue Biblique* 80/4, 514-530.

Jackson, B. S.: "Reflections on Biblical Criminal Law", *The Journal of Jewish Studies* 24/1, 8-38.

Jackson, B. S.: "The Problem of Exod. XXI 22-5 (Ius talionis)", *Vetus Testamentum* 23, No. 3, 273-304.

Jacob, E.: "Quelques travaux récents sur le prophétisme", *RHPhR* 53, no. 3-4, 415-425.

Janzen, W.: *Mourning Cry and Woe Oracle*, (Berlin, 1972). – R: *BiOr* 30, 91-92 (C. van Leeuwen).

Kluger, Rivkah Schärf: *Satan in the Old Testament*, transl. by H. Nagel. (Evanston, Ill., 1967). – R: *OLZ* 68, 591-592 (Hans Bardtke).

Kutsch, E.: *Verheissung und Gesetz Untersuchungen zum sogenannten 'Bund' im Alten Testament*. (Berlin, W. de Gruyter). xii, 230 S. = Beiheft zur *ZATW*, 131.

Leloir, L.: "Valeurs permanentes du Sacerdoce lévitique. Mise au point", *EthL* 49, No. 1, 178-179.

Lemaire, A.: "Le sabbat á l'époque royale israélite", *Revue Biblique* 80, no. 2, 161-185.

Levin, L.: "Whither Conservative Liturgy?", *Judaism* 22, No. 4, 433-439.

Levinson, N. Peter: *Die Kultsymbolik im Alten Testament und im nachbiblischen Judentum*. (Stuttgart, 1972). – R: *Anthropos* 68, 316 (Joseph Henninger).

Loader, J. A.: "An Explanation of the Term *proselūtos*", *Novum Testamentum* 15, 270-277.

Louys, D.: "David dansant devant l'Arche 2Sam 6" *Vav Revue du Dialogue* 7, no. 3, 9-22.

Ludwig, T. M.: "The Traditions of the Establishing of the Earth in Deutero-Isaiah", *JBL* 92/3, 345-357.

Lust, J.: "The Mantic Function of the Prophet", *Bijdragen, Tijdschrift voor Filosofie en Theologie* 34/3, 234-250.

McCarter, P. K.: "The River Ordeal in Israelite Literature", *HThR* 66, No. 4, 403-412.

McCarthy, Dennis J.: "Further Notes on the Symbolism of Blood and Sacrifice", *JBL* 92, No. 2, 205-210.

Memmi, A., W. Ackermann, N. Zoberman, S. Zoberman: "Pratique religieuse et identité juive", *RFS* 14/2, 242-270.

Mettinger, T. N. D.: *Solomonic State Officials. A Study of the Civil Government Officials of the Israelite Monarchy*. (IBHR, 1971, p. 92). – R: *JSS* 18, 155-156 (R. E. Clements). *JNES* 32, 499 (J. Ouellette). *BibZ* 17, 300-303 (J. Scharbert). *ZDMG* 123, 378-379 (W. Richter). *ThRv* 69, 278-282 (H. Cazelles). *OLZ* 68, 593-596 (G. Pfeifer).

Milch, R. J.: "An Encounter with the *Akedah*", *Judaism* 22/4, 397-399.

Mölle, Herbert: *Das 'Erscheinen' Gottes im Pentateuch. Ein literaturwissenschaftlicher Beitrag zur alttestamentlichen Exegese*. (Bern, Herbert Lang/Frankfurt a. M., Peter Lang). xx, 268 S. = Europäische Hochschulschriften, XXIII/18.

Mulhall, M M.: "Aaron and Moses: Their Relationship in the Oldest Sources of the Pentateuch", *DisAbIn A* 34/4, 2018. (The autho's summary of his diss., Catholic University of America, 1973).

Negretti, Nicola: *Il settimo giorno. Indagine oritico teologica delle tradizioni presacerdotali e sacerdotali circa il sabato biblico.* (Roma, Biblical Institute Press). 341 p. = Analecta Biblica, 55.

Neusner, J.: *The idea of purity in ancient Judaism.* The Haskell lectures, 1972-1973. With a critique and a commentary by M. Douglas. (Leiden, E. J. Brill). xiv, 153 p. = Studies in Judaism and Late Antiquity, I.

Ohana, M.: "Agneau pascal et circoncision: le problème de la halakha premishnaique dans le Targum palestinien", *VeTes* 23, 385-399.

Olan, L. A.: "A New Prayer Book. Conservative Judaism Defines Itself", *Judaism* 22, No. 4, 418-425.

Paul, Shalom M.: *Studies in the Book of the Covenant in the Light of Cuneiform and Biblical Law.* (Leiden, 1970). – R: *BiOr* 30, 449-452 (H. P. H. Petschow).

Peterson, D. L.: "Israelite Prophecy and Prophetic Traditions in the Exilic and Post-Exilic Periods", *DisAbIn A* 34/1, 409-410. (The author's summary of his diss., Yale University, 1972).

Phillips, A.: "Some Aspects of Family Law in Pre-Exilic Israel", *Vetus Testamentum* 23/3, 349-361.

Potin, J.: *La fête juive de la Pentecôte.* Etude des textes liturgiques (*IBHR*, 1971). – R: *JThS* 24/1, 221-223 (J. B. Segal).

von Rad, Gerhard: *Das Opfer des Abraham.* (München, Chr. Kaiser Verlag). 96 S. = Kaiser Traktate, 6. – R: *BiOr* 30, 448-449 (Miloś Bić).

Ribar, J. W.: "Death Cult Practices in Ancient Palestine", *DisAbIn A* 34, No. 4, 1800-1801. (The author's summary of his diss., University of Michigan, 1973).

Riskin, S.: " 'Modern' Prayer: A What Sacrifice?", *Judaism* 22, No. 4, 426-432.

Roberts, J. J.: "The Davidic Origin of the Zion Tradition", *JBL* 92/3, 329-344.

Rücker, Heribert: *Die Begründungen der Weisungen Jahwes im Pentateuch.* (Leipzig, St. Benno Verlag). xxxiii, 165 S. = Erfurter theologische Studien, 30.

Sanders, E. P.: "R. Akiba's View of Suffering", *JQR* 63, No. 4, 332-351.

Sawyer, J. F. A.: "Hebrew Words for the Resurrection of the Dead", *Vetus Testamentum* 23/2, 218-234.

Schäfer, P.: *Die Vorstellung vom heiligen Geist in der rabbinischen Literatur,* (München, 1972). – R: *Kirjath Sepher* 48, 434-437 (J. Heinemann).

Scharbert, J.: "Die Geschichte der *bārûk* – Formel", *Biblische Zeitschrift* 17, Jeft 1, 1-28.

Schoneveld, J.: "Le sang du cambrioleur. Exode XXII 1, 2", *Festschrift de Liagre Böhl* (q. v. sub I-7), 335-340.

Schottroff, W.: *Der altisraelitische Fluchspruch.* (Neukirchen-Vluyn, 1969). – R: *BiOr* 30, 452-453 (R. Frankena).

Séd, N.: "Les traditions secrètes et les disciples de Rabban Yoḥanan ben Zakkaï", *RHR* 184/1, 49-66.

van Selms, A.: "Temporary Henotheism", *Festschrift de Liagre Böhl* (q. v. sub I-7), 341-348.

Sendrail, M.: "Le sens de la maladie dans l'antiquité hébraïque", *BAGB* 4, No. 1, 85-101.

Seybold, K.: "Das Herscherbild des Bileamorakels. Num. 24, 15-19", *Theologische Zeitschrift* 29/1, 1-19.

Sherwin, B. L.: "Bar-Mizvah", *Judaism* 22/1, 53-65.

Silberg, Moshe: *Talmudic Law and the Modern State.* Translated by Ben-Zion Bokser. Edited by Marvin S. Wiener. (New York, Burning Bush Press). xiii, 224 p.

Silver, A. M.: "The Second Day Yom Tov of Galut in Israel", *Tradition* 13/3, 124-136.

Singer, S. A.: "Moses: Faith and Law", *Judaism* 22, 38-44.

Snaith, N.: "A Note on Numbers XVIII 9", *Vetus Testamentum* 23, No. 3, 373-375. (*min-hāēš* to read *min-hā išeh*!)

Soler, J.: "Sémiotique de la nourriture dans la Bible", *AESC* 28/4, 943-955.

Stemberger, Günter: "Zur Auferstehungslehre in der rabbinischen Literatur", *Kairos* 15, Heft 3-4, 238-266.

Stendebach, F. J.: "Das Verbot des Knochenzerbrechens bei den Semiten", *BibZ* 17/1, 29-38, Bibliographie (1 S.) (With reference to Exod. 12: 46).

Stolz, F.: "Aspekte religiöser und sozialer Ordnung im alten Israel. Zusammenhang religiöser und sozialer Ordnung", *ZEE* 17/3, 145-159.

Towner, W. S.: "Form-Criticism of Rabbinic Literature", *JoJeS* 24/2, 101-118.

Towner, W. S.: *The rabbinic 'enumeration of scriptural examples'.* A study of a rabbinic pattern of discourse with special reference to *Makhilta d'R. Ishmael.* (Leiden, E. J. Brill). xii, 276 p. = Studia Post-Biblica, XXII.

Tropper, D.: "Bet Din Shel Kohanim", *The Jewish Quarterly Review* 63, No. 3, 204-221.

Vogels, W.: "Covenants between Israel and the Nations", *Eglise et Théologie* 4/2, 171-196.

Weinberg, J. P.: "Das *beit'ābōt* im 6.-4. Jh. v. u. Z.", *Vetus Testamentum* 23, No. 4, 400-414.

Weinfeld, M.: *Deuteronomy and the Deuteronomic School*, (Oxford, Clarendon Press, 1972). xviii, 467 p. R: – *JQR* 63/3, 272-276 (S. C. Reif). *BiOr* 30, 86-87 (J. H. Hospers).

Weinfeld, M.: "To the Origin of Apodictic Law in Ancient Israel", *Tarbiz* 41/4, 349-360 (in Hebrew, with a summary in English).

Weinfeld, M.: "The Origin of the Apodictic Law. An Overlooked Source" (= The Hittite and Assyrian 'Instructions') *Vetus Testamentum* 23/1, 63-75.

Werblowsky, R. J. Zwi: "Tora als Gnade", *Kairos* 15, Heft 1-2, 156-163.

Westermann, C.: "Anthropologische und theologische Aspekte des Gebets in den Psalmen", *LitJb*, Heft 2, 83-96.

Zerbib, M.: "Conférence sur Simhat-Tora", *Vav, Revue du Dialogue* 7, no. 3, 38-43.

4. PHILOSOPHY

Altmann, A.: "Eternality of Punishment: A Theological Controversy within the Amsterdam Rabbinate in the Thirtees of the Seventeenth Century", *PAAJR* 40, 1-88.

Baer, Richard A., jr.: *Philo's Use of the Categories Male and Female.* (Leiden, 1970). – R: *OLZ* 68, 146-148 (H.-F. Weiss).

Ben-Shlomo, Y.: "L'influence de Gershom Scholem", *Ariel* no. 28, 25-28.

Blumberg, H.: "Theories of Evil in Medieval Jewish Philosophy", *HUCA* 43, 149-168.

Blumenthal, D. R.: "The Commentary of R. Hoter ben Shelomo to the Thirteen Principles of Maimonides", *DisAbIn, A* 33/7, 3755. (The author's summary of his diss., Columbia University, 1972).

Bowler, M. G.: "Rosenzweig on Judaism and Christianity: The Two Govenant Theory" *Judaism* 22/4, 475-481.

Breton, S.: "Âme spinoziste, âme néo-platonicienne", *RPhL* 71, no. 10, 210-224 (with English Summary).

Breton, S.: *Politique, religion, écriture chez Spinoza.* (Lyon, Profac), 94 p.

Brykman, G.: "Spinoza et la séparation entre les hommes", *Revue de Métaphysique et de Morale* 78/2, 174-188.

Burggraeve, R.: "Il contributo di E. Levinas al personalismo sociale", *Salesianum* 35/4, 569-599.

Carmy, S.: "Halakhan, Tradition and History", *Tradition* 13/3, 161-168. (A review article on N. Rotenstreich: *Tradition and Reality. The Impact of History on Modern Jewish Thought*, New York, 1972).

Chouchena, E.: "L'arbre de la connaissance", *Les Nouveaux Cahiers* 8, No. 32, 36-38.

Cohen, R.: "En relisant Maïmonide: Du naturel de l'homme", *Les Nouveaux Cahiers* 8 (No. 32), 18-26.

Davidson, H.: "The Active Intellect in the *Cuzari* and Hallevi's Theory of Causality", *REJ* 131, 351-396.

Fabro, C.: "Una nuova edizione di Spinoza", *Humanitas* 28/2, 118-120.

Fischel, H. A.: *Rabbinic literature and Greco-Roman philosophy. A study of Epicurea and rhetorica in early Midrashic writings.* (Leiden, E. J. Brill). xii, 201 p. = Studia Post-Biblica, XXI.

Giuletti, G.: "Recenti Studi Spinoziani" (II), *Rivista Rosminiana di Filosofia e di Cultura* 67/1, 27-43.

Gordon, J.: "Maïmonide, Aristote ou le sens de l'histoire", *Les Nouveaux Cahiers* 8, no. 31, 22-27.

Granatstein, M.: "Theodicy and Belief", *Tradition* 13/3, 36-47.

Greenberg, G.: "Religion and History According to Samuel Hirsch", *HUCA* 43, 103-124.

Greenberg, S.: "Lifetime Education as Conceived and Practiced in the Jewish Tradition", *RelEd* 68/3, 339-347.

Greive, H.: "Jehuda Halevi und die philosophische Position des Abraham ibn Ezra", *Judaica* 29/4, 141-148.

Greive, Hermann: *Studien zum jüdischen Neuplatonismus. Die Religionsphilosophie des Abraham Ibn Ezra.* (Berlin, W. de Gruyter). v, 225 p., Bibliographie (17 p.). = Studia Judaica. Forschungen zur Wissenschaft des Judentums, 7.

Günther, H.: "Walter Benjamin und die Theologie", *Stimmen der Zeit* 191, Heft 1, 33-46.

Hendel, R. J.: "Maimonides' Attitude towards Sacrifices", *Tradition* 13-14/4-1, 163-179.

Hilliard, F. H.: "A Re-examination of Buber's Address on Education", *BJES* 21, No. 1, 40-49.

Kahn, J. G.: " 'Connais-toi toi-même' à la manière de Philon", *RHPhR* 53, no. 3-4, 293-307, 1 pl.

Kaplan, E. K.: "Language and Reality in Abraham J. Heschel's Philosophy of Religion", *JAAR* 41/1, 94-113.

Kaplan, F.: "Le salut par l'obéissance et la nécessité de la révélation chez Spinoza", *RMM* 78/1, 1-17.

Kaplan, L.: "The Religious Philosophy of Rabbi Joselh Solovetchik", *Tradition* 14, No. 2, 43-64.

Lewis, C.: "From Adam's Serpent to Abraham's Ram", *Judaism* 22, No. 4, 392-396.

Mack, B. L.: *Logos und Sophia. Untersuchungen zur Weisheitstheologie im hellenistischen Judentum.* (Göttingen, Vandenhoeck & Ruprecht). 22 S. = Studien zur Umwelt des Neuen Testaments, 10.

Mancini, I.: "Ernst Bloch. II. Filosofia della religione", *RFNS* 65, no. 4, 661-710.

Mancini, I.: "Ernst Bloch. I. Teoria della speranza", *RFNS* 65, no. 3, 423-470.

Mesch, B.: "Joseph ibn Caspi, Fourteenth Century Philosopher and Exegete", *DisAbIn, A* 33/7, 3761. (The author's summary of his diss., Brandeis University, 1972).

Mijušković, B.: "Spinoza's Ontological Proof", *Sophia* 12/1, 17-24.

Mühlenberg, E.: "Das Proble der Offenbarung in Philo von Alexandrien", *ZNTW* 64, No. 1-2, 1-18.

Munk, E.: "Chema Israël", *Les Nouveaux Cahiers* 8, No. 32, 27-30.

Nikiprowetzky, V.: "L'exégèse de Philon d'Alexandrie" *RHPhR* 53/3-4, 309-329. 309-329.

Peli, P.: "Blessings: The Gateway to Prayer", *Tradition* 14/2, 65-80.

Pelli, M.: "The Impact of Deism on the Hebrew Literature of the Enlightenment in Germany", *JoJeS* 24/2, 127-146.

Petitdemange, G.: "Existenz und Offenbarung in den ersten Werken von Franz Rosenzweig", *Judaica* 30, 12-36, 71-77.

Philon d'Alexandrie: *De providentia, I-II.* Introduction, traduction et notes par M. Hadas-Lebel. (Paris, Editions du Cerf). 373 p. bibliographie (3 p.), index. = Les oeuvres de Philon d'Alexandrie, 35.

Plessner, M.: "La signification du *Kitāb Ma'ānī al-Nafs*, attribué à R. Baḥya ibn Paquda, et sa place dans l'histoire de la pensée juive", *Kirjath Sepher* 48/3, 491-498 (en Hhébreu).

Poliakov, L.: "Freud e Mosè", *Comunità* 27 (170), 303-321.

Reines, A. J.: "Maimonides' Concept of Providence and Theodicy", *Hebrew Union College Annual* 43, 169-206.

Rosenzweig, F.: "Les bâtisseurs. A propos de la Loi", *Les Nouveaux Cahiers* 8, No. 32, 44-52.

Roshwald, M.: "De l'idée de Terre Promise", *Diogène*, No. 82, 59-89.

Roth, S.: "Towards a Definition of Humility", Tradition 13-14, No. 4-1, 5-22.

Sacks, J.: "Alienation and Faith", *Tradition* 13-14, No. 4-1, 137-162.

Sandmel, S.: "The Enjoyment of Scripture: An Esthetic Approach", *Judaism* 22, No. 4, 455-467.

Schlanger, Jacques: *La Philosophie de Salomon ibn Gabirol. Etude d'un Néoplatonisme*. (Leiden, 1968). – R: *OLZ* 68, 596-599 (H. Simon).

Scholem, G.: "Der Name Gottes und die Sprachtheorie der Kabbala", *Eranos-Jahrbuch* 39, 243-299.

Seckinger, D. S.: "Martin Buber and the One-Sided Dialogical Relation", *Journal of Thought* 8/4, 295-301.

Sermoneta, J. B.: *Un glossario filosofico ebraico-italiano del XIIIe secolo*, (Roma, Ateneo, 1969). 565 p. – R: *Kirjath Sepher* 48/3, 438-444 (S. Rosenberg – L. Cuomo).

Simon, I.: "Les serments médicaux et les prières médicales dans la tradition hébraïque", *RHMH*, No. 101, 15-18; No. 102, 15-18.

Solomon, A.: "Eros-Thanatos: A Modification of Freudian Instinct Theory in the Light of Torah Teachings", *Tradition* 14, No. 2, 90-102, Bibliography (2 p.).

Soss, N. M.: "Old Testament Law and Economic Society", *Journal of the History of Ideas* 34/3, 323-344.

Spero, S.: "Is the God of Maimonides Truly Unknowable?", *Judaism* 22, No. 1, 66-78.

Stitskin, L. D.: "From the Pages of Tradition: Religion and Philosophy Lead to the Truth. Letter of Maimonides to his Disciple Joseph Ben Judah Ibn Aknin", *Tradition* 13/3, 154-160.

Stitskin, L. D.: "Maimonides' Letter on Apostacy. The Advent of the Messiah and Shivat Zion (Return to Zion)", *Tradition* 14, No. 2, 103-112.

Thomas, C. F.: "Philosophy and Theology" (= A. Heschel), *Theology Today* 30, No. 3m 272-277.

Vajda, G.: "Le 'Kalām' dans la pensée religieuse juive du Moyen Age", *RHR* 183, no. 2, 143-160.

Vajda, G.: "Le problème de la souffrance gratuite selon Yūṣuf al-Basīr", *REJ* 131, 269-322.

Vermes, P.: "Buber's Understanding of the Divine Name Related to Bible, Targum and Midrasch", *JoJeS* 24/2, 147-166.

Weaver, M.: "πνεῦμα in Philo of Alexandria", *DisAbIn, A* 33, No. 11, 6445. (The author's summary of his Diss., Univ. of Notre Dame, 1973).

Zac, S.: "Essence du judaisme et liberté de conscience", *Les Nouveaux Cahiers* no. 34, 14-299.

Zlotnick, D.: "The Commentary of Rabbi Abraham Azulai to the Mishnah", *PAAJR* 40, 147-168.

5. HISTORY AND GENERAL

Ackroyd,Peter R.: *Exile and Restoration. A Study of Hebrew Thought of the Sixth Century B.C.* (London, 1968). – R: *OLZ* 68, 141-142 (G. Wallis).

Ahlström, G. W.: "Syncretism and Religious Parties in Ancient Israel", *History of Religions* 12/4, 372-377.

Albright, W. F.: "From the Patriarchs to Moses. I. From Abraham to Joseph", *BibArch* 36/1, 5-33.

Albright, W. F.: "From the Patriarchs to Moses. II. Moses out of Egypt", *BibArch* 36/2, 48-76.

Allony, N.: "The Reaction of Moses ibn Ezra (= MIE) to the Arabiyya ('Arabism')", in: *XXIXe Congrès International des Orientalistes, Résumés des Communications*, Sections 1-5. (Paris, Y. Hervouet), p. 50.

Asmussen, J. P.: *Studies in judeo-Persian Literature*. Translated from the Danish. (Leiden, E. J. Brill). vii, 135 p., 5 facs. in the text, 20 pl. = Studia Post-Biblica, XXIV.

Attai, R.: *Les juifs d'Afrique du Nord. Bibliographie*. (Leiden, E. J. Brill). xxxiv, 248 p., xii p.

Avi-Yona, M.: "Recherches des synagogues", *Ariel* no. 28, 29-43.

Baron, Salo W.: *A Social and Religious History of the Jews*. Volume XV: *Late Middle Ages and Era of European Expansion (1200-1650). Resettlement and Exploration*. (London, American University Publishers Group). 550 p.

Barr, J.: "Ugaritic and Hebrew *šbm*", *Journal of Semitic Studies* 18/1, 17-39.

Beem, H.: "Het Sefer Zikaron van Harlingen en zijn achtergrond" (The Sefer Zikaron of Harlingen and its Background), *StuRos* 7, 186-191.

Bentwich, J. S.: "The State of Religion in Israel", *Judaism* 22, No. 2, 151-156.

Berman, M.: "Rabbi Edward Nathan Calish and the Debate Over Zionism in Richmond, Virginia", *AJHQ* 62/3, 295-305.

Blidstein, G. J.: "A Note on the Function of 'The Law of the Kingdom is Law' in the Medieval Jewish Community", *JJS* 15, 213-219.

Boecker, Hans Jochen: *Die Beurteilung der Anfänge des Königtums in den deuteronomistischen Abschnitten des 1. Samuelbuches*. (Neukirchen-Vluyn, 1969). – R: *OLZ* 68, 360-362 (G. Wallis).

Bokser, B. Z.: "Justin Martyr and the Jews", *JQR* 64, 97-122.

Busink, Th. A.: *Der Tempel von Jerusalem von Salomo bis Herodes. Eine Archäologisch-Historische Studie unter Berücksichtigung des Westsemitischen Tempelbaus*. (Leiden, 1970). – R: *BiOr* 30, 79-84 (André Parrot).

Byatt, A.: "Josephus and Population Numbers in First Century Palestine" *PEQ* 105, No. 1, 51-60.

Cantera, J.: "Notas sobre el judeoespañol de Oriente", *Filologia Moderna* 13 (no. 46-47), 105-115.

Cantera Burgos, F. – C. Carrete Parrondo: "Las juderias medievales en la provincia de Guadalajara", *Sefarad* 33/1, 3-44, 4 tav.

Coogan, M. D.: "Patterns in Jewish Personal Names in the Babylonian Diaspora", *JSJ* 4, 183-191.

Cross, Frank M.: *Canaanite Myth and Hebrew Epic. Essays in the History of the Religion of Israel.* (Cambridge, Mass., Harvard University Press). xviii, 376 p.

Des Places, E.: "Le 'Dieu incertain' des Juifs", *Journal des Savants* no. 4, 289-294.

Farine, A.: "Charity and Study Societies in Europe of the Sixteenth-Eighteenth Centuries", *JQR* 64, 16-47, 164-175.

Fisher, A.: "The Outsider and Orthodox Judaism", *Tradition* 13, No. 3, 48-66.

Fohrer, G.: *History of Israelite Religion.* Translated by David E. Green. (London, S.P.C.K.) 416 p. – R: *BiOr* 30, 447 (C. van Leeuwen).

Friedemann, Ch.: "La Loi dans la pensée d'Isaac (1883-1946)", *REJ* 131, 127-159.

Fritz, V.: "Zur Erwähnung des Tempels in einem Ostrakon von Arad", *Die Welt des Orients* 7/1, 137-140.

Garte, E.: "The Theme of Resurrection in the Dura-Europos Synagogue Paintings", *JQR* 64, 1-15, 14 fig.

Golb, N.: "A Judeo-Arabic Court Document of Syracuse A. D. 1020", *JNES* 32, No. 1-2, 105-123.

Goldman, B.: *The Sacred Portal: A Primary Symbol in Ancient Judaic Art* (Detroit, 1966). – R: *JQR* 64/2, 176-179 (J. Gutmann).

Goldstein, I.: "Interfaith Relations in Israel", *Judaism* 22, No. 2, 202-209.

Gomez-Menor Fuentes, J.: "Un judio converso de 1498: Diego Gómez de Toledo (Samuel abolafia) y su proceso inquisitorial", *Sefarad* 33/1, 45-110, 1 tav.

Goodblatt, D. M.: "Rabbinic Academic Institutions in Sasanian Babylonia", *DisAbIn, A* 33/8, 4288. (The author's summary of his diss., Brown University, 1972).

Greenberg, G.: "Zur Verteidigung Formstechers", *Judaica* 29/1, 24-35, Bibliographie (1 S.)

Greenberg, G.: "Samuel Hirsch's American Judaism", *AJHQ* 62/4, 362-382.

Hauser, A. J.: "A Study of Representative approaches to the Historical Question of Saul's Rise to the Monarchy", *DisAbIn A* 33/12, 7014. (The Author's summary of his diss., University of Iowa, 1972).

Hengel, Martin: *Judentum und Hellenismus. Studien zu ihrer Begegnung unter besonderer berücksichtigung Palästinas.* (Tübingen, J. C. B. Mohr). xi, 693 S. = Wissenschaftliche Untersuchungen zum Neuen Testament, 10.

Herrmann, Siegfried: *Geschichte Israels in alttestamentlicher Zeit.* (München, Chr. Kaiser). 426 S., 8 Karten.

Janssen, Enno: *Das Gottesvolk und seine Geschichte. Geschichtsbild und Selbstverständnis im palästinensischen Schrifttum von Jesus ben Sirach bis Jehuda ha-Nasi.* (Neukirchen-Vluyn, 1971). – R: *BiOr* 30, 271-272 (Gerhard F. Hasel).

Kreissig, Heinz: *Die sozialökonomische Situation in Juda zur Achämenidenzeit.* (Berlin, Akademie-Verlag). 132 S. = Schriften zur Geschichte und Kultur des Alten Orients, 7.

Landau, L.: "Un mythe tenace: la 'conspiration juive' ", *NouCa* no. 34, 34-42.

Leivestad, R.: "Das Dogma von der prophetenlosen Zeit", *New Testament Studies* 19/3, 288-299.

Lemaire, A.: "Asriel, *šr'l*, Israel et l'origine de confédération israélite", *VeTes* 23/2, 239-243.

Lemaire, A.: "Note épigraphique sur la pseudo-attestation du mois ṣḥ", *Vetus Testamentum* 23/2, 243-245.

Lifshitz, B.: "L'ancienne synagogue de Tibériade, sa mosaïque et ses inscriptions", *JSJ* 4, 43-55.

Lipiński, E.: "L'étymologie de 'Juda' ", *Vetus Testamentum* 23, no. 3, 380-381.

Long, Burke O.: "The Effect of Divination upon Israelite Literature", *JBL* 92, 489-497.

Losier, M. A.: "Witness in Israel of the Hebrew Scriptures in the Context of the Ancient Near East", *DisAbIn, A* 33/11, 6441. (The author's summary of his diss., University of Notre Dame, 1973).

Maier, Johann: *Geschichte der jüdischen Religion.* Von der Zeit Alexander des Grossen bis zur Aufklärung mit einem Ausblick auf das 19./20. Jahrhundert. (Berlin, W. de Gruyter, 1972). xix, 641 S. – R: *Anthropos* 68, 654-655 (Karl Hoheisel). *JSJ* 4, 84-86 (J. M. Baumgarten).

Maler, B.: "¿Que traduccion del tercer mandamiento utilizo Maestre Roldán?", *Sefarad* 33/1, 145-151.

Marmur, Dow (ed.): *Reform Judaism. Essays on Reform Judaism in Britain.* Dedicated to Rabbi Werner Van der Zyl. (London, Reform Synagogues of Great Britain). xvii. 257 p., 1 front.

Marshall, I. H.: "The Jewish Dispersion in New Testament Times", *Faith and Thought* 100/3, 237-258, bibliography.

Mayes, A. D. H.: "Israel in the Pre-Monarchy Period", *Vetus Testamentum* 23, No. 2, 151-170.

Mendenhall, George E.: *The Tenth Generation. The Origins of the Biblical Tradition.*) Baltimore, The John Hopkins University Press). xviii, 248 p. – R: *Interpretation* 27, 469-474 (W. L. Holladay).

Middendorp, Th.: *Die Stellung Jesu Ben Siras zwischen Judentum und Hellenismus.* (Leiden, E. J. Brill). xvi, 183 p.

de Moor, J. C.: *New Year with Cannanites and Israelites.* – R: *Syria* 49, 471-472 (A. Caquot). *CBQ* 35, 257 (C. Stuhlmueller). *JAOS* 93, 589-591 (D. Marcus).

Muffs, Yochanan: *Studies in the Aramaic Legal Papyri from Elephantine.* (New York, KTAV Publ. Co.) xi, 311 p. = Studia et Documenta ad iura Orientis Antiqui pertinentia, VIII.

Nai Rnee, S.: "Jewish Assimilation: The Case of Chinese Jews", *Comparative Studies in Society and History* 15/1, 115-126.

Nedava, J.: "Who were the 'Biryoni' ", *JQR* 63, 317-322.

Nemoy, L.: "Ibn Kammūnah's Treatise on the Differences between the Rabbinites and the Karaites", *JQR* 63/3, 222-246 (cont.)

Neusner, J.: "Babylonian Jewry and Shapur II's Persecution of Christianity from 339 to 379 A.D.", *HUCA* 43, 77-102, bibliography (4 p.)

Neusner, J.: *Eliezer ben Hyrcanus. The tradition and the man.* Part 1: *The tradition.* Part 2: *Analysis of the tradition The man.* (Leiden, E. J. Brill). xix, 500 p., and xiii, 528 p. = Studies in Judaism and Late Antiquity, III and IV.

Neusner, J.: " 'Pḫarisaic-Rabbinic' Judaism: a clarification", *History of Religions* 12/3, 250-270.

Neusner, J.: "The Written Tradition in the Pre-Rabbinic Period", *JSJ* 4, 56-65.

Noack, Bent: *Spätjudentum und Heilsgeschichte.* (Stuttgart, 1971). – R: *OLZ* 68, 263-264 (W. Beltz).

Noah, Mordecal M. (ed. and tr.): *The Book of Yashar (Sefer Ha-Yashar).* Translated from the Hebrew. (New York, Hermon Press). xxiv, 267 p.

Ohata, K.: "Ashtarte Belief in Ancient Israel" (in Japanese), *Journal of Religious Studies* 46 (No. 213), 1-16 (with a summary in English).

Orrieux, C.: "Israël et l'Orient ancien", *Cahiers d'Histoire* 18/1, 61-68. (Bulletin bibliographique).

Pelli, M.: "Isaac Satanow's 'Mishlei Asaf', as Reflecting the Ideology of the German Hebrew Haskalah", *ZRGG* 25, 225-242.

Redford, D. B.: "Studies in Relations between Palestine and Egypt during the First Millenium B. C. II. The Twenty-Second Dynasty", *JAOS* 93/1, 3-17.

Rosenbloom, J. R.: "Social Science Concepts of Modernization and Biblical History: The Development of the Israelite Monarchy", *JAAR* 40/4, 437-444.

Roshwald, M.: "Marginal Jewish Sects in Israel" (II), *IJMMES* 4, No. 3, 328-354.

Schmidt, Johann Michael: *Die jüdische Apokalyptik. Die Geschichte ihrer Erforschung von den Anfängen bis zu den Textfunden von Qumran.* (Neukirchen-Vluyn, 1969). – R: *OLZ* 68, 476-478 (G. Delling).

Schmitt, Armin: *Entrückung – Aufnahme – Himmelfaht. Untersuchungen zu einem Vorstellungsbereich im Alten Testament.* (Stuttgart, Kathol. Bibelwerk). xiv, 378 S. = Forschungen zur Bibel, 10.

Schreckenberg, Heinz: *Die Flavius-Josephus Tradition in Antike und Mittelalter.* (Leiden, 1972). – R: *BiOr* 30, 273-274 (M. Delcor).

Ségré, A.: "Le judaïsme et la sécularisation", *SIDJCh* 6/2, 4-18.

Shatzmiller, J.: *Recherches sur la communauté juive de Manosque au Moyen Age, 1241-1329.* Préface de Georges Duby. (Paris-La Haye, Mouton). 183 p., bibliographie (3 p.) = Etudes juives, XV.

Siegert, F.: "Gottesfürchtige und Sympathisanten", *JSJ* 4, 109-164.

Silver, D. J.: "Moses and the Hungry Birds", *JQR* 64/2, 123-153.

in der Smitten, Wilhelm Th.: "Zur jüdischen Königsideologie während des Hellenismus", *BiOr* XXX, No. 1-2, 10-13.

Soggin, J. Alberto: *Das Königtum in Israel. Ursprünge, Spannungen, Entwicklung.* (Berlin, 1967). – R: *OLZ* 68, 144-145 (H.-J. Zobel).

Solodukho, Y. A.: *Soviet Views of Talmudic Judaism.* Five papers in English translation. Edited with a commentary by J. Neusner. (Leiden, E. J. Brill). xiv, 110 p. = Studies in Judaism and Late Antiquity, II.

Steinsalz, A.: "Religion in the State of Israel", *Judaism* 22, No. 2, 140-150.

Tamani, G.: "La biblioteca ebraica del cardinal Domenico Grimani", in: *XXIXe Congrès International des Orientalistes. Résumés des Communications*, Sections 1-5. (Paris, Y. Hervouet), p. 55.

Treu, K.: "Die Bedeutung des Griechischen für die Juden im römischen Reich", *Kairos* XV/1-2, 123-144.

Ussishkin, D.: "King Solomon's Palaces", *BibArch* 36/3, 78-105.

Vajda, Georges: *Deux commentaires Karaïtes sur l'Ecclésiaste.* (Leiden, 1971). – R: *BiOr* 30, 269-270 (M. Delcor).

Vajda, G.: "Les études hébraïques", *Journal Asiatique* 261, 83-87.

Vattioni, F.: "L'inscription 177 de Beth She'arim et le livre de Néhémie", *Revue Biblique* 80/2, 261-263.

de Vaux, R.: *Histoire ancienne d'Israël.* Vol. 2: *La période de Juges.* Préface de R. Tournay. (Paris, Librairie Lecoffre). 159 p. = Etudes Bibliques.

de Vaux, R.: *Histoire ancienne d'Israël. Des origines à l'installation en Canaan.* (Paris, Gabalda, 1971). 674 p. – R: *Vetus Testamentum* 23/1, 117-126 (S. Herrmann). *Syria* 49, 461-464 (A. P.). *JBL* 92, 285-287 (A. E. Glock). *Revue Bibli-*

que 80, 82-92 (A. Malamat). *CBQ* 35, 417-420 (E. J. Ciuba). *BiOr* 30, 444-446 (M. Delcor).

Vermes, Geza: "Ḥanina ben Dosa. A Controversial Galilean Saint from the First Century of the Christian Era" (II), *JoJeS* 24, 51-64.

Weinberg, J. P.: "The Palestinian civic- and temple community of the 6th – 4th centuries B.C.", *Drevnii Vostok* (Erevan), 149-161. (In Russian, with an English summary on p. 234).

Weippert, H.: "Das geographische System der Stämme Israels", *Vetus Testamentum* 23, No. 1, 76-89.

Weippert, M.: "Fragen des israelitischen Geschichtsbewusstseins", *Vetus Testamentum* 23/4, 415-442.

Weippert, Manfred: "Menahem von Israel und seine Zeitgenossen in einer Steleninschrift des Assyrischen Königs Tiglathpileser III aus dem Iran", *ZDPV* 89, 26-83, 1 Abb.

Witakowski, Witold: "Religion of the Jewish Colony in Elephantine", *Euhemer* XVII/2 (88), 23-34.

Yadin, Yigael: *Bar Kochba, de herontdekking van de legendarische held van de laatste joodse opstand tegen het Romeinse Keizerrijk*. Translated into Dutch from the English edition by R. J. Demaree. (Bussum, 1971). – R: *BiOr* 30, 447-448 (Siegfried H. Horn),

Yaron, Z.: "Redemption: A Contemporary Jewish Understanding", *EcRev* 25/2, 169-179.

Zafrani, H.: "Le Judaïsme marocain et sa culture", *Les Nouveaux Cahiers* 8, No. 32, 53-58.

Zeitlin, S.: "The Plague of Pseudo-Rabbinic Scholarship", *The Jewish Quarterly Review* 63/3, 187-203.

Zeron, A.: "Einige Bemerkungen zu M. F. Collins: 'The Hidden Vessels in Samaritan Tradition' " *JSJ* 4, 165-168.

Zobel, H.-J.: "Das Selbstverständnis Israels nach dem Alten Testament", *ZATW* 85/3, 281-294.

V. CHRISTIANITY

1. ORIGINS

Abel, E. L.: "Jewish-Christian Controversy in the Second and Third Centuries A.D.", *Judaica* 29/3, 112-125.

Aletti, J. N.: "D'une écriture à l'autre. Analyse structurale d'un passage d'Origène: Commentaire sur Jean, livre II, § 13-21", *RchSR* 61/1, 27-47 (with a summary in English).

Bagatti, B.: *Excavations in Nazareth*. Vol. I. *From the Beginning till the XII Century*. Translated from the Italian by E. Hoade. (Jerusalem, 1969). – R: *BiOr* 30, 262-263 (Siegfried H. Horn).

Barbaglio, G.: "Esperienza storica ed esperienza di fede: interpretazione biblica", *Humanitas* 28/3, 167-177.

Barnes, T. D.: "Porphyry Against the Christians: Date and the Attribution of Fragments", *JThS* 24/2, 424-442.

Barrett, C. K.: *A Commentary on the Second Epistle to the Corinthians*. (London, A. & C. Black). xvi, 354 p. = Black's New Testament Commentaries.

Barth, G.: "Zwei vernachlässigte Gesichtspunkte zum Verständnis der Taufe im Neuen Testament", *ZThK* 70/2, 137-161.

Bartlett, D. L.: "Exorcism Stories in the Gospel of Marc", *DisAbIn A* 33/12, 7010. (The author's summary of his diss., Yale University, 1972).

Bartsch, H.-W.: "La critique de l'idéologie dans l'Evangile relevée dans le récit de la Passion", *ArFi* (= Demitizzazione e Ideologia, Padova), 219-240.

Baumbach, G.: "Die Stellung Jesu im Judentum seiner Zeit", *FZPhTh* 23, Heft 3, 285-305.

Ben-Chorin, S.: "Hoffnungskraft und Glaube in Judentum und biblischer Prophetie", *Evangelische Theologie* 33/1, 103-112.

Berger, K.: " 'Gnade' im frühen Christentum. Eine traditionsgeschichtliche und literatursoziologische Fragestellung", *NeTT* 27, 1-25.

Berger, K.: "Materialien zu Form und Ueberlieferungsgeschichte neutestamentlicher Gleichnisse", *Novum Testamentum* 15/1, 1-37.

Betz, Otto: "Neues Testament, Spätjudentum und Qumran", in: U. Mann (Hrsg.): *Theologie und Religionswissenschaft* (Darmstadt, Wissenschaftliche Buchgesellschaft) 300-317.

Beutler, J.: "Glaube und Zeugnis im Johannesevangelium", *Bijdragen* 34/1, 60-68.

Boismard, M.-E.: "Aenon, près de Salem (*Jean*, III, 23)", *Revue Biblique* 80/2, 218-229.

Bornkamm, G.: *Qui est Jésus de Nazareth?* Traduit de l'allemand. (Paris, Seuil). 254 p., bibliographie.

Bouwman, G.: "La Samarie chez Luc, Actes des Apôtres", *Bijdragen* 34/1, 40-59. (Deutsche Zusammenfassung).

Bouyer, L.: "Liturgie juive et liturgie chrétienne", *Istina* 17/2, 132-146.

Bowker, John: *Jesus and the Pharisees*. (London, Cambridge University Press). xi, 192 p. (Greek and Semitic source material in translation).

Bring, Ragnar: *Christus und das Gesetz. Die Bedeutung des Gesetzes des Alten Testaments nach Paulus und seun Glauben an Christus*. (Leiden, 1969). – R: *BiOr* 30, 93-94 (Hans Bardtke).

Brown, S. K.: "James: A religio-Historical Study of the Relation between Jewish, Gnostic and Catholic Christianity in the Early Period through an Investigation of the Traditions about James the Lord's Brother", *DisAbIn, A* 33/7, 3755-3756. (The author's summary of his diss., Brown University, 1972).

Brox, N.: "*Sōtēria* and *Salus*. Heilsvorstellungen in der Alten Kirche", *EvTh* 33, Heft 3, 253-279.

Brox, Norbert: "Zum Problemstand in der Erforschung der altchristlichen Pseud-epigraphie", *Kairos* XV, 10-23.

Brunner, Hellmut: "Eine altägyptische Idealbiographie in christlichem Gewande", *ZÄSA* 99, No. 2, 88-94.

Bultmann, R.: *L'Histoire de la Tradition Synoptique*, suivie du Complément de 1971. (Paris, Editions du Seuil). 724 p., index.

von Campenhausen, H. F.: "Einheit und Einigkeit in der Alten Kirche", *EvTh* 33, Heft 3, 280-293.

Castro, S.: "Los tiempos sagrados en la Biblia", *Revista de Espiritualidad* 32, no. 126, 7-35.

Cavalletti, S.: "Liturgie juive, liturgie chrétienne", *SIDJC* VI/1, 4-25.

Clarke, G. W.: "Double-Trials in the Persecution of Decius", *Historia* 22/4, 650-663.

Clowney, E. P.: "The Final Temple", *The Westminster Theological Journal* 35, No. 2, 156-189.

Colaclides, P.: "Acts 17, 28 A and Bacchae 506", *Vigiliae Christianae* 27, No. 3, 161-164.

Colella, P.: "Les abréviations ṭ et *HR*", *Revue Biblique* 80/4, 547-558.

Copeland, E. L.: "*Nomos* as a Medium of Revelation, Paralleling *Logos*, in Ante-Nicene Christianity", *StuTh* 27/1, 51-61.

Cullmann, O.: "Salvezza in Cristo. Problema e promessa", *Humanitas* (Brescia) XXVIII/1, 11-31.

Cutrone, E. J.: "The Anaphora of the Apostles: Implications of the Mar Eša'ya Text", *ThSt* 34/4, 624-642.

Daoust, J.: "Pline le jeune et les chrétiens du Pont-Bithynie", *Bible et Terre Sainte*, No. 152, 20-22.

Dautzenberg, G.: "Der Glaube im Hebräerbrief", *Biblische Zeitschrift* 17, Heft 2, 161-177.

Dauvillier, J.: "La parabole du Bon Pasteur et les Droits de l'Antiquité", *L'Année Canonique* 17, 269-278.

Davids, Adelbert: "Irrtum und Häresie. *l Clem. – Ignatius von Antiochien – Justinus*", *Kairos* 15, Heft 3-4, 165-187.

Delobel, J.: "La rédaction de Lc., IV, 14-16a et le *Bericht vom Anfang*", in: *L'Evangile de Luc. Problèmes littéraires et théologiques. Mémorial Lucien Cerfaux.* (Gembloux, J. Duculot), pp. 203-223.

Denaux, A.: "L'hypocrisie des Pharisiens et le dessein de Dieu. Analyse de Lc., XIII, 31-33", in: *L'Evangile de Luc. Problèmes littéraires et théologiques. Mémorial Lucien Cerfaux.* (Gembloux, J. Duculot), pp. 245-285.

Dörrie, Heinrich: "L. Kalbenos Tauros. Das Persönlichkeitsbild eines platonischen Philosophen um die Mitte des 2. Jhs. n. Chr.", *Kairos* XV, 24-35.

Duchatelez, K.: "La 'condescendance' divine et l'histoire du salut", *NRTh* 95, No. 6, 593-621.

Duchatelez, K.: "Le principe de l'économie paptismale dans l'antiquité chrétienne", *Istina* 17/3, 327-358.

Dulaey, M.: "Le symbole de la baguette dans l'art paléochrétien", *REAg* 19, No. 1-2, 3-38, 4 pl.

Duplacy, J.: "p75 (Pap. Bodmer XIV-XV) et les formes les plus anciennes du texte de Luc", in: *L'Evangile de Luc. Problèmes littéraires et théologiques. Mémorial Lucien Cerfaux.* (Gembloux, J. Duculot), pp. 111-128.

Dupont, J.: "Les discours de Pierre dans les Actes et le chapitre XXIV de l'Evangile de Luc", in: *L'Evangile de Luc. Problèmes littéraires et théologiques. Mémorial Lucien Cerfaux.* (Gembloux, J. Duculot), pp. 329-374.

Durable, A. M.: "Jesus d'après Flavius Joséphe", *Bible et Terre-Sainte*, no. 154, 22-23.

Emerton, J. A.: "The Problem of Vernacular Hebrew in the First Century A.D. and the Language of Jesus", *JThS* 24/1, 1-23, bibliography (2 p.)

Engemann, J.: "Anmerkungen zu spätantiken Geräten des Alltagslebens mit christlichen Bildern, Symbolen und Inschriften", *JACh* 15, 154-173, 11 Taf.

Eno, R. B.: "Origen and the Church of Rome", *The American Ecclesiastical Review* 167/1, 41-50.

Ferwerda, R.: "Le serpent, le noeud d'Hercule et le caducée d'Hermès. Sur un passage orphique chez Athénagore", *Numen* 20/2, 104-115.

Flora, J. R.: "A Critical Analysis of Walter Bauer's Theory of Early Christian Orthodoxy and Heresy", *DisAbIn, A* 33/9, 5276. (The author's summary of his diss., The Southern Baptist Theological Seminary, 1972).

Francke, J.: *Van sabbat naar zondag. De rustdag in Oud en Nieuw Testament.* (Amsterdam, Ton Bolland). 210 p.

Frend, W. H. C.: *Martydom and Persecution in the Early Church. A Study of a Conflict from the Maccabees to Donatus.* (Oxford, 1965). – R: *Gnomon* 45/7, 691-697 (C. Andresen).

Frend, W. H. C.: "The Old Testament in the Age of the Greek Apologists A.D. 130-180", *SJTh* 26/2, 128-150.

Frey, Louis: *Analyse ordinale des évangiles synoptiques.* (La Haye, Mouton). 384 p. = Mathématiques et sciences de l'homme, XI.

Galvin, R. J.: "Addai and Mari revisited: the State of the Question", *EphLit* 87/4-5, 383-414.

George, A.: "Le sens de la mort de Jésus pour Luc", *Revue Biblique* 80/2, 186-217.

Geudtner, O.: *Die Seelenlehre der chaldäischen Orakel.* (Meisenheim am Glan, Hain-Verlag, 1971). viii, 78 S. – R: *Gnomon* 45/3, 236-240 (M. Baltes)

Grassi, J. A.: "Underground Christians in the Earliest Church", *The American Ecclesiastical Review* 167/1, 11-19.

Grillmeier, A.: *Le Christ dans la tradition chrétienne. De l'âge apostolique à Chalcédoine (451).* (Paris, Ed. dy Cerf). 624 p., bibliographie (8 p.) = Coll. Cogitatio Fidei, 72.

Guillet, J.: "Jésus-Christ, prêtre et prophète", *Studia Missionalia* 22, 331-344.

Gunther, J. J.: *St. Paul's opponents and their background. A. study of apocalyptic and Jewish sectarian teachings.* (Leiden, E. J. Brill). x, 323 p. (= Novum Testamentum, Supplem. XXXV).

Gutmann, J.: "Les origines de l'art chrétien seraient-elles juives?", *SIDJC* VI, no. 1, 35-37.

Güttgemanns, E.: "Narrative Analyse synoptischer Texte", *Linguistica Biblica*, Heft 25-26, 50-73. (English summary).

Hahn, F.: "Die Frage nach dem historischen Jesus", *TThZ* 82/4, 193-205.

Hengel, M.: "Historische Methoden und theologische Auslegung des Neuen Testaments" *KD* 19/2, 85-90.

Hinz, C.: " 'Jesus und der Sabbat' ", *Kerygma und Dogma* XIX/2, 91-108.

van der Horst, P. W.: "Macrobius and the New Testament. A Contribution to the Corpus Hellenisticum", *NoTes* 15, 220-232.

Hughes, P. E.: "Hebrews 6: 4-6 and the Peril of Apostasy", *WThJ* 35/2, 137-155.

Hurley, J. B.: "Did Paul Require Veils or the Silence of Women? A Consideration of I Cor. 11: 2-16 and I Cor. 14: 33b-36", *WThJ* 35/2, 190-220.

Kasper, W. et alii: "Die Entstehung des Auferstehungsglaubens. Diskussionbeiträge", *ThQ* 153/3, 229-283.

Kehl, A.: "Beiträge zum Verständnis einiger gnostischer und frühchristlicher Psalmen und Hymnen", *JACh* 15, 92-119.

Keresztes, P.: "The Jews, the Christians, and Emperor Domitian", *Vigiliae Christianae* 27/1, 1-28.

Kettler, Franz-Heinrich: "Funktion und Tragweite der historischen Kritik des Origenes an den Evangelien", *Kairos* 15, 36-49.

Klein, R.: *Das frühe Christentum im römischen Staat.* (Darmstadt, 1971). – R: *Klio* 55, 321-325 (R. Günther).

Kysar, R.: "The Source Analysis of the Fourth Gospel. A Growing Consensus?", *NoTes* 15/2, 134-152.

Lackner, W.: "Ein epigraphisches Zeugnis für den Praeses Ciliciae Marcianus in der Passion des Iulianos von Anazarbos", *VigXChr* 27/1, 53-55.

Lai, P. H.: "Production du sens par la foi. Autorités religieuses contestées/fondées. Analyse structurale de Matthieu 27, 57 – 28, 20", *RchSR* 61/1, 65-96 (with a summary in English).

Lamirande, E.: "Jérusalem céleste", *Dictionnaire de Spiritualité Ascétique et Mystique*, t. 8, fasc. 54-55, col. 944-958.

Lanata, G.: "Gli Atti del Processo contro il Centurione Marcello", *Byzantion* 42/2, 509-522.

Ligier, L.: "Le sacerdoce chrétien: nouveauté évangélique et sacramentalité missionnaire", *StMis* 22, 345-370.

Löning, Heinrich: *Die Saulustradition in der Apostelgeschichte.* (Münster, Verlag Aschendorff). vi, 225 S. = Neitestamentliche Abhandlungen, N. F., 9.

Lührmann, D.: "Pistis im Judentum", *ZNTW* 64, 19-38.

Luschnat, O.: "Sextus-Sprüche und Kleitarchos, der Alexanderhistoriker", *Theologia Viatorum* 11, 127-142.

Marichal, R.: Autour des graffiti du Paedagogium", *Revue des Etudes Latines* 50, 84-93.

Marshall, H.: "Palestinian and Hellenistic Christianity: Some Critical Comments", *NTS* 19/3, 271-287.

Mees, M.: "Ausserkanonische Parallelstellen zu den Gerichtsworten Mt. 7, 21-23; Lk. 6, 46; 12, 26-28 und ihre Bedeutung für die Formung der Jesusworte", *VetChr* 10/1, 79-102.

Mees, M.: "Petrustraditionen im Zeugnis kanonischen und ausserkanonischen Schrifttums", *Augustinianum* 13/2, 185-203.

Mellon, C.: "La parabole. Manière de parler, manière d'entendre", *RchSr* 61/1, 49-63 (with a summary in English).

Merkel, H.: *Die Widersprüche zwischen den Evangelien. Ihre polemische und apologetische Behandlung in der Alten Kirche bis zu Augustin.* (IBHR, 1971). – R: *Erasmus* 25, 15-18 (F. F. Bruce).

Merklein, H.: "Zur Tradition und Komposition von Eph 2, 14-18", *Biblische Zeitschrift* 17/1, 79-102.

Michel, Otto: "Synoptische Evangelien und johanneische Schriften", in: U. Mann (Hrsg.): *Theologie und Religionswissenschaft* (Darmstadt, Wissenschaftliche Buchgesellschaft) 286-299.

Michel, O., S. Safrand, R. Le Déaut, M. de Jonge and J. van Goudoever: *Studies on the Jewish Background of the New Testament.* (Assen, 1969). – R: *OLZ* 68, 364-366 (W. Wiefel).

Minnerath, R.: *Les Chrétiens et le monde (Ier et IIe s.).* (Paris, Lecoffre-Gabalda). xi, 352 p.

Molthagen, J.: *Der römische Staat und die Christen im zweiten und dritten Jahrhundert.* (Göttingen, Vandenhoeck & Ruprecht, 1970). 132 S. = Hypomnemata, 28. – R: *Gnomon* 45/2, 215-217 (F. Millar).

Morin, J.-A.: "Les deux derniers des Douze: Simon le Zélote et Judas Iskariôth", Revue Biblique 80/3, 332-358.

Mourlon Beernaert, P.: "Jésus controversé. Structure et théologie de Marc 2,1 – 3,6", *NRTh* 95/2, 129-149.

Müller, K.: "Menschensohn und Messias. Religionsgeschichtliche Vorüberlegungen zum Menschensohnproblem in den synoptischen Evangelien", *BibZ* 17/1, 51-66.

Nakhnikian, G.: "Salvation in Plato and St. Paul: An Essay in Normative Ethics", *CJPh* II/3, 325-344.

Nedungatt, G.: "The Covenanters of the Early Syriac-Speaking Church", *OChP* 39, 191-215, 419-444.

Neirynck, F.: "La matière marcienne dans l'Evangile de Luc", in: *L'Evangile de Luc. Problèmes littéraires et théologiques. Mémorial Lucien Cerfaux.* (Gembloux, J. Duculot), pp. 157-201.

de Pablo Maroto, D.: "Pecado y santidad en la Iglesia primitiva", *Revista de Espririturalidad* 32 (127), 135-161.

Pagels, E. H.: *The Johannine Gospel in Gnostic Exegesis: Heracleon's Commen-*

tary on John. (Nashville, Tenn., Abingdon). 128 p. = SBL Monograph Series, 17.

Pesch, R.: "La rédaction lucanienne du logion des pécheurs d'hommes (Lc., V, 10 c)", in: *L'Evangile de Luc. Problèmes littéraires et théologiques. Mémorial Lucien Cerfaux*. (Gembloux, J. Duculot), pp. 225-244.

Reiling, J.: *Hermas and Christian prophecy. A study of the elevanth Mandate*. (Leiden, E. J. Brill). x, 197 p. = Novum Testamentum Supplements, XXXVII.

Renehan, R.: "Classical Greek Quotations in the New Testament", in: *The Heritage of the Early Church, Essays in Honor of G. V. Florovsky* (q. v. sub I-7), 17-46.

Reutterer, R.: "Legendenstudien um den heiligen Hippolytos", *ZKTh* 95, Heft 3, 286-310.

Revel-Neher, E.: *Présence juive dans l'iconographie paléo-chrétienne*. (L'Arche, no. 189, 1972). – R: *SIDJC* VI/1, 38-39 (J. M. Des Rochettes).

Richardson, C. C.: "A New Solution to the Quartodeciman Riddle", *The Journal of Theological Studies* 24/1, 74-84.

Robichon, M.: "Jésus et la politique", *Bible et Terre Sainte* No. 149, 19-20.

Roloff, J.: "Auf der Suche nach einem neuen Jesusbild. Tendenzen und Aspekte der gegenwärtigen Diskussion", *ThLZ* 98/8, 561-572.

Rordorf, W.: *Sabbat et dimanche dans l'Eglise ancienne*. (Neuchâtel, 1972). – R: *ThLZ* 98/10, 765-766 (W. Wiefel).

Roslon, J. W.: "La foi chrétienne antique concernant le salut selon les inscriptions funéraires", *SThV* 11/1, 109-125 (en polonais).

Rougier, L.: "La civilisation de l'Antiquité et le Christianisme", *La Pensée et les Hommes* 17/5, 143-151. (With reference to the work under the same title by Marcel Simon, published 1972).

Rougier, L.: *La genèse des dogmes chrétiens*. (Paris, A. Michel, 1972). 312 p. – R: *NRTh* 95/5, 557-559 (L. A. Richard).

Saake, H.: "Der Tractatus pneumatico-philosophicus des Origenes in *Peri archōn* 1, 3", *Hermes* 101, 91-114.

Saake, H.: "Paulus als Ekstatiker. Pneumatologische Beobachtungen zu 2 Kor. XII 1-10", *NoTes* 15/2, 153-160.

Samain, E.: "La notion de ἀρχή dans l'oeuvre lucanienne", in: *L'Evangile de Luc. Problèmes littéraires et théologiques. Mémorial Lucien Cerfaux*. (Gembloux, J. Duculot), pp. 299-328.

Savignac, J. de: "Sur le fragon rouge d'Apocalypse XII", in: *XXIXe Congrès Intern. des Orientalistes, Résumés des Communications*, Sections 1-5, (Paris, Y. Hervouet), p. 33.

Schein, B. E.: "Our Father Abraham", *DisAbIn A* 34/1, 411. (The author's summary of his diss., Yale University, 1972).

Schmitt, A.: "Ps 16, 8-11 als Zeugnis der Auferstehung in der Apg", *Biblische Zeitschrift* 17/2, 229-248.

Schoedel, W. R.: "Christian 'Atheism' and the Peace of the Roman Empire", *Church History* 42/3, 309-319.

Schubert, Kurt: "Geschichte und Heilsgeschichte", *Kairos* XV, Heft 1-2, 89-101.

Schubert, Ursula: "Christus, Priester und König. Eine politisch-theologische Darstellungsweise in der frühchristlichen Kunst", *Kairos* 15, Heft 3-4, 201-237, 18 Abb. auf Taf.

Schwanz, P.: *Imago Dei als christologisch-anthropologisches Problem in der Geschichte der Alten Kirche von Paulus bis Clemens von Alexandrien*, 1970. – R: *ZKTh* 95/3, 340-342 (C. Beukers).

Simon, M.: "Early Christianity and Pagan Thought: Confluences and Conflicts", *RelSt* 9/4, 385-399.

Sobosan, J. G.: "The Trial of Jesus", *Journal of Ecumenical Studies* 10/1, 70-93 (with summaries in French, German, Spanish and Italian).

de Solages, B.: *La composition des évangiles de Luc et de Matthieu et leurs sources*. (Leiden, E. J. Brill). 320 p., errata slip.

Spicq, C.: "Note sur μορφή dans les papyrus et quelques inscriptions", *Revue Biblique* 80/1, 37-45.

Stöger, A.: "Das Johannesevangelium aktuell?", *Theologische – Praktische Quartalschrift* 121, 226-235.

Strauss, David Friedrich: *The Life of Jesus Critically Examined*. Edited with an Introduction by Peter C. Hodgson. (London, SCM Press). xviii, 812 p.

Strobel, A.: "Die Friedenshaltung Jesu im Zeugnis der Evangelien: christliches Ideal oder christliches Kriterium?", *ZEE* 17/2, 97-106.

Ternant, P.: "L'Esprit du Christ et l'intervention humaine dans l'envoi en mission. A l'époque néo-testamentaire", *NRTh* 95/4, 367-392.

Thümmel, H. G.: "Zur Deutung der Mosaikkarte von Madeba", *ZDPV* 89, Heft 1, 66-79.

Tielsch, E.: "Die Wende vom antiken zum christlichen Glaubensbegriff. Eine Untersuchung über die Entstehung, Entwicklung und Ablösung der antiken Glaubensvorstellung und -definition in der Zeit von Anaxagoras bis zu Augustin (500 vor bis 400 nach Chr.)", *Kant-Studien* 64/2, 159-199.

Trocme, Etienne: *Jésus de Nazareth vu par les témoins de sa vie*. (Neuchâtel, 1972). – R: *BiOr* 30, 94-95 (P. J. Cools).

van Unnik, W. C.: "Elements artistiques dans l'Evangile de Luc", in: *L'Evangile de Luc. Problèmes littéraires et théologiques. Mémorial Lucien Cerfaux*. (Gembloux, J. Duculot), pp. 129-140.

van Unnik, W. C.: "L'aphthonia de Dieu dans la littérature chrétienne primitive", *MKNAW* 36/2, 3-55 (en néerlandais).

van Unnik, W. C.: *Sparsa collecta. Collected essays.* Part 1: *Evangelia, Paulina, Acta.* (Leiden, E. J. Brill). x, 409 p. = Novum Testamentum, Supplements, XXIX.

Vawter, B.: "Le développement de l'expression de la foi dans la communauté en prière dans le Nouveau Testament", *Concilium*, No. 82, 25-31.

Vereno, Matthias: "Paulus zwischen Judentum und Christentum. Religionswissenschaft im Spannungsfeld der Bekenntnisse. Eine Betrachtung zu Schalom Ben-Chorin's Paulus-Buch" (= *Paulus. Der Völkerapostel in jüdischer Sicht*, 1970), *Kairos* 15, Heft 1-2, 145-155.

Vezin, G.: *L'Apocalypse et la fin des temps. Etude des influences égyptiennes et asiatiques sur les religions et les arts.* (Paris, Ed. de La Revue Moderne). 188 p., 80 pl.

Vilanova, E.: "Le développement de l'expression de la foi dans la communaité en prière à l'époque apostolique", *Concilium*, No. 82, 33-42.

Wedderburn, A. J. M.: "Philo's 'Heavenly Man' ", *Novum Testamentum* 15, 301-326.

Wells, P.: "Les images bibliques de la Bible dans I Pierre 2, 9-10", *EtEv* 33/1, 20-25.

White, P. S.: *Prophétie et prédiction. Une étude herméneutique des citations de l'Ancien Testament dans les sermons des Actes.* (Univ. de Lille III, Service de reproduction des thèses). 471, 34 p., bibliographie (21 p.). (Thèse, Fac. des Lettres et Sciences Humaines, Strasbourg, 5 déc. 1970).

Young, F. M.: "Temple Cult and Law in Early Christianity. A Study in the Relationship between Jews and Christians in the Early Centuries", *NTS* 19/3, 325-338.

Zehrer, F.: "Sinn und Problematik der Schriftverwendung in der Passion", *Theologisch-Praktische Quartalschrift* 121/1, 18-25.

Zehrer, F.: "Zum Judasproblem", *Theologisch-Praktische Quartalschrift* 121, Heft 3, 259-264.

2. PATRISTIC LITERATURE

de Aldama, J. A.: "Boletín de literatura antigua cristiana", *EsEc* 48, no. 185, 271-283.

Alvarez Turienzo, S.: "Exploración en turno a la doctrina del hombre y al humanismo agustiniano", *La Ciudad de Dios* 186, no. 2, 165-250.

Arbesmann, R.: "The Attitude of Saint Augustine towards Labor", *The Heritage of the Early Church, Essays in Honor of G. V. Florovsky* (q. v. sub I-7), 245-259.

Argenio, R.: "Le Prefazioni a Symmachum di Prudenzio", *Rivista di Studi Classici* 21 (60), 17-28.

Armas, G.: "Algunas figuras del pastor de lamas, en los escritos de san Agustín", *Augustinus* 18 (no. 70), 157-164.

Astruc, C.: "Un feuillet retrouvé du Parisinus Coislin. gr. 58 (fragment de S. Grégoire de Nysse, *Oratio de Abraham*/BHG 2354)", *AB* 91/3-4, 415-418.

Athanase d'Alexandrie: *Sur l'Incarnation du Verbe*. Introduction, texte critique, traduction, notes et index par C. Kannengiesser. (Paris, Editions du Cerf). 484 p. = Sources Chrétiennes, 199.

Aubineau, M.: "Textes chysostomiens dans les mss athonites: Dochiariou 12 et Koutloumous 29, 30, 54, 55", *Kleronomia* 6/1, 97-104.

Aubineau, M.: "Une homélie de Grégoire d'Antioche (570-593), retrouvée dans le *Vaticanus gr.* 1975", *Byzantion* 42/2, 595-597.

Aubineau, M.: "Une homêlie pascale attribuée à Sant Athanase d'Alexandrie, dans le Sinaiticus gr. 492", in: *Zetesis* (q. v. sub I-7), 578-668.

Aubineau, M. (ed., tr.): Hésychius de Jérusalem, Basile de Séleucie, Jean de Béryte, Pseudo-Chrysostome, Leonce de Constantinople: *Homélies pascales*. (Paris, Ed. du Cerf, 1972). 543 p., 6 pl. – R: *REL* 50, 323-324 (P. Petitmengin).

Backes, I.: "Das trinitarische Glaubensverständnis beim hl. Athanasius d. Gr.", *TThZ* 82/3, 129-140.

Barbel, J.: Gregor von Nyssa, Die grosse katechetische Rede: *Oratio catechetica magna*. (Stuttgart, Anton Hiersemann, 1971). viii, 231 S. = Bibliothek der griechischen Literatur, 1. – R: *Erasmus* 25/9-10, 266-268 (A. Kemmer).

Barnes, T. D.: *Tertullian. A Historical and Literary Study*. (Oxford, Clarendon Press, 1971). xii, 320 p. – R: *RHR* 183, No. 1, 76-80 (J. Fontaine).

Barwick, K.: "Elementos estoicos en san Agustin. Huellas varronianas en el *De dialectica* de Agustin", *Augustinus* 18, No. 70, 101-129.

Basilius Von Caesarea: *Briefe*. Zweiter Teil. Eingeleitet, übersetzt und reläutert von W.-D. Hauschild. (Stuttgart, Anton Hiersemann Verlag). x, 192 S. = Bibliothek der griechischen Literatur, Abteilung: Patristik, Band 3.

Bentivegna, J.: "The Matter as 'Milieu Divin' in St. Irenaeus", *Augustinianum* 12/3, 543-548.

Berger, K.: "Der traditionsgeschichtliche Ursprung der *traditio legis*", *VigChr* 27, No. 2, 104-122.

Bergeron, R.: "La doctrine eucharistique de l'*Enarr. in Ps. XXXIII* d'Augustin", *REAg* 19, 101-120.

di Bernardino, A.: "Maestri cristiani del III secolo nell'insegnamento classico", *Augustinianum* 12/3, 549-556.

Beumer, J.: "Die ältesten Zeugnisse für die römische Eucharistirfeier bei Ambrosius von Mailand", *ZKTh* 95/3, 311-324.

Blázquez, N.: "Filosofia y vivencia religiosa en san Agustín", *Augustinus* 18 (no. 69), 23-31.

Boularand, E.: "Tertullien et la conversion de la culture antique", *BLE* 73, no. 4, 279-289.

Boularand, E.: "Un ouvrage monumental sur Hilaire de Poities avant l'exil" *BLE* 73/3, 193-202 (= Jean Doignon: *Hilaire de Poitiers avant l'exil*, thèse, Paris, Etudes Augustiniennes, 1971, 668 p.)

Bovon-Thurneysen, A.: "Ethik und Eschatologie im Philipperbrief des Polycarp von Smyrna", *ThZ* 29/4, 241-256.

Braun, R.: "Un nouveau Tertullein: problèmes de biographie et de chronologie", *REL* 50, 67-84. (A critical review of T. D. Barnes, *Tertullian. A Historical and Literary Study*, Oxford, 1971, 320 p.)

Brioso, M.: "Géneros y fórmulas. Cuestiones formales en torno a un tipo de expresión formular en el cristianismo primitivo", *Emerita* 41/1, 57-73.

Brown, Peter: *Religion and Society in the Age of Saint Augustine*. (London, Faber and Faber, 1972). 352 p. – R: *BiOr* 30, 505 (J. N. Bakhuizen van den Brink).

Brox, N.: "*Non ulla gens non christiana* (zu Tertullian, *Ad nat.* 1, 8, 9f.)", *VigChr* XXVII/1, 46-49.

Bruce, F. F.: "Eschatology in the Apostolic Fathers", in: *The Heritage of the Early Church, Essays in Honor of G. V. Florovsky* (q. v. sub I-7), 77-89.

Brunner, G.: *Die theologische Mitte des Ersten Klemensbriefes. Ein Breitrag zur Hermeneutik früchristlicher Texte*. (Frankfurt a.M., Josef Knecht, 1972). ix, 177 S. = Frankfurter Theologische Studien, 11. – R: *ZKTh* 95/2, 212-215 (N. Brox).

Bruns, J. E.: "The *Altercatio Jasonis et Papisci*, Philo, and Anastasius the Sinaite", *ThSt* 34/2, 287-294.

Byrnes, R. G.: "The Fallen Soul as a Plotinian Key to a Better and Fuller Understanding of the Character of Time and History in the Early Works of Saint Augustine", *DisAbIn A* 33, No. 8, 4466. (The author's summary of his Diss., Fordham University, 1972).

Cantalamessa, R.: "Christianesimo e Impero Romano nel pensiero dei Padri Anteniceni. Per una valutazione storica della 'Svolta Costantiniana' ", *Augustinianum* 12/3, 373-390.

Capánaga, V.: "Inter pretación agustiniana del amor. Eris y Agape", *Augustinus* 18 (71-72), 317-354.

Cataldo, G. B.: "Semantica e intersoggettività della parola in S, Agostino", *Sapienza* 26/2, 170-184.

Cazier, P.: "Le *Livre des règles* de Tyconius. Sa transmission du *De doctrina christiana* aux *Sentences* d'Isidore de Séville", *REAg* 19/3-4, 241-261.

Cherchi, P.: "Un eco ciceroniana in S. Agostino", *REAg* 19, no. 3-4, 303-304.

Chesnut, G. F., Jr.: "Fate, Fortune, Free will and Nature in Eusebius of Caesarea", *Church History* 42/2, 165-182.

Chrysostome Jean (Saint) "Septième catéchèse adressée aux néophytes", *ŽMP* no. 2, 70-75.

Cignelli, L.: "Il titolo Cristo-Speranza nell'esegesi patristica", *SBF* 23, 105-150.

Coman, J.: "Elements d'anthropologie dans les oeuvres de saint Justin, martyr et philosophe", *CRFO* 25 (84), 317-337.

Coman, J.: "Esprit critique dans la littérature patristique", *Theologia* 44, no. 1-2, 263-277.

Conomis, N. C.: "Greek in Isidore's *Origines*", *Glotta* 51, Heft 1-2, 101-112.

Coquin, R. G.: "Le Testamentum Domini: problème de tradition textuelle", in: *XXIXe Congrès International des Orientalistes. Résumés des Communications*, Sections 1-5. (Paris. Y. Hervouet), p. 38.

Courcelle, P.: "Ambroise de Milan face aux comiques latins", *Revue des Etudes Latines* 50, 223-231.

Courtonne, Y.: *Un témoin du IVe siècle oriental. Saint Basil et son temps d'après sa correspondance*. (Paris, Les Belles Lettres). 559 p.

Covi, D.: "Valor y finalidad del sexo según san Agustín. La Etica sexual en el paraíso según san Agustín", *Augustinus* 18 (no. 69), 3-21.

Crocco, A.: "La metodologia filosofica di S. Agostino", *Sapienza* 26/1, 5-26.

Crouzel, H.: "A Letter from Origen 'to Friends in Alexandria' ", in: *The Heritage of the Early Church, Essays in Honor of G. V. Florovsky* (q. v. sub I-7), 135-150. (With Latin text and English translation).

Crouzel, H.: "Chronique origénienne", *Bulletin de Littérature Ecclésiastique* 73/2, 146-149.

Crouzel, H.: "Deux textes de Tertullien concernant la procédures et les rites du mariage chrétien", *BLE* 74/1, 3-13.

Daniélou, J.: "Metempsychosis in Gregory of Nyssa", in: *The Heritage of the Early Church, Essays in honor of G. V. Florovsky* (q. v. sub I-7), 227-243.

Delcourt, M.: "Alogeuesthai", *RBPhH* 51/1, 51-55.

D'Elia, F.: "Componente mistica e senso della storia nella 'conversio' di Cassiodoro", *Sapienza* 26/1, 84-90.

Del Ton, G.: "Timori e speranze per l'avenire. Meditando il De Civitate Dei", *Divinitas* 17/1, 5-18.

Desideri, P.: "Il *Dione* e la politica di Sinesio", *Atti della Academia delle Scienze di Torino* 107/2, 551-593.

Doignon, J.: *Hilaire de Poitiers avant l'exil. Recherches sur la naissance, l'enseignement et l'épreuve d'une foi épiscopale en Gaule au milieudu IVe siècle.* (Paris, Etudes Augustiniennes, 1971). 666 p. – R: *Bijdragen* 34/1, 93-98 (P. Smulders). *REAg* 19, 194-197 (R. Savon).

Donnelly, D. H.: "Augustine and Romanitas", *DisAbIn A* 34/4, 2015. (The author's summary of his diss., Graduate Theological Union, 1973).

Dumortier, J.: "Une homélie chrysostomienne suspecte", *Mélanges de Science Religieuse* 30/4, 185-191.

Evans, C. F.: "Tertullian's References to Sentius Saturninus and the Lukan Census", *JThS* 24/1, 24-39.

Evans, D. B.: *Leontius of Byzantium. An Origenist Christology*, 1970. – R: *BZ* 66/1, 95-99 (S. Otto).

Fernández Marcos, N.: "El torno al estudio del griego de los cristianos", *Emerita* 41/1, 45-56 (with English summary).

Ferrari, L. G.: "Astronomy and Augustine's Break with the Manichees", *REAg* 19, no. 3-4, 263-276.

Flury, P.: "Das sechste Gedicht des Paulinus von Nola", *VigChr* 27/2, 129-145.

Fonkič, B. L. et A. P. Každan: "Nouvelle édition des Actes de la Laure du Mont-Athos et sa signification pour la byzantinologie", *VV* 34, 32-54.

Forlin Patrucco, M.: "Povertà e ricchezza nell'avanzato IV secolo: la condanna ei mutui in Basilio di Cesarea", *Aevum* 47, 225-234.

Fortin, E. L.: "The viri novi of Arnobius and the Conflict between Faith and Reason in the Early Christian Centuries", in: *The Heritage of the Early Church, Essays in Honor of G. V. Florovsky* (q. v. sub I-7), 197-226.

Froehlich, K.: "Montanism and Gnosis", in: *The Heritage of the Early Church, Essays in Honor of G. V. Florovsky* (q. v. sub I-7), 91-111.

Gaško, P.: "Le jeûne et la prière dans les oeuvres de Basile de Césarée", *ŽMP* no. 2, 75-78 (en russe).

van der Geest, J. E. L.: *Le Christ et l'Ancien Testament chez Tertullien. Recherche terminologique.* (Nijmegen, Dekker en Van de Vegt). xv, 258 p. = Latinitas Christianorum Primaeva, 22.

Gelsomino, V.: "Da Cicerone a Prudenzio: genesi di un'*invenzione* dantesca", *GIF* 4, no. 1, 1-24.

Green, R. P. H.: "Some Types of Omagery in the Poetry of Paulinus of Nola", *VigChr* XXVII/1, 50-52.

Grosdidier de Matons, J.: "A propos d'une édition récente du *χριστ` ο ς*

Grosdidier de Matons, J.: "A propos d'une édition récente du χριστὸς πάσχων", in: *Travaux et Mémoires* 5, 363-372.

Grossi, V.: "Regula veritatis e narratio battesimale in Saint' Ireneo", *Augustinianum* 12/3, 437-463.

Grossi, V.: "Un contributo agli studi su Clemente Alessandrino", *Augustinianum* 13/1, 149-152. (A propos de Salvatore R. C. Lilla: *Clement of Alexandria. A Study on Christian Platonism and Gnosticism*, Oxford Univ. Press, 1971).

Hagner, D. A.: *The Use of Old and New Testaments in Clement of Rome*. (Leiden, E. J. Brill). xii, 393 p. = Supplements to Novum Testamentum, 34.

Hamman, A.: "Existe-t-il un langage trinitaire chez les Pères Apostoliques?", *Augustinianum* 13/3, 455-458.

Harb, P.: "Nouvelles preuves en faveur de l'authenticité Ḥazzayonne de la Lettre sur les trois degrés", in: *XXIXe Congrès International des Orientalistes. Résumés des Communications*, Sections 1-5. (Paris, Y. Hervouet), pp. 42-43.

Harkins, P. W.: "Chrysostom's Postbaptismal Instructions", in: *The Heritage of the Early Church, Essays in Honor of G. V. Florovsky* (q. v. sub I-7), 151-165.

Heron, A.: "The Two Pseudo-Athanasian Dialogues Against The Anomoeans", *JThS* 24/1, 101-122.

Hörner, H.: *Auctorum incertorum, vulgo Basilii vel Gregorii Nysseni, sermones de creatione hominis, sermo de paradiso*. (Leiden, E. J. Brill, 1972). clxxiv, 101 p. R: *BZ* 66/1, 91-95 (E. Amand de Mendieta).

Jansma, T.: "Ephraem on Exodus II, 5: Reflections on the Interpkay of Human Freewill and Divine Providence", *OChP* 39/1, 5-28.

Jurado, M. R.: "El concepto de mundo en ElCristianismo (2ª mitad del s. III)", *EsEc* 48 (No. 184), 65-85.

Kannengiesser, C.: "Athanasius of Alexandria and the Foundation of Traditional Christology", *ThSt* 34/1, 103-113.

Kannengiesser, C.: "Athanase édité par Robert W. Thomson", *Recherches de Science Religieuse* 61/2, 217-232.

Kissel, W.: "Eine falsch verstandene Laktanz-Stelle (*De opificio dei* 19, 10)", *VigChr* 27/2, 123-128.

Klijn, A. F. J., and G. J. Reinink: *Patristic evidence for Jewish-Christian sects*. (Leiden, E. J. Brill). x, 313 p. = Novum Testamentum, Supplements, XXXVI.

Knauber, A.: " 'Aus apostolischer Überlieferung...' (Liturgiekonstitution Art. 106). Zur Frühgeschichte der sonntäglichen Eucharistieverpflichtung", *ThG* 63/4-5, 308-321.

Kopeček, T. A.: "Social/Historical Studies in the Cappadocian Fathers", *DisAbIn*, *A* 33/8, 4288-4289. (The author's summary of his diss., Brown University, 1972).

Kötting, B.: "Zur Frage der 'Successio apostolica' in frühkirchlicher Sicht", *Catholica* 27, 234-247.

Kowalczyk, S.: "La métaphysique du bien selon l'aception de St. Augustin", *EstAg* 8, no. 1, 31-51.

Lackner, W.: "Zum Zusatz Epiphanios' von Salamis *Panarion*, Kap. 64", *Vigiliae Christianae* 27/1, 56-58.

Lactance: *Institutions divines.* Livre V. Introduction, texte critique, traduction, commentaire par P. Monat. 2 tomes. (Paris, Ed. du Cerf). 259 et 310 p. = Sources chrétiennes, 204 et 205.

Lambert, B.: *Bibliotheca Hieronymiana manuscripta. La tradition manuscrite des oeuvres de Saint Jérôme.* (La Haye, M. Nijhoff, 1969-1970). 3 tomes. – R: *Gnomon* 45/1, 46-50 (I. Opelt).

Laoye, J. A.: "Augustine's Apologetic Use of the Old Testament as Reflected Especially in the 'De civitate dei' ", *DisAbIn, A* 33/9, 5279. (The author's summary of his diss., The Southern Baptist Theological Seminary, 1972).

Lapointe, G.: *La Célébration des martyrs en Afrique d'après les sermons de saint Augustin*, (Montreal, 1972). – R: *StRel* 3/1, 76-78 (E. Lamirande).

Lash, C.: "L'onxtion postbaptismale de la 14e homélie de Théodore de Mopsueste: une interpolation syriaque?", in: *XXIXe Congrès Intern. des Orientalistes. Résumés des Communications*, Sections 1-5, (Paris, Y. Hervouet), pp. 43-44.

Laufs, J.: "Der Friedensgedanke bei Augustinus. Untersuchungen zum XIX. Buch des Werkes De civitate Dei", *Hermes, Einzelschriften*, No. 27, 1-146.

Lee, G. M.: "Gregor v. Nazianz, Oratio XV, In Machabaeorum Laudem 4", *ZNTW* 64, No. 1-2, 152-153.

Leroy, M.-V.: "Le Christ de Chalcédoinde", *Revue Thomiste* 73/1, 75-93. (A propos de T. *Šagi-Bunić: 'Deus perfectus et Homo perfectus' a Concilio Ephesino ad Chalcedonense*).

Liébaert, J.: *Les enseignements moraux des Pères apostoliques.* (Gembloux, Duculot, 1970). xiii, 294 p. – R: *NRTh* 95/5, 559 (P. Bacq).

Lilla, S. R. C.: Clement of Alexandria. *A Study in Christian Platonism and Gnosticism.* (Oxford University Press, 1971). xiv, 266 p. – R: *RHR* 183/1, 70-76 (A. Méhat).

Maloney, R. P.: "The Teachings of the Fathers on Usury: an Historical Study on the Development of Christian Thinking", *VigChr* 27, 241-265.

Manferdini, T.: "El problema de la comunicación inteligible según san Agustin", *Augustinus* 18 (no. 69), 33-61.

Marcovich, M.: "Hippolytus: *Refutatio*, X. 33.9 (p. 290.9-15 Wendland) Again", *JThS* 24/1, 195-196.

Marotta, E.: "I riflessi biblici nell'orazione ad Origene di Gregorio il Taumaturgo", *VetChr* 10/1, 59-77.

Mees, M.: "Text- und Bibelvarianten im Paidagogos des Clemens von Alexandrien", *Augustinianum* 12/3, 425-435.

Meijering, E. P.: "Die 'physische Erlösung' in der Theologie des Irenäus", *NAK* 53, 147-159.

Meijering, E. P.: "Some Observations on Irenaeus' Polemics against the Gnostics", *NeTT* 27, 26-33.

Meijering, E. P.: "The Doctrine of the Will and of the Trinity in the Orations of Gregory of Nazianzus", *NeTT* 27/3, 224-234.

Miller, R. H.: "Enlightenment through the Bath of Rebirth: The Experience of Christian Initiation in Late Fourth Century Jerusalem", *DisAbIn, A* 33/7, 3761-3762. (The author's summary of his diss., Fordham University, 1972).

Mortley, R.: *Connaissance religieuse et herméneutique chez Clément d'Alexandrie.* (Leiden, E. J. Brill). vi, 255 p.

Mortley, R.: "The Theme of Silence in Clement of Alexandria", *JThS* 24/1, 197-202.

Murray, R.: "The Lance which Re-opened Paradise, a Mysterious Reading in the Early Syriac Fathers", *OChP* 39/1, 224-234.

Nautin, P.: "Ciel, pneuma et lumière chez Théophile d'Antioche (notes critiques sur Ad Autol. 2, 13)", *VigChr* 27/3, 165-171.

Nautin, P.: Etudes de chronologie hiéronymienne (393-397)", *REAg* 19, 69-86, 213-239. (Cf. *ibidem*, 18, 209-218).

O'Connell, R. J.: "*Confessions*VII, IX, 13 – XXI, 27. Reply to G. Madec", *REAg* 19, 87-100. (Cf. *ibidem*, 16/1, 79-137).

Opelt, I.: "Hilarius von Poitiers als Polemiker", *Vigiliae Christianae* 27/3, 203-217.

Orbe, A.: "Supergrediens angelos (S. Ireneo, Adv. haer. V, 36, 3)", *Gregorianum* 54/1, 5-59.

Orlandi, T.: "Patristica copta e patristica greca", *VetChr* 10, No. 2, 327-341.

Orozz Reta, J.: "Experiencias eclesiales en la conversión de san Agustin", *Augustinus* 18 (no. 70), 131-144.

Outtier, B.: "Recueils arméniens et géorgiens d'oeuvres attribuées à saint Ephrem le syrien", in: *XXIXe Congrès intern. des Orientalistes. Résumés des Communications*, Sections 1-5. (Paris, Y. Hervouet), pp. 45-46.

Pegueroles, J.: "El fundamento del conocimiento de la verdad en San Augustin: la *memoria Dei*", *Pensamiento* 29 (no. 113), 5-35.

Peñamaria, A.: "Biblia y padres. Las Comunicaciones del Coloquio de Estrasburgo", *Estudios Eclesiásticos* 48 (no. 184), 99-110. (Presentation of André Benoit et Pierre Prigent (ed.): *La Bible et les Pères*, Paris, P.U.F., 1971, 280 p.)

Petit, P.: "Emerveillement, prière et esprit chez saint Basile le Grand", *ColCis* 35, 81-108, 218-238.

Petitmengin, P.: "Tertullianus redivivus", *REAg* 19, No. 1-2, 177-185. (Critical remarks on T. D. Barnes, *Tertullian. A historical and literary study*, Oxford, 1971).

Pincherle, A.: "Orarium e sudarium", *Rivista di Storia e Letteratura Religiosa* 9, no. 1, 52-56.

de Plinval, G.: "L'Heure est-elle vanue de redécouvrir Pélage?", *REAg* 19, No. 1-2, 158-162.

Poirier, M.: "Vescovo, clero e laici in una comunità cristiana del III secolo negli scritti di San Cipriano", *RSLR* 9/1, 17-36.

Popma, K. J.: "Patristic Evaluation of Culture", *Philosophia Reformata* 38, 97-113.

Popova, T. V.: "Les particularités littéraires de la *Vita Constantini* d'Eusèbe de Césarée", *VV* 34, 122-129 (en russe).

Prete, S.: "Confessioni Trinitarie in alcuni Atti di martiri del sec. II (Giustino, Apollonic, Policarpo)", *Augustinianum* 13/3, 469-482.

Prete, S.: "Some *loci* in Ancient Latin Hagiography", in: *The Heritage of the Early Church, Essays in Honor of G. V. Florovsky* (q. v. sub I-7), 307-319.

Prigent, P. et R. Stehly: "les fragments du *De Apocalypsi* d'Hippolyte", *ThZ* 29, Heft 5, 313-333.

Quacquarelli, A.: "L'antimonarchianesimo di Tertulliano e il suo presunto montanismo", *VetChr* 10/1, 5-45.

Quacquarelli, A.: *L'Ogdoade patristica e suoi riflessi nella liturgia e nei monumenti.* (Bari, Adriatica Editrice). 110 p., 28 fig., bibliografia (5 p.)

Quacquarelli, A.: "Sulla dossologia trinitaria dei Padri Apostolici", *VetChr* 10, no. 2, 211-241.

Reinhardt, W. W.: "Time and History in the Thought of Hilary of Poitiers", *DisAbIn A* 34/4, 2020-2021. (The author's summary of his diss., Vanderbilt University, 1973).

Renoux, C.: "Les Memre sur Nicomédie d'Ephrem de Nisibe: Témoignages littéraires et tradition manuscrite syriaque et arménienne", in: *XXIXe Congrès International des Orientalistes. Résumés des Communications*, Sections 1-5, (Paris, Y. Hervouet), pp. 46-47.

Riga, P. J.: "penance in St. Ambrose", *Eglise et Théologie* 4, No. 2, 213-226.

Roncoroni, A.: "Note al *De virginitate* di Avito di Vienne", *Athenaeum* 51, no. 1-2, 122-134.

Sabattini, P. T. A.: "Storia e leggenda nei *Peristephanon* di Prudenzio", *Rivista di Studi Classici* 21 (60), 39-77, bibliografia (2 p.)

Sabattini, T. A.: "S. Cipriano nella tradizione agiografica", *Rivista di Studi Classici* 21/2, 181-204.

Sabugal, S.: "El titulo *Christós* en los Padres Apostólicos u Apologistas griegos", *Augustinianum* 12/3, 407-423.

Salvien de Marseille: *Oeuvres*. Tome I: *Les Lettres, les Livres de Timothée à l'Eglise*. Introduction, texte critique, traduction et notes par G. Lagarrigue. (Paris, Ed. du Cerf, 1971). 348 p. = Sources chrétiennes, 176. – R: *REL* 50, 319-320 (J. P. Weiss). *REAg* 19, 200-201 (L. Brix).

Sansterre, J.-M.: "Eusèbe de Césarée et la naissance de la théorie 'césaropapiste' ", *Byzantion* 42/2, 532-594 (suite et fin. Cf. *ibidem*, 42/1 (1972), 131-195).

Santer, M.: "Hippolytus: *Refutatio Omnium Haeresium*, X. 33.9", *JThS* 24/1, 194-195.

Scazzoso, P.: "L'umanesimo di S. Basilio", *Augustinianum* 12, no. 3, 391-405.

Scazzoso, P.: "Riflessioni sull'Ecclesiologia Orientale", *Vita Monastica* 27 (112-113), 38-119.

Scazzoso, P.: "San Basilio e la Sacra Scrittura", *Aevum* 47, no. 3-4, 210-224.

Schatkin, M.: "St. John Chrysostom's Homily on the Protopaschites: Introduction and Translation", in: *The Heritage of the Early Church, Essays in Honor of G. V. Florovsky* (q. v. sub I-7), 167-186.

Schäublin, C.: "Textkritisches zu den Briefen des Hieronymus", *Museum Helveticum* XXX/1, 55-62.

Schindler, A.: "Querverbindungen zwischen Augustins theologischer und kirchenpolitischer Entwicklung 390-400", *ThZ* 29, 95-116.

Schmöle, K.: "Gnosis und Metanoia. Die anthropologische Sicht der Busse bei Klemens von Alexandrien", *TThZ* 82/5, 304-312.

Schwarte, K. H.: *Die Vorgeschichte der augustinischen Weltalterlehre*. (Bonn, Habelt, 1966). – R: *Gnomon* 45/1, 40-45 (C. Andresen).

Schwartz, J.: "Celsus redivivus", *RHPhR* 53, no. 3-4, 399-405.

Serr, J.: "Les charismes dans la vie de l'Englise. Tèmoignages patristiques", *Foi et Vie* 72, no. 4-5, 33-42.

Sesboüé, B.: "Les chrétiens devant l'avortement d'après le témoignage des Pères de l'Eglise", *Etudes*, no. août-sept., 262-282.

Siclari, A.: "L'Antropologia di Nemesio di Emesa nella critica moderna", *Aevum* 47, no. 5-6, 477-497.

Sieben, H.-J.: "Athanasius über den Psalter. Analyse seines Briefes an Marcellinus. Zum 1600. Todesjahr des Bischofs von Alexandrien", *ThPh* 48/2, 157-173.

Sieben, H.-J.: "Zur Entwicklung der Konzilsidee", *Theologie und Philosophie* 48, Heft 1, 28-64.

Stalder, K.: "Apostolische Sukzession und Eucharistie bei Clemens Romanus, Irenäus und Ignatius von Antiochien", *IKZ* 63/2-3, 100-128.

Stead, G. C.: " 'Eusebius' and the Council of Nicaea", *JThS* 24, No. 1, 85-100.

Stuiber, A.: "Ein griechischer Textzeuge für das *Opus imperfectum in Matthaeum*", *VigChr* 27/2, 146-147.

Swartley, W. M.: "The Imitatio Christi in the Ignatian Letters", *VigChr* 27/2, 81-103. (In opposition to the article by Theodor Preiss: "La mystique de l'imitation", published in *RHPhR* 17, 1938, 197-241).

Taylor, J.: "St. Basil the Great and Pope St. Damasus I", *The Downside Review* 304, 186-203; 305, 262-274.

Tetz, M.: "Markellianer und Athanasios von Alexandrien", *ZNTW* 64, 75-121.

Thomson, R. W.: *The Teaching of Saint Gregory: An Early Armenian Catechism.* (Harvard University Press, 1970). – R: *BZ* 66/1, 88-91 (M. G. de Durand).

Timothy, H. B.: *The Early Christian Apologists and Greek Philosophy, Exemplified by Irenaeus, Tertullian and Clement of Alexandria.* (Assen, Van Gorcum). iv, 103 p. = Wijsgerige teksten en studies, 21.

Tyloch, Witold: "Un receil des textes messianiques provenant de la IVe grotte de Qumran", *Euhemer* XVII/4 (90), 25-32. (4Q Testimonia. En polonais).

Unger, D. J.: "The Divine and Eternal Sonship of the Word According to St. Irenaeus of Lyons", *Laurentianum* 14/3, 356-408.

van Unnik, W. C.: "The Interpretation of 2 Clement 15.5", *Vigiliae Christianae* XXVII/1, 29-34.

de Veer, A. C.: "Aux origines du *De natura et origine animae* de Saint Augustin", *REAg* 19, 121-157.

Verheijen, L. M. J.: "Contributions à une édition critique améliorée des Confessions de Saint Augustin", *Augustiniana* 22 (1972), 35-52; 23, 334-368 (suites, à suivre).

Vilela, A.: "Le presbyterium selon saint Ignace d'Antioche", *BLE* 73/3, 161-186.

Vogt, H.-J.: "Les partis dans l'histoire de l'Eglise: Athanase et ses contemporains", *Concilium* no. 86, 35-46.

Yarnold, E. J.: " 'Ideo et Romae Fideles Dicuntur Qui Baptizati Sunt': A Note on *De Sacramentis* I. 1", *JThS* 24/1, 202-207.

Zaphiris, G.: "Connaissance naturelle de Dieu d'après Athanase d'Alexandrie", *Kleronomia* 6/1, 61-96.

3. APOCRYPHA

Agourides, S.: "Les livres d'Henoch, I", *Theologia* 44, no. 3-4, 513-560 (en grec, à suivre).

Asmussen, J. P.: "Der apokryphe dritte Korintherbrief in der armenischen Tradition", *AOD* 35, 51-55.

Bammel, E.: "Joh. 7: 35 in Manis Lebensbeschreibung", *Novum Testamentum* 15, 191-192.

Böhlig, A.: "Zur Apokalypse des Petrus", *Göttinger Miszellen*, Heft 8, 11-13.

Dalmais, I. H.: "Apocryphes et Imaginaire chrétien", *Bible et Terre-Sainte* 154, 12-20.

Decroix, J.: "Les manuscrits des Apocryphes de la Bible", *Bible et Terre-Sainte* no. 154, 2-11, bibliographie.

Dehandschutter, B.: "L'Evangile selon Thomas: témoin d'une tradition prélucanienne?", in: *L'Evangile de Luc, Problèmes littéraires et théologiques. Mémorial Lucien Cerfaux*, (Gembloux, J. Ducolot), pp. 287-297.

Devoti, D.: "L'antropologia di Eracleone attraverso la figura del Battista", *AAST* 107, no. 2, 709-756.

van Esbroeck, M.: "Apocryphes géorgiens de la Dormition", *Analecta Bollandiana* 91, no. 1-2, 55-75.

Ford, A. E.: *L'Evangile de Nicodème. Les versions courtes en ancien français et en prose.* (Genève, Droz). 111 p. = Publications romanes et françaises, 125.

Garitte, G.: " 'Protevangelii Iacobi'. Versio arabica antiquior" *Le Muséon* 86, no. 3-4, 377-396. (Cod. Sin. Ar. 535, fol. 347 r.-v., texte et traduction latine).

Maillot, A.: "Eloge de Marcion", *Foi et Vie* 72, no. 5-6, 29-34.

Mara, M. G. (ed.): *Evangile de Pierre*. (Paris, Les Editions du Cerf). 224 p. = Sources Chrétiennes, 201.

Martin, L. H., Jr.: "Note on 'The Treatise on the Resurrection' (Cg I,3) 48.3-6", *VigChr* 27/4, 281.

Martin, L. H., Jr.: "The Anti-Philosophical Polemic and Gnostic Soteriology in *The Treatise on the Resurrection* (CGI, 3)", *Numen* 20/1, 20-37.

Martin, L. H., Jr., "*The Treatise on the Resurrection* (CGI, 3) and Diatribe Style", *VigChr* 27, 277-280.

Mueller, D.: "Kingdom of Heaven or Kingdom of God", *VigChr* 27, No. 4, 266-276.

Nickelsburg, G. W. E., Jr.: "Narrative Traditions in the Paralipomena of Jeremiah and 2 Baruch", *CBQ* 35/1, 60-68.

Orbe, A.: "Cristologia de los Ofitas (S. Iren., adv. haer. I, 30, 11-14)", *EsEc* 48 (185), 191-230.

Orbe, A.: "El Diácono del Jordán en el sistema de Basilides", *Augustinianum* 13, no. 2, 165-183.

Richardson, C. C.: "The Cospel of Thomas: Gnostoc or Encratite?", in: *The Heritage of the Early Church, Essays in Honor of G. V. Florovsky* (q. v. sub I-7), 65-76.

Schenke, Hans Martin: "Die Taten des Petrus und der zwölf Apostel. Die erste Schrift aus Nag-Gammadi-Codex VI", *ThL* 98/1, 13-19.

Zelzer, K.: "Zu den lateinischen Fassungen der Thomasakten. 2. Überlieferung und Sprache", *Wiener Studien* 5 (1971), 161-179.

Zelzer, K.: "Zu den lateinischen Fassungen der Thomasakten. 1. Gehalt, Gestaltung, zeitliche Einordnung", *Wiesner Studien* 5 (1971), 161-179.

4. MONASTICISM

Anson, Peter: *The Call of the Desert. The Solitary Life in the Christian Church.* (London, SPCK/ = The Society for Promoting Christian Knowledge/). xx, 278 p.

Bartelink, G. J. M.: "Les oxymores *desertum civitas et desertum floribus vernans*", *StuMon* 15/1, 7-15.

Borias, A.: "Une nouvelle édition de la Règle de Saint Benoit", *RHS-RAM* 49 (No. 193), 117-128.

Bouet, P.: "Le millénaire monastique du Mont Saint-Michel", *Cahiers de Civilisation Médiévale* 16/1, 51-58.

Bradley, B.: "Jean le Solitaire (d'Apamée)", in: *Dictionnaire de Spiritualité Ascétique et Mystque*, t. 8, fasc. 54-55, col. 764-772.

Brock, S. P.: "Early Syrian Ascetism", *Numen* 20/1, 1-19.

Colless, B. E.: "La vie ascétique selon Jean de Dalyatha", in: *XXIXe Congrès Intern. des Orientalistes, Résumés des Communications*, Sections 1-5, (Paris, Y. Hervouet), p. 38.

Dimier, A. et alii: "Bulletin de spiritualité monastique. IV, du XIe au XVIe siècle", *ColCis* 35/4, [351]-[373].

Fernández, Q.: "Desarrollo económico del Monasterio de Gradfes (León)", *EsAg* 8, no. 1, 117-136.

Gorce, D.: "Die Gastfreundlichkeit der altchristlichen Einsiedler und Mönche", *JACh* 15, 66-91.

Gribomont, J.: "Jérome (saint)", *Dictionnaire de Spiritualité Ascétique et Mystique*, t. 8, fasc. 54-55, col. 901-918.

Gribomont, J.: "Rome et les moines. Le principal document sur l'Office divin au VIe siècle remis en question", *Maison-Dieu* no. 114, 135-140.

Griffe, E.: "A propos de canon 33 du Concile d'Elvire", *Bull. de Littérature Ecclésiastique* 73/2, 142-145.

Gross, K.: "Plus Amari quam Timeri. Eine antike politische Maxime in der Benediktinerregel", *VigChr* 27/3, 318-329.

Heun, Eugen: "Askese und Fasten bei den alten Christen", *Die Medizinische Welt*, Nr. 7, 3-19.

Jaspert, B.: "Benedikt von Nursia: der Vater des Abendlandes? Kritische Bemerkungen zur Typologie eines Heiligen", *Erbe und Auftrag* 49, 90-104, 190-207.

Leroy, J., I. H. Dalmais, P. et S. Riché: "Saint Syméon le Stylits: ascèse et sainteté. Le Chateau de Syméon", *BTS* no. 147, 2-17.

Linage Conde, A.: "Analecta cartusiana", *Studia Monastica* 15, no. 1, 143-146.

Mähler, M.: "Evocations bibliques et hagiographiques dans la Vie de saint Benoit par saint Grégoire", *ReBén* 83, 398-429.

Manning, E.: "Une nouvelle édition de la Règle de S. Benoit", *RHE* 68/2, 457-464.

Meinardus, O.: "A Note on Some Maronite Monasteries in the Wādī Qadīsha", *Orientalia Suecana* 21, 9-25.

Mioni, E.: "Jean Moschus", in: *Dictionnaire de Spiritualité Ascétique et Mystique*, t. 8, fasc. 54-55, col. 632-640.

Morard, Françoise-E.: "*Monachos*, Moine. Histoire du terme grec jusqu'au 4e siècle. Influence bibliques et gnostiques", *FZPhTh* 20, 329-415.

Palomares Ibañez, J. M.: "Aspectos de la historia del convento de San Pablo de Valladolid', *AFP* 43, 91-135.

Peifer, C.: "An International Congress on the Regula Benedicti", *Studia Monastica* 15, No. 1, 129-133.

Quecke, Hans: "Briefe Pachoms in koptischer Sprache. Neue deutsche Übersetzung", in: *Zetesis* (Fs de Strijker), 655-663.

Regnault, L.: "Jean de Gaza", in: *Dictionnaire de Spiritualité Ascétique et Mystique*, t. 8, fasc. 54-55, col. 536-538.

Sauget, J. M.: "Un nouveau témoin de collection d'Apophthegmata Patrum: le Paterikon du Sinaï Arabe 547", *Le Muséon* 86, 5-35.

von Severus, E.: "Eléments théologiques de la Règle de saint Benoit et tendances théologiques fondamentales actuelles", *ColCis* 35/3, 199-209.

Stiernon, D.: "Jean de Jérusalem", in: *Dictionnaire de Spiritualité Ascétique et Mystique*, t. 8, fasc. 54-55, col. 565-574.

Verheijen, L. M. J.: "Eléments d'un commentaire de la Règle de saint Augustin", *Augustiniana* 23, 306-333 (suite, à suivre).

Villegas, F.: "La *Regula cuiusdam Patris ad monachos*. Ses sources littéraires et ses rapports avec la *Regula monachorum* de Colomban", *RHS* (= *RAM*) 49, 3-35, 135-144.

de Vogüé, A.: "Le prêtre et la communauté monastique dans l'Antiquité", *Maison-Dieu* no. 115, 61-69.

de Vogüé, Adalbert: "L'anecdote pachômienne du 'Vaticanus graecus' 2091. Son origine et ses sources", *RHS/RAM* 49, 401-419.

de Vogüé, A.: "La Vie arabe de saint Pachôme et ses deux sources présumées", *AB* 91, no. 3-4, 379-390.

de Vogüé, A.: "Le nom du supérieur de monastère dans la règle pachomienne. A propos d'un ouvrage récent", *StuMon* 15/1, 17-22. (A propos de F. Ruppert: *Das pachomianische Mönchtum und die Anfänge klösterlichen Gehorsams*, Münsterschwarzach, 1971).

de Vogüé, A.: " 'Ne juger de rien par soi-même'. Deux empunts de la Règle colombanienne aux Sentences de Sextus et à S. Jérôme", *RHS (= RAM)* 49/2, 129-134.

de Vogüé, A.: "Per ducatum Evangelii. La règle de saint Benoit et l'Evangile", *ColCis* 35/3, 186-198.

Wathen, A.: "Monasticism: Qumran and Christian", *Benedictines* 28, No. 3-4, 58-68, 92.

Zeller, W.: "Die kirchengeschichtliche Sicht des Mönchtums im Protestantismus, insbesondere bei Gerhard Tersteegen", *Erbe und Auftrag* 49/1, 17-30.

Zimmermann, G.: *Ordensleben und Lebensstandard. Die cura corporis in den Ordensvorschriften des abendländischen Hochmittelalters.* (Münster, Aschendorffsche Verlag). xvi, 577 p. – R: *Erasmus* 25 (19-20), 693-695 (H. Schipperges).

5. CHURCHES, THEOLOGY

Allegra, G. M.: "La Sutra del Messia", *Rivista Biblica* 21/2, 165-186.

Astruc, C.: "Une fausse attribution réparée (L'opuscule de 'Psellos' *Σίς τούς λέγοντας ορον ειναι Θανάτον* restitué à Théophylacte Simokattes)", *Travaux et Mémoires* 5, 357-361.

Aubineau, M.: "Syméon le Nouveau Théologien, Traités théologiques et éthiques: Notes de lecture", *RPhLHA* 47/1, 50-60.

Bálint, S.: "Die Verehrung des hl. Johannes des Evangelisten im alten Ungarn", *ÖZV* 27/4, 303-320.

Bartikian, H.: "Encore une fois sur l'origine du nom Pauliciens", *REArm* 9, 445-451. (See under Yuzbashian, K., below!)

Bauer, J. B.: "Anpassung und Veränderung in der Alten Kirche", *Wort und Wahrheit* 26, Heft 2, 99-111.

Berbuir, E.: "Die Herausbildung der kirchlichen Ämter von Gehilfen und Nachfolgern der Apostel", *WissWeis* 36/2-3, 110-128.

Bilaniuk, P. B. T.: "The Mystery of *theosis* or Divinization", in: *The Heritage of the Early Church, Essays in Honor of G. V. Florovsky* (q. v. sub I-7), 337-359.

Blanchetière, F.: "Aux sources de l'anti-judaisme chrétien", *RHPhR* 53, no. 3-4, 353-398.

Böcher, O.: "Kirche und Konfession nach dem Neuen Testament. Zur Frage nach Legitimität und Illegitimität der Konfessionalität", *JEB* 16, 33-47, Bibliographie.

Bordenave, J., et M. Vialelle: *Aux racines du mouvement cathare: La mentalité religieuse des paysans de l'Albigeois médiévale.* (Toulouse, Privat). 350 p.

Börtnes, J.: "Hagiographical Transformation in the Old Russian Lives of Saints", *Scando-Slavica* 18, 5-12.

du Bourguet, P.: "Une assimilation abusive: copte = chrétien (d'Egypte)", in: *XXIXe Congrès International des Orientalistes. Résumés des Communications,* Sections 1-5. (Paris, Y. Hervouet), pp. 41-42.

Brandmüller, W.: "Laien auf der Kanzel. Ein Gegenwartsproblem im Licht der Kirchengeschichte", *ThG* 63, 321-342.

Bröker, Werner: *Politische Motive naturwissenschaftlicher Argumentation gegen Religion und Kirche im 19. Jahrhundert, dargestellt am "Materialisten" Karl Vogt (1817-1895).* (Münster, Aschendorff). iv, 260 S. = Beiträge zur Theologie, 35.

Le Brun, J.: "Autour du quiétisme. Correspondance inédite de l'abbé Bossuet (1696-1699)", *RHE* 68/1, 67-101.

Byčkov, V. V.: "L'icône comme catégorie de l'esthétique byzantine", *Vizantijskij Vremennik* 34, 151-168 (en russe).

Canard, M.: "Le conte de l'Ile-baleine et son utilisation dans la polémique byzantine contre les pauliciens", *REArm* 9, 379-384.

Canivet, P.: "Un nouveau nom sur la liste épiscopale d'Apamée: l'archevêque Photius en 483", in: *Traveaux et Mémoires* 5, 243-258.

Carey, J. J.: "Hans Küng and Karl Barth: One Flesh or One Spirit?", *JES* 10/1, 1-16 (with summaries in French, German, Spanish and Italian).

Chadwick, H.: "The Status of Ecumenical Councils in Anglican Thought", in: *The Heritage of the Early Church. Essays in Honor of G. V. Florovsky* (q. v. sub I-7), 393-408.

Chaillou, J.: "Cathares en Charente et en Saintong?", *Cahiers d'Etudes Cathares* 24 (59), 30-31.

Chenu, M. D.: "Contestation sans schisme dans l'Eglise médiévale", *Concilium*, no. 88, 47-54.

Clasen, S.: "Theologische Anliegen und historische Wirklichkeit in franziskanischen Heiligenlegenden. Ein Beitrag zur Hagiographie des Mittelalters", *wissweis* 36/1, 1-44.

Collarini, M.: "Dimensioni dell'unità della Chiesa in Cipriano di Cartagine", *Laurentianum* 14/1, 251-278.

Colless, B. E.: "The Mysticism of John Saba", *Orientalia Christiana Periodica* 39/1, 83-102.

Colpe, Carsten: "Häretische Patriarchen bei Eutychios", *JACh* 14 (1971), 48-60. – R: *Le Muséon* 86, 217-219 (A. de Halleux).

Coppens, J.: "Le prophète eschatologique. L'annonce de sa sa venue. Les relectures", *EThL* 49-5-35.

Cramer, Maria: *Koptische Hymnologie in Deutscher Übersetzung*, (Wiesbaden, 1969). – R: *BiOr* 30, 49-55 (F. Rofail Farag).

D'Alatri, M.: "Ordo Paenitentium ed eresia in Italia", *Collectanea Franciscana* 43, 181-197.

Dalmais, I. H.: "L'Esprit Saint et le mystère du salut dans les épiclèses eucharistiques syriennes", *Istina* 17/2, 147-154.

Dando, M.: "Survivances gnostiques dans un texte latin de la Gaule Méridionale du Haut Moyen Age: L'*Adrian et Epictitus*", *CEC* 24 (58), 3-24, bibliographie.

Delpoux, C.: "Les Comtes de Toulouse et le Catharisme. Raymond VI", *CEC* 24 (57), 39-62 (suite, 31e partie).

Demetriades, J. M.: "Nicetas of Byzantium and His Encounter with Islam: A Study of the 'Ανατροπή and the Two *Epistles* to Islam", *DisAbIn A* 34/1, 403. (The author's summary of his diss., Hartford Seminary Foundation, 1972).

Dupuy, B.: "L'infaillibilité selon Hans Küng", *RDCCIF* 79, 33-40.

Duvernoy, J.: "Une source familière de l'hérésiologie médiévale: Le tome II des *Beiträge* de Döllinger", *RHR* 183/2, 161-177. (Une table de concordance des textes et de leurs sources médiévales).

Dvornik, F.: "Photius, Nicholas I and Hadrian II", *Byzantinoslavica* 34, No. 1, 33-50.

Dykmans, M.: "De Jean XXII au Concile de Florence ou les avatars d'une hérésie gréco-latine", *RHE* 68/1, 29-66.

Ellis, E. E.: "La fonction de l'eschatologie dans l'Evangile de Luc", in: *L'Evangile de Luc. Problèmes littéraires et théologiques*. Mémorial Lucien Cerfaux. (Gembloux, J. Duculot), pp. 141-155.

van Els, T. J. M.: *The Kassel Manuscript of Bede's Historia Ecclesiastica Gentis*

Anglorum and its Old English Material. (Assen, 1972). xxxi, 277 p. – R: *Studia Neophilologica* 45/1, 173-174 (O. Arngart).

Eyice, S. et J. Noret: "S. Lucien, disciple de S. Lucien d'Antioche. A propos d'une inscription de Kirsehir (Turquie)", *AB* 91/3-4, 363-377.

Farag, F. R.: "The Technique of Research of a Tenth-Century Christian Arab Writer: Severus Ibn al-Muqaffa", *Le Muséon* 86, 37-66.

Farrar, R. S.: "Structure and function in representative Old English Saints' Lives", *Neophilologus* 57/1, 83-93.

Feghali, J.: "Origine et formation du mariage dans le Droit des Eglises de langue syriaque", *AnCan* 17, 413-431.

Fiey, J. M.: "Chrétientés syriaques du Horāsān et du Ségestān", *Le Muséon* 86, No. 1-2, 75-104.

Frend, W. H. C.: "Severus of Antioch and the Origin of the Monophysite Hierarchy", in: *The Heritage of the Early Church, Essays in Honor of G. V. Florovsky* (q. v. sub I-7), 261-275.

Gardberg, C. J.: *Late Nubian Sites. Churches and Settlements.* With an Introduction by T. Säve-Söderbergh. (Stockholm, 1970). – R: *OLZ* 68, 454-457 (William Y. Adams).

Garsoïan, N. G.: "Le rôle de la hiérarchie chrétienne dans les rapports diplomatiques entre Byzance et les Sassanides", in: *XXIXe Congrès Intern. des Orientalistes, Résumés des Communications*, Sections 1-5, (Paris. Y. Hervouet), p. 42.

Gaudemet, J.: "De la liberté constantinienne à une Eglise d'Etat", *RDC* 23, 59-76.

Gaudemet, J.: "Sur la co-responsabilité", *L'Année Canonique* 17, 533-541.

Gautier, P.: "L'édit d'Alexis Ier Comnène sur la réforme du clergé", *REByz* 31, 165-201.

Gautier, P.: "Les lettres de Grégoire, higoumène d'Oxia" (d'après *Vaticanus graecus* 573), *REByz* 31, 203-227.

Gerest, C.: "Mouvements spirituels et institutions ecclésiales (essai historique)", *Concilium* no. 89, 35-50.

Golub, I.: "L'autograph de l'ouvrage de Križanić *Bibliotheca Schismaticorum Universa* des archives de la Congrégation du Saint Office à Rome", *OChP* 39/1, 131-161.

Goodall, J. A.: "Icons and Spirituality: An Essay in Interpretation", *One in Christ* 9/3, 284-293.

Gouillard, J.: "Constantin Chrysomallos sous le masque de Syméon le Nouveau Théologien", *Travaux et Mémoires* 5, 313-327.

Granata, A.: "La dottrina dell'elemosina nel sermone *Pro sanctimonialibus de Paraclito* di Abelardo", *Aevum* 47, 32-59.

Gross, J.: "Uber die Stellung des Papstes. 'Der Gefangene des Vatikans' ", *ZRGG* 25, 112-125.

Gunther, J. J.: "The Fate of the Jerusalem Church. The Flight to Pella", *Theologische Zeitschrift* 29/2, 81-94.

Hage, W.: "Die oströmische Staatskirche und die Christenheit des Perserreiches", *ZKG* 84/2-3, 174-187.

Halkin, F.: "Sainte Elisabeth d'Héraclée, abbesse à Constantinople", *AB* 91/3-4, 249-264.

Harrington, Wilfrid: *The Path of Biblical Theology*. (Dublin, Gill and MacMillan). ix, 438 p.

Haulotte, E.: "Unités de base selon le Nouveau Testament", *Cultures et Foi*, no. 25, 11-28.

Houssiau, A.: "Le lien conjugal dans l'Eglise ancienne", *L'Année Canonique* 17, 569-577.

Huber, Paul: *Bild und Botschaft. Byzantinische Miniaturen zum Alten und Neuen Testament*. (Zürich, Atlantis Verlag). 4to. 204 S., 98 Taf. (davon 33 farb.).

Jaspert, B.: "Die Ursprünge der päpstlichen Unfehlbarkeitslehre", *ZRGG* 25/2, 126-134. (Regarding B. Tierney: *Origins of Papal Infaillibility 1150-1350. A Study on the Concept of Inafaillibility, Sovereignty and Tradition in the Middle Ages*, Leiden, 1972).

Jaubert, A.: "Inafaillible: observations sur le langage du Nouveau Testament", *RDCCIF* 79, 93-101.

Jenkins, D.: "What does Salvation Mean to Christians Today?", *Ecumenical Review* 25/2, 180-190.

Jolivet, J.: *Arts du langage et théologie chez Abélard*, (Paris, J. Vrin, 1969), 390 p. – R: *CCM* 16/1, 75-76 (M. Hubert).

Kane, G. S.: "*Fides quaerens intellectum* in Anselm"s Thought", *SJTh* 26/1, 40-62.

Kannengiesser, C.: "Athanasius von Alexandrien, seine Beziehungen zu Trier und seine Rolle in der Geschichte der christlichen Theologie", *TThZ* 82/3, 141-153.

Kawerau, Peter: *Das Christentum des Ostens*. (Stuttgart, W. Kohlhammer, 1972). 298 p. = Die Religionen der Menschheit, 30. – R: *Anthropos* 68, 314-315 (Johann Kraus).

Kazakova, N. A.: "Maxime le Grec dans l'historiographie soviétique", *Voprosy Istorii* No. 5, 149-157.

Khalil-Kussaim, S.: "Date de la composition de l'évangéliaire rimé de ᶜAbdīšūᵓ", *MUSJ* 47, 173-181.

Kieckhefer, R. A.: "Repression of Heresy in Germany, 1348-1520", *DisAbIn A*

34/2, 691. (The author's summary of his diss., University of Texas at Austin, 1972).

Klauser, T.: "Rom und der Kult der Gottesmutter Maria", *Jahrbuch für Antike und Christentum* 15, 120-135, 3 Abb., 2 Taf.

Kochev, N.: "Ideyno-teoretičeskie korni isikhazma", *Etudes Balkaniques* 9, No. 1, 48-61.

Kontakia of Romanos, Byzantine melodist, Vol. II: *On Christian life.* Translated and annotated by Marjorie Carpenter. (Columbia, University of Missouri Press). 4to. xiv, 310 p.

Kooy, V. E.: "God and Nature in John Scotus erigena: An Examination of the Neoplatonic Elements and their Greek Patristic Sources in the Ontological System of John Scotus Erigena", *DisAbIn, A* 33/8, 4478. (The author's summary of his diss., Claremont Graduate School, 1972).

Kottje, R.: "Ein bisher unbekanntes Fragment der Historia Eclesiastica Gentis Anglorum Bedas", *ReBén* 83, 429-432.

Krajcar, J.: "Simeon of Suzdal's Account of the Council of Florence", *OChP* 39, No. 1, 103-130.

Krautheimer, R.: *Early Christian and Byzantine Architecture.* (Penguin Books, 1965). xx, 390 p., illus. – R: *BZ* 66/1, 120-132 (H. Hallensleben).

Kümmel, W. G.: "Luc en accusation dans la théologie contemporaine", in: *L'Evangile de Luc. Problèmes littéraires et théologiques. Mémorial Lucien Cerfaux.* (Gembloux, J. Duculot), pp. 149-165.

Küng, H.: "La préhistoire de *Infaillible? Une interpellation*", *RDCCIF* 79, 14-31.

Laurent, V.: *Les Mémoires du Grand Ecclésiarque de l'Eglise de Constantinople Sylvestre Syropoulos sur le Concile de Florence (1438-1439).* (Paris, C.N.R.S., 1971). xxv, 715 p., 10 pl. = Publications de l'Institut Français d'Etudes Byzantines. – R: *RThL* 4/1, 112-115 (A. de Halleux).

Lemaire, A.: "L'Eglise apostolique et les ministères", *Revue de Droit Canonique* 23, 19-46.

Lépissier, J.: "Quelques passages de l'*Izbornik* de 1076 avec leur source grecque", *Byzantinoslavica* 34/1, 28-32.

van der Lof, L. J.: "Der fanatische Arianismus der Wandalen", *ZNTW* 64, No. 1-2, 146-151.

Lozinskij, M.: "Sur l'histoire des *Paterik* (Vies des Pères du désert et récits hagiographiques)", *ŽMP* no. 3, 72-75.

Luscombe, D.,E.: *The School of Peter Abelard*, (Cambridge University Press, 1969), xiii, 360 p. – R: *CCM* 16/1, 79-81 (R. Javelet).

McDermott, J. M.: "Hilary of Poitiers: The Infinite Nature of God", *Vigilliae Christianae* 27, 172-202.

McGinn, B.: "Joachim and the Sibyl. An Early Work of Joachim of Fiore from Ms. 322 of the Bibliotheca Antoniana in Padua", *CCC* 24/2, 97-138.

Machilek, F.: "Ergebnisse und Aufgaben moderner Hus-Forschung. Zu einer neuen Biographie des Johannes Hus", *ZOfg* 22/2, 302-330. (A propos de M. Spinka: *John Hus, a biography*, Princeton University Press, 1968, 344 p.)

Macomber, W. F.: "A Theory on the Origins of the Syrian Maronite and Chaldean Rites", *OChP* 39/1, 235-242.

Maiberger, P.: "*Das Buch der kostbaren Perle*" von Severus Ibn al-Muqaffà. Einleitung und arabischer Text. (Wiesbaden, F. Steiner Verlag, 1972). – R: *Erasmus* 25, 339-343 (M. Cramer).

Maisonneuve, H.: "La pape et l'Eglise", *L'Année Canonique* 17, 623-646.

Maloney, G. A.: *Russian Hesychasm. The Spirituality of Nil Sorskij*. (The Hague, Mouton). 302 p. = Slavistic Printings and Reprintings, 269.

Maron, G.: "Geschichtliche Aspekte neuzeitlicher Konfessionalität", *Jahrbuch des Evangelischen Bundes* 16, 48-59.

Martimort, A.-G.: *Le Gallicanisme*. (Paris, Presses Universitaires de France). 128 p. = Coll. "Que sais-je?".

Mazzini, I.: "Lettera del Concilio di Arles (314) a papa Silvestro tradita dal codex Parisinus Latinus 1711. (Dubbi intorno alla sua autenticità)", *VigChr* 27, 282-300.

Mencucci, V.: "I moti popolari di inspirazione religiosa nel medioevo", *Humanitas* 28/4, 286-300, bibliogr.

Mian, F.: "Maiestatis communio", *Augustinianum* 13/2, 205-214.

Michalowski, Kazimierz: *Faras. Centre artistique de la Nubie chrétienne*. (Leiden, 1966), (und) –: *Faras. Die Kathedrale aus dem Wüstensand*. (Einsiedeln, 1967). – R: *OLZ* 68, 457-461 (E. Blumenthal).

Mikkers, E.: "Jean de Ford", *Dictionnaire de Spiritualité Ascétique et Mystique*, t. 8, fasc. 54-55, col. 516-527.

Miquel, P.: "Deux témoins de l'expérience de Dieu: Saint Bernard et Pierre le Vénérable", *ColCis* 35/2, 108-120.

Molnar, A.: *Jan Hus, Testimone della Verità*. (Torino, Editrice Claudiana). 237 p., 20 tav., bibliografia (6 p.)

Moore, R. I.: "Nicétas, émissaire de Dragovitch, a-t-il traversé les Alpes?", *Annales du Midi* 85, 85-90.

Našturel, P. Ş.: "Quatre martyrs de Noviodonum (Scythie mineure)", *Analecta Bollandiana* 91, No. 1-2, 5-8, 1 pl.

Nautin, P.: "L'évolution des ministères au IIe et au IIIe siècle", *RDC* 23, 47-58.

Nersès Šnorhali: *Jésus Fils unique du Père*. Introduction, traduction de l'arménien et notes par I. Kéchichian. (Paris, Ed. du Cerf). 252 p., 1 pl., 1 carte. = Sources chrétiennes, 203.

Nichols, R. L.: "Metropolitan Filaret of Moscow and the Awakening of Orthodoxy", *DisAbIn, A* 33/8, 4316-4317. (The author's summary of his diss., University of Washington, 1972).

Noethlichs, K. L.: "Zur Einflussnahme des Staates auf die Entwicklung eines christlichen Klerikerstandes. Schicht- und berufsspezifische Bestimmungen für den Klerus im 4. und 5. Jahrhundert in den spätantiken Rechtsquellen", *JACh* 15, 136-153.

Noret, J.: "La vie grecque ancienne de S. Marūtā de Mayferqaṭ", *Analecta Bollandiana* 91, 77-103.

Nowak, Edward: *Le chrétien devant la souffrance*. Etude sur la pensée de Jean Chrysostome. (Paris, Editions Beauchesne). 4to. 240 p. = Théologie historique, 19.

Palgen, Rudolf: "Der Schöpfungsbericht der Beatrice", *Kairos* 15, Heft 1-2, 50-60.

Pelikan, J.: " 'Council or Father or Scripture': The Concept of Authority in the Theology of Maximus Confessor", in: *The Heritage of the Early Church, Essays in Honor of G. V. Florovsky* (q. v. sub I-7), 277-288.

Phaire, B. R.: "Papal Motivations for an Asian Apostolate (1245-1254). An Analysis", *BisAbIn, A* 33/11, 6262. (The author's summary of his diss., New York University, 1972).

Pontal, O.: "Recherches sur le costume des clercs des origines au XIVe siècle d'après les décrets des conciles et des synodes", *AnCan* 17, 769-796.

Popov, I. V.: "Saint Apmphiloque, éveque d'Iconium", *Bogoslovskie Trudy* 9, 15-79, bibliographie. (En russe).

Quecke, H.: "Ein neues koptisches Anaphora-Fragment (Bonn, Univ.-Bibl. So 267)", *OChP* 39/1, 216-223, 2 Taf.

Rahner, K.: "Kirchliche und ausserkirchliche Religiosität", *Stimmen der Zeit* 191, Heft 1, 3-13.

Recio, A.: "Fragmentos de sarcofagos romano-cristianos en Andalucía", *Antonianum* 48/2-3, 343-360, 4 pl.

Reiche, R.: "Einige lateinische Monatsdiätetiken aus Wiener und St. Galler Handschriften", *Sudhoffs Archiv* 57/2, 113-141.

Reymond, E. A. E. – J. W. B. Barns (ed.): *Four Martydoms from the Pierpont Morgan Coptic Codices*. (London, Oxford University Press). xii, 278 p.

van Riet, G.: "Le problème du mal dans la philosophie de la religion de Saint Thomas", *RPhL* 71, No. 9, 5-45.

Rijk, C. A.: "Importance des relations judéo-chrétiennes pour la liturgie chrétienne", *SIDJC* VI/1, 26-32.

Riou, A.: *Le Monde et l'Eglise selon Maxime le Confesseur.* (Paris, Beauchesne). 279 p., bibliogr. (7 p.), 4 index. = Théologie historique, 22.

Roché, D.: "Catharisme et science spirituelle", *Cahiers d'Etudes Cathares* 24 (60), 3-14.

Roché, Deodat: "L'Initiation cathare", *Cahiers d'Etudes Cathares* 24, no. 59, 3-11.

Van Roey, A.: "L'Oeuvre littéraire de Pierre de Callinique, patriarche jacobite d'Antioche († 591)", in: *XXIXe Congrès International des Orientalistes. Résumés des Communications*, Sections 1-5. (Paris, Y Hervouet), p. 49.

Roques, R.: "Jean Scot (Erigène)", *Dictionnaire de Spiritualité Ascétique et Mystique*, t. 8, fasc. 54-55, col. 735-761.

de Rossi, I. B. – A. Ferrua: *Inscriptiones christianae urbis Romae septimo saeculo antiquiores.* Vol. V: *Coemeteria reliqua viae Appiae.* (Vatican, Pont. Institutm Archaeolog. Christian), 1971). viii, 442 p., 39 pl. – R: *Vetera Christianorum* 10/1, 180-194 (C. Carletti).

Rückert, H.: *Vorträge und Aufsätze zur historischen Theologie* 1972. – R: *Erasmus* 25/3-4, 79-81 (F. F. Bruce).

Ryan, J. D.: "The Interrelation of the Oriental Mission and Crusade Activities of the Papacy under Nicholas IV (1288-1292)", *DisAbIn, A* 33/11, 6263. (The author's summary of his diss., New York University, 1972).

Samir, K.: "Le Recueil Ephrémien Arabe des 52 homélies", *OChP* 39, no. 2, 307-332, bibliographie (2 p.)

Šanjek, F.: "Albigeois et 'chrétiens' bosniaques", *RHEF* 59 (163), 251-267.

Santos, A.: "La espiritualidad bizantina", *Manresa* 45 (no. 174), 27-60.

Schlink, E.: "Die Bedeutung der orthodoxen Kirche für die ökumenische Bewegung", *ÖkRs* 22/4, 430-441.

Schmid, H. H.: "Schöpfung, Gerechtigkeit und Heil. 'Schöpfungstheologie' als Gesamthorizont biblischer Theologie", *ZThK* 70/1, 1-19.

Schmieschen, P. M.: "Anselm and the Faithfulness of God", *Scotish Journal of Theology* 26/2, 151-168.

Schmitz-Valckenberg, G.: *Grundlehren katharischer Sekten des 13. Jahrhunderts.* Eine theologische Untersuchung mit besonderer Berücksichtigung von *Adversus Catharos et Valdenses* des Moneta von Cremona. (München, Ferdinand Schöning, 1971). xx, 351 p. – R: *Speculum* 48/2, 404-406 (R. E. Lerner).

Schneemelcher, W.: "Das Konstantinische Zeitalter. Kritisch-historische Bemerkungen zu einem modernen Schlagwort", *Kleronomia* 6/1, 37-60.

Schulze, Bernhard: "Das Weltbild des Patriarchen Photios nach seinen Homilien", *Kairos* 15, Heft 1-2, 101-115.

Scobie, C. H. H.: "The Origins and Development of Samaritan Christianity", *NTS* 19, No. 4, 390-414.

Sed, N.: "Le docétisme des Odes de Salomon", in: *XXIXe Congrès International des Orientalistes. Résumés des Communications*, Sections 1-5. (Paris, Y. Hervouet), p. 48.

Sims-Williams, N.: "A Sogdian Fragment of a Work of Dadišo Qaṭraya", *Asia Major* 18, No. 1, 88-105.

Smolík, J.: "Truth in History According to Hus' Conception", *Communio Viatorum* 15/2-3, 97-109.

Somogyi, A.: "Ein kirchenslawischer Kodex von Ungarn", *Etudes Balkaniques* 8/2, 65-79.

Steitz, Heinrich: "Kirchengeschichte der Frühzeit", in: U. Mann (Hrsg.): *Theologie und Religionswissenschaft* (Darmstadt, Wissenschaftliche Buchgesellschaft), 332-356.

Stiernon, D.: "Jean de Karpathos", *Dictionnaire de Spiritualité Ascétique et Mystique*, t. 8, fasc. 54-55, col. 589-592.

Strayer, J. R.: *The Albigensian Crusades*, (New York, The Dial Press, 1971), 201 p. – R: *Speculum* 48/2, 411-415 (F. L. Cheyette).

Suhl, Alfred: "Der Philomenbrief als Veispiel paulinischeer Paränese", *Kairos* 15, Heft 3-4, 267-279.

Tarnay, A.: "Auteurs et sources de la chronique des Observantins hongrois", *ITK* 77, no. 2-3, 135-147 (en hongrois).

Testa, P. E.: "Reazione delle correnti religiose giudaiche e cristiane sulla distruzione di Gerusalemme (I-II secolo d. C.)", *Rivista Biblica* 21/3, 301-324.

Theunissen, W. P.: *Ikonen*. (Den Haag, Uitgeversmij Succes). 4to. 43 p., 30 pl.

Thomas, R. (ed.): *Petrus Abaelardus: Dialogus inter Philosophum, Judaeum et Christianum*, (Stuttgart, 1970), 171 p. – R: *CCM* 16/1, 83-84 (M. de Candillac).

Trout, J. M. III: "Alan of Lille and the Art of Preaching in the Twelfth Century", *DisAbIn, A* 33/8, 4292-4293. (The author's summary of his diss., Rutgers University, 1972).

Tsuji, S. G.: " 'Le passage de la mer Rouge': étude iconographique d'un des panneaux sculptés des portes de Sainte – Sabine à Rome", *Orient* 8, 53-79, 6 pl.

Turner, C. J. G.: "A Slavonic Version of John Cantacuzenus's *Against Islam*", *SEER* 51 (122), 113-127.

Vandermarck, W.: "Natural Knowledge of God in Romans: Patristic and Medieval Interpretation", *ThSt* 34/1, 36-52.

Varona García, M. A.: "Fragmento de un salterio visigótico en el archivo de la Real Chancillería de Valladolid", *RABM* 76, 405-412.

Vattioni, F.: "Le iscrizioni siriache antiche", *Augustinianum* 13/2, 279-338. (Supplements H. J. W. Drijvers: *Old Syriac/Edessean/Inscriptions*, Leiden, 1972).

Velimirović, Miloś (ed.): *Studies in E. tern Chant*, III. (London, Oxford University Press). viii, 187 p., 5 pl.

Vogel, C.: "*Laica communione contentus*. Le retour du presbytre au rang des laïcs (Eléments du dossier)", *RevSR* 47/1, 56-122.

Vogel C.: "Titre d'ordination et lien du presbytre à la communauté locale dans l'Eglise ancienne", *Maison-Dieu* 115, 70-85.

Vööbus, A.: "Nouvelles sources de l'Octateuque clémentin Syriaque", *Le Muséon* 86, 105-109.

Vööbus, A.: "The Discovery of New Important *mēmrē* of Gīwargī, the Bishop of the Arabs", *JSS* 18/2, 235-237.

Vööbus, A.: "The Origin of the Monophysite Church in Syria and Mesopotamia", *Church History* 42/1, 17-26.

van der Walt, B. J.: "Eisegesis-Exegesis, Paradox and Nature-Grace: Methods of Synthesis in Medieval Philosophy", *PhRef* 38, 191-211.

Walter, C.: "Pictures of the Clergy in the Theodore Psalter", *Revue des Etudes Byzantines* 31, 229-242, 2 pl.

Weissmahr, B.: "Gibt es von Gott gewirkte Wunder? Grundsätzliche Ueberlegungen zu einer Verdrängten Problematik", *Stimmen der Zeit* 191/1, 47-61.

Werth, R. N.: "Die gotischen Bezeichnungen für 'Hoherpriester' ", *ZVS* 87, Heft 2, 248-268.

Yuzbashian (= Juzbašjan), K. N.: "Photius et l'origine du nom 'Pauliciens' ", *VON* no. 8, 87-90 (en russe).

Yuzbashian, K.: "De l'origine du nom *Pauliciens*", *REArm* 9, 355-377.

VI. ISLAM

1. PRE-ISLAMIC ARABIA

Aggoula, B.: "Remarques sur les inscriptions hatréennes" (II), *MUSJ* 47, 1-83.

van Beek, Gus W.: *Hajar Bin Humeid. Investigations at a Pre-Islamic Site in South Arabia.* With Contributions by A. Jamme (and others). (Baltimore, 1969). – R: *OLZ* 68, 480-484 (Walter W. Müller).

Beeston, A. L. F.: "Kingship in Ancient South Arabia", *JESHO* 15, 256-268.

Beeston, A. F. L.: "The Heart of Shanfarā", *Journal of Semitic Studies* 18, 257-258.

Bibby, T. G.: *Preliminary Survey in East Arabia 1968.* (Reports of the Danish Archeological Expedition to the Arabian Gulf. Volum Two). With one chapter by Holger Kapel. 4to. 67 p., 66 fig. = Jutland Archaeological Society Publications, XII.

Dalgleish, K.: "Some aspects of the treatment of emotion in the *dīwān* of al-Aʿshā", *JAL* 4, 97-111.

Dentzer, J.-M.: "Le sanctuaire de Baalshamîn à Palmyre", *Revue Archéologique*, no. 2, 315-320.

Garbini, G.: "Nuove iscrizioni sabee", *Annali dell'Istituto Orientali di Napoli* 33/1, 31-46, 4 tav.

Hammond, P.: "The Snake Monument at Petra", *AJAS* I/1, 1-29, 5 fig.

Hammond, Philip C.: *The Nabateans, Their History, Culture and Archaeology.* (Gothenburg, Paul Åström Förlag). 129 p., 4 maps. = Studies in Mediterranean Archaeology, 42.

Höfner, Maria: *Inschriften aus Sirwāh, Haulān* (I. Teil). (Wien, Verlag der Österreichischen Akademie der Wissenschaften). 81 p., 17 Taf. = ÖAW, Philos.-Historische Klasse, Sitzungsberichte, 291/1. Sammlung Eduard Glaser, VIII.

Jamme, A.: "Documentation Sud-Arabe, VIII", *Rivista degli Studi Orientali* 48, no. 1-4, 1-13.

Klengel, Horst: *Syria Antiqua. Vorislamische Denkmäler der Syrischen Arabischen Republik.* (Leipzig, 1971). – R: *Syria* 49, 454-455 (A. P.)

Lankester Harding, G.: *An Index and Concordance of Pre-Islamic Names and Inscriptions.* (University of Toronto Press, 1971). – R: *BiOr* 30, 284-288 (A. G. Loundine).

Loundine, A. G.: "Deux inscriptions sabéennes de Mârib", *Le Muséon* 86, No. 1-2, 179-192.

Lüling, Günter: *Die einzigartige Perle des Suwaid b. Abi Kahil al-Yaškuri*. 2. Teil. *Über die eindeutige Christlichkeit dieses in der vorislamischen 'Heidenzeit' hochgerühnten Gedichtes*. (Erlange, H. Lüling). 52 p. = Abhandlungen zur Christlichen Altarabischen Literatur, 1.

Nöldeke, Theodor: *Geschichte der Perser und Araber zur Zeit der Sasaniden*. Aus der arabischen Chronik des Tabari übersetzt und mit ausführlichen Erläuterungen und Ergänzungen versehen. Photomechanischer Nachdruck der Erstausgabe 1879. (Leiden, E. J. Brill). xxviii, 503 S.

Puech, E.: "L'inscription de la citadelle d'Amman", *Revue Biblique* 80, no. 4, 531-546, 1 pl.

Ryckmans, Jacques: "Etudes d'épigraphie sud-arabe en russe, 9 (année 1972)", *BiOr* XXX, 193-194.

Ryckmans, J.: "Le repas rituel dans la religion sud-arabe", *Festschrift de Liagre Böhl* (q. v. sub I-7), 327-334.

Ryckmans, J.: "Les inscriptions anciennes de l'Arabie du Sud. Points de vue et problèmes actuels", *Oosters Genootschap in Nederland* 4, 75-110.

Ryckmans, Jacques: "Un rite d'*istisqā*ᵓ au temple sabéen de Marib", *AIPHOS* 20, 379-388.

Schaffer, Brigitte (Hrsg.): *Sammlung Eduard Claser, VII*. Sabäische Inschriften aus verschiedenen Fundorten. (Wien, Hermann Böhlaus Nachf., 1972). 65 p., 11 Taf. = ÖAW, Philos.-Hist. Klasse, Sitzungsberichte, 282/1. – R: *Anthropos* 68, 647 (J.H.)

Schneider, R.: "Deux inscriptions Sudarabiques du Tigré", *BiOr* 30, 385-389, pl. XIV-XVI (9 photos).

Seyrig, H.: "Les dieux syriens en habit militaire", *AAAS* 21, no. 1-2, 67-76, 2 pl.

Shahîd, Irfan: *The Martyrs of Najrân: New Documents*. (*IBHR*, 1971). – R: *Orientalia* 42, 462-466 (R. Köbert).

Vattioni, F.: "Aspetti del culto del Signore dei cieli", *Augustinianum* 12/3, 479-515; 13/1, 37-73.

Winnett, F. V. and W. L. Reed: "An archaeological-epigraphical survey of the Hāᵓil area of Northern Saᶜūdi Arabia", *Berytus* 22, 53-100.

Wright, G. R. H.: "The Date of the Khaznet Firᶜaun at Petra in the Light of an Iconographic Detail", *PEQ* 105/1, 83-90, 1 pl.

2. SCRIPTURES, EARLY ISLAM

Atallah, W.: "De quelques prétendues idoles, *baǧǧa, šaǧǧa*, etc.", *Arabica* 20, 160-167.

Audebert, C.: "Notes sur les recherches autour de l'(*l'i*^{c}*ǧāz) I*^{c}*ǧāz* en Egypte au cours des vingt dernières années", *CLOS* 1-2, 29-37.

Austin, R. W.: " 'I seek God's pardon ...' ", *Studies in Comparative Religion* 7, 92-94.

Basetti-Sani, Giulio: "Satana nel Corano", *Sacra Doctrina* (Bologna), 587-653.

Basetti-Sani, Giulio: "Su alcune interpretazioni cattoliche di Muhammad", *Renovatio* 8, 606-624.

Beeston, A. F. L.: "Ships in a Quranic Simile", *Journal of Arabic Literature* 4, 94-96.

Bellamy, J. A.: "The mysterious letters of the Koran: old abb-reviations of the *Basmalah*", *JAOS* 93, 267-285.

Bohdan, L.: "Die Anschauungen über die Arbeit im Koran", *ZRGG* 25, Heft 2, 97-111.

Bravmann, M. M.: *The Spiritual Background of Early Islam. Studies in Ancient Arab Concepts.* (Leiden, 1972). – R: *BiOr* 30, 288-291 (G. H. A. Juynboll).

Calasso, G.: "Note su *waswasa*, 'sussurrare', nel Corano e nei *ḥadīt*", *AION* 23 (33), 233-246.

Cameron, A. J.: *Abû Dharr al-Ghifârî. An examination of his image in the hagiography of Islam.* (London, Luzac). xvi, 175 p. = Oriental Translation Fund, New Series, 43.

Corbin, H.: " 'Et son Trône était porté sur l'eau ...' (Qorân 11/9)", in: *In Principio. Interprétations des premiers versets de la Genèse*, (Paris, Etudes Augustiniennes, Centre des religions du livre), pp. 293-304. (Genèse, 1, 2 dans l'ésoterisme islamique).

Cragg, Kenneth: *The Event of the Qurʾān. Islam in its Scripture.* (London, 1971). (and) the same: *The Mind of the Qurʾān*, (London, 1973). – R: *Arabica* 20, 322-323 (M. Arkoun).

Cragg, K.: *The Event of the Qurʾān. Islam in its Scripture.* (London, 1971). – R: *WI* 14, 247-248 (S. D. Goitein).

Cuperus, W. S.: *Al-Fātiḥa dans la pratique réligieuse musulmane du Maroc à partir du 19ième siècle.* (Utrecht, Elikwijk), 188 p. (With a Summary in Dutch).

Dorra-Haddad, J.: "Coran, prédication nazaréenne", *Proche-Orient Chrétien* 23, no. 2, 148-155. (A propos de M. Roncaglia: "Eléments ébionites et elkésaites dans le Coran", *ibid.*, 21, 101-128).

Gaudefroy-Demombynes, Maurice: *Mahomet.* 2e éd. (Paris, 1969). – R: *OLZ* 68, 375-376 (C. E. Bosworth).

Juynboll, G. H. A. *The Authenticity of the Tradition Literature Discussion in Modern Egypt.* (Leiden, 1969). – R: *OLZ* 68, 270-271 (Johann Fück). *WI* 14, 221 (A. Schimmel).

Juynboll, G. H. A.: "The Qurrāʾ in Early Islamic History", *JESHO* 16, 113-129.

Kamińska, H.: "Les noms d'Allah dans le Coran. Essai d'une analyse statistique", *Studia Religioznawcze* no. 8, 49-69 (en polonais, rés. en russe, anglais, allem.)

Köbert, R.: "Zur Ansicht des frühen Islam über das Mönchtum (*rahbānīya*)", *Orientalia* 42, 520-524.

Köbert, R.: "Zur Bedeutung von *ṣibġa*(!) in Koran 2, 138", *Orientalia* 42, 518-519.

Der Koran. Aus dem Arabischen. Übersetzung von Max Henning. Einleitung von Ernst Werner und Kurt Rudolph. Textdurchsicht, Anmerkungen, Register von Kurt Rudolph. (Leipzig, 1968). – R: *OLZ* 68, 154-156 (H. Gätje).

Lapis, B.: "Die Anschauungen über die Arbeit im Koran", *ZRGG* 25, Heft 2, 97-111.

Magnin, J. M.: "Notes sur l'ébionisme", *PrOCh* 23, no. 3-4, 233-265. (A propos de M. Roncaglia: "Eléments ébionites et elkesaïtes dans le Coran", *ibid.* 21 (1971), 101-126, et de J. Dorra-Haddad: "Coran, prédication nazaréenne", *ibid.* 23, 148-155).

Marston Speight, R.: "Attitudes toward Christians as Revealed in the Musnad of al-Ṭayālisī", *The Muslim World* 63/4, 249-268.

Meier, Fritz: "Ein Profetenwort gegen die Totenbeweinung", *Der Islam* 50, 207-229.

Nagel, T.: "Das Problem der Orthodoxie im frühen Islam", *Bonner Orientalistische Studien*, N. S., 27/1 (Studien zum Minderheitenproblem im Islam), 7-44.

Napoli, G.: "Maria nel Corano", *SBF* 23, 206-241.

Newby, G. D.: "Sūrat al-ikhlāṣ", in: *Orient and Occident. Essays presented to C. R. Gordon* (q. v. sub I-7), 127-130.

Noth, A.: *Quellenkritische Studien zu Themen, Formen und Tendenzen frühislamischer Geschichtsüberlieferung.* 1: *Themen und Formen.* (Bonn, Selbstverlag des Orientalischen Seminars der Universotät). 210 S. = Bonner Orientalistische Studien, N. S., 25.

O'Shaughnessy, T. J.: "God's Throne and the Biblical Symbolism of the Qurʾān", *Numen* 20, 202-221.

Paret, Rudi: *Der Koran, Kommentar und Konkordanz* (Stuttgart, 1971). – R: *WI* 14, 218-219 (S. D. Goitein).

Robson, J.: "Aspects of the Qur'anic Doctrine of Salvation", in: *Man and his Salvation. Studies in Memory of S. G. F. Brandon* (Manchester University Press), 205-219.

Saiyidain, K. G.: "Qurān's Invitation to Think", *Islam and the Modern Age* 4, No. 2, 5-27.

Schmucker, W.: "Die christiliche Minderheit von Nağrān und die Problematik ihrer Beziehungen zum frühen Islam", *BOS* 27/1 (= *Studien zum Minderheitenproblem im Islam*), 183-281.

Schützinger, H.: "Die arabische Jeremia-Erzählung und ihre Beziehungen zur jüdischen religiösen Ueberlieferung", *ZRGG* 25/1, 1-19.

Speight, R. Marston: "Attitudes toward Christians as revealed in the *Musnad* of al-Ṭayālisī", *MW* 63, 249-268.

Speight, R. M.: "The Will of Sa^cd b. a. Waqqāṣ: The Growth of a Tradition", *Der Islam* 50, 249-267.

Wessels, Antonie: *A Modern Arabic Biography of Muhammad*, (Leiden, 1972). – R: *Arabica* 20, 314-315 (Ch. Pellat).

Zain-ul-Abedeen: "Man's Nature and Destiny: the Qur'anic View", *Religion and Society* 20, No. 3, 18-25.

Zain-ul-Abedeen: "Man's Nature and Destiny: What Do the Mufassirin Say?", *Religion and Society* 20, No. 3, 26-34.

3. THEOLOGY AND PHILOSOPHY

Abdou, M M. I.: *Les bases de La certitude chez Averroes*. (Lille, Service de reproduction des thèse, Univ. de Lille III). T. 1: 435 p., t. 2: 548 p., index. (Thèse, Univ. de Paris 1, 1e 12 juin 1973).

Abu Shanab, R. E.: "Avicenna and Ockham on the Problem of Universals", *Pakistan Philosophical Journal* 11, 1-14.

Ahmed, Ziauddin: "Aḥmad B. Ḥanbal and the Problems of *īmān*", *Islamic Studies* 12, 161-170.

Ahmed, Ziauddin: "Some Aspects of the Political Theology of Aḥmad b. Ḥanbal", *IslSt* 12, 53-66.

Alfarabi: *Book of Letters (Kitāb al-Ḥurūf). Commentary of Aristotle's Metaphysics*. Arabic Text, Edited with Introduction and Notes by M. Mahdi. (Beirut, 1969). – R: *OLZ* 68, 50-56 (G. G. Hana).

Alich, Salih H.: "Arapsko-islamska filozofija: definicija i značaj kroz historiju" (Arabo-Islamic Philosophy: Its Meaning and Role in History), *Izraz* XVII/10, 313-336, Bibliography (3 p.) (In Serbo-Croatian).

Antes, Peter: *Zur Theologie der Schi^ca*. Eine Untersuchung des *Ǧāmi^c al-asrār wa manba^c al-anwār* von Sayyid Ḥaidar Āmolī. (Freiburg/Br., 1971). – R: *BiOr* 30, 291-292 (K. Rudolph).

Arkoun, Muhammad: *Essais sur la pensée islamique*. (Paris, Ed. G.-P. Maisonneuve et Larose). 350 p.

Askari, Hasan: "Unity and Alienation in Islam": *The Ecumenical Review* 25, No. 2, 191-201.

Askari, Hasan: "Worship and Prayer", *Islam and the Modern Age* 4, No. 1, 20-37.

Atallah, W.: "Un rituel de serment chez les Arabes: *al-yamīn al-ġamūs*", *Arabica* XX, No. 1, 63-73.

Bausani, A.: "Cosmologia e religione nell'Islam", *Scientia* 108, no. 9-12, 723-767. (The same article also in English).

Belguedj, M. S.: "Ben Badis et le mu'tazilisme", *Revue de l'Occident Musulman et de la Mediterranée* 13-14, 75-86.

Berman, L. V.: "The Hebrew Versions of Averroes' Middle Commentary on the Nicomachean Ethics", in: *XXIXe Congrès International des Orientalistes, Résumés des Communications*, Sections 1-5. (Paris, Y. Hervouet), pp. 50-51.

Bernand, M.: "La Notion de ᶜIlm chez les premiers muᶜtazilites", *Studia Islamica* 37, 27-56 (suite).

Burki, Riffat: "Iqbal and Tauhid", *Iqbal Review* 14, No. 3, 9-15.

Burki, Riffat: "The Concept of Time in Iqbal's Thought", *JRCI* 6, 103-128.

Carré, O.: "Bulletin d'islamologie. Quelques ouvrages récents sur la pensée et la philosophie arabo-musulmanes", *RSPhTh* 57, 657-674.

Corbin, H.: "Per il concetto di filosofia irano-islamica", *Conoscenza Religiosa* (1973), 424-431.

Courtenay, W. J.: "The critique on natural causality in the mutakallimun and nominalism", *HThR* 66, 77-94.

Cragg, Kenneth: " 'In the Name of God ...' ", *Islam and the Modern Age* 4, No. 1, 1-10.

Endress, Gerhard: *Proclus Arabus: Zwanzig Abschnitte aus der Institutio Theologica in arabischer Uebersetzung*. Eingeleitet, herausgegeben und erklärt. (Wiesbaden, In Komm. bei Franz Steiner). 348 xii, 90 S. = Beiruter Texte und Studien, Band 10.

van Ess, J.: *Frühe muᶜtazilitische Häresiographie*. Zwei Werke des Nāšiᵓ al-akbar. (Wiesbaden, F. Steiner, 1971). – R: *Erasmus* 25, 389-390 (W. Montgomery Watt). *Arabica* 20, 92-93 (G. Vajda).

Farooqi, Hafiz Abbadullah: "Iqbal's Philosophy of Life", *Iqbal Review* 14, No. 3, 27-44.

Farooqi, Abbadullah: "The Impact of Khawaja Hafiz on Iqbal's Thought", *Iqbal Review* 14, No. 1, 33-60.

al-Fārūqī, I. R.: "The Essence of Religious Experience in Islam", *Numen* 20, 186-201.

Gardet, L.: "Quelques réflexions sur un problème de théologie et philosophie musulmanes: toue-puissance divine et liberté humaine", *ROMM* 13-14, 381-394, 381-394.

Gardet, L.: "The Religious and Philosophical Attitude of Ibn-i Sina (and its Hellenic Sources)", *JPHS* 21, 149-163.

al-Geyoushi, Muhammed Ibraheem: "Al-Tirmidhi's Conception of the Areas of Interiority", *IslQuart* 16, 168-188.

al-Ghazālī, Abū Ḥāmid: *Al Maqṣad al-asnā fī Sharḥ Maᶜānī Asmāᵓ Allāh al-Ḥusnā.* Arabic text with Introduction by Fadlou A. Shehadi. (Beyrouth, 1971). – R: *BiOr* 104-105 (M. van Damme).

Gräf, Erwin: "Brauch/ᶜ*urf* und Sitte/ᶜ*āda* in der islamischen Jurisprudenz", in: *Festschrift zum 65. Geburtstag von Helmut Petri* (Wien, Böhlau), 122-144.

Hawi, Sami S.: "A Twelfth-Century Philosophy of Science", *Pakistan Philosophical Journal* 11, 15-36.

Hawi, Sami S.: "Ibn Ṭufail's Ḥayy ibn Yaqẓān: Its Structure, Literary Aspects and Method", *IsCul* 47 191-211.

Horten, Max: "The System of Islamic Philosophy in General", *Is1St* 12, 1-36. (Translated from German by V. J. Hager).

Hourani, G. F.: Islamic Rationalism: The Ethics of ᶜAbd al-Jabbār, (Oxford, 1971). – R: *JRAS* 1, 56-57 (J. N. Mattock).

Ibn Abī d-Dunyā: *The Noble Qualities of Character.* Edited with an Introduction and Notes by James A. Bellamy. (Wiesbaden, Franz Steiner Verlag). xiv, 110, 150 (Arabic Text) p., 3 pl. = Bibliotheca Islamica, 25.

[Ibn al-Nafis:] *The Theologus Autodidactus* of Ibn al-Nafīs.-*ar-Risāla al-Kāmilīya fī s-sīra an-nabawīya.* Edited with an Introduction, Translation and Notes by the late M. Meyerhof and J. Schacht. (Oxford, 1968). – R: *OLZ* 68, 487-489 (J. van Ess).

Israili, Shamoon: "Iqbal: a Progressive", *Indo-Iranica* 26, No. 2-3, 127-142.

Jadaane, F.: "Les conditions socio-culturelles de la philosophie islamique", *Studia Ismanica* 38, 5-60.

Jarzebowski, T.: "Astronomical Works of al-Biruni", *Afghanistan* 26, No. 2, 6-14.

Jomier, J.: "Le prophétisme musulman", *Studia Missionalia* 22, 237-254.

Khundmiri, S. Alam: "Man's Nature and Destiny: philosophic view in Islam", *Religion and Society* 20/3, 35-42.

King, D.,A.: "Al-Khalili's auxiliary tables for solving problems of spherical astronomy", *JHA* 4, 99-110.

King, D. A.: "Ibn Yunus' very useful tables for reckoning time by the sun", *AHES* 10, 342-394.

van Koningsveld, P. S.: "ᶜUmar ibn al-Muẓaffar ibn Rūzbahān ibn Ṭāhir Šams ad-Dīn Abu 'l-Mafākhir (fl. 615 H) and his Study of *Kitāb al-Miğisṭī*", *Der Islam* 50, 168-169.

Livingston, J. W.: "Naṣīr al-Dīn al-Ṭūsī's *al-Tadhkirah*: A Category of Ismanic Astronomical Literature", *Centaurus* 17, 260-275.

Mahdi, Muhsin: "Alfarabi on Philosophy and Religion", *The Philosophical Forum* 4/1, 5-25.

Marquet, Y.: *La Philosophie des Iḫwān al-safā. De Dieu à l'homme*. (Thèse, Univ. Paris IV, 1971. Univ. Lille III, Service de reproduction des thèse). 680 p., bibliographie.

Muñoz Jimenez, R.: "Muhammad ᶜAbduh: su obra y su doctrina teológica", *Ciencia Tomista* 100/3-4, 535-563 (to be continued).

Nasr, S. H.: "The Meaning and Role of 'Philosophy' in Islam", *Studia Islamica* 37, 57-80.

Nasr, Seyyed Hossein: "The Meaning and Role of Philosophy in Islam", *JRCI* 6, No. 1-2, 5-28.

Nasr, Seyyed Hossein: "The Significance of Comparative Philosophy for the Study of Islamic Philosophy", *IsMA* 4/1, 11-19. (Published also in *SCR* 7, 212-218).

an-Naubaḫtī, al-Ḥasan ibn Mūsā: *Les sectes shiites*. Traduction de l'arabe, étude et commentaire par S. M. Prozorov. (Moskva, Izd. Nauka). 255 p., 1 pl., bibliographie (7 p.), index. (En russe).

Nettler, Ronald L.: "A controversy on the problem of perception: The religious outlooks in Islam", *HumIs* I, 133-156.

Paret, Rudi: "Der Islam", in: U. Mann (Hrsg.): *Theologie und Religionswissenschaft* (Darmstadt, Wissenschaftliche Buchgesellschaft) 144-161.

Pellat, Ch.: "L'astrolable sphérique d'al-Rudani", *Bulletin d'Etudes Orientales* 26, 7-83.

Pingree, D.: "The Greek Influence on Early Islamic Mathematical Astronomy", *JAOS* 93, 32-43.

Rasheed, Ghulam Dastagir: "Iqbal and the Concept of Perfect Man", *Indo-Iranica* 26, No. 2-3, 124-126.

Riad, E.: "A propos d'une définition de la colère chez al-Kindī", *Orientalia Suecana* 22, 62-65.

Riad, E.: "Miskawayh sur la colère", *Orientalia Suecana* 21, 34-52.

Said, Subhi: "On the musattribution of the word *al-Ḥujja* to Abū ᶜAbdallāh al-Husayn b. Khālawayh", *IslQuart* 17, 125-139.

Schimmel, Annemarie: "A 'sincere Muhammadan's' way to salvation", in: *Man and his Salvation. Studies in Memory of S. G. F. Brandon* (Manchester University Press), 221-242.

Schipperges, H.: "Zur Typologie eines 'Avicenna Hispanus' ", *Sudhoffs Archiv* 57, 99-101.

Schmitz, R. und Fariborz Moattar: "Zur Biobliographie Ismāᶜil Ǧorǧānīs (1040-1136). Der 'Schatz des Königs von Ḫwārazm' ", *Sudhoffs Archiv* 57, 337-360.

Schuon, F.: "Dilemmas of theological speculation, with special reference to Moslem scholasticism", *IslQuart* 17, 36-63.

Sheikh, M. Saeed: "Al-Ghazali's Influence on the West", *Pakistan Philosophical Journal* 11, 53-67.

Spies, Otto: "Islam und Syntagē", *Oriens Christianus* 57, 1-30.

Stepanyants, M. T.: "Problems of Ethics in Mohammad Iqbal's Philosophy", *Iqbal Review* 14/1, 1-8.

Strohmaier, G.: "Diogenesanekdoten auf Papyrus und in arabischen Gnomologien", *ArPap* 22, 285-288.

Swartz, Merlin: "A seventh-century (A. H.) Sunni creed: The ᶜAqīda Wāsitīya of Ibn Taymīya", *HumIs* I, 91-131. ("Introduction", pp. 91-103, "The Translation", pp. 103-131).

Swerdlow, N.: "Al-Battānī's Determination of the Solar Distance", *Centaurus* 17, 97-105.

Tamer, Aref (ed.): *La Quaṣīda šāfīya* [!]. Texte arabe établi et annoté. (Beyrouth, 1967). – R: *OLZ* 68, 484-487 (E. Wagner).

Veselovsky, N.: "Copernicus and Nasir al-Din al-Tusi", *Journal for the History of Astronomy* 4, 99-130.

Watt, W. Montgomery: *The Formative Period of Islamic Thought.* (Edinburgh, The University Press). xii, 424 p.

Waugh, E.: "Jealous Angels: Aspects of Muslim Religious Language", *OJRS* 1, No. 2, 56-72.

Wein, Clemens: *Die islamische Glaubenslehre* (ᶜAqīda) *des Ibn Taimiya.* (Bonn, Inaugural-Dissertation zur Erlangung der Doktorwürde der Philosophischen Fakultät der Rheinischen Friedrich-Wilhelms-Universität zu Bonn). 132 p.

Widengren, G.: "La légende des Sept Dormants dans les écrits des Frères Purs", *Archivio di Filosofia* (= Demitizzazione e Ideologia, Padova), 509-526.

Zimmermann, Friedrich W. und H. Vivian B. Brown: "Neue arabische Übersetzungstexte aus dem Bereich der spätantiken griechischen Philosophie", *Der Islam* 50, 313-324.

4. MYSTICISM

Ali, Hafiz, Mohammad Tahir: "Shaikh Muhibbullah of Allahabad: Life and Times", *IsCul* 47, 241-256.

Ansari, Nagmuddin: "Some Notes on the Life, Works, and Thoughts of Shaykh Saduddin Ahmad Ansari", *Afghanistan* 25/4, 32-45.

Arberry, A. J.: *A Sufi Martyr.* The Apologia of ᶜAin al-Quḍāt al-Hamadhānī, Translated with Introduction and Notes. (London, 1969). – R: *OLZ* 68, 376-378 (A. Schimmel). *WI* 14, 229-230 (J. van Ess).

al-Attas, S. M. N.: *The Mysticism of Ḥamzah Fanṣūri* (Kuala Lumpur, 1970). – R: *WI* 14, 231-233 (A. Schimmel).

el-Azma, Nazeer: "Some notes on the impact of the story of the Miᶜrāj on Sufi literature", *MW* 63, 93-104.

Baljon, J. M. S.: *A Mystical Interpretation of Prophetic Tales by an Indian Muslim.* Shāh Walī Allāh's *Taʾwīl al-aḥādīth*, translated. (Leiden, E. J. Brill). ix, 67 p. = Religious Texts Translation Series Nisaba, 2.

Chabbi, J.: "ᶜAbd al-Ḳādir al-Djīlānī, personnage historique", *Studia Islamica* 38, 75-106.

Cordun, V.: "les saints thaumaturges d'Ada Kaleh", *Turcica* 3, 100-116, bibliographie (24 réfer.)

Fahd, T.: "De Petrus Alfonsy à Idris Shah", *REI* 41, 165-179.

Gilsenan, Michael: *Saint and Sufi in Modern Agypt. An Essay in the Sociology of Religion.* (Oxford, Clarendon Press). 248 p., 1 pl. = Oxford Monographs on Social Anthropology.

Güven, Rasih: "Origin of Islamic Mysticism", *JRCI* 6, No. 1-2, 79-98.

Ibish, Yussuf: "La teoria del viaggiare di Ibn ᶜArabī", *Conoscenza Religiosa* (1973), 418-423.

Ibn ᶜAṭāʾillāh: *Ṣūfī aphorisms* (Kitāb al-ḥikam). Translated with an introduction and notes by V. Danner. Foreword by M. Lings. (Leiden, E. J. Brill). xiv, 88 p.

Imanaga, S.: "A Study of Sufism in Chinese Islam", *The Hirosima University Studies, Literature Department*, 32/1, 46-64, (2)-(3) (English summary). (In Japanese).

Kaleshi, Hasan: "L'Ordre des Sa'diya en Yougoslavie", in: *XXIXe Congrès International des Orientalistes. Résumés des Communications*, Sections 6-7. (Paris, Y. Hervouet), p 36.

Kassim, Mahmoud: "La problème de la prédestination et du libre arbitre chez Leibniz et Ibn ᶜArabi", *Annuals of Faculty of Dar al-Ulūm* 1972-1973, 1-26.

Khalid, M. B.: "Thoughts on Sufism", *JRCI* 6, No. 1-2, 65-78.

Khan, Sahibzada Shaukat Ali: "A rare manuscript of Jāmī", *Islamic Culture* 47, 327-333.

Kobayashi, S.: "The Formation of the Sufi Orders in Egypt", *The Toyoschi Kenkyu* 32/2, 62-85 (in Japanese, with English summary, p. 3).

Landolt, H.: "Der Briefwechsel zwischen Kāšānī and Simnānī über *waḥsat al-wuǧūd*", *Der Islam* 50, 29-81.

de Laugier de Beaurecueil, S.: "La structure du *Livre des étapes* de Khwāja ᶜAbdallāh Anṣārī", *Afghanistan* 26/3, 35-83.

Lings, M.: *A Ṣūfī Saint of the Twentieth Century – Shaikh Aḥmad al-ᶜAlawī* (London, 1970). – R: *WI* 14, 233-234 (A. Schimmel).

Makdisi, George: "Ibn Taimīya: A Sūfī of the Qādirīya Order", *The American Journal of Arabic Studies* 1, 118-129.

Michon, J. L.: *Le soufi marocain Ahmad Ibn ᶜAjība (1746-1809) et son Miᶜrāj; glossaire de la mystique musulmane.* (Paris, Librairie J. Vrin). 321 p., 1 pl. (facsimilé), bibliographie (10 p.) = Etudes Musulmanes, XIV.

Moinul Haq, S.: "The Origin and Growth of Sufism (a brief survey)", *JPHS* 21, 79-108.

Nasr, Seyyed Hossein: *Sufi Essays* (London, 1972). – R: *WI* 14, 251-253 (Annemarie Schimmel).

Nwyia, Paul (ed.): *Trois oeuvres inédites de mystiques musulmans: Šaqīq al-Balḫī,* Ibn ᶜAṭā, Niffarī. (Beyrouth, Dar el-Marchreq, Librarie Orientale). 343 p. (in Arabic). = Recherches publiées sous la direction de l'Institut de Lettres Orientales, Nouvelle Série, A, Langue Arabe et pensée islamique, 7.

Paul, H. C.: "*Bāul* – poets on *Chāri* – *Chandra* (or four states of the mind)", *JASB* 18, 1-53.

Rahman, M.: "The Language of the Sufis", *Indo-Iranica* 26, No. 2-3, 72-92.

Reinert, Benedikt: *Die Lehrevom tawakkul in der klassischen Sufik.* (Berlin, 1968). – R: *OLZ* 68, 156-158 (A. Schimmel).

Ripoli, A. M.: "Doctrina del amor y misticismo estético en Ibn al-ᶜArabi de Murcia", *RIE* 31 (122), 125-139.

Schimmel, Annemarie: "The Sufi Ideas of Shaykh Ahmad Sirhindi", *Die Welt des* Islams 14, 199-203.

Trimingham, J. Spencer: *The Sufi Orders in Islam.* (Oxford, 1971). – R: *BiOr* 30, 491-492 (J. W. Fück), *JRAS* 1, 58-59 (R. J. Austin).

Utas, Bo (ed.): *Ṭarīq ut-taḥqīq.* A critical edition, with a history of the text and a commentary. (Lund, Studentlitteratur). 245 p., 53 (Persian text) p. = Scandinavian Institute of Asian Studies, Monograph Series, 13.

Weischer, B. M.: "Mysticism in the East and West", *Iqbal Review* 14, No. 1, 24-32.

Whinfield, E. H.: *Teachings of Rumi. The Masnavi.* (London, The Octagon Press). xii, 330 p.

5. HISTORY AND GENERAL

al-ᶜAbbādī, A. M.: *El reino de Granada en la época de Muhammad V.* (Madrid, Instituto de Estudios Islámicos). xvi, 260 p.

Abel, A.: " 'Réfutation d'un agarène' de Barthélémy d'Edesse", *Studia Islamica* 37, 5-26.

Abel, A.: "Rôle de la structure juridique dans le developpement et le déclin de l'état musulman arabe", *RSJB* 31, 533-554.

Abu Jāber, Faiz: "The Status of Women in Early Arab History", *Islam and the Modern Age* 4/2, 67-76.

Achrapov, I. und L. Rempel': *Teznoi Schtuk Afrasiaba* (Geschnittener Stuck vom Afrasiab), (Taškent, 1971). – R: *BiOr* 30, 301 (B. Brentjes).

Ahmed, Ziauddin: "Some Aspects of the Political Theology of Aḥmad B. Ḥanbal", *IslSt* 12, 53-66.

Ali, Ahmed: *Ghālib.* Selected Poems translated with an introduction. (Roma, 1969). – R: *OLZ* 68, 505-509 (A. Schimmel).

Alich, Salih H.: "Neumanichäismus und verwandte heterodoxe Bewegungen in Vorderasien", *Balcanica* IV, 95-110.

Allana, G.: "Iqbal as a Political Philosopher", *Iqbal Review* 14, No. 3, 61-68.

Alparslan, Ali: "Ecoles calligraphiques turques", *Islam Tetkikleri Enstitusu Dergisi* 5, 265-278.

Anand, Mulk Raj: "The Turkish Heritage in Painting", *Marg* 26, No. 4, 2-16.

And, Metin: *Geleneksel Türk Tiyatrosu* (Kukla-Karagöz-Ortaoyunu). (Ankara, 1969). – R: *OLZ* 68, 278-279 (Otto Spies).

Andrews, W. G.: "A critical-interpretive approach to the Ottoman Turkish Ġazel", *IJMES* 4, 97-111.

Arié, R.: *L'Espagne musulmane au temps des Nasrides (1232-1492)* (Paris, Boccard). 528 p., 12 pl.

Arié, R.: "Remarques sur quelques aspects de la civilisation hispano-musulmane", *BAEO* 9, 131-150.

Arié, Rachel: *Miniatures Hispano-Musulmanes.* Recherches sur un manuscrit arabe illustré de l'Escurial. (Leiden, 1969). – R: *OLZ* 68, 387-390 (V. Kubíčková).

Arnaldez, R.: "Controverse d'Ibn Hazm contre Ibn Nagrila le juif", *ROMM* 13-14, 41-48.

Asad, Talal: *The Kababish Arabs. Authority and Consent in a Nomadic Tribe.* (London, C. Hurst, 1970). xvi, 263 p., 16 tab., 13 fig., 2 maps. – R: *Anthropos* 68, 336-338 (Joseph Henninger).

Aširov, N.: "L'Islam et les relations nationales. Attitude de l'Islam envers la nation et la question Nationale", *Nauka i Religija* no. 10, 54-59 (en russe).

Atil, E.: *Ceramics from the World of Islam*. (Washington, Smithsonian Institution). 225 p., 101 pl. =Freer Gallery of Arts, Fiftieth Anniversary Exhibition, III.

Atil, Esin: "Ottoman Miniature Painting under Sultan Mehmed II", *Ars Orientalis* 9, 103-120.

el-Awa, Mohamed: "The Place of Custom (ᶜ*urf*) in Islamic Legal Theory", *Islamic Quarterly* 17, 177-182.

Bacqué-Grammont, J. L.: "Une lettre du prince ottoman Bâyazîd b. Mehmed sur les affaires d'Iran en 1480", *StuIr* 2, 213-234.

Baer, Eva: "Early Muslim Architecture", *OLZ* 68, 117-126. (A review article with regard to K. A. C. Creswell: *Early Muslim Architecture, Umayyads A. D. 622-750*. Vol. I, 1 u. 2. With a Contribution on the Mosaics of the Dome of the Rock in Jerusalem and of the Great Mosue in Damascus by M. Gautier-Van Berchem. 2nd ed. (Oxford, 1969).

Baldick, J.: "The Authenticity of ᶜIrāqī's ᶜUshshāq-nama", *Studia Iranica* 2, 67-78.

Balić, Smail: *Kultura Bošnjaka. Muslimanska komponenta*. (Die Kultur der Bosniaken. Die muslimische Komponente). (Wien, A. Holzhausens NFG). 247 S., 14 Taf. (davon 1 farbig). (Deutsche Zusammenfassung, S. 195-204).

Balić, Smail: "Österreich und das islamische Kulturerbe", *Österreichische Osthefte* 15, 275-282.

Balogun, Isma'il A. B.: "The Life and work of the Mujaddid of West Africa, ᶜUthmān b. Fūdī, popularly known as Usumanu Ḍan Fodio", *IslSt* 12, 271-292.

Barkow, J. H.: "Muslims and Maguzawa in North Central State, Nigeria: an ethnographic comparison", *CJAS* 7, 59-76.

Basetti-Sani, G.: "Francesco d'Assisi e l'Islam", *Renovatio* 8, 47-72, 233-240.

Baştav, Şerif: "La bataille rangée de Malazgirt et Romain Diogène", *Cultura Turcica* 8-10, 132-152.

Bausani, A.: "The Life and Work of Iqbal", *Iqbal Review* 14, No. 3, 45-60.

Bayerle, G.: *Ottoman Tributes in Hungary, according to Sixteenth Century Tapu Registers of Novigrad*. (Paris-The Hague, Mouton). 228 p., 8 maps. = Near and Middle East Monographs, VIII.

Bazin, M.: "Qom, ville de pèlerinage et centre régional", *Revue Géographique de l'Est* 13, 77-136, 4 pl., bibliographie.

Begović, Mehmed: "Sur l'application du droit pendant le règne turc dans nos pays", *Balcanica* 4, 361-367.

Beldiceanu, N.: *Recherche sur la ville ottomane au XVe siècle Etude et actes*. (Paris, Adrien Maisonneuve). 466 p., 81 fac. = Bibliothèque archéologique et historique de l'Institut Français d'Archéologie d'Instanbul, XXV.

Belkhayat-Clement, Fouzia: "La notion du contrôle social chez Ibn Khaldûn", *IBLA* 131, 25-52.

Bencheikh, J. E.: "Un outrageur politique au IIIe/IXe siècle: Ibn Bassām al-Abartā°ī (m. vers 302 h.)", *Arabica* 20, 261-291.

Berque, J.: "Cadis de Kairouan d'après un manuscrit tunisien", *ROMM* 13-14, 97-108.

Berque, J.: "Tradition and Innovation in the Maghreb", *Daedalus* 102, No. 1, 239-250.

Bilgrami, Rafat: "Akbar's Mahdar of 1579", *Islamic Culture* 47, 231-240.

Bogdanović, D.: "Les étymologies iraniennes des orientalismes dans la langue serbo-croate", *Balcanica* 4, 631-637.

Bolland, R. and A. Polak: "Manufacture and Use of some Sacred Woven Frabrics in a North-Lombok Community", *Tropical Man* 4 (1971), 149-170.

Bormans, M.: "A propos d'une récente fatwâ relative au statut familial des émigrés algériens", *ROMM* 13-14, 131-140.

Borrmans, M.: "Perspectives Algériennes en matière de droit familial", *Studia Islamica* 37, 129-153.

Borrmans, M.: "Statut personnel et droit familial en pays musulmans", *Proche-Orient Chrétien* 23/2, 133-147.

Bosworth, C. F.: "The Heritage of Rulership in early Islamic Iran and the search for dynastic connections with the past", *Iran* 11, 51-62.

Bosworth, Clifford Edmund: "°Ubaidallāh b. Abī Bakra and the 'Army of Destruction' in Zābulistan (79/698)", *Der Islam* 50, 268-283.

Bouhdiba, A.: *Islam et sexualité*. (Thèse, Univ. de Paris, 1972. Lille, Service de reproduction des thèses, Univ. de Lille III). 601 p., bibliographie (48 p.)

Boullata, I. J.: "The beleaguered unicorn: a study of Tawfīq Ṣāyigh", *JAL* 4, 69-93

Boullata, Kamal: "Classical Arab Art and Modern European Painting: a Study in Affinities", *MW* 63, 1-14.

Bourouiba, Rachid: "La doctrine almohade", *ROMM* 13-14, 141-158.

Bourouiba, R.: "Note sur les plans des mosquées", *Revue d'Histoire et de Civilisatio de Maghreb* 10, 41-55.

Brentjes, B.: "Drei figurative verzierte Kenotaphe aus Aserbaidshan", *BiOr* 30, 389-390, Taf. XVII-XVIII.

Brett, M.: "Problems in the Interpretation of the History of the Maghreb in the Light of Some Recent Publications", *JAH* 13/3, 489-506.

Bulliet, R. W.: "The Political-Religious History of Nishapur in the Eleventh Century", in: *Islamic Civilization, 950-1150*, ed. D. S. Richards (Oxford), 71-91.

Bürgel, J. Ch.: "Psychosomatic methods of cures in the Islamic Middle Ages", *HumIs* I, 157-172. ("References", pp. 171-172).

Burgoyne, M H.: "Ṭarīq Bāb al-Ḥadīd: A Mamlūk Street in the Old City of Jerusalem", *Levant* 5, 12-35.

Burns, R. I.: *Islam under the Crusaders. Colonial survival in the 13th-century kingdom of Valencia.* (Princeton, N.J., Princeton University Press). xxxi, 475 p.

Busse, Heribert: "The revival of Persian Kingship under the Buyids", in: *Islamic Civilization, 950-1150*, ed. D. S. Richards (Oxford), 47-69.

Cagman, Filiz: "Ottoman Turkish Miniatures", *Marg* 26, No. 4, 29-52.

Caroe, O.: "The Gauhar Shah *muṣallā* (mosque) in Herat", *Asian Affairs* 4 (60), 295-298.

Carré, O.: "A propos de la sociologie politique d'Ibn Khaldûn", *Revue Française de Sociologie* 14, 115-124.

Chalmeta, P.: "Le problème de la féodalité hors l'Europe chrétienne: Le cas de l'Espagne musulmane", in: *Actas del II Coloquio Hispano-Tunecino* (Madrid), 91-116.

Chambers, R. L.: "The education of a nineteenth-century Ottoman *âlim*, Ahmed Cevdet Pasha", *IJMES* 4, 440-464.

Charbel, P.: "Il sacrificio di communione tra gli arabi", *Bibbia e Oriente* 15, no. 3, 129-138.

Charpentier, C.-J.: "The Use of Haschish and Opium in Afghanistan", *Anthropos* 68, 482-490, 3 fig., bibliography.

Chartier, M.: "Khalid Muhammad Khalid, héraut de la liberté perdue", *IBLA* 36/1, 1-24. (= Penseurs musulmans contemporains, 1).

Chartier, M.: "La rencontre Orient-Occident dans la pensée de trois philosophes égyptiens contemporains: Ḥasan Ḥanafī, Fuʾād Zakariyyā, Zakī Naǧīb Maḥmūd", *Oriente Moderno* 53, 605-642.

Chelhod, J.: "La parenté et le mariage au Yémen", *L'Ethnographie* 67, 47-90.

Chelhod, J.: "Les cérémonies du mariage au Yémen", *Objets et Mondes* 13, no. 1, 3-34.

Connick Carlisle, Roxane: "Women Singers in Darfur, Sudan Republic", *Anthropos* 68, 785-800, 2 pl. (with bibliography).

Constantelos, D. J.: "The Moslem Conquests of the Near East as revealed in the Greek Sources of the Seventh and the Eight Centuries", *Byzantion* 42/2, 325-357.

Cooper, L. H.: "Genius and Invention: Artists and Artisans of Iran", *Apollo* 97 (133), 296-303.

Corbin, H.: "Juvenilité et chevalerie en Islam Iranien", *Eranos-Jahrbuch* 40, 311-356.

Corbin, H.: "L'initiation ismaélienne ou l'ésoterisme et le verbe", *Eranos-Jahrbuch* 39, 41-142.

Coulson, N. J.: *Succession in the Muslim Family*, (Cambridge University Press, 1971). – R: *BiOr* 30, 105 (E. Ashtor).

Cremers, W.: "Schamanistische Überbleibsel in der heutigen anatolischen Folklore", *Turcica* 3, 49-58.

Czeglédy, K.: "Gardizi on the History of Central Asia (746-780)", *AOH* 27, 257-267.

Dagorn, R.: "Quelques réflexions sur les inscriptions arabes des nécropoles kairouanaises", *ROMM* 13-14, 239-258.

Dahsiar, S.: "On the Popular Belief of Indonesia", *Bunka* 37, No. 3-4, 110-120 (in Japanese, with English summary).

Damis, John: "Early Moroccan reactions to the French protectorate: The cultural dimension", *HumIs* I, 15-31

Dankoff, Robert: "The Alexander romance in the *Dīwān Lughāt at-Turk*", *Humaniora Islamica* I, 233-244.

Davidian, H.: "The application of some basic psychological theories in the Iranian cultural context", *ISSJ* 25, 532-546.

Delanoue, G.: "Endoctrinement religieux et idéologie ottomane: l'addresse de Muḥammad ᶜAbduh au Cheikh al-Islam, Beyrouth, 1887", *ROMM* 13-14, 293-312.

Delanoue, G.: "Une épître de Ḥasan al-Bannā aux Frères Musulmans. Translation de la *Risālat at-taᶜlīm*", *CLOS* 1-2, 55-83.

Dilger, Konrad: *Untersuchungen zur Geschichte des osmanischen Hofzeremoniells im 15. und 16. Jahrhundert.* (München, 1967). – R: *OLZ* 68, 379-383 (M. Ferdinandy).

Diyarbekirli, N.: "Vestiges de croyances altaïques dans l'art seldjoukide", *Turcica* 3, 59-70.

Djaït, H.: *La personnalité et le devenir arabo-islamiques.* (Paris, Les Editions du Ceuil). 301 p. = Coll. Esprit.

Dodd, P. C.: "Family honor and the forces of change in Arab society", *IJMES* 4, 40-54.

Doi, A. R. I.: "The Arab Concept of Ifriqiya and the Planting of Islam in Africa", *Africa Quarterly* 12, 202-214.

Donohue, J. J.: "Three Buwayhid Inscriptions", *Arabica* 20, 74-80.

Dressendörfer, Peter: *Islam unter der Inquisition. Die Morisco Prozesse in Toledo (1575-1610).* (Wiesbaden, 1971); – R: *BiOr* 30, 107-110 (H. Beinart).

Dujčev, I.: "Contribution à l'histoire de la conquête turque en Thrace aux dernières décades du XIVe siècle", *EtBalk* 9, 80-92.

Dumont, P.: "Littérature et sous-developpement: les 'romans paysans' en Turquie", *AESC* 28, 745-764.

Ebied, R. Y. and M. J. L. Young: "Shams al-Dīn al-Jazarī and his *al-Maqānāt al-zayniyyah*", *ALUOS* 7, 54-60.

Ende, W.: "Schiitische Tendenzen bei sunnitischen Sayyids aus Ḥaḍramaut: Muḥammad b. ᶜAqīl al-ᶜAlawī (1863-1931)", *Der Islam* 50, 82-97.

Ergil, Doğu: "Secularisation as Class Conflict: the Turkish Example", *Asian Affairs* 6 (62), 69-80.

Esin, Emel: "Ṭabarī's report on the warfare with the Türgiš and the testimony of eighth century Central Asian art", *CAJ* 17, 130-149.

Esin, E.: "The Cosmic Symbolism of the Dracontine Arch and Apotropaic Mask in Turkish Symbolism", *AARP* 4, 32-51.

van Ess, J.: "Libanesische Miszellen, 5: Drusen und Black Muslims", *Die Welt des Islams* 14, 203-213.

Fahd, T.: "Genèse et cause des saveurs d'après l'Agriculture Nabatéenne", *ROMM* 13-14, 319-329.

Fahndrich, H. E.: "The *Wafayāt al-aᶜyān* of Ibn Khallikān: a new Approach", *JAOS* 93, 432-445.

Faroghi, S.: "Social mobility among the Ottoman *ᶜulamâ*ᵓ in the late sixteenth century", *IJMES* 4, 204-218.

al-Fārūqī, I. R.: "Islam and Art", *Studia Islamica* 37, 81-109.

Faruqi, Ziya-ul-Hasan: "A Note on the Wahabīyah", *Islam and the Modern Age* 4, No. 1, 38-50.

Fazlur Rahman: "Islam and the New Constitution of Pakistan", *JAAS* 8, 190-204.

Fazlur Rahman: "Islamic Thought in the Indo-Pakistan Subcontinent and the Middle East", *JNES* 32, 194-200.

Fehérvári, Géza: *Islamic Pottery*. A comprehensive study based on the Barlow Collection. (London, Faber). 4to. 191 p., 138 pl.

Fischel, W. J.: "Pre-Islamic Civilization of Iran as seen by Ibn Khaldun", *BICF* 1, No. 2, 25-39.

Fisher, Alan W.: "Muscovite-Ottoman relations in the sixteenth and seventeenth centuries", *HumIs* I, 207-217.

Flemming, Barbara: "Bemerkungen zur türkischen Prosa vor der Tanẓīmāt-Zeit", *Der Islam* 50, 157-167.

de Fouchécour, C. H.: *La description de la nature dans la poésie lyrique persane du XIe siècle. Inventaire et analyse des thèmes.* (Paris, 1969). – R: *OLZ* 68, 63-66 (A. Schimmel).

Freeman-Grenville, G. S. P. and B. G. Martin: "A Preliminary List of the Arabic Inscriptions of the Eastern African Coast", *JRAS* 98-122.

Gaál, E.: "Aladdin and the wonderful lamp", *AOH* 27, 291-300.

Gabrieli, Francesco: "La poèsie religieuse de l'ancien Islam", *Revue des Etudes Islamiques* 41, 7-50.

Garton, T.: "Islamic Elements in Early Romanesque Sculpture in Apulia", *AARP* 4, 100-116.

Gellner, E.: "Post-Traditional Forms in Islam: The Turf and Trade, and Votes and Peanuts", *Daedalus* 102/1, 191-206.

Gerresch, C.: "Un récit des Mille et Une Nuits: Tawaddud, petite encyclopédie de l'Islam médiéval", *BIFAN* 35/1, 57-175.

Gibb, Sir Hamilton: *The Life of Saladin.* From the works of ᶜUmād ad-Dīn and Bahāᵓ ad-Dīn. (Oxford, Clarendon Press). vi, 76 p.

Glatzer, B.: "The Madrasah of Shah-i-Mashad in Badgis", *Afghanistan* 25, No. 4, 46-68.

Gökbilgin, T.: "Kâtip Çelebi, interprète et rénovateur des traditions religieuseș au XVIIe s.", *Turcica* 3, 71-79.

Gökbilgin, Tayyib: "L'Empire Ottoman: formation, évolution, disparition", *RSJB* 31, 555-564.

Gordon, Laura Mavis: "A young Croat's encounter with an exotic Muslim culture: A Serbo-Croatian travel epic of the nineteenth century", *HumIs* I, 189-205. (= [Matija Mažzuranić:] *Pogled u Bosnu, ili kratak put u onu krajinu, učenjen po jednom domorodcu*, Zagreb, 1842).

Gottschalk, H. L.: "Beiträge zur Mamluken-Geschichte", *Die Welt des Islams* 14, 192-199.

Gottschalk, H. L., B. Spuler und H. Kähler: *Die Kultur des Islams* (Frankfurt, 1971). – R: *WI* 14, 225-226 (O. Spies).

Grandguillaume, G.: "Régime économique et structure du pouvoir: le système des foggara du Touat", *ROMM* 13-14, 437-457.

Grand-Henry, J.: "Divination et poésie populaire arabe en Algérie: à propos de quelques *būqāla* inédites", *Arabica* 20/1, 53-62.

Grignaschi, M.: "La *Nihāyatu-l-arab fi akhbāri-l-Furs-wa-lᶜArab* et les *Siyaru mulūki-l-ᶜAğam* du Ps. Ibn-al-Mugaffaᶜ", *BEO* 26, 83-184.

Grignaschi, M.: "Les règles d'Ardașīr b. Bâbak pour le gouvernement du Royaume", *ITED* 5, 95-112.

Grindal, B. T.: "Islamic Affiliations and Urband Adaptation: The Sisala Migrant in Accra, Ghana", *Africa* 43/4, 333-346.

Grohmann, Adolf: *Arabische Paläographie*. II. Teil. (Wien, 1971). – R: *BiOr* 30, 488-489 (A. F. L. Beeston).

Grohmann, Adolf: *Arabische Paläographie*, I. (Wien, 1967). – R: *OLZ* 68, 151-153 (H. Simon).

von Grunebaum, G. E. u. a.: *Der Islam*, II. *Die islamischen Reiche nach dem Fall von Konstantinople*. (Frankfurt am Main, Fischer Taschenbuch-Verlag, 1971). – R: *BiOr* 30, 490 (B. Brentjes).

Guichard, P.: "Un Seigneur Musulman dans l'Espagne chrétienne: Le Ra'is de Crevillente (1243-1318)", in: *Mélanges de la Casa de Velazquez* (Paris, Ed. E. de Boccard), T. IX, 283-334.

Guillaume, G.: "Soliman-le-Magnifique, l'apogée de la peinture turque et Ivan Stchoukine", *ArtsAs* 26, 271-290.

Guilmain, J.: "A Note on the 'Arabesques' in the Diatessaron, Florence, Bibl. Laur., Orient 81", *Art Bulletin* 55, 38-39.

Ha'iri, Abdul-Hadi: "Afghānī on the Decline of Islam", *Die Welt des Islams* 14, 116-128. (For part 1 see *ibid.*, 13, 121-125)'

Hamidullah Muhammad: "Constitutional Problems in Early Islam", *Islam Tetkikleri Enstitusu Dergisi* 5, 15-35.

Hamidullah, Muhammad: "Le premier empire musulman du temps du Prophète et de ses trois successeurs", *RSJB* 31, 509-532.

Hartmann, A.: "La conception gouvernementale du calife an-Nāṣir li-Dīn Allāh", *Orientalia Suecana* 22, 52-61.

Harvey, L. P.: "The *alfaquî in La dança general de la muerte*", *Hispanic Review* 41, 498-510.

Hasan, Ahmad: "Modern Trends in *ijmā*ᶜ", *Islamic Studies* 12, 121-153.

Hathaway, R. L.: "The art of epic epithets in the 'Cantar de mio Cid' ", *Hispanic Review* 41, 311-321.

Hauziński, Jerzy: "Asasyni – radykalna sekta islamu we wspolczesnei historiografii" (The Assassins: a radical sect in Islam in contemporary historiography), *Euhemer* XVII/2 (88), 35-45. (In Polish).

Hazai, G.: *Das Osmanisch-Türkische im XVII. Jahrhundert*. Untersuchungen an den Transkriptionstexten von Jakob Nagy de Harsány. (Budapest, Akadémiai Kiadó). 498 p. = Bibliotheca Orientalis Hungarica, XVIII. (The text, in Turkish, Latin and German, contains material of relevance to Islam, mystic orders, etc.)

Hazard, J. N.: "Socializing Islamic Law in Africa", *L'Année Canonique* 17, 543-554.

Hernández Giménez, F.: "La travesía de la Sierra de Guadarrama en el acceso a la raya musulmana del Duero", *al-Andalus* 38, fasc. 2, 415-454.

Heyd, Uriel: *Studies in Old Ottoman Criminal Law*. Edited by V. L. Ménage. (Oxford, Clarendon Press). xxxii, 340 p.

Hillenbrand, R.: "Reflections en O. Aslanapa's *Turkish art and architecture*", *IslQuart* 17, 75-91.

Hoenerbach, W.: *Dichterische Vergleiche der Andalus-Araber*. I und II. (Bonn, Selbstverlag des Orientalischen Seminars der Universität Bonn). xvi, 244 S. = Bonner Orientalistische Studien, N. S., 26.

Holt, P. M.: "The Sultanate of al-Mansur Lachin (696-8/1296-9)", *BSOAS* 36, 521-532.

Holt, P. M., Ann K. S. Lambton and B. Lewis (Ed.): *The Cambridge History of Islam*. Vol. I: *The Central Islamic Lands*. Vol. II: *The Further Islamic Lands. Islamic Society and Civilisation*. (Cambridge University Press, 1971). – R: *Arabica* 20, 95-97 (M. Arkoun).

Hourani, A. H. and S. M. Stern (Ed.): *The Isilamic City. A Colloquium*. (Oxford, 1970) (and) D. S. Richards (Ed.): *Islam and the Trade of Asia* (Oxford, 1970). – R: *WI* 14, 221-224 (A. Schimmel).

Ibn al-Faqīh al-Hamadānī: *Abrégé du livre des pays*. Traduit de l'arabe par H. Massé. (Damas, Institut Français de Damas). v, 440 p.

Idris, H. R.: "Du šīʿisme d'al-Raqīq", *Arabica* 20, 191-192.

Ilter, Fügen: "An East Anatolian Building from the Age of Timur: Yelmaniye Medrese", *Anadolu* 17, 109-122.

Inal, Güner: "A Manuscript of the Shāhnāmeh from the Period of Shāh Ismāʿīl and its Influence on the Later Shāhnāmeh Illustrations", *STY* 5, 530-545.

"Iran prestigieux empire", *Missi* (Lyon), no. 4, 112-134. (L'Islam et le mouvement shi^{c}ite en Iran).

Jäschke, G.: "Die Gründung der türkischen Republik. Anfang der Reformen Kemal Atatürks", *Belleten* 37, 471-473.

Jennings, R. C.: "Loans and credit in early 17th century Ottoman Judicial records: the Sharia Court of Anatolian Kayseri", *JESHO* 16, 168-216.

Johansen, B.: "Religiöse Traditionen und koloniale Struktur in Marokko", *Das Argument* 15, 308-331.

Johanson, U.: "Die guten Sitten beim Essen und Trinken: Bericht von einem Feldforschungspraktikum über Gastfreundschaft, Konsumptionsnormen und Wirtschaftsdenken im Wandel bei türkischen Gastarbeitern", *Sociologus* 23, 41-70.

Juynboll, G. H. A.: "The Date of the Great *fitna*", *Arabica* 20, 142-159.

Kaba, L.: "Islam, Society and Politics in Pre-colonial Baté", *BIFAN* 35, No. 2, 323-344.

el-Kafrawy, M. A. A. and J. D. Latham: "Perspective of Abū al-ᶜAtāhiya", *Islamic Quarterly* 17, 160-176.

Kakuk, S.: *Recherches sur l'histoire de la langue Osmanlie des XVIe et XVIIe siècles. Les éléments osmanlis de la langue hongroise.* (Budapest, Akadémiai Kiadó). 660 p. = Bibliotheca Orientalis Hungarics, XIX.

Kennedy, E. S.: *A Commentary upon Biruni's Kitāb Taḥdīd al Amākin.* (Beirut, American University of Beirut). xx, 270 p., illus.

Khalid, M. B.: "The Caravan of Islam on the Indo-Pakistan Sub-Continent", *JRCI* 6, 177-187.

Khalidi, Tarif: "Islamic biographical dictionaries: a preliminary assessment", *MW* 63, 53-65.

Kissling, H. J.: "Über eine Goldmünze Sulṭān Muṣṭafā's I", *Die Welt des Islams* 14, 163-170.

Klein-Franke, F.: "The geomancy of Aḥmad b. ᶜAlī Zunbul: a study of the Ambic Corpus Hermeticum", *Ambix* 20, 26-35.

Knappert, J.: "A Swahili Islamic Prayer from Zaire", *Orientalia Lovaniensia Periodica* 4, 197-201.

Knappert, J.: *Swahili Islamic Poetry.* 3 vols. (Leiden, 1971). – R: *JRA* 5, 59-60 (N. Q. King).

Korson, J. H.: "Some Aspects of Social Change in the Muslim Family in West Pakistan", *CAS* 3, 138-155.

Kosay,Hâmit Zübeyr: "Die türkischen Museen in der republikanischen Ära", *Cultura Turcica* 8-10, 86-109.

Krawulsky, Dorothea: *Briefe und Reden des Abū Ḥāmid Muhammad al-Gazzālī, übersetzt und erläutert.* (Freiburg/Br., 1971). – R: *BiOr* 30, 297-298 (Kurt Ru-

Krüger, E.: "Die Reisetagebücher Nāṣir ad-Nīns: ein autobiographisches Zeugnis?", *Die Welt des Islams* 14, 171-191.

Kuran, Aptullah: "Early Works of the Architect Sinan", *Belleten* 37, 545-556.

Lacoste, C.: "Hituels de pèlerinages féminins dans l'Islam rural contemporain", in: *XXIXe Congrès International des Orientalistes. Résumés des Communications,* Sections 1-5. (Paris, Y. Hervouet), p. 86.

de La Granja, F.: "El 'Kitāb Tuḥfat al Mugtarib bi-Bilād al-Magrib' ", *RIEI* 17, 123-130.

Lamei, Saleh Mostafa: *Moschee des Farağ ibn Barquq in Kairo.* Mit einem Beitrag von Ulricj Haarmann. (Glückstadt, J. J. Augustin, 1972). 66 p. in 4°, 73 Abb. =Abhandlungen des Deutschen Archäologischen Instituts Kairo, Islamische Reihe, 3. – R: *Anthropos* 68, 334 (Inge Hofmann).

Laoust, H.: "Les agitations religieuses à Baghdad aux IVe et Ve siècles de l'Hégire", in: *Islamic Civilisation, 950-1150*, ed. D. S. Richards (Oxford), 169-185.

Lapidus, I. M.: "The Evolution of Muslim Urban Society", *CSSH* 15, 21-50.

Laroui, Abdallah: "Cultural problems and social structure: The Campaign for Arabization in Morocco", *HumIs* I, 33-46.

Laroui, Abdallah: "For a methodology of Islamic studies. Islam seen by G. Von Grunebaum", *Diogenes* 83, 12-39.

Latham, J. D.: "Towns and Cities of Barbary: the Andalusian Influence", *IslQuart* 16, 189-204.

Latifi, D.: "Rationalism and Muslim Law", *Islam and the Modern Age* 4, No. 4, 43-70.

Lawrence, B. B.: "Shahrastani on Indian Idol Worship", *Studia Islamica* 38, 61-73.

Lehfeldt, W.: "Zur serbokroatischen Übersetzung arabisch-islamischer Termini in einem Text des 15./16. Jahrhunderts", *ZsBalk* 7, 23-54.

Lelong, M.: "Unanimité et pluralisme dans la pensée islamique d'aujourd hui", *ROMM* 15-16, 127-138.

Levey, M.: *Early Arabic Pharmacology. An Introduction based on ancient and medieval sources.* (Leiden, E. J. Brill). viii, 187 p.

Le Tourneau, R.: "Nouvelles orientations des Berbères d'Afrique du Nord 950-1150", in: *Islamic Civilisation 950-1150*, Ed. D. S. Richards (Oxford), 127-153.

Levtzion, N.: "Conversion to Islam: Some Notes for a Comparative Study", in: *XXIXe Congrès International des Orientalistes. Résumés des Communications,* Sections 1-5. (Paris, Y. Hervouet), pp. 88-89.

Lewcock, R. and G. R. Smith: "The Early Mosques in the Yemen: A Preliminary Report", *AARP* 4, 117-130.

Lewis, B.: *Islam in History. Ideas, Men and Events in the Middle East.* (London, Alcove Press). 349 p.

Little, D. P.: "The historical and historiographical significance of the detention of Ibn Taymiyya", *IJMES* 4, 311-327.

Lombard, M.: *L'Islam dans sa première grandeur (VIIIe – XIe siècle).* (Paris, 1971). – R: *BiOr* 30, 103-104 (Renate Jacobi).

Lorandi, M.: "I modelli orientali dei castelli federiciani: i Qasr omayyadi e la loro influenza nella genesi dell'architettura sveva", *BAMPI* 58, 9-26.

Louis, André: "Les prestations réciproques en milieu berbère du Sud tunisien", *Anthropos* 68, 456-472, summarium en angl., bibliographie (2 p.)

McDonough, Sheila: "On teaching Islam to undergraduates", *HumIs* I, 261-277, bibliography.

McNeill, William H. and Marilyn Robinson Waldman (ed.): *The Islamic World.* (London, Oxford University Press). xviii, 468 p., maps. = Readings in World History, 6.

Magnarella, P. J. and Orhan Türkdoğan: "Descent affinity and ritual relations in Eastern Turkey", *AmAnth* 75, 1626-1633.

Makdisi, George: "The Madrasa in Spain: some remarks", *ROMM* 15-16, 153-158.

Makdisi, George: "The Sunni Revival", in: *Islamic Civilisation, 950-1150*, Ed. D. S. Richards (Oxford), 155-168

Mantran, R.: "La bataille de Lépente vue par un chroniqueur ottoman", *CLOS* 1-2, 183-189.

Mantran, R.: "L'echo de la bataille de Lépente à Constantinople", *ARSC* 28, 396-405.

Mantran, Robert: *L'Expansion Musulmane (VIIe – XIe siècles*). (Paris, 1969). – R: *OLZ* 68, 269-270 (Bertold Spuler).

Manzanares de Cirre, M.: "El otro mundo en la literatura aljamiado-morisca", *Hispanic Review* 41, 599-608.

Ma^coz, Moshe: *Ottoman Reform in Syria and Palestine 1840-1861.* The Impact of the Tanzimat on Politics and Society. (Oxford, 1968). – R: *OLZ* 68, 275-278 (Erika Glassen).

Maqbul Ahmad, S.: "Al-Biruni and the Decline of Science and Technology in Medieval Islam, and his Contributions to Geography, with Special Reference to India", *Afghanistan* 26/2, 91-96.

Marsigli, Luigi Ferdinando: *Stato militare dell'Impero Ottomano. L'état militaire de l'Empire Ottoman.* Einführung Manfred Kramer, Register Richard F. Kreutel. (Graz, Akademische Druck- und Verlagsanstalt, 1972). – R: *BiOr* 30, 492-494 (Heidrun Wurm).

Marsot, A. Lutfi al-Sayyid: "The political and economic functions of the ᶜulamāᵓ in the 18th century", *JESHO* 16, 130-154.

Marx, E.: "Circumcision feasts among the Negev Bedouins", *IJMES* 4, No. 4, 411-427, bibliography.

Mason, Herbert: "Arab Algerian literature revisited", *Humaniora Islamica* I, 77-87.

Massé, H. (trad.): ᶜImād ad-Dīn al-Isfahānī: *Conquète de la Syrie et de la Palestine par Saladin. (al-Fatḥ al-qussī fi l-fatḥ al-qudsī*). (Paris, Paul Geuthner, 1972). 460 p.

Masumi, M. Saghir Hasan: "Burhān al-Sharīᶜah's 'al-Muḥīṭ al-Burhānī' ", *ITED* 5, 67-73.

Matkovski, A.: "L'Islam aux yeux des non-musulmans des Balkans", *Balcanica* 4, 203-211.

Matuz, J.: "Der Niedergang der anatolischen Seldschuken: die Entscheidungsschlacht am Kösedağ", *CAJ* 17, 180-199.

Merigoux, J. M.: "Un précurseur du dialogue islamo-chrétien: Frère Ricoldo (1243-1320)", *Revue Thomiste* 73, 609-621.

Mieli, Aldo: *La science arabe et son rôle dans l'évolution scientifique mondiale.* Réimpression anastatique augmentée d'une bibliographie avec index analytique par A. Mazahéri. (Leiden, 1966). – R: *BiOr* 30, 292-295 (Paul Kunitzsch).

Millward, W. G.: "Aspects of Modernism in Shi^{c}a Islam", *Studia Islamica* 37, 111-128.

Moneim, M. N. F.: "L'Islam et l'avortement", *Cahiers Universitaires Catholiques*, No. 5, 17-20.

Monfouga-Nicolas, Jacqueline: *Ambivalence et culte de possession.* Contribution à l'étude du Bori hausa. Préface de Roger Bastide. (Paris, Editions Anthropos, 1972). xix, 384 p., 8 pl., 2 cartes. = Ouvrage publié avec le concours du Centre National de la Recherche Scientifique. – R: *Anthropos* 68, 654-655 (A. Retel-Laurentin).

Mottahedeh, R.: "Administration of Būyid Qazwīn", in: *Islamic Civilization, 950-1150*, ed. D. S. Richards (Oxford), 33-45.

Mukhtār, ^{c}Abd al-Mun^{c}im: "On the survival of the Byzantine administration in Egypt during the first century of the Arab rule", *AOH* 27, 309-319.

Müller-Christensen, Sigrid: "Zwei Seidengewebe als Zeugnisse der Wechselwirkung von Byzanz und Islam", in: *Artes Minores, Dank an Werner Abegg* (q. v. sub I-7).

Mushirul Haq: "Muslim Understanding of Hindu Religion", *Islam and the Modern Age* 4, No. 4, 71-77.

Muslehuddin, Mohammad: "Islamic Jurisprudence and the Rule of Necessity and Need", *IslSt* 12, 37-52, 103-120.

Nasr, Seyyed Hossein: "The Significance of the Void in the art and architecture of Islam", *IslQuart* 16, 115-120.

Nasr, Seyyed Hossein: "The Western World and its Challenges to Islam", *IslQuart* 17, 3-25.

Nemeth, J.: "Das Wolga-bulgarische Wort baqšĭ 'gelehrter Herr' In Ungarn", *ITED* 5, 165-170.

Nemoy, L.: "Nicholson's Islamic Poetry", *JQR* 63/4, 361-362.

Noer, Deliar: *The Modernist Muslim Movement in Indonesia, 1900-1942.* (London, Oxford University Press). xii, 390 p. = East Asian Historical Monographs.

Norris, H. T.: *Saharan Myth and Saga.* (Oxford, Clarendon Press, 1972). xv,

240 p., 6 pl., map. = Oxford Library of African Literature. – R: *Anthropos* 68, 335-336 (Inge Hofmann).

Nosowski, J.: "L'Islam et la chrétienté aux temps de l'empire des califes", *SThV* 11/1, 223-240 (en polonais).

Noth, A.: "Die literarisch überlieferten Verträge der Eroberungszeit als historische Quellen für die Behandlung der unterworfenen Nicht-Muslims durch ihre neuen muslimischen Oberherren", *BOS* 27/1 (= Studien zum Minderheitenproblem im Islam), 282-314.

Noth, A.: "Zur Verhältnis von kalifaler Zentralgewalt und Provonzen in umaiyadischer Zeit: die '*Sulh*' – '*ᶜAnwa*' Traditionen für Ägypten und den Iraq", *Die Welt des Islams* 14, 150-162.

Ögel, S.: *Der Kuppelraum in der türkischen Architektur.* (Leiden-Instanbul, 1972). – R: *BiOr* 30, 494-499 (J. M. Rogers).

Oman, G.: "La Necropoli islamica di Dahlak Kebir (Mar Rosso)", *AION* 23 (33), 561-569.

Öney, Gönül: "The Influence of Early Islamic Stucco Work in Iran on Anatolian Seljuk Art", *Belleten* 37 (147), 267-277.

Orozbaev, P. R.: "Anticlerical and atheistic trends in the work of Barpy Alykulov", *VMUF* No. 3, 87-92.

Palokruševa, G.: "Conséquences ethniques de l'Islamisation des Miacs en Macédoine", *Ethnologia Slavica* 5, 37-47.

Pantúčková, E.: "Zur Analyse eines der historischen Bestandteile von Ahmedis Iskendername", *Archiv Orientální* 41, 28-41.

Papadopoulo, A.: "Esthétique de l'art musulman. La peinture", *AESC* 28, 681-710.

Pauliny, J.: "ᶜŪğ ibn ᶜAnāq, ein sagenhafter Riese. Untersuchungen zu den islamischen Riesengeschichten", *Graecolatina et Orientalia* 5, 249-268.

Pavón Maldonado, B.: "La formación del arte hispanomusulmán", *Al-Andalus* 38, fasc. 1, 195-242.

Plancke, M.: "Islamic education in Tunisia (ca. 800 – 1574)", *Humaniora Islamica* I, 5-14.

Plaskowicka-Rymkiewicz, St.: "Une étude sur la stylistique turque: quelques motifs poétiques dans les oeuvres des poètes du XIIIe siècle: Sultan Veled, Ahmed Fakih et Ṣeyyad Hamza", *RO* 35, 137-154.

Polak, A.: "Some Aspects of a Process of Change in an Indonesian Community", *Tropical Man* 4, 108-116.

Poonawala, Ismail K.: "The Church of Saint George at Urfa (Edessa)", *BSOAS* 36, 109-115.

Puin, G. R.: "Aspekte der wahhabitischen Reform auf der Grundlage von Ibn Gannāms 'Rauḍat al-afkār' ", *BOS* 27/1 (Studien zum Minderheitenproblem im Islam), 45-99.

Rafikov, A. Ch.: *Očerki Istorii Knigopečatanija v Turzii* (A brief history of book-printing in Turkey)' (Leningrad, Izd. Nauka). 218 p.

Rahmani, Aftab Ahmad: "The Life and Works of Ibn Ḥajar al-ᶜAsqalānī", *IsCul* 47, 57-74, 159-174, 257-273.

Redjala, Mbarek: "Une copie de la *Muqaddima* de l'exemplaire du *Kitāb al-ᶜibar* offert par Ibn Ḥaldūn à l'Université al-Qarawiyīn de Fès", *RHT* 3, 193-201.

Rekaya, M.: "Māzyār: résistance ou intégration d'une province iranienne au monde musulman au milieu du IXe siècle apr. J.C.", *Studia Iranica* 2, no. 2, 143-192, bibliographie.

Renda, Günsel: "The Miniatures of Silsilename, No. 1321, in in the Topkapĭ Saray Museum Library", *STY* 5, 481-495.

Riaz, Muhammad: "Chivalry in Islamic History", *JRCI* 6, 145-158.

Richards, D. S.: "The Early History of Saladin", *Islamic Quarterly* 17, 140-159.

Rikin, W. M.: *Ngabersihan, als knoop in de tali parenti. Bijdrage tot het verstaan van de besnijdenis der Sundanezen.* (Meppel, Ramco Offset). 194 p. (with a summary in English).

Rizvi, S. S. A. and Noel Q. King: "Some East African Ithna-Asheri *Jamaats* (1840-1967)", *JRA* 5/1, 12-22.

Rizvić, Muhsin: *Književno Stvaranje Muslimanskih Pisaca u Bosni i Hercegovini u Doba Austro-Ugarske Vladavine.* (Literary Activity of Muslim Writers in Bosnia and Hercegovina during Austro-Hungarian Rule). 2 volumes. (Sarajevo, Svjetlost). 316 and 306 p. = Akademija Nauka i Umjetnosti Bosne i Hercegovine, Djela, Knjiga XLVI.

Rogers, J. M.: "The 11th Century – A Turning Point in the Architecture of the Mashriq?", in: *Islamic Civilisation, 950-1150*, ed. D. S. Richards (Oxford), 211-249.

Röhrborn, Klaus: *Untersuchungen zur Osmanischen Verwaltungsgeschichte.* (Berlin, Walter de Gruyter). xii, 177 S. = Studien zur Sprache, Geschichte und Kultur des Islamischen Orients, Beihefte zur Zeitschrift *Der Islam*, N.F., Band 5.

Rosenthal, Franz: *A History of Muslim Historiography*. 2nd revised edition. (Leiden, 1968). – R: *OLZ* 68, 153-154 (H. Simon).

Rosenthal, F.: *Four Essays on Art and Literature in Islam*. (Leiden, E. J. Brill, 1971). vii, 121 p. = The L. A. Mayer Memorial Studies in Islamic Art and Archaeology, 2. – R: *BiOr* 30, 297 (J. W. Fück).

Roux, J. P.: "Turquie d'hier et d'aujourd'hui", *Objets et Mondes* 13, 107-116.

Roux, J.-P.: "Une survivance des traditions turco-mongoles chez les Séfévides", *RHR* 183/1, 11-18.

Ruiz Figueroa, M.: "Dos narraciones de Al Yaḥiẓ, prosista clasico del siglo IX", *EsOr* 8/3, 278-285.

Šabanović, Hazim: *Književnost Muslimana Bosne i Hercegovine na Orijentalnim Jezicima. Biobibliografija.* (Literature of the Muslims of Bosnia and Hercegovina in Oriental /= Arabic, Turkish, and Persian/ Languages. A Biobibliography). [Edited by Ahmed S. Aličić]. (Sarajevo, Svjetlost). 728 p. = Kulturno Nasljedje (Cultural Heritage).

Sadan, J.: "A propos de martaba: remarques sur l'étiquette dans le monde musulman médiéval", *REI* 41, 51-69.

Sadat, Deena R.: "Âyân and Ağa: the transformation of the Bektashi corps in the eighteenth century", *MW* 63, 206-219.

Salim, Gholamreza: "Rashid ed-Din Fazlollah's Contribution to the Advancement of Education in his Time with particular Reference to his Interest in Medical Training", *JRCI* 6, 137-142.

Samb, Amar: "L'Islam et le Christianisme, par Cheikh Moussa Kamara. Traduction et annotations", *BIFAN* 35/2, 269-322.

Sánchez-Albornoz, Claudio: *La España Musulmana, según los autores Islamitas y Christianos medievales.* Tercera edición. 2 vol. (Madrid, Espasa-Calpe). Vol. 1: 558 p., 38 tav., 8 cart. Vol. 2: 637 p., 72 tav., 7 cart.

Santiago Simón, E.: *Un fragmento de la obra de Ibn al-Šabbāṭ (s. XIII) sobre al-Andalus. R. Lourido Díaz: La rebelión de los 'Abid, en 1778, y su desintegración como milicia especial.* (Granada, Sem. de Historia del Islam, Universidad). 160 p. = Cuadernos de Historia del Islam, 5.

Scarcia, G.: "Kuh-e Khwagè: forme attuali del Mahdismo iranico", *Oriente Moderno* 53, 755-764.

Scerrato, Umberto: *Arte Islamica a Napoli.* Opere delle Raccolte Pubbliche Napoletane. Catalogo. (Napoli, 1968). – R: *OLZ* 68, 56-57 (Eva Baer).

Schaendlinger, A. C.: *Osmanische Numismatik. Von den Anfängen des Osmanischen Reiches bis zu seiner Auflösung 1922.* (Braunschweig, Klinkhardt & Biermann). 4to. v, 178 S., 17 Taf. = Handbücher der mittelasiatischen Numismatik, 3.

Scheindlin, Raymond P.: "Poetic structure in Arabic: Three poems by al-Mu^c^tamid Ibn ^c^Abbād", *HumIs* I, 173-186.

Schimmel, Annemarie: *Islamic Literature of India.* (Wiesbaden, Otto Harrassowitz). iv, 60 p. = A History of Indian Literature.

Schmedding, Brigitta: "Ein islamisches Seidengewebe des 12. Jahrhunderts", in: *Artes Minores, Dank an Werner Abegg* (q. v. sub I-7).

Schützinger, H.: "Die Schelmengeschichten in Tausendundeiner Nacht als Ausdruck der ägyptischen Volksmeinung", *RhJV* 21, 200-215.

Seljuq, A.: "Ibn Khaldū's Study of Physical Environment", *JPHS* 21, 219-226.

Sezgin, Fuat: *Geschichte des arabischen Schrifttums*. I: *Qurʾānwissenschaften, Ḥadīṯ, Geschichte, Fiqh, Dogmatik, Mystik bis ca 430 H.* (Leiden, 2967). – R: *OLZ* 68, 150-151 (Johann Fück).

Sezgin, Ursula: *Abū Miḥnaf, ein Beitrag zur Historiographie der Umaiyadischen Zeit.* (Leiden, 1971). – R: *BiOr* 30, 102-103 (G. H. A. Juyboll).

Shaban, M. A.: *Islamic History (A. D. 600-750/A. H. 132), A New Interpretation.* (Cambridge, 1971). – R: *Arabica* 20, 102-103 (M Arkoun).

Shah, Mir Hussain: "Beruni and his Follower, Gardezi, on the Festivals of the Hindus", *Afghanistan* 26/3, 90-94.

Shaw, S. J.: "A promise of reform: two complementary documents", *IJMES* 4, 359-365.

Siraždinov, S. Ch. (ed.): *Iz istorii točnych nauk na srednevekovom bližnem i srednem vostoke* (Aus der Geschichte der Naturwissenschaften im mittelalterlichen Nahem und Mittleren Osten), (Taškent, 1972). –R: *BiOr* 30, 304 (B. Brentjes).

Siroux, M.: "L'évolution des antiques mosquées rurales de la région d'Ispahan", *ArtsAs* 26, 65-112.

von Sivers, Peter: "The realm of justice: Apocalyptic revolts in Algeria (1849-1879)", *HumIs* I, 47-60.

Smith, J. I.: "Continuity and Change in the Understanding of 'Islam' ", *IsMA* 4, No. 2, 42-66. (Published also in *IslQuart* 16, 121-139).

Soliman, Ahmad el-Said: "Quelques survivances païennes dans la littérature populaire des Turcs musulmans", *Abr Nahrain* 13, 1-15.

Sönmez, Emel: "The Novelist Halide Edib Adivar and Turkish Feminism", *Die Welt des Islams* 14, 81-115.

Sourdel, D.: "Les conceptions imamites au début du XIe siècle d'après le Shaykh al-Mufīd", in: *Islamic Civilization*, ed. by D. S. Richards (Oxford), 187-200.

Sourdel-Thomine, J.: "Renouvellement et tradition dans l'architecture Saljuqide", in: *Islamic Civilisation, 950-1150*, Ed. D. S. Richards (Oxford), 251-263.

Southern, R. W.: "Dante and Islam", in: *Relations between East and West in the Middle Ages*, Edited by Derek Baker (Edinburgh University Press), 133-145.

Soze, A. A. A. K.: "Background and Nature of Guru Nanak's Mission: An Islamic Viewpoint", *IsMA* 4/1, 51-65.

Spies, Otto (ed.): *Das Buch At-Tašwīq aṭ-ṭibbī* des Ṣāʿid ibn al-Ḥasan. Ein arabisches Adab-Werk über die Bildung des Arztes, (und) Schah Ekram Taschkandi: *Übersetzung und Bearbeitungdes Kitāb at-Tašwīq at-Ṭibbī* des Ṣāʿid ibn al-Ḥasan. Ein medizinisches Adabwerk aus dem 11. Jahrhundert. (Bonn, 1968). – R: *OLZ* 68, 370-375 (G. Strohmaier).

Spiridonakis, B. S.: *Empire Ottoman. Inventaire des mémoires et documents aux archives de Ministère des Affaires Etrangères de France.* (Thessaloniki, Institute for Balkan Studies). 536 p. = Institute for Balkan Studies, Publications, No. 132.

Spuler, B.: "L'Iran et l'Islam", in: *XXIXe Congrès International des Orientalistes. Résumés des Communications.* Sections 1-5. (Paris, Y. Hervouet), p. 134.

Spuler, U.: "Nurculuk. Die Bewegung des 'Bediüzzaman' Said Nursi in der modernen Türkei", *BOS* 27/1 (= Studien zum Minderheitenproblem im Islam), 100-182.

Spuropoulos, A. G.: "Quelques hommes de lettres originaires de l'Acarnanie pendant la domination turque", *Gregorios Palamas*, no. 636, 329-336 (em grec).

Stchoukine, I.: "Qāsim ibn ᶜAlī et ses peintures dans les *Aḥsan al-Kibār*", *ArtsAs* 28, 45-54.

Stewart, C. C. and E. K. Stewart: *Islam and Social Order in Mauritania. A Case Study from the Nineteenth Century.* (Oxford, Clarendon Press). xviii, 204 p., 1 fig., 7 pl., 4 maps. = Oxford Studies in African Affairs.

Strika, V.: "Note introduttive a un'estetica islamica: la miniatura persiana", *Rendiconti Accad. Lincei* 28, 699-727.

Talbi, M.: "Les contacts culturels entre l'Ifriqiya hafside (1230-1569) et le Sultanat nasride d'Espagne (1232-1492)", in: *Actas del II Coloquio Hispano-Tunecino* (Madrid), 63-90.

Tedeschi, S.: Il capostipite della dinastia dei sultani di Dahlak", *Africa* (Roma) 28, 65-72.

Tibawi, A. L.: "*The Cambridge History of Islam*: A critical review", *IslQuart* 17, 92-100.

Timm, K.: " 'Islam noir', 'Historische Ethnologie' und ein 'Kulturwandel' in Westafrika", *EAZ* 14/1, 17-53.

Titley, N.: "Development of fourteenth-fifteenth century painting in Khorasan, Iran, and Turkey", *Marg* 26/4, 17-28.

Townson, Duncan: *Muslim Spain.* (London, Cambridge University Press). 48 p., 56 illus. and maps. =Cambridge Introduction to History of Mankind, Topic Book.

Turk, Afif: "El reino de Zaragoza en el siglo XI de Cristo (V de la hégira)", *RIEI* 17, 7-122.

Ullmann, Manfred: *Die Natur- und Geheimwissenschaften im Islam.* (Leiden, E. J. Brill, 1972). xiii, 500 p. = Handbuch der Orientalistik, 1 Abt., Ergänzungsband Vi, 2 Ab. – R: *BiOr* 30, 490-491 (J. N. Mattock).

Ünal, Rahmi Hüseyin: "Deux caravansérails peu connus de l'époque pré-ottomane au sud de Karaman (Konya)", *AARP* 3, 59-69.

Urvoy, D.: "Sur l'évolution de la notion de ǧihād dans l'Espagne musulmane", *Mélanges de la Casa de Velazques* 9, 335-371.

Urvoy, D.: "Une étude sociologique des mouvements religieux dans l'Espagne musulmane de la chute du califat au milieu du XIIIe siècle", *MCV* 8 (1972), 223-293.

Vázquez de Benito, M. de la C.: "El manuscrito n. XXX de la collectión Gayangos", *BAEO* 9, 73-124.

Voll, J.: "Islam: Its Future in the Sudan", *The Muslim World* 63, No. 4, 280-296.

Waardenburg, Jacques: "Changes of perspective in Islamic studies over the last decades", *HumIs* I, 247-260.

Waardenburg, J.: "Tendences d'histoire des religions dans l'Islam au Moyen Age", in: *XXIXe Congrès International des Orientalistes. Résumés des Communications*. Sections 1-5. (Paris, Y. Hervouet), p. 108.

Wagner, Ewald: *Abū Nuwās. Eine Studie zur arabischen Literatur der frühen Abbasidenzeit.* (Wiesbaden, 1965). – R: *OLZ* 1-274 (Manfred Fleischhammer). mer).

Wagner, Ewald: "Eine Liste der Heiligen von Harar", *ZDMG* 123, Heft 2, 269-292.

Walker, W. S. and Ahmet E. Uysal: "Am ancient God in Modern Turkey: some Aspects of the Cult of Hĭzĭr", *JAF* 86, 286-289.

Watt, W. Montgomery: "L'influence de l'Islam sur l'Europe médiévale", *REI* 41, 127-156 (fin).

Watt, W. Montgomery: *The Influence of Islam on Medieval Europe* (Edinburgh, 1972). – R: *WI* 14, 248-250 (O. Spies). *Arabica* 20, 327-330 (M. Arkoun).

Wielandt, Rotraud: *Offenbarung und Geschichte im Denken moderner Muslime.* (Wiesbaden, 1971). – R: *BiOr* 30, 296 (G. H. A. Juynboll). *WI* 14, 255-257 (W. Ende).

Wilber, D. N.: "Le Masǧid-i ǧāmiᶜ de Qazwin", *Revue des Etudes Islamiques* 41, 199-229.

Yalaoui, M.: "Les relations entre Fatimides d'Ifriqiya et Omeyyades d'Espagne à travers le diwan d'Ibn Hānī", in: *Actas del II Coloquio Hispano-Tunecino* (Madrid), 13-30.

Yalman, Nur: "Some observations on secularism in Islam: the cultural revolution in Turkey", *Daedalus* 102/1, 139-168.

Yanuck, M.: "The Indian-Muslim Self-Image: Nine Historians in Search of a Past", *IsMA* 4, No. 4, 78-94.

Yildiz, Hakki Dursun: "Die geistigen und psychischen Grundlagen des Unabhängigkeitskrieges", *Cultura Turcica* 8-10, 70-85.

Začinović, Jusuf: "Zidne dekoracije Ferhadije džamije u Sarajevu", (Mural decorations of Ferhadiya mosque in Sarajevo), *Naše Starine* 13, 221-232.

VII. HINDUISM

Adiceam, M. E.: *Contribution à l'étude d'Aiya Nār-Śāstā.* (Pondichéry, Institut Français d'Indologie, 1967). – R: *Erasmus* 25 (11), 336-337 (O. von Hinüber).

Antes, P.: "Das Neue im modernen Hinduismus", *Zeitschrift für Missionsw. und Religionswissenschaft* 57/2, 99-116.

Arapura, J. G.: "Māyā and the Discourse about Brahman", in: M. Sprung (ed.): *The Problem of Two Truths in Buddhism and Vedānta* (Dordrecht, D. Reidel Co.) 109-121.

Arya, U.: *Ritual Songs and Folksongs of the Hindus of Surinam*. (Leiden, 1968). – R: *OLZ* 68, 285-287 (W. Ruben).

Beane, W. C.: "The Cosmological Structure of Mythical Time: Kālī Śakti", *History of Religions* 13/1, 54-83.

Bechert, H.: "The Cult of Skandakumāra in the Religious History of South India and Ceylon", in: *Association Internationale des Etudes Tamoules, Compte-rendu de la troisième conférence internationale, Paris, 1970* (Pondichéry, Institut Français d'Indologie), 199-207.

Bhaktivinoda, T.: "Life of Śrī Caitanya", *Indian Philosophy and Culture* 18, No. 1, 4-15.

Bhaktivinoda, T.: "Precepts of Śrī Caitanya", *Indian Philosophy and Culture* 18, No. 1, 16-39.

Bhattacharji, S.: *The Indian Theogony: A Comparative Study of Indian Mythology from the Vedas to the Puranas* (Cambridge Univ. Press, 1970). – R: *JRAS* 1, 74-75 (T. Ling).

Biardeau, M.: "Le sacerdoce dans l'hinduisme classique", *StMis* 22, 187-200.s

The Bilvamaṅgalastava. Edited and translated with an introduction by F. Wilson. (Leiden, E. J. Brill). x, 172 p.

Bodewitz, H. W.: *Jaiminīya Brāhmaṇa I, 1-65.* Translation and Commentary. With a Study °Agnihotra and Prāṇāgnihotra°. (Leiden, E. J. Brill). xix, 357 p. = Orientalia Rheno-Traiectina, 17.

Boetzelaar, J. M. van: "Hindoeïstische wijsbegeerte", in: *Oosterse filosofie* (Assen, Van Gorcum) 15-26.

Bon, B. H.: "Philosophy and Religion", *Indian Philosophy and Culture* 18/4, 354-357.

Brooks, R. W.: "Some Uses and Implications of Advaita Vedānta's Doctrine of Māyā", in: M. Sprung (ed.): *The Problem of Two Truths in Buddhism and Vedānta* (Dordrecht, D. Reidel Co.) 98-108.

de Bruyne, J. L.: *Rudrakavi's Great Poem of the Dynasty of Rāṣṭrauḍha*. Cantos 1-12 and 18-20, introduced, translated and annotated. (Leiden, 1968). – R: *OLZ* 68, 501-503 (J. Deleu).

Caitanyadāsa, R.: "Śrī Caitanya's Gift of Divine Name", *Indian Philosophy and Culture* 18/1, 85-98.

Cardona, G.: "A New Translation of the Mahābhāṣya", *OLZ* 68, 229-238. (A review article on S. D. Joshi: *Patañjali's Vyākaraṇa-Mahābhāṣya Samarthāhnika (P. 2.1.1)*, edited with Translation and Explanatory Notes, Poona, 1968.

Cocagnac, A. M.: "L'Hindouisme, hier et aujourd'hui. Une invasion mystique", *ICI*, No. 429, 21-24.

Cornelis, E.: "L'homme tel que l'Inde le conçoit selon ses sources classiques", *Concilium*, no. 86, 39-50.

Dandekar, R. N.: *Some Aspects of the History of Hinduism*. (Poona, 1967). – R: *OLZ* 68, 283-285 (I. Fišer).

Dange, S. A.: "The Thunder: Cow and the 'Asyavāmīya'", *Journal of the University of Bombay* 41 (77), 28-51.

Delfendahl, B.: "Le culte chamêtre dans un village de l'Inde. Description systématique", *L'Ethnographie* no. 66, 29-55.

Derrett, J. D. M.: *Dharmaśāstra and Juridical Literature*. (Wiesbaden, Otto Harrassowitz). iv, 75 p. = A History of Indian Literature, Part of Vol. IV.

Derrett, J. D. M.: *History of Indian Law (Dharmaśāstra)*. (Leiden, E. J. Brill). vi, 39 p. = Handbuch der Orientalistik, Zweite Abteilung, Band III, 1. Abschnitt.

Deutsch, E. and J. A. B. van Buitenen: *A Source Book of Advaita Vedānta*, (Honolulu, 1971). – R: *IIJ* 15, 138-140 (J. F. Staal).

Dhavamony, M.: "Priesthood in Early Hinduism", *Studia Missionalia* 22, 165-185.

Dubey, S. P.: "The Concept of Soul in Hinduism", *Religion and Society* 19, No. 4, 16-32.

Fuchs, S.: "Priests and Magicians in Aboriginal India", *StMis* 22, 201-236, bibliography.

Gail, A. J.: "Die neun Abschnitte Bhāratavarṣas. Eine textgeschichtliche Untersuchung", *WZKS* 17, 5-20.

Gaṅgādhara: *Gaṅgādasa-Pratāpavilāsa-Nāṭakam*. A Historical Sanskrit Play, edited by B. J. Sandesara and P. A. M. Bhojak. (Baroda, Oriental Institute). xv, 82 p., 4 pl. = Caekwad's Oriental Series, 156.

Gnoli, R.: *Abhinavagupta. Luce delle sacre Scritture (Tantrāloka)*. (Turino, Unione Tipogr. Ed. Torinese, 1972). 900 p. = Classici delle Religioni, 25.

Gonda, J.: *The Vedic God Mitra* (Leiden, 1972). – R: *IIJ* 15, 223-232 (F. B. J. Kuiper).

Goudriaan, T.: "Tamburu and his Sisters", *WZKS* 17, 49-95.

Hacker, P.: "Vrata", *Nachrichten der Akademie der Wissenschaften in Göttingen, Philos.-hist. Klasse*, Heft 5, 107-142.

Haich E.: *Force Sexuelle et Yoga*. Préface du Helmut Speer. (Lausanne, Ed. du Signal), 188 p.

Hara, M.: "The King as a Husband of the Earth (mahīpati)", *AsiSt/EtAs* 27/2, 97-114.

Hasan, K. A.: "The Hindu Dietary Practices and Culinary Rituals in a North Indian Village: An Ethnomedical and Structural Analysis", *Ethnomedizin* I/1, 43-70.

Hiatt, L. R.: "The Pattini Cult of Ceylon: A Tamil Perspective", *SoCoR* 20, no. 2, 231-249, bibliography.

Hiltebeitel, A.: "The Mahabharata and Hindu Eschatology", *History of Religions* 12/2, 95-135.

Höfer, A. and B. P. Sarestha: "Ghost Exorcism among the Brahmans of Central Nepal", *CAJ* 17/1, 51-77, bibliography.

Hoffmann, Karl: *Der Injunktiv im Veda. Eine synchronische Funktionsuntersuchung.* (Heidelberg, 1967). – R: *OLZ* 68, 75-84 (W. Thomas).

Hooykaas, C.: *Religion in Bali.* (Leiden, E. J. Brill). 4to. x, 31 p., 48 pl. = Iconography of Religions, XIII, fasc. 10.

Kurup, K. K. N.: "The Cult of Teyyam and Hero Worship", *Folklore* (Calcutta) 14, No. 1, 1-25: No. 2, 45-68: No. 3, 85-101.

Larson, G. J.: "Mystical Man in India", *JSSR* 12, No. 1, 1-16, bibliography.

Lauf, Detlef-I.: *Das Bild als Symbol im Tantrismus. Indische Tantras als praktische Führer zur seelischen Ganzheit des Menschen.* (München, Heinz Moos). Quarto. 76 p., 72 Abb.

Lazari-Pawlowska, I.: "The Models of Hindu Perfection", *Etyka* No. 12, 25-56 (in Polnish with Russian and English Summaries).

Lingat, Robert: *Les sources du droit dans le système traditionnel de l'Inde*. (Paris-La Haye, 1967). – R: *OLZ* 68, 503-504 (L. Skurzak).

Mahapatra, Manamohan: "The Badu: a Service-Caste at the Lingaraj Temple at Bhubaneswar", *CAS* 3, 96-108.

Mahāraj, B. H. B.: "Śrī Caitanya's Concept of Divine Love", *Indian Philosophy and Culture* 18/1, 108-125.

Mahāraj, B. H. B.: "Śrī Caitanya's Concept of Finite Self", *Indian Philosophy and Culture* 18/1, 47-69.

Meillasoux, C': "Y a-t-il des castes aux Indes?", *Cahiers Internationaux de Sociologie* 54, 5-29, bibliographie.

Mesquita, R.: "Yāmunamuni: Leben, Datierung und Werke", *Wiener Zeitschrift für die Kunde Südasiens und Archiv für indische Philosophie* XVII, 177-193.

Mette, A.: *Piṇḍ'esaṇā. Das Kapitel der Oha-nijjutti über den Bettelgang.* (Wiesbaden, Akademie der Wissenschaften und der Literatur). 242 S., Bibliographie (5 S.) = AWL, Abhandlungen der geistes- und sozialwissenschaftlichen Klasse, 11.

Mishra, V. B.: *Religious beliefs and practices of North India during the early medieval period.* (Leiden, E. J. Brill). xx, 191 p. = Handbuch der Orientalistik, Zweite Abteilung, Ergänzungsband III.

Müller, Niklas: *Glauben, Wissen und Kunst der alten Hindus.* (Leipzig, 1968). R: *OLZ* 68, 281-282 (H. Goetz).

Mylius, K.: "Die gesellschaftliche Entwicklung Indiens in jungvedischer Zeit nach den Sanskrit-Quellen. III. Der ideologische Überbau. Mit einem Anhang: Das vedische Opferritual", *EAZ* 14/3, 425-499, Bibliographie.

Nath, G.: "Śrī Caitanya's Concept of Theistic Vedanta", *Indian Philosophy and Culture* 18/1, 70-84.

O'Flaherty, Wendy Doniger: *Ascetism and Eroticism in the Mythology of Śiva.* (London, Oxford University Press). xiv, 386 p., 16 illus. = School of Oriental and African Studies.

Pallis, M.: "Consideration on Tantrik Spirituality", *JOR* 34-35, 41-51.

Parvulescu, A.: "Lat. *nubo: nubes* et le mythe d'Indra", *AUBCO* 22, 157-164.

Pocock, D. F.: *Mind, Body and Wealth. A Study of Belief and Practice in an Indian Village.* (Oxford, Vasil Blackwell). xv, 187 p., map.

Ras, J. J.: "The Panji Romance and W. H. Rassers' Analysis of its Theme", *BTLV* 129, 411-456.

Reddy, A. M.: "On the Role of Ritual Friendship in the Mobility of Wealth in the Visakhapatnam Agency", *Man in India* 53/3, 243-255, bibliography.

Rolland, P.: "Le Mahavrata. Contribution à l'étude d'un rituel solennel védique", *NAWG* Heft 3, 51-79.

Sarasvatī, S.: "Śrī Kṛṣṇa Caitanya's Concept of the Godhead", *Indian Philosophy and Culture* 18/1, 40-46.

Schmidt, Hanns-Peter: *Bṛhaspati und Indra. Untersuchungen zur vedischen Mythologie und Kulturgeschichte.* (Wiesbaden, 1968). – R: *OLZ* 68, 177-181 (J. Gonda).

Schneider, U.: *Der Somaraub des Manu. Mythus und Ritual.* (Wiesbaden, 1971). – R: *WZKS* 17, 205-206 (H. Krick).

Sharma, B. N. K.: *The Brahmasūtras and their Principal Commentaries. A Critical Exposition*. Vol. I. (Bombay, 1971). – R: *WZKS* 17, 208 (E. Steinkellner).

Sharma, U.: "Theodicy and the Doctrine of Karma", *Man* 8/3, 347-364, Bibliography.

Singh, S. B.: "Syncretic Icons in Uttar Pradesh", *East and West* 23, No. 3-4, 339-346, 3 pl.

Sivaraman, K.: "The Meaning of Moksha in Contemporary Hindu Thought and Life", *EcRev* 25/2, 148-157.

Srinivasan, D.: "Samdhyā: Myth and Ritual", *Indo-Iranian Journal* 15, 161-178.

Stephenson, G.: "Die westöstliche Yoga-Synthese", *ZMRW* 57/2, 117-118. (Besprechung des Werkes von Sri Aurobindo: *Die Synthese des Yoga*, Bellnhausen, Verlag Hinder und Deelmann, 1972, 965 S.)

Vana, L.: "Śrī Caitanya's Concept of Bhakti", *Indian Philosophy and Culture* 18/1, 99-107.

Wilson, F. (ed.): *The Bilvamangalastava*. Edited and Translated with an introduction. (Leiden, E. J. Brill). x, 172 p.

Yocum, G. E.: "Shrines, Shamanism and Love Poetry: Elements in the Emergence of Popular Tamil Bhakti", *JAAR* 41/1, 3-17.

VIII. BUDDHISM

Abe, M.: "Buddhist *Nirvana*: Its Significance in Contemporary Thought and Life", *EcRev* 25/2, 158-168.

Alsdorf, Ludwig: *Die Āryā-Strophen des Pali-Kanons*. (Wiesbaden, 1968). – R: *OLZ* 68, 280-281 (H. Kopp).

Ames, M. M.: "Westernization of Modernization: The Case of the Sinhalese Buddhism", *SoCoR* 20/2, 139-170.

Bastow, David: "Continuity and Diversity in Early Buddhism", in: *The Cardinal Meaning, Essays in Comparative Hermeneutics: Buddhism and Christianity* (The Hague, Mouton) 103-125.

Bechert, H.: "Buddhistische Sozialethik und Kulturwandel in Ceylon und Südostasien", *Le Muséon* 86, 499-519.

Bechert, H.: "Contradictions in Sinhalese Buddhism", *CAS* 4, 7-17.

Bechert, H.: "Sangha, State, Society, 'Nation': Persistence of Traditions in 'Post-Traditional' Buddhist Societies", *Daedalus* 102/1, 85-95.

Beyer, Stephan: *The Cult of the Tara. Magic and Ritual in Tibet*. (Berkeley and Los Angeles, University of California Press). xxii, 542 p., 54 fig., 16 pl.

Bhattacharya, Kamaleswar: "*L'ātman-brahman dans le bouddhisme ancien*. (Paris, Ecole Française d'Extrême-Orient). 4to. 179 p. = Publications de l'EFEO, 90.

Bloss, L. W.: "The Buddha and the Nāga: A Study in Buddhist Folk Religiosity", *History of Religions* 13/1, 36-53.

Bortolaso, G.: "Lo Zen penetra neol'Occidente", *La Civiltà Cattolica*, No. 2948, 156-161.

Chang, A.: "Fan Chen and his Treatise on the Destruction of the Soul", *Chinese Culture* 14/4, 1-8.

Ch'en, Kenneth K. S.: *The Chinese Transformation of Buddhism*. (Princeton, N.J., Princeton University Press). 345 p.

Coedès, G. et C. Archaimbault: *Les trois mondes. Traibhûmi Brah R'van*. (Paris, Ecole Française d'Extrême Orient). xvii, 294 p. Quarto. = Publications de l'EFEO, 89.

Cousins, L. S.: "Buddhist Jhāna", *Religions* (London) 3, No. 2, 115-131.

Demiéville, P.: *Choix d'études bouddhiques (1929-1970)*. (Leiden, E. J. Brill). xli, 497 p., portr. (Note liminaire d'Yves Hervouet).

Dönmé, Konchog Tänpä: *Spiritual Guide to the Jewel Island* by Konchog Tänpä Dönmé, disciple and spiritual son of Jamyang Zhäpa, a scholar of the epoch of the Seventh Dalai Lama (1708-1757). Translated by Blanche C. Olschak and Thupten Wangyal. (Zürich, Buddhist Publications). 224 p.

Doržiev, Z. et A. Kondratov: "Sanctuaires de Lhassa", *Nauka i Religija* (Moskva), No. 4, 91-96.

Eimer, Helmut und Pema Tsering: "T'e'u raṅ mdos ma", *Serta Tibeto-Mongolica, Festschrift für Walther Heissig* (Wiesbaden), 47-87.

Enomiya-Lassalle, Hugo M.: *Zen unter Christen. Östliche Meditation und christliche Spiritualität.* (Graz, Verlag Styria). 78 p.

Ensink, J.: *De groote weg naar het licht. Een keuze uit de literatuur van het Mahayāna-Buddhisme, uit het Sanskrit vertaald en toegelicht.* Tweede, herziene en uitgebreide druk. (Amsterdam, Wetenschappelijke Uitgeverij). 183 p.

Eracle, J.: *La Doctrine bouddhique de la terre pure. Introduction à trois Sûtra bouddhiques.* (Paris, Dervy-Livres). 117 p.

Evans-Wentz, W. Y.: *Tibetan Yoga and Secret Doctrines or Seven Books of Wisdom of the Great Path, according to the Late Lama Kazi Dawa-Samdup's English Rendering, arranged and edited with Introductions and Annotations to serve as a Commentary.* (Oxford, 1967). – R: *OLZ* 68, 85-86 (J. Schubert).

Falk, N. E.: "Wilderness and Kingship in Ancient South Asia", *History of Religions* 13/1, 1-15.

Fernando, C.: "How Buddhists and Catholics of Sri Lanka See Each Other: A Factor Analytic Approach", *SoCoR* 20/2, 321-332.

Fernando, T.: "The Western-Educated Elite and Buddhism in British Ceylon. A Neglected Aspect of the Nationalist Movement", *CAS* 4, 18-29.

Forte, A.: "Il 'Monastero dei grandi Chou' a Lo-Yang", *AION* 33, no. 3, 417-429.

Fozdar, J. K.: *The God of Buddha.* (New York, Asia Publishing House). xii, 184 p.

Frauwallner, E.: "Abhidharma-Studien. V. Der Sarvādtivādaḥ. Eine entwicklungsgeschichtliche Studie", *WZKS* XVII, 97-121 (Fortsetzung folgt).

Frédéric, Louis: *Südost-Asien. Tempel und Skulpturen.* Deutsch von Sibylle von Reden. (Essen, 1968). – R: *OLZ* 68, 93-94 (J. W. de Jong).

Gaulier, S.: "Expressions iconographiques des croyances eschatologiques dans la région de Koutcha, d'après deux boîtes funéraires de la collection Pelliot", in: *XXIXe Congrès International des Orientalistes. Résumés des Communications,* Sections 6-7. (Paris, Y. Hervouet), p. 2-3.

Geiger, W.: *Kleine Schriften zu Indologie und Buddhismuskunde.* Herausgegeben von H. Bechert. (Wiesbaden, Franz Steiner). xxxiii, 707 S. = Glasenapp-Stiftung, 6.

Gimaret, D.: "A propos de S. M. Stern et S. Walzer: *Three Unknown Buddhist Stories in an Arabic Version*, Oxford, Cassirer, 1971, 38 p., plus 23 p. de texte arabe", *Arabica* 20, 186-191.

Gokhale, B. G.: "Anagarika Dharmapala. Toward Modernity through Tradition in Ceylon", *CAS* 4, 30-39.

Goldstein, M. C.: "The Circulation of Estates in Tibet: Reincarnation, Land and Politics", *JAS* 32/3, 445-455.

Gombrich, R.: "Le clergé bouddhiste d'une circonscription kandienne et les élections générales de 1965", *SoCoR* 20/2, 257-266.

Gorakshkar, S.: "An Inscribed Image of Hayagriva-rTamgrin from Tibet in the Prince of Wales Museum", *BMWI* No. 12, 70-72, 1 photo.

Govinda, Lama Anagarika: *Der Weg der weissen Wolken*. Erlebnisse eines buddhistischen Pilgers in Tibet. (Zürich, 1969). – R: *OLZ* 68, 612-613 (J. W. de Jong).

Guenther, H.: "Saṁvṛti and Paramārtha in Yogācāra According to Tibetan Sources", in: M. Sprung (ed.): *The Problem of Two Truths in Buddhism and Vedānta* (Dordrecht, D. Reidel Co,) 89-97.

Hoang-Thĭ-Bich (Thich Man-Oa-La): *Étude et traduction du Gakudôyôjin-Shû. Recueil de l'application de l'esprit a l'étude de la Voie du maître de Zen, Dôgen*. (Genève, Droz). iv, 224 p. = Centre de Recherches d'Histoire et de Philologie de la IVe Section de l'Ecole Pratique des Hautes Etudes, II. Hautes Etudes Orientales, 4.

Houtart, F.: "Champ religieux et champ politique dans la société singhalaise", *SoCoR* 20/2, 105-138.

Humbach, Helmut: *Die aramätische Inschrift von Taxila*. (Wiesbaden, 1969). – R: *BiOr* 30, 466-467 (H. J. W. Drijvers).

Iida, Shotaro: "The Nature of Saṁvṛti and the Relationship of Paramārtha to it in Svātantrika-Mādhyamika", in: M. Sprung (ed.): *The Problem of Two Truths in Buddhism and Vedānta* (Dordrecht, D. Reidel Co.) 64-77.

Ingram, P. O.: "The Zen Critique of Pure Land Buddhism", *JAAR* 41, No. 2, 184-200.

Italiaander, Rolf: *Sokagakkai, Japans neue Buddhisten*. (Erlangen, Verlag der Evang.-Luther. Mission). 423 p., illus.

Izutsu, T.: "Sense and Nonsense in Zen Buddhism", *Eranos-Jahrbuch* 39, 183-215.

Johnston, W.: *Zen et Connaissance de Dieu*. (Paris, Desclée de Brouwer). 187 p.

Kajiyama, Y.: "Three kinds of affirmation and two kinds of negation in Buddhist philosophy", *WZKS* XVII, 161-175.

Kaufmann, R.: "Vietnamesen: Hinterindien, Süd-Vietnam. Kulttänze in einer buddhistischen Pagode bei Huê", *Encyclopaedia Cinematographica*, Film E 2027 (Göttingen, Inst. für d. Wiss. Film), 15 p.

Kloppenborg, R. (tr.): *The sūtra on the Foundation of the Buddhist Order (Catuṣpariṣatsūtra)*; Relating the Events from the Bodhisattva's Englighternment up to the Conversion of Upatiṣya (Śāriputra) and Kolita (Maugdalyāyana). (Leiden, E. J. Brill). xvi, 123 p. = NISABA. Religious Text Translation Series, I.

Knechten, H.: "Die deutschen buddhistischen Katechismen", *ZMRW* 57, Heft 3, 207-223, Bibliographie (2 p.)

Kuznetsov, B. I.: *Rgyal Rabs Gsal Ba'i Me Long* (The Clear Mirror of Royal Genealogies). (Leiden, 1966). – R: *OLZ* 68, 300-301 (Johannes Schubert).

Lafleur, W. R.: "Saigyô and the Buddhost Value of Nature", *History of Religions* 13, 93-128, 227-248.

Lamotte, E.: "Der Verfasser des Upadeśa und seine Quellen", *Nachrichten der Akademie der Wissenschaften in Göttingen, Philos.-hist. Klasse*, Heft 2, 29-50.

Lauf, D. I.: "Vorläufiger Bericht über die Geschichte und Kunst einiger lamaistischer Tempel und Klöster in Bhutan", *EZZ* 3/2, 41-85.

Leach, E.: "Buddhism in Post-Colonial Political Order in Burma and Ceylon", *Daedalus* 102/1, 29-54.

Li-kouang, L.: *Dharma-Samuccaya. Compendium de la Loi.* 3e partie. (Chapitres XIII à XXXVI). (Paris, A. Maisonneuvel). 568 p., and 48 p. = Annales du Musée Guimet, tome 75. (Publié avec le concours du CNRS).

Lin, Li-Kouang (ed. et tr.): *Dharma-Samuccaya. Compendium de la loi.* Texte sanscrit édité avec la version tibétaine et les versions chinoises et traduit en français. 3e partie: Ghapitres 13 à 36. (Paris, Adrien Maisonneuvel). vi, 567 p.

Lotz, J. B.: "Der Koan als Meditationsweg für Christen", *Erbe und Auftrag* 49, Heft 5, 382-391.

Malalgoda, K.: "The Buddhist-Christian Confrontation in Ceylon 1800-1880", *SoCoR* 20/2, 171-200.

Massao, A.: "Zen and Nietzsche", *The Eastern Buddhist* 6, No. 2, 14-32.

Masson, J.: "Le bouddhisme ancien face au brahmane et au sacrifice", *StMis* 22, 123-144.

Maten, E. P.: *Budhasvāmin's Bṛhatkathāślokasaṃgraha.* A literary study of an ancient Indian Narrative. (Leiden, E. J. Brill). viii, 116 p. = Orientalia Rheno-Traiectina, XVIII.

Matilal, Bimal Krishna: "A Critique of the Mādhyamika Position", in: M. Sprung (ed.): *The Problem of Two Truths in Buddhism and Vedānta* (Dordrecht, D. Reidel Co.) 54-63.

Mette, A.: "Vedhas in Lalitavistara und Divyāvadāna. Beschreibung des schönen Körpers in Sanskrit und Prakrit", *WZKS* 17, 21-42

Mitomo, K.: "Anuśaya as conceived in Abhidharma-Buddhism", *JIBS* 22, No. 1, 501-506 (in Japanese).

Morgan, F. B.: "Vocation of Monk and Layman. Signs of Change in Thai Buddhist Ethics", *CAS* 4, 68-77.

Murti, T. R. V.: "Saṁvṛti and Paramārtha in Mādhyamika and Advaita Vedānta", in: M Sprung (ed.): *The Problem of Two Truths in Buddhism and Vedānta* (Dordrecht, D. Reidel Co.) 9-26.

Niyogi, P.: "Organisation of Buddhist Monastaries in Ancient Bengal and Bihar", *JIH* 51 (153), 531-557.

Obeyesekere, G.: "The Goddess Pattini and the Lord Buddha: Notes on the Myth of the Birth of the Deity", *SoCoR* 29/2, 217-229, bibliography.

Obschak, Blanche Christine and Gesche Thupten Wangyal: *Mystic At of Ancient Tibet.* (London, Allen & Unwin), 224 p., ill.

Pao, K.: "The Lama Temple and Lamaism in Bayin Man", *Monumenta Serica* 29, 659-684.

Paslick, R. H.: "Dialectic and Non-Attachment: the structure of Hermann Hesse's Siddhartha", *Symposium* 27/1, 64-75, 2 fig.

Pathirana-Wimaladharma, K.: "Some Observations on the Religious Festivals, Village Rituals and the Religiosity of the Sinhala Rural Folk in the N.C.P. Ceylon", *SoCoR* 20/2, 267-285, bibliography.

Piker, S.: "Buddhism and Modernisation in Contemporary Thailand", *CAS* 4, 51-67.

Regamey, C.: "Encore à propos du lalitavistara et de l'épisode d'Asita", *Asiatische Studien* 27/1, 1-34.

Reynolds, C. J.: "The Buddhist Monkhood in Nineteenth Century Thailand", *DisAbIn* A 34/3, 1221-1222. (The author's summary of his diss., Cornell University).

Reynolds, F.: "Three Recent Books on Religion in South Asia", *HoR* 13/2, 160-164 (= A. K. Warder: *Indian Buddhism*; R. Gombrich: *Precept and Practice: Traditional Buddhism in the Rural Highlands of Ceylon*; M. Singer: *When a Great Tradition Modernizes: An Anthropological Appproach to Indian Civilization*).

Reynolds, F. E.: "Tradition and Change in Theravada Buddhism. A Bibliographical Essay Focused on the Modern Period", *CAS* 4, 94-104.

Reynolds, F. E.: "Sacral Kingship and National Development. The Case of Thailand", *CAS* 4, 40-50.

Ruegg, D. S.: *La théorie du tathāgatagarbha et du gotra: études sur la sotériologie et la gnoséologie du bouddhisme*, (Paris, 1969). – R: *IIJ* 15, 292-299 (J. Takasaki).

Schmithausen L.: "Spirituelle Praxis und philosophische Theorie im Buddhismus", *ZMRW* 57/3, 161-186.

Schmithausen, L.: "Zu D. Seyfort Rueggs Buch: *La Théorie du Tathāgatagarbha et du Gotra.* (Besprechungsaufsatz)", *WZKS* 17, 123-160.

Seneviratne, H. L.: "L'ordination buddhiste à Ceylan", *SoCoR* 20/2, 251-256.

Sharma, U.: "Theodicy and the Doctrine of Karma", *Man* 8/3, 347-364.

Simon, Pierre J. et Ida Simon-Barouh: *Hâù bóng. Un culte viêtnamien de possession transplanté en France.* (Paris-La Haye, Mouton). 87 p., 15 phot. = Cahiers de l'Homme, n.s., 13.

Sinha, Nirmal Chandra: *Tibet – Considerations on Inner Asian History.* (Calcutta, 1967). – R: *OLZ* 68, 205-206 (H. Bräutigam).

Smith, B. L.: "Sinhalese Buddhism and the Dilemmas of Reinterpretation", *CAS* 3, 1-25.

Smith, C. T.: "Notes on Chinese Temples in Hong Kong", *JHKRAS* 13, 133-139. 133-139.

Smith, J. I.: "Early Muslim Accounts of Buddhism in India", *Studies in Islam* 10, ‹No. 1-2, 87-100.

Snellgrove, D. L.: *Four Lamas of Dolpo. Autobiographies of Four Tibetan Lamas (15th-18th Centuries). I: Introduction and Translations.* (Oxford, 1967). – R: *HJ* 15, 68-74 (J. W. de Jong).

Sprung, M.: "The Mādhyamika Doctrine of Two Realities as a Metaphysic", in: the same (ed.): *The Problem of Two Truths in Buddhism and Vedānta* Dordrecht, D. Reidel Co.) 40-53.

Sprung, Mervyn (ed.):. *The Problem of Two Truths in Buddhism and Vedānta.* (Dordrecht, D. Reidel Publishing Co.) viii, 125 p.

Staviskii, B. J. (ed.): *Buddiiskii Kul'tovyi Zentr Kara-Tepe v Starom Termeze* (= Das buddhistische Kultzentrum Kara Tepe in Alt-Termes. (Moskau, Nauka, 1972). 174 p. – R: *BiOr* 30, 500-501 (B. Brentjes).

Steinkellner, E.: "Buddhaparinịrvāṇastotram", *Wiener Zeitschrift für die Kunde Südasiens und Archiv für indische Philosophie* XVII, 43-48.

Steinkellner, Ernst: *Dhrmakirti's Retubinduh. I: Tibetischer Text und rekonstruierter Sanskrit-Text. II; Übersetzung und Anmerkungen.* (Wien, 1967). – R: *OLZ* 68, 190-192 (Johannes Schubert).

Stephens, K.: "Hai Jui: Ming Patriot, Spark for Revolution and God", *JHKRAS* 13, 144-146.

Stevenson, I.: "Characteristics of Cases of the Reincarnation Type in Ceylon", *CAS* 3, 26-39.

Streng, F. J.: "The Significance of Pṛatītyasamutpāda for Understanding the Relationship between Saṁvṛti and Paramārthasatya in Nāgārjuna", in: M. Sprung (ed.): *The Problem of Two Truths in Buddhism and Vedānta* (Dordrecht, D. Reidel Co.) 27-39.

Swearer, D.: "Three Modes of Zen Buddhism in America", *Journal of Ecumenical Studies* 10/2, 290-303.

Swearer, D. K.: "Control and Freedom: The Structure of Buddhist Meditation in the Pāli suttas", *PhEW* 23/4, 435-455.

Swearer, D. K.: "Thai Buddhism: Two Responses to Modernity", *CAS* 4, 78-93.

Takeuchi, A.: "Der Mensch in der Nähe zur Natur. Zum Denkeen des japanischen Zen-Meisters Dogen", *ZRGG* 25/1, 20-31.

Tambiah, S. J.: *Buddhism and the Spirit Cults in Northeast Thailand*, (Cambridge University Press), 388 p. – R: *SovEtn*, No. 3, 186-187 (E. V. Ivanova).

Teo, W. K. H.: "Self-Responsibility in Existentialism and Buddhism", *IJPhR* 4, No. 2, 80-91.

Thomas, D.: "The Concept of Soul in Buddhism", *Religion and Society* 19, No. 4, 33-42.

Vetter, T. E.: "Het boeddhisme", in: *Oosterse filosofie* (Assen, van Gorcum/ Amsterdam-Brussel, Intermediair) 27-39.

Vos, F.: "De verlichting in Zen: het ontdekken van de eigen Boeddha-natuur", *Oosterse filosofie* (Assen, Van Gorcum) 52-65.

Waddell, N.: "The Zen Sermons of Bankei Yotaku", *The Eastern Buddhist* 6, No. 2, 129-151.

Warder, A. K.: "Is Nāgārjuna a Mahāyānist?", in: M. Sprung (ed.): *The Problem of Two Truths in Buddhism and Vedānta* (Dordrecht, D. Reidel Co.) 78-88.

Weller, Friedrich: "Der Arme Heinrich in Indien", *OLZ* 68, 437-448.

Werner, Karel: "Authenticity in the Interpretation of Buddhism" in: *The Cardinal Meaning, Essays in Comparative Hermeneutics: Buddhism and Christianity* (The Hague, Mouton) 161-193.

Wilhelm, H.: "On Ming Orthodoxy", *Monumenta Serica* 29, 1-26.

Willemen, Charles: "The Prefaces to the Chinese Dharmapadas, Fa-chü Ching and Ch-u-yao Ching", *T'oung Pao* 59, 203-219.

Wilson, H. A.: "An 'Anatomy' of the Buddhist Renaissance in Ceylon in the Work of K. N. Jayatilleke", *SoCoR* 20/2, 201-215.

Yalman, N.: "On the Meaning of Food Offerings in Ceylan", *SoCoR* 20/2, 287-302.

Yamaori, T.: "Fasting and Charismatic Rebirth", *Bunka* 37, No. 3-4, 146sq. (In Japanese, English symmary, pp. 396-397).

Yuyama, A.: *A Bibliography of the Sanskrit Texts of the Saddharmapuṇḍarīka-sūtra* (Canverra, 1970). – R: *IIJ* 15, 140-144 (J. May).

Zago, M.: "Le bonze dans le bouddhisme Theravâda Lao", *StMis* 22, 145-163.

Zukovskaja, N. L.: "Le mandala comme objet du culte dans le lamaïsme", *SMAE* 29, 71-79 (en russe).

IX. CHINESE RELIGIONS

Ahern, Emily M.: *The Cult of the Dead in a Chinese Village*. (Stanford, Calif., Stanford University Press). xiv, 280 p., 8 pl.

Bauer, Wolfgang: *Das Bild in der Weissage-Literatur Chinas*. Prophetische Texte im politischen Leben vom Buch der Wandlung bis zu Mao Tse Tung. (München, Heinz Moos). Quarto. 74 p. = Welt der Bilder, 4.

Böttger, W.: "Chinesische Drachengewänder aus dem Fundus des Leipziger Museums für Völkerkunde", *JMVL* 29, 163-190.

Chang, Carsun: *Wang Yang-Ming: Idealist Philosopher of Sixteenth-Century China*. (Jamaica, 1962). – R: *OLZ* 68, 402-403 (W. Eichhorn).

Chen, E. M.: "Is there a doctrine of physical immortality in the Tao Te Ching?", *HoR* XII/3, 231-249.

Chen, Hsiang-shui: "The Ancestors Tablet: Inheritance and wealth in the Determination of Ancestor Position", *BIES* 36, 141-164.

Cheng, C. Y.: "Religious Reality and Religious Understanding in Confucianism and Neo-Confucianism", *IPhQ* 13/1, 33-61.

Chiao, J. W.: "Zum Wortfeld 'Tod', 'sterben' und 'tot' in der chinesischen Sprache", *MonSer* 30, 338-391.

Ching, J.: "Beyond Good and Evil. The Culmination of the Thought of Wang Yang-ming (1472-1529)", *Numen* 20/2, 125-134.

Ching, J.: "Neo-Confucian Utopian Theories and Political Ethics", *Monumenta Serica, Journal of Oriental Studies* 30, 1-56.

Chuang, Ying-chang: "Temples, Ancestral Halls and Patterns of Settlement in Chushan", *BIES* 36, 113-140.

Demiéville, P.: *Choix d'études sinologiques (1921-1970)*. (Leiden, E. J. Brill). xli, 633 p., partr. (Note liminaire par Yves Hervouet).

Eder, Matthias: *Chinese Religion*. (Tokyo, The Society of Asian Folklore). vii, 204 p. Quarto. = Asian Folklore Studies, Monographs, 6.

Elorduy, C.: "La Gnosis Taoísta del Tao Te Ching", *Montalban* 2, 145-302.

von Erdberg-Consten, E.: "Time and Space in Chinese Cosmology", *PhQCS* I62, 120-131.

Jackson, A.: "Tibetan Bön Rites in China: A Case of Cultural Diffusion", *Ethnos* 38, 71-92.

Kaltenmark, Max: *Lao Tzu and Taoism*. Translated from the French by R. Greaves. (Stanford, Calif., 1969). – R: *OLZ* 68, 514-516 (D. Holzman).

Keightly, D. N.: "Religion and the Rise of Urbanism", *JAOS* 93, 527-538. (A review article on Paul Wheatley: *The Pivot of the Four Quarters. A Preliminary Enquiry into the Origins and Character of the Ancient Chinese City*, Chicago, 1971).

Kent, George W.: *Worlds of Dust and Jade. 47 Poems and Ballads of the Third Century Chinese Poet* Ts'ao Chih, translated, with an Introduction. (New York, 1969). – R: *OLZ* 68, 513-514 (D. Holzman).

Lidin, O. G.: *The Life of Ogyū Sorai. A Tokugawa Confucian Philosopher*. (Lund, Studentlitteratur). 209 p. = Scandinavian Institute of Asian Studies, Monograph Series, 19.

Lindell, K.: "Stories of Suicide in Ancient China", *Acta Orientalia* (Copenhagen) 35, 167-239.

Liu, J. T. C.: "How Did a Neo-Confucian School Become the State Orthodoxy?", *PhEW* 23/4, 483-505.

Lombard-Salmon, C.: "A propos de quelques cultes chinois particuliers à Java", *ArAs* 26, 243-264, 18 fig.

Miyakawa, H.: "Taoist Trends in the Five Dynasties Period", *The Toho Shukyo* no. 42, 13-34 (in Japanese, with English summary).

Pasternak, B.: "Chinese Tale-Telling Tombs", *Ethnology* 12/3, 259-273.

Peyraube, A.: "Trois études sur les religions chinoises", *ASR* 18 (35), 151-157. (A propos de H. Doré: *Manuel des superstitions chinoises*, rééd. 1970; R. Van Gulik: *La Vie sexuelle dans la Chine ancienne*, 1971; H. Maspéro: *Le Taoïsme et les religions chinoises*, 1971).

Prunner, Gernot: *Papiergötter aus China*. (Hamburg, Museum für Völkerkunde). 5 p., 16 Taf. = Wegweiser zur Völkerkunde, 14.

Rubin, Vitali: "The End of Confucianism?", *T'oung Pao* 59, 68-78.

Sawaguchi, T.: "Taoism in the Literary Works *Lè-fù* of the Hàn and Wei Periods", *The Toho Shukyo* no. 42, 1-12 (in Japanese, with English summary).

Schub, D.: "Der chinesische Steinkeris. Ein Beitrag zur Kenntnis der Sino-tibetischen Divinationskalkulationen", *ZentSt* 7, 353-423.

See, Chinben: "Religious Sphere and Social Organization: An Exploratory Model on the Settlement of Changhua Plain", *BIES* 36, 191-208.

Shih, J.: "Non è forse Confucio un profeta?", *Studia Missionalia* 22, 105-121.

Soper, Alexander Coburn: *Textual Evidence for the Secular Arts of China in the Period from Liu Sung through Sui (A.D. 420-618)*. Excluding Treatises on Painting. (Ascona, 1967). – R: *OLZ* 68, 304-306 (W. Eichhorn).

Tang, Chün-i: "Cosmologies in Ancient Chinese Philosophy", *ChStPh* 5, No. 1, 4-47.

Tang, Chün-I: "Religious Beliefs and Modern Chinese Culture. Part II. The Religious Spirit of Confucianism", *ChStPh* 5/1, 48-85.

Weber-Schäfer, Peter: *Altchinesische Hymnen.* Aus dem "Buch der Lieder" und den "Gesängen von Chᵓu" übertragen und erläutert. (Köln, 1967). – R: *OLZ* 68, 399-401 (R. Felber).

Yu, D. C.: "Chinese Folk Religion", *History of Religions* 12, No. 4, 378-387. (A review article).

Zürcher, E.: "Hoofdlijnen van de klassieke Chinese wijsbegeerte", *Oosterse filosofie* (Assen, Van Gorcum) 40-51.

X. JAPANESE RELIGIONS

Akimoto, N.: "The Institutional Relation of the Manor and the Official Priest, *Kando-no-mori* of *Kasuga* Shrine in the Middle Age" (in Japanese), *NKK* No. 31, 1-33 (cont.)

Creemers, Wilhelmus H. M.: *Shrine Shinto after World War II*. (Leiden, 1968). – R: *OLZ* 68, 403-404 (M. Ch. Haguenauer).

Ellwood, R. S., Jr.: "Shinto and the Discovery of History of Japan", *JAAR* 41, No. 4, 493-505.

Hirohata, S.: "The Myth of Visiting the Land of the Dead", *JJE* 38/1, 1-8. (In Japanese with an English summary).

Ikeda, Hiroko: *A Type and Motif Index of Japanese Folk-Literature*. (Helsinki, Academia Scientiarum Fennica, 1971). 377 p., map. = FF Communications, 209. – R: *Anthropos* 68, 331-332 (Matthias Eder).

Kiley, C. J.: "State and Dynasty in Archaic Yamato", *The Journal of Asian Studies* 33/1, 25-49.

Krempien, R.: *Towazugatari. Übersetzung und Bearbeitung eines neuaufgefundenen literarischen Werkes des Kamakura-Zeit*. (Freiburg/Br., Schwarz Verlag). iv, 333 S. = Ostasiatische Untersuchungen, 1.

Lucas, Heinz: *Japanische Kultmasken. Der Tanz der Kraniche*. (Kassel, 1965). – R: *OLZ* 68, 306-308 (I. L. Kluge).

Matsumoto, N.: "Etude historique sur les Shidoso (prêtres ordonnés illégalement) à l'époque Nara", *JHAKU* 20, 62-92 (en japonais).

Miyata, N.: "On the Structure of the 'Miroku World' in Japan", *JReS* 47, No. 1, 29-50 (in Japanese, with English summary, pp. 106-107).

Numazawa, K.: "Das Priestertum im Schintoismus", *Studia Missionalia* 22, 67-104.

Rotermund, H. O.: "Sôka-gakkai. Idéologie d'une nouvelle secte japonaise", *RHR* 184, no. 2, 137-157.

Spae, J.: "Japanese Religiosity and the Spiritual Values of the East", *Bulletin des Sciences* 4, 676-696.

Steenstrup, C.: "The Imagawa Letter. A Muromachi Warrior's Code of Conduct which Became a Tokugawa Schoolbook", *MoNi* 28/3, 295-316.

Tetsui, Y.: "The Myths of Hiruko and Hinokagutsuchi as Compared with some Ancient Myths in China", *BSSJ* No. 25, 175-188, English summary, pp. 9-10. (In Japanese).

Yoshio, W.: "Kinship Systems in Northern Okinawa: A Case Study in Kawata Folk Village", *JJE* 38/2, 120-172. (In Japanese, with English summary).

XI. MINOR RELIGIONS

Balyuzi, H. M.: *Edward Granville Browne and the Bahá'í Faith* (London, 1970). – R: *WI* 14, 230-231 (J. van Ess).

Kazemi, F.: "Some Preliminary Observations on the Early Development of Babism", *The Muslim World* 63/2, 119-131.

McLeod, W. H.: *Gurū Nānak and the Sikh Religions.* (Oxford, 1968). – R: *OLZ* 68, 393-395 (J. Gonda).

Nijenhuis, J.: "Bahá'í: World Faith for a Modern Man?", *Journal of Ecumenical Studies* 10/3, 532-551.

Oliver, V. L.: "Caodaism: A Vietnamese Example of Sctarian Development", *DisAbIn, A* 33/9, 5280-5281. (The author's summary of his diss., Syracuse University, 1972).

Simundson, D. N.: "John Ballou Newbrough and the *Oahspe* Bible", *DisAbIn A* 34/1, 259. (The author's summary of his diss., University of New Mexico, 1972).

INDEX

Abásolo, J. A. 37
al-ᶜAbbādī, A. M. 164
Abdou, M. M. I. 157
Abe, M. 189
Abegg, W. 30
Abel, A. 164
Abel, E. L. 105, 120
Abela de la Rivière, M. Th. 38
Abraham, A. T. 103
Abrahams, I. 94
Abramovitz, M. 105
Abū Jāber, F. 164
Abu Shanab R. E. 157
Achrapov, I. 164
Ackermann, W. 107
Ackroyd, P. R. 114
Adam, A. 21, 103
Adam, J. P. 79
Adams, W. Y. 145
Adiceam, M. E. 184
Adler, A. 38
al-Afghānī, S. J. 10
Afshar, I, 3
Aggebracht, A. 58
Aggoula, B. 153
Agourides, S. 139
Ahern, E. M. 197
Ahlström, G. W. 114
Ahmed, Z. 157, 164
ᶜAin al-Qudāt al- Hamadhānī 162
Airoldi, N. 93
Akataev S. N. 74
Akimoto, N. 200
Aland, B. 85
Alavi, B. 3
Albeck Ch. 105
Albright, W. F. 114
de Aldama, J. A. 128
Aldred C. 58
Aletti, J. N. 120
Alexandre, E. 85
Alfarabi 157, 160
Alfonsi, L. 79
Ali, A. 164
Ali, F. A. 66
Ali, E. 161
Alich, S. H. 9, 157, 164
Aličić, A. S. 179
Allam, S. 58
Allana G. 164
Allegra, G. M. 142
Allegro, J. M. 103
Allony, N. 114
Almagro Gorbea, M. J. 37
Alonso Díaz, J. 105
Alparslan, A. 164
Alsdorf, L. 189
Alsdorf-Bollee, A. 38
Alster, B. 66
Altendorf, H. D. 14
Altermüller, B. 58
Althaus, H. 18
Altheim, F. 31
Altmann, A. 110
Alvarez Turienzo, S. 128
Amad G. 56
Amand de Mendieta, E. 133
Ambanelli, I. 93
Ames, M. M. 189
Amiet, P. 66, 74
Amsler, S. 93
Anand, M. R. 164
Anati, E. 37
And, M. 164
Andresen, C. 123 137
Andrews, W. G. 164
Ankum, J. A. 32
Annequin, J. 24
Ansari, N. 161
Anson, P. 140
Antes, P. 157, 184
Antiseri, D. 18
Anton, F. 38
Antweiler, A. 18
Anus, P. 58
Arapura, J. G. 184
Arberry, A. J. 162
Arbesmann, R. 128
Archaimbault, C. 189
Archer, D. 18
Archi, A. 76
d'Arès, J. 103
Argenio R. 129
Arié, R. 164
Arinze, F. A. 38
Arkoun, M. 155, 157, 172, 180, 182
Armas, G. 129
Arnal, J. 37
Arnaldez, R. 164
Arnaud, D. 66
Arngart, O. 145
Aro, J. 66
Ardzinba, V. G. 79
Arya, U. 184
Asad, T. 164
Aschwanden, H. 38
Aširov, N. 164
Ashtor, E. 168
Askari, H. 157, 158
Asmussen, J. P. 114, 139
Assmann, J. 58
Astour, M. 89
Astruc, C. 129, 142
Asuni, T. 21
Atallah, W. 154, 158
Athanase d'Alexandrie 129
Atil, E. 165
Attai, R. 114
al-Attas, S. M. N. 162
Attfield, R. 18
Aubert, J. F. 58
Aubet, M. E. 85
Aubineau, M. 129, 142
Audebert, C. 155
Aufenanger H. 38
Aujolat, N. 79
Aurobindo, Sri 188
Austin, R. J. 163
Austin R. W. 155
Austin, W. H. 18
Auvray, P. 93
Avi-Yona, M. 114
el-Awa, M. 165
Awolalu, J. O. 38
el-Azma, N. 162

van Baaren, Th. P. 3, 31
Baars, W. 93
Babajan, F. S. 24
Babolin, A. 18
Backes, I. 129
Bacq, P. 134
Bacqué-Grammont, J. L. 165
Badawy, A. M. 58, 64, 65
Bader, G. 93

Baer, A. 66
Baer, E. 165, 179
Baer, R. A., Jr. 110
Bargatti, B. 120
Bagnall, R. S. 64
Baillet, M. 103
Bakan, D. 16
Baker, D. 180
Bakhuizen van den Brink, J. N. 25, 130
Bakry, H. S. K. 58
Baldick, J. 165
Balić, S. 2, 3, 165
Balil, A. 85
Bálint, S. 142
Baljon, J. M. S. 162
Balkan, K. 76
Balogun, I. A. B. 165
Baltes, M. 123
Baltzer, D. 93
Balyuzi, H. M. 202
Bammel, E. 139
Bammer, A. 79
Banī-Ādam, H. 3
Banks, R. 16
Banti, L. 53
Baqués Estapé, L. 58
Barb, A. A. 24
Barbaglio, G. 120
Barbel, J. 129
Bardtke, H. 2, 3, 31, 93, 95, 100, 103, 107, 121
Barguet, P. 62
Barkow, J. H. 165
Barnes, R. H. 39
Barnes, T. D. 120, 129, 130, 136
Barns, J. W. B. 64, 149
Baron, S. W. 114
Barr, J. 114
Barrett, C. K. 120
Barschel, B. 53
Barta, W. 58, 59, 60
Bartelink, G. J. M. 140
Barth, G. 120
Barthélemy, D. 3
Bartikian, H. 142
Bartlett, D. L. 120
Bartsch, H. W. 120
Baruch, J. Z. 93
Barucq, A. 60
Barwick, K. 129
Basave, A. 16
Bascom, W. 39
Basetti-Sani, G. 155, 165
Başgöz, I. 31
Basile de Séleucie 129
Basilius von Caesarea 129
Baskakov, N. A. 24
Basta, M. 59
Baştav, Ş. 165
Bastide, R. 21, 176
Bastomsky, S. J. 105
Bastow, D. 189
Bateni, N. R. 4
Bauer, J. 73, 74
Bauer, J. B. 143
Bauer, W. 197
Baumbach, G. 120
Baumer, I. 24
Baumgarten, J. M. 116
Baumgartner, W. 2
Bausani, A. 4, 158, 165
Bayer, O. 4
Bayerle, G. 165
Bayliss, M. 66
Bazin, L. 4
Bazin, M. 165
Beane, W. C. 184
Beauchamp, P. 93
Becher, H. 39, 47
Bechert, H. 34, 184, 189
Beck, J. C. 39
Becker, J. 93
Beckingham, C. F. 31
Beckman, B. 24
Becquelin, P. 39
Bee, R. E. 93
van Beek, G. W. 153
Beek, M. A. 34, 93
Beem, H. 114
Beeston, A. F. L. 153, 155, 171
Begović, M. 165
Béguin, G. 24
Behrens, H. 37
Behrsing, S. 4
Beidelman, T. O. 32
Beierwaltes, W. 18
Beldiceanu, N. 165
Belenizkii, A. M. 74
Belguedj, M. S. 158
Belkhayat-Clement, F. 166
Bellamy, J. A. 155, 159
Beltz, W. 117
Beljawski, W. A. 66
Bell, L. 59
Bellamy, J. A. 4
Belmont, N. 21
Bencheikh, J. E. 166
Ben-Chorin, S. 120, 128
Benoit, A. 4, 136
Benoit, P. 103
Ben-Shlomo, Y. 110
Bentivegna, J. 129
Bentwich, J. S. 114
Benz, E. 24, 39
Benzi, M. 39
Berbuir, E. 143
Berciu, I. 92
Berger, K. 103, 120, 129
Berger, P. L. 21
Berger, P. R. 66
Bergeron, R. 129
vanden Berghe, L. 74, 76
Bergsma, H. M. 39
Berlev, O. D. 61
Berman, L. V. 158
Berman, M. 114
Berman, S. J. 105
Bernand, M. 158
Bernard, P. 4
di Bernardino, A. 129
Berndt, R. M. 39
Bernhardt, K. H. 93
Bernini, G. 93
Berque, J. 166
le Berre, M. 4
Bertagaev, T. A. 24
Berthe, L. 43
Bethge, H. G. 85
Betz, O. 120
Beuken, W. A. M. 93
Beukers, C. 127
Beumer, J. 130
Beutler, J. 120
Beyer, S. 189
Bhaktivinoda, T. 184
Bhattacharji, S. 184
Bhattacharya, K. 189
Bhojak, P. A. M. 185
Bianchi, B. 4
Bianchi, H. 105
de Bianchi, M. R. 39
Biardeau, M. 184
Bibby, T. G. 153
Bić, M. 108
Bichir, G. 24
Bidou, P. 39
Biebuyck, D. 39
Biezais, H. 31
Biggs, R. D. 66
Bilaniuk, P. B. T. 143
Bilgrami, R. 166
Binet, J. 34
Biobaku, S. O. 31
al-Bīrūnī, 31, 159, 175
Bischofberger, O. 39
Bisi, A. M. 85
Bissoli, C. 4
Bijlefeld, W. A. 4

Bizarri, E. 53
Björkman, G. 59
Black, M. 33, 94
Blackman, M. B. 39
Blanchetière, F. 143
Blankenberg-van Delden, C. 59
Blaškovič, J. 7
Blau, J. 94
Blázquez, J. M. 85
Blázquez, N. 130
Bleeker, C. J. 2, 7, 24, 31, 59
Bleich, J. D. 105
Blenkinsopp, J. 101
Blidstein, G. J. 114
Blixen, O. 39
Bloch, R. 53
Blondeau, A. M. 4
Bloss, L. W. 189
Blue, L. 31
Blumberg, H. 110
Blumenthal, D. R. 110
Blumenthal, E. 4, 148
Boccassino, R. 39
Böcher, O. 105, 143
Bodewitz, H. W. 184
Boecker, H. J. 114
de Boer, P. A. H. 94
den Boer, W. 79, 83
Boertien, M. 105
van Boetzelaar, J. M. 184
Bogaers, J. E. 53
Bogaers, P. M. 96
Bogdanović, D. 166
Bogoljubov, M. N. 74
Bogoslovskij, E. 59
Bohdan, L. 155
Böhlig, A. 139
Boismard, M. E. 121
Bokser, B.-Z. 109, 114
Bolland, R. 166
Bolton, R. 40
Bon, B. H. 184
Bonnafé, P. 40
Bonnard, P. E. 94
Bonneau, D. 59
Booth, H. J. 16
Bordenave, J. 143
Borger, R. 66, 70, 75
Borghouts, J. F. 59. 64
Borias, A. 140
Börker-Klähn, J. 66
Bormans, M. 166
Bornkamm, G. 121
Boros, L. 33
Borrás, G. M. 1
Börtnes, J. 143
Bortolaso, G. 189
Boswinkel, E. 89
Bosse-Griffiths, K. 59
Bosworth, C. E. 155, 166
Bottéro, J. 66
Böttger, W. 197
Boucher, S. 80
Bouet, P. 140
Bouhdiba, A. 167
Boularand, E. 130
Boullata, I. J. 166
Boullata, K. 166
Bourget, P. 43
van Bourgondiën, W. 4
du Bourguet, P. 5, 143
Bourouiba, R. 166
Bouttier, M. 5
Bouwman, G. 121
Bouyer, L. 121
Bouzek, J. 80
Bovon-Thurneysen, A. 130
Bowker, J. 24, 121
Bowler, M. G. 110
Bowman, A. K. 64, 90
Bowman, R. A. 74, 75
Boyle, J. A. 25
Bradbury, R. E. 40
van den Braden, A. 86
Bradley, B. 140
Braham, A. 80
Brain, J. L. 40
Brand, R. 40
Brandmüller, W. 143
Brandon, S. G. F. 1, 5, 31
Braun, R. 130
Bräutigam, H. 194
Bravmann, M. M. 155
Brechtken, J. 18
Breebaart, A. B. 85
Breech, E. 94
Brentjes, B. 31, 166, 171, 181
Bresciani, E. 59
Brestou, P. 86
Breton, S. 86, 110
Brett, M. 166
Breydy, M. 25
Brierbrier, M. L. 59
Bright, J. 94
Bring, R. 121
Brinkman, J. A. 32, 67
Brioso, M. 130
Brix, L. 137
Brock, S. P. 5, 94, 140
Brockington, L. H. 94
Brockway, D. 5
van den Broek, R. 86
Broekhuis, J. 59
Bröker, W. 143
Bromley, M. 40
Brommer, F. 80
Brooks, R. W. 185
Brown, H. V. B. 161
Brown, L. B. 16
Brown, P. 130
Brown, S. K. 121
Browne, G. M. 86
Brox, N. 121, 130
Bruce, F. F. 125, 130, 150
Brugman, J. 31
le Brun, J. 143
Brunner, F. 86
Brunner, G. 130
Brunner, H. 121
Bruno, J. 16
Bruns, J. E. 130
de Bruyne, J. L. 185
Brykman, G. 110
Buccellati, G. 32
Buchwald, W. 34
Budd, P. J. 105
Budde, L. 80
van Buitenen, J. A. B. 185
Bulliet, R. W. 166
Bulman, J. M. 94
Bultmann, R. 121
Bunge, J. G. 94
Bunte, W. 105
Burchard, Ch. 103
Bureau, R. 40
Bürgel, J. Ch. 167
Burggraeve, R. 110
Burgoyne, M. H. 167
Burhoe, R. W. 18
Burki, R. 158
Burnand, Y. 80
Burney, C. 76
Burns, J. B. 25
Burns, R. I. 167
Burridge, K. 40
Burton, A. 86
Busink, Th. A. 114
Buss, R. J. 25
Busse, H. 167
Büttner, M. 21
Buxton, J. 40
Byatt, A. 114
Byčkov, V. V. 143
Bynum, W. F. 19
Byrnes, R. G. 130

Cacoullos, W. R. 80
Cagman, F. 167
Cagni, L. 31, 67, 69
Cahen, C. 5

Caitanyadāsa, R. 185
Calame, C. 80
Calasso, G. 155
Callmer, J. 54
Calmeyer, P. 2, 67, 75
Cameron, A. J. 155
Cameron, G. G. 74
von Campenhausen, H. F. 121
Canard, M. 5, 143
de Candillac, M. 151
Canivet, P. 143
Cantalamessa, R. 130
Cantera, J. 115
Cantera Burgos, F. 115
Capánaga, V. 130
de Capitani, F. 86
Caplice, R. 5, 66, 67, 70
Capps, W. H. 5
Caquot, A. 117
Cardona, G. 185
Carey, J. J. 143
Carletti, C. 150
Carneiro Da Cunha, M. 40
Carmy, S. 110
Caroe, O. 167
Carr, G. L. 105
Carré, O. 158, 167
Carroll, J. W. 17
Carruba, O. 76
Carter, A. T. 21
Carter, C. 77
Carter, H. 60
Carter, T. H. 56
Cassin, E. 67
Cassuto, U. 94
Castellani, G. 3
Castellino, G. R. 67
Castiglione, L. 57, 86
Castro, S. 121
Cathcart, K. J. 94, 95
Cataldo, G. B. 130
Cauvin, J. 37
Cavalletti, S. 121
Cazelles, H. 94, 107
Cazemier, L. J. 60
Cazier, P. 131
Cébeillac, M. 80
Cefaux, L. 32
de Certeau, M. 5
Ceyssens, R. 40
Chabbi, J. 162
Chadwick, H. 143
Chaillou, J. 143
Chalmeta, P. 167
Chambers, R. L. 167
Chambers, W. V. 94
Chandra, M. 25
Chang, A. 189
Chang, C. 197
Charbel, P. 167
Charlesworth, J. H. 95
Charpentier, C. J. 167
Chartier, M. 167
Charvát, P. 68
Chaudenson, R. 38
Chaumont, M.-L. 74
Chelhod, J. 167
Chen, E. M. 197
Ch'en, K. K. S. 189
Chen, H.-sh. 197
Cheng, C. Y. 197
Chenu, M. D. 144
Cherchi, P. 131
Chesnut, G. F., Jr. 131
Cheyette, F. L. 151
Chiao, J. W. 197
Chikovani, M. I. 25
Child, H. 25
Ching, J. 197
Chouchena, E. 111
Christ, K. 5
Christmann-Franck, L. 76
Chrysostome J. (St.) 131
Chuang, Y.-ch. 197
Ciafardone, R. 19
Cignelli, L. 131
Ciuba, E. J. 119
Civil, M. 1, 70
Claburn, W. E. 95
Clanton, G. 21
Clark, L. V. 5
Clarke, G. W. 121
Clasen, S. 144
Clements, R. E. 107
Clerc, G. 88
Clews, R. A. 23
Clifford, R. J. 34, 95
Closs, A. 25
Clowney, E. P. 121
Coats, G. W. 95
Cocagnac, A. M. 185
Cocquerillat, D. 67
Cody, A. 106
Coedès, G. 189
Cogan, M. 56
Cohen, C. B. 19
Cohen, R. 111
Colaclides, P. 121
Colella, P. 121
Collarini, M. 144
Colles, D. 25
Colless, B. E. 140, 144
Colpe, C. 2, 86, 144
Coman, J. 131
Comhaire-Sylvain, S. 40
van Compernolle, R. 67
Connick Carlisle, R. 167
Conomis, N. C. 131
Constantelos, D. J. 167
Coogan, M. D. 115
Cook, B. F. 80
Cools, P. J. 106, 127
Cooper, J. S. 72
Cooper, L. H. 167
Coote, R. B. 57
Copeland, E. L. 121
Coppel, W. G. 40
Coppens, J. 5, 13, 15, 144
Coquin, R. G. 131
Corbin, H. 155, 158, 168
Cordun, V. 162
Cornelis, E. 185
Cornelius, F. 76
Corzannet, F. 40
Couchy, L. H. 5
Couchy, M. 5
Coulson, N. J. 168
Coupez, A. 40
Courcelle, P. 131
Couroyer, B. 56, 60
Courtès, P. C. 25
Courtenay, W. J. 158
Cortois, J. C. 56
Courtonne, Y. 131
Cousins, L. S. 189
Covi, D. 131
Cowan, H. K. J. 40
Cragg, K. 155, 158
Crockett, J. D. 16
Craigie, P. G. 95
Cramer, M. 144
Cremers, W. 168
Crawford, H. E. W. 67
Crawford, M. P. 21
Creemers, W. H. M. 200
Creswell, K. A. C. 165
Crocco, A. 131
Cross, F. M. 115
Crouzel, H. 131
Crozet, R. 98
Crumrine, N. R. 41
Cullmann, O. 122
Cuperus, W. S. 155
Cutrone, E. J. 122
Czeglédy, K. 168

Dagorn, R. 168
Dahsiar, S. 168
D'Alatri, M. 144
Dalgleish, K. 153

Dalley, S. 67
Dalmais, I. H. 139, 141, 144
Damis, J. 168
Dammann, E. 5, 6, 34, 41, 43
van Damme, M. 159
Dancy, J. C. 100
Dandamaev, M. A. 74
Dandekar, R. N. 185
Dando, M. 144
Dange, S. A. 185
Daniélou, J. 6, 131
Dankoff, R. 168
Danner, V. 162
Daoust, J. 122
Daumas, F. 6
Dautzenberg, G. 122
Dauvillier, J. 122
David, A. R. 60
David, M. 31, 32, 67
Davidian, H. 168
Davids, A. 122
Davidson, H. 111
Davies, T. W. 25
Deckers, J. G. 86
Decroix, J. 139
Degen, R. 78, 93, 95
Dehandschutter, B. 6, 139
Delanoue, G. 168
Delcor, M. 95, 118
Delcourt, M. 131
Delfendahl, B. 185
D'Elia, F. 131
Della Capanna, G. P. 41
Delling, G. 118
Del Monte, G. F. 77, 78, 79
Delobel, J. 122
Delpoux, C. 144
Del Ton, C. 131
Deluz, A. 41
Demaree, R. J. 119
Demargne, P. 25
Demetriades, J. M. 144
Demiéville, P. 189, 197
Denaux, A. 122
De Nerve, A. 21
Deng, F. M. 41
Denis, A. M. 100
Dennis, G. 54
Dentzer, J. M. 153
Dequeker, L. 103
Derchain, Ph. 60, 64
Derrett, J. D. M. 185
Deshayes, J. 6
Desideri, P. 132
Desparmet, R. 4
Despina, M. 95
Des Places, E. 87, 115
Desroche, H. 21
Des Rochettes, J. M. 126
Detienne, M. 80
Deuel, L. 32
Deutsch, E. 185
Devauges, J. B. 80
Devish, R. 41
Devoti, D. 139
Deyts, S. 80
Dhavamony, M. 2, 6, 185
Diener, L. 62
Dietrich, A. 6, 57
Dietrich, W. 6
van Dijk, J. 67
van Dijk, J. J. A. 69
Di Lella, A. A. 97
Dilger, K. 168
Dimier, A. 140
Dioszegi, V. 25
Diouf, N. 41
Dirat, M. 80
Dirksen, P. B. 95
Diyarbekirli, N. 168
Djaït, H. 168
Dobbelaere, K. 21
Dobrača, K. 6
Dodd, P. C. 168
Doi, A. R. I. 168
Doignon, J. 130, 132
Domenach, J. M. 25
Donaldson, J. 106
Donat, P. 37
Dönme, K. T. 190
Donne, J. B. 4
Donnelly, D. H. 132
Doré, H. 198
Doresse, M. 60
Donohue, J. J. 168
Dorra-Haddad, J. 155, 156
Dörrie, H. 86, 122
Doržiev, Z. 190
Dossin, G. 68
Douglas, M. 108
Doutreloux, A. 33
Downes, R. M. 41
Dräger, L. 41
Dragojlović, D. 86
Draževa, R. D. 25
Dressendörfer, P. 168
Drew-Bear, T. 80
van Driel, G. 68
Drijvers, H. J. W. 6, 31, 152
Driver, G. R. 72, 74
Dubarle, D. 80
Dubey, S. P. 185
Dubuisson, D. 54
Ducharelez, K. 122
Duchesne-Guillemin, J. 37
Dujčev, I. 169
Dulaey, M. 122
Dumas, A. 16
Dumont, P. 169
Dumortier, J. 132
Dunand, F. 86
Dunand, M. 86
Dunant, Ch. 86
Dunayevsky, I. 56
Dunkly, J. W. 8
Dunn, S. P. 27
Duplacy, J. 6, 122
Dupont, J. 122
Dupont-Sommer, A. 32, 103
Dupré, W. 19
Dupuy, B. 144
Dupuy, B. D. 106
Durable, A. M. 122
de Durand, G. M. 6, 138
During, Caspers, E. C. L. 68
Duvernay, J. 25
Duvernoy, J. 144
Dux, G. 21
Dvornik, F. 144
Dykmans, M. 144

Ebeling, E. 2
Ebied, R. Y. 169
Edel, E. 60
Eder, M. 197, 200
Edwards, I. E. S. 56
Edzard, D. O. 2, 32, 68
Ehlen, P. 19
Ehrman, A. 95
Eibl-Eibesfeldt, I. 6, 41
Eichhorn, W. 197, 198
Eichler, B. L. 68
Eickelpasch, R. 25
Eilers, W. 25
Eimer, H. 190
Eisleb, D. 51
Eissfeldt, O. 6, 7, 34, 89, 95, 97, 103, 106
Elbert, S. H. 46
Elenga, L. 41
Eliade, M. 1
Elliger, K. 32
Ellis, E. E. 144
Ellis, R. S. 68
Ellul, J. 21
Ellwood, R. S., Jr. 200
Elon, M. 106
Elorduy, C. 197
Eloy, L. 54
van Els, T. J. M. 144
Embree, R. A. 17

Emerton, J. A. 95, 122
d'Encarnação, J. 54
Ende, W. 169, 182
Endelman, J. E. 9
Endress, G. 158
Engel, F. A. 37
Engemann, J. 80, 122
Engl, E. 41
Eno, R. B. 123
Enomiya-Lasalle, H. M. 190
Ensink, J. 190
Eracle, J. 190
van Erdberg-Consten, E. 197
Erdheim, M. 41
Ergil, D. 169
Ermakov, I. M. 22
Ernst, Y. 7
van Esbroeck, M. 139
Esin, E. 169
Espinoza Soriano, W. 41
van Ess, J. 158, 159, 169, 202
Etienne, P. 42
Evans, C. F. 132
Evans, D. B. 132
Evans-Pritchard, E. E. 32, 42
Evans-Wentz, W. Y. 190

Fabro, C. 111
Fahd, T. 162, 169
Fahim, H. M. 22
Fahndrich, H. E. 169
Fales, F. M. 68
Falk, N. E. 190
Fannon, P. 95
Fantar, M. 56
al-Fārābī 157, 160
Farag, F. R. 144, 145
Farber, W. 68
Farber-Flügge, G. 68
Farīd, Sh. 89
Farine, A. 115
Faroghi, S. 169
Farrar, R. S. 145
Farooqi, H. A. 158
al-Fārūqī, I. R. 158, 169
Faruqi, Z. ul-H. 169
Fasciano, D. 81
Fass, J. 7
Fatás, G. 1
Faulkner, J. E. 22
Faulkner, R. O. 60, 64
Fauth, W. 87
Fazlur Rahman 169
Feachem, R. 42
Fecht, G. 60
Fédry, J. 26
Feenstra, R. 32
Feer, M. 42
Feghali, J. 145
Fehérvári, G. 169
Felber, R. 199
Felbermayer, F. 42
Fellows, D. 51
Fendler, M. 95
Fernández, Q. 140
Fernández Marcos, N. 132
Fernando, C. 190
Fernando, T. 190
Ferrara, A. J. 68
Ferrari, L. G. 132
Ferron, J. 56, 60
Ferwerda, R. 123
Festugière, J. A. 81
Feustel, R. 37
Fichte, H. 42
Fiey, J. M. 145
Figge, H. H. 42
Filliozat, J. 7
Finet, A. 68
Finkelstein, J. J. 56, 67
Fischel, H. A. 111
Fischel, W. J. 169
Fischer, E. 42
Fischer, H. 60
Fischer, H. J. 42
Fischer, K. M. 87
Fisher, A. 115
Fisher, A. W. 169
Fisher, J. 115
Fishwick, D. 81
Fitzmyer, J. A. 103
Flasche, R. 42
Fleischer, R. 87
Fleischhammer, M. 182
Flemming, B. 7, 169
Flew, A. 19
Flora, J. R. 123
Florovsky, G. 4, 32
Foard, L. C. 19
Foerster, W. 87
Flury, P. 132
Fohrer, G. 1, 33, 95, 115
Fonkič, B. L. 132
Fontaine, J. 85, 129
Ford, A. E. 139
Forde, D. 40
Forge, A. 32
Forlin Petrucco, M. 132
Forni, G. 87
Forno, M. 42
Forte, A. 87, 190
Fortin, E. L. 132
Fossier, R. 22
Fóti, L. 60
Foubert, J. 26
de Fouchécour, C. H. 170
Fouquet, A. 87
Fozdar, J. K. 190
Fraenkel, A. 7
Francke, J. 123
Frank, B. 7
Frankena, R. 68
Franklin, K. J. 42
Frauwallner, E. 190
Frazier, A. M. 17
Frédéric, L. 190
Freeman-Grenville, G. S. P. 170
Freiman, A. 7
Frend, W. H. C. 123, 145
Freudenstein, E. G. 106
Frey, L. 123
Freydank, H. 68, 72
Frézouls, E. 4
Frickel, J. 85, 87
Friedberg, C. 43
Friedmann, Ch. 115
Friedrich, G. 1
Frison, L. 19
Fritsch, Ch. T. 3, 5, 105
Fritz, V. 115
Frobenius, L. 43
Froehlich, K. 132
Frostin, P. 7
Fuchs, S. 185
Fück, J. 13, 33, 155, 180
Fück, J. W. 163, 178
Fuerst, W. J. 100
Fuks, L. 7
van Funk, W. P. 87

Gaál, E. 170
von Gabain, A. 32
Gabrieli, F. 7, 170
Gadd, C. J. 56
Gagé, J. 81
Gager, J. G. 87
Gail, A. J. 185
Galand, L. 7
Galand-Pernet, P. 7
Gallardo, M. D. 26
Gallus, A. 9
Galvin, A. D. 43
Galvin, R. J. 123
Gamer-Wallert, I. 56
Gamoran, H. 106
Gangādhara 185
Ganghoffer, R. 4
Garbini, G, 153
Garcia de la Fuente, O. 56, 103

Gardberg, C. J. 145
Gardet, L. 158, 159
Gardin, J. C. 4
Garelli, P. 56
Garitte, G. 89, 139
Garsoïan, N. G. 145
Garte, E. 115
Garton, T. 170
Gasche, H. 71
Gaško, P. 132
Gass, P. 43
Gaster, Th. H. 77
Gäters, A. 54
Gaube, H. 74
Gaudefroy-Demobynes, M. 155
Gaudemet, J. 145
del Gaudio, G. 43
Gaulier, S. 26, 190
Gautier, P. 145
Gautier-van Berchem, M. 165
Gawlikowski, M. 87
van der Geest, J. E. L. 132
Geiger, W. 190
Gelb, I. J. 1, 32
Gellner, E. 170
Gelsomino, V. 132
Genicot, L. 7
George, A. 123
George, B. 60
Georgiev, V. I. 54
Gerest, C. 145
Gerhardt, L. 43
Gerleman, G. 95
Gerresch, C. 170
Gersch, S. E. 87
Gese, H. 7, 26
de Geus, C. H. J. 76
Geudtner, O. 123
al-Geyoushi, M. I. 159
Géza, K. 69
Ghalioungui, P. 60
al-Ghazālī, a. Ḥ. 159
Ghirshman, R. 75
Giangrande, G. 81
Gibb, Sir H. (A. R.) 170
Gibbons, J. A. 87
Gibbs, D. R. 17
Gigante, M. 81
Gil, M. 106
Gilbert, M. 95
Gilman, S. 17
Gilsenan, M. 162
Gimaret, D. 191
Gimbutas, M. 37
Girard, R. 26
Girodon, P. 43
Giuletti, G. 111
Giveon, R. 60
Glassen, E. 175
Glatzer, B. 170
Glock, A. E. 118
Gloria, H. 43
Glueck, N. 32
Gnoli, R. 185
Göbl, R. 75
Goedicke, H. 60, 64
Goetz, J. 26
Goitein, S. D. 155
Gökbilgin, T. 170
Gokhale, B. G. 191
Golb, N. 115
Goldberg, A. 96
Goldman, B. 115
Goldstein, I. 115
Goldstein, M. C. 191
Golub, I. 145
Gombrich, R. 191
Gomez-Menor Fuentes, J. 115
Gomez-Tabanera, J. M. 37
Gonda, J. 186
Goodall, J. A. 145
Goodblatt, D. M. 115
Gooding, D. W. 102
Goodridge, R. M. 22
Goody, J. 43
Gorakshkar, S. 191
Gorce, D. 140
Gordon, C. H. 32
Gordon, H. J. 61
Gordon, J. 111
Gordon, L. M. 170
Görg, M. 106
Ǧorǧānī, I. 161
Gossiaux, P. P. 8, 43
Gottschalk, H. L. 170
van Goudoever, J. 125
Goudriaan, T. 186
Gouillard, J. 145
Gouin, P. 4
Govinda, L. A. 191
Goyon, J.-C. 61
de Graaf, J. 22
Graefe, E. 61
Gräf, E. 159
Gragg, G. 69
Grambo, R. 26
Gramsch, B. 37
Granata, A. 145
Granatstein, M. 111
Grandguillaume, G. 170
Grand-Henry, J. 171
Grant, M. 1
Grassi, J. A. 123
Gratzl, K. 22
Gravand, H. 43
Gravel, P. 19
Gray, J. 7
Green, A. R. W. 56
Green, R. P. H. 132
Greenberg, G. 111, 115
Greenberg, S. 106, 111
Greenfield, J. C. 77
Greenfield, S. A. 19
Gregor von Nyssa 129
Greive, H. 111
Gribomont, J. 140
Grieshammer, R. 61
Griffe, E. 141
Griffin, D. 19
Grignaschi, M. 170
Grillmeier, A. 123
Grimm, D. 96
Grindal, B. T. 171
Grisward, J. H. 26
Grienewegen-Frankfort, H. A. 56
Grohmann, A. 171
Groos, K. 8
Gropp, G. 75
Grosdidier de Matons, J. 132, 133
Gross, H. 106
Gross, J. 146
Gross, K. 141
Grossfeld, B. 96, 106
Grossi, V. 133
Gröteke, F. 54
Grothus, J. 77
Grumelli, A. 22
von Grunebaum, G. E. 3, 171
Grünert, H. 37
Guarducci, M. 81
Guariglia, G. 38, 44
Guenther, H. 191
Guhl, M. C. 17
Guhr, G. 37
Guiart, J. 43
Guichard, P. 171
Guillaume, G. 171
Guillaumont, A. 8
Guillén, J. 81
Guillet, J. 123
Guilmain, J. 171
Guiraud, H. 81
Guittard, C. 81
van Gulik, R. 198
Günther, H. 111
Günther, J. J. 123

Günther, R. 124
Gurney, O. R. 71
Güterbock, H. 77
Güterbock, H. G. 77
Gutmann, D. 17
Gutmann, J. 115, 123
Güttgemanns, E. 123
Güven, R. 162
Gysseling, M. 53

Haaf, E. 43
Haag, E. 96
Haag, H. 93
Haardt, R. 87, 89
Haarmann, U. 173
Haas, V. 77, 78
Haase, R. 31, 77
Haberland, E. 33
Habib, G. 69
Habicht, Ch. 84
Hachmann, R. 69
Hacker, P. 186
Hadas-Lebel, M. 112
Hadot, P. 87
Hage, W. 146
Hager, V. J. 159
Hagner, D. A. 133
Haguenauer, M. Ch. 200
Hahn, F. 123
Hahn, R. A. 8
Haich, E. 186
Ha'iri, A.-H. 171
Hajdenova, V. 87
Haldar, A. 57
Halkin, F. 146
Hallensleben, H. 147
de Halleux, A. 144, 147
Hallo, W. W. 69
Hallock, R. T. 75
Hambis, L. 8
Hamidullah, M. 171
Hamilton, D. G. 17
Hamman, A. 133
Hammer, R. J. 100
Hammerschmidt, E. 8
Hammond, N. G. L. 56
Hammond, P. 153
Hammond, Ph. C. 153
Hanfmann, G. M. A. 57
Hanson, P. D. 96
Hara, M. 26, 186
Haran, M. 106
Harb, P. 133
Harjula, B. 43
Harkins, P. W. 133
Harmatta, J. 11, 31, 75
Harner, M. J. 33
Harper, P. O. 31
Harrington, D. J. 8
Harrington, W. 146
Harris, E. E. 19
Harrison, T. 43
Hart III, G. L. 26
Hartman, S. S. 75
Hartmann, A. 171
Hartmann, G. 43
Hartmann, H. 43
Hartog, J. 44
Harvey, L. P. 171
Harwood, A. 44
Hasan, A. 171
Hasan, K. A. 186
Hasel, G. F. 96, 100, 106, 116
Hasler, J. A. 8
Hassan, A. 61
Hasting, W. K. 64
Hathaway, R. L. 171
Hatt, J. J. 54
Haug, W. 26
Haulotte, E. 146
Hauschild, W. D. 129
Hauser, A. J. 115
Häusler, A. 37
Haussig, W. 3
Hauziński, J. 171
Hawi, S. S. 159
Hawkins, J. D. 77
Hayano, D. M. 44
Hayes, J. L. 8
Hayes, W. C. 61
Hazai, G. 8, 35, 171
Hazanov, A. M. 54
Hazard, J. N. 171
Hazel, J. 1
Heath, D. B. 44
Hebga, M. 26
Hecker, K. 78
Heerma van Voss, M. 8, 59, 61, 65
Heichelheim, F. M. 57
Heidenreich, R. 87
Heimpel, W. 69
Heineman, J. 108
Heinen, H. D. 44
Heinrich, E. 75
Heintz, B. 44
Heintz, J. G. 96
Heissig, W. 15, 33
Helck, W. 2, 57, 61
Helck, W. A. 62
Helfrich, K. 44
Hendel, R. J. 111
Henderson, R. N. 44
Hengel, M. 115, 123
Henkel, O. V. 54
Hennemann, G. 19
Hennig, J. 106
Henning, M. 156
Henninger, J. 107, 154, 164
Henrichs, A. 88
Henry, P. 88
Herbert, K. 88
Herdner, A. 77
Héritier-Izard, F. 44
Hermanns, M. 44
Hermisson, H. J. 96
Hernández Giménez, F. 172
Heron, H. 133
Herrmann, F. 24
Herrmann, J. 37
Herrmann, S. 116, 118
Herrmann, W. 57
Hertz, R. 22
Hervouet, Y. 189, 197
Hésychius de Jérusalem 129
Heun, E. 44, 141
de Heusch, L. 26, 33
Heyd, U. 172
Hyler, A. 65
Hiatt, L. R. 186
Hillenbrand, R. 172
Hilliard, F. H. 111
Hiltebeitel, A. 186
Himmelmann, N. 88
Hinnels, J. R. 31
Hinton, R. T. 19
Hintze, F. 33
von Hinüber, O. 184
Hinz, C. 124
Hinz, W. 11, 75
Hirohata, S. 200
Hirsch, H. 69
Hirschberg, W. 8, 15
Hlopin, I. H. 75
Hoang-Thi-Bich 191
Hochegger, H. 8, 44
Hochenegg, H. 44
Hodžas, S. I. 61
Hoenerbach, W. 172
Hoenig, S. B. 103
Höfer, A. 186
Höfer, M. 7
Hofer, F. 2
Hoffman, W. M. 17
Hoffmann, J. G. H. 8
Hoffmann, K. 186
Hoffner, H. A., Jr. 32
Höfler, O. 54
Hofman, E. 9
Hofmann, I. 61, 62, 65, 177
Höfner, M. 153

Hoftijzer, J. 9
Höftmann, H. 9
Hoge, D. R. 17
Hoheisel, K. 3, 6, 9, 116
Hohnschopp, H. 44
Holladay, W. L. 117
Holland, J. A. B. 19
Holleman, A. W. J. 88
Holm, O. 9
Holt, P. M. 9, 172
Höltker, G. 51
Holzman, D. 198
Homès-Fredericq, D. 57
Honko, L. 33
Hooykaas, C. 26, 186
Horcasitas, F. 44
Horgan, M. P. 103
Horn, S. H. 57, 101, 119, 120
Horbostel, W. 88
Hörner, H. 133
Hornung, E. 59, 61, 62
van der Horst, P. W. 124
Horten, M. 159
Horwitz, W. J. 96
Hospers, J. H. 9, 110
Hourani, A. H. 172
Hourani, G. F. 159
Houssiau, A. 146
Houtart, F. 191
Houwink ten Cate, Ph. H. J. 78, 79
Hruška, B. 69
Huard, P. 62
Hubbeling, H. G. 19
Huber, H. 44
Huber, P. 146
Hubert, M. 146
Hudson, H. 19
Hughes, P. E. 124
Hügli, A. 33
Hultkranz, Å. 9, 45
Humbach, H. 75, 191
Hummel, G. 22, 35
Hummel, S. 54
Humphrey, C. 45
Humphreys, W. L. 96
Hurbon, L. 45
Hurley, J. B. 124
Huxley, G. 81
Hvidberg-Hansen, O. 69

Ibish, Y. 162
Ibn Abī d-Dunyā 159
Ibn al-Faqīh al-Hamadānī 172
Ibn al-Nafīs 159
Ibn ᶜAṭāᵓillāh 162
Ibn Ḥajar al-ᶜAsqalānī 178
Ibn Taymīya 161
Ichon, A. 46
Idris, H. R. 172
van Iersel, B. 96
Iida, Sh. 191
Ikbal Ali Shah 33
Ikeda, H. 200
Ilogu, E. 45
Ilter, F. 172
ᶜImād ad-Dīn al-Isfahānī 175
Imanaga, S. 162
Inal, G. 172
Ingram, P. O. 191
Ionova, Ju. V. 26
Isaacman, A. 45
Ishida, T. 106
Israili, Sh. 159
Italiaander, R. 191
Ivanjan, E. A. 22
von Ivanka, E. 4
Ivanova, C. V. 195
Iversen, E. 88
Izco Ilundain, J. A. 96
Izutsu, T. 191

Jackson, A. 197
Jackson, B. S. 106
Jacob, E. 107
Jacobs, L. 96
Jacobsen, Th. 96
Jacobsohn, H. 62
Jacques, F. 81
Jadaane, F. 159
Jageneau, R. 45
Jäkel, S. 82
James, T. G. H. 62
Jamke, W. 19
Jamme, A. 153
Jankuhn, H. 37
Jansma, T. 133
Janssen, E. 116
Janssen, J. J. 3
Jantzen, U. 57
Janzen, W. 107
Jarzebowski, T. 159
Jäschke, G. 172
Jaspert, B. 141, 146
Jaubert, A. 146
Javelet, R. 147
Jawad, A.-J. 69
Jean de Béryte 129
Jeanneret, R. 81
Jelgersma, H. C. 62
Jellicoe, S. 5, 96
Jenkins, D. 146
Jenni, E. 3
Jennings, R. C. 172
Jesi, F. 26
Jestin, R. R. 68, 69
Jirku, A. 77
Jobst, W. 82
Johansen, B. 172
Johansen, U. 33
Johanson, U. 172
Johnson, C. B. 19
Johnston, T. F. 45
Johnston W. 191
Jolivet, J. 146
Jomier, J. 159
Jones, B. W. 96
de Jong, J. W. 9, 190, 191, 194
de Jonge, K. 45
de Jonge, M. 125
Jonkers, E. J. 82, 88
Jouffroy, H. 4
Judenko, K. 45
Jurado, M. R. 133
Jürs, F. 81
Juynboll, G. H. A. 155, 156, 172, 180, 182
Juzbašjan, K. N. 152

Kaba, L. 173
el-Kafrawy, M. A. A. 173
Kaganoff, N. M. 9
Kahle, P. 33
Kähler, H. 170
Kabl-Fuhrtman, G. 20
Kahn, J. G. 111
Kaiser, O. 57, 96, 97
Kajiyama, Y. 191
Kákosy L. 61, 62
Kakuk, S. 173
Kaleshi, H. 162
Kalish, R. A. 17
van der Kam, J. 97
Kamanzi, Th. 40
Kamentzky, C. 26
Kamhi, D. J. 97
Kamińska, H. 156
Kammenhuber, A. 77
Kampman, A. A. 9, 34
Kane, G. S. 146
Kannengiesser, C. 94, 133, 146
Kaoukabani, B. 88
Kaoze, S. 45
Kapel, H. 153
Kapelrud, A. S. 77
Kaplan, E. K. 111
Kaplan, F. 111
Kaplan, L. 111

Kaplony-Heckel, U. 9
Karadžić, V. St. 27
Kartomi, M. J. 26
Kasper, W. 124
Kasprús, A. 45
Kassim, M. 162
Kater-Sibbes, G. J. F. 88
Kathcart, K. J. 77
Kaufmann, R. 191
Kawerau, P. 146
Kayambo, Ka Ch. 45
Kayser, H. 62
Kazakova, N. A. 146
Každan, A. P. 132
Kazemi, F. 202
Kearney, P. J. 97
Kéchichian, I. 149
Keel, O. 97
Keep, A. E. 63
Kehl, A. 124
Keightly, D. N. 198
Keizer, L. S. 88
Kellens, J. 75
Keller, C.-A. 97
Kemmer, A. 129
Kemp, B. J. 62
Kemp, P. 19
Kempinski, A. 56
Kennedy, E. S. 173
Kennedy, G. 7
Kent, G. W. 198
Kerns, T. A. 27
Keresztes, P. 124
Kessler, W. 103
Kettler, F. H. 124
Khalid, M. B. 162, 173
Khalidi, T. 173
Khalil-Kussaim, S. 146
Khan, S. Sh. A. 162
Khundmiri, S. A. 159
Kibicho, S. G. 45
Kieckhefer, R. A. 146
Kiefer, Th. M. 45
Kienast, B. 69
Kiwada, I. M. 97
Kiley, C. J. 200
Kilson, M. 46
Kil-Sung, Ch. 46
Kim, N. V. 46
Kimpianga, K. M. 46
King, D. A. 159
King, N. Q. 178
King, R. H. 20
Kirk, G. S. 27
Kirschbaum, E. 2
Kirshenblatt-Gimblett, B. 9
Kirtley, B. F. 46
Kisch, G. 10
Kissel, W. 133
Kissling, H. J. 173
Kitchen, K. A. 62
Kjelström, R. 46
Klengel, H. 5, 56, 70, 77, 78, 153
Klauser, T. 147
Klein, R. 124
Klein-Franke, F. 173
Kleywegt, A. J. 81
Klijn, A. F. J. 133
Klíma, J. 31, 32, 56, 66, 70, 77
Klíma, O. 31, 75, 76
Klímová, D. 27
Kloppenborg, R. 192
Kluge, I. L. 200
Kluger, R. Sch. 107
Knappert, J. 173
Knust, Th. A. 11
Knauber, A. 133
Knechten, H. 192
Kobayashi, S. 162
Köbert, R. 10, 154, 156
Koch, K. 97
Köcher, F. 70
Kochev, N. 147
Köchler, H. 20
Koehler, L. 2
Kohutnicki, B. 49
Kolmaš, J. 10
Komoróczy, G. 70
Kondratov, A. 190
Köngas, M. 27
van Koningsveld, P. Sj. 10, 97, 159
Kooy, V. E. 147
Kopeček, T. A. 133
Kopp, H. 189
Kornrumpf, H. J. 2, 10
Kornrumpf, J. 10
Korson, J. H. 173
Kosay, H. Z. 173
Koskenniemi, S. 10
Kötting, B. 134
Kottje, R. 147
Kowalczyk, S. 134
Krajcar, J. 147
Kramer, M. 175
Krštev, K. N. 22
Kratz, U. 33
Kraus, F. R. 31, 68, 70
Kraus, J. 146
Krause, M. 87, 88
Krautheimer, R. 147
Krawulsky, D. 173
Krecher, J. 70
Kreissig, H. 116
Krempien, R. 200
Kreutel, R. F. 175
Krick, H. 187
Kriss, R. 35
Kristeller, P. O. 10
Kronenfeld, D. B. 46
Krstić, N. 27
Krüger, E. 173
Kübel, P. 88
Kudsi-Zadeh, A. A. 10
Kubičkova, V. 164
Kuhlmann, K. P. 62
Kühne, C. 78
Kuiper, F. B. J. 186
Kümmel, H. M. 67, 70, 72, 78, 79
Kümmel, W. G. 147
Küng, H. 147
Kunitzsch, P. 176
Kuper, H. 46
Kuran, A. 173
Kurup, K. K. N. 186
Kurz, O. 20
Kusunoki, M. 33
Kutsch, 97, 107
Kutscher, R. 70
Kuz'mina, E. E. 75
Kuznetsov, B. I. 192
Kvastad, N. B. 27
Kysar, R. 124

La Barre, W. 27
Labat, R. 3, 70
Labib, P. 88
Labreque, Y. 92
Lackner, W. 124, 134
Lacoste, C. 7, 173
Lactance 134
Ladiges, P. M. 46
Laessøe, J. 2
Laeyendecker, L. 24
Lafleur, W. R. 192
Lafrance, Y. 81
de La Fuente, N. R. 46
Lagarrigue, G. 137
Lagercrantz, S. 46
de La Granja, F. 173
Lai, P. H. 124
Laing, R. D. 17
Lambert, B. 134
Lambert, M. 25
Lambert, W. G. 70
Lambton, A. K. S. 172
Lamei, S. M. 173
Lamirande, E. 124, 134

Lamotte, E. 192
Lanata, G. 124
Landau, D. 116
Landolt, H. 162
Lane, E. 46
Lang, D. M. 76
Langdon M. K. 81
Langholf, V. 82
Langosch, K. 33
Lankester, H. G. 153
Lansing, J. W. 20
Laoust, H. 174
Laoye, J. A. 134
Laperrousaz, E. M. 103
Lapidge, M. 88
Lapidus, I. M. 174
Lapis, B. 156
Lapointe, G. 134
Lapp, P. W. 97
de Lapparent, A. 4
Larés, M. 97
Laroche, E. 76, 78, 79
Laroui, A. 174
Larson, G. J. 186
Lash, C. 134
Latham, J. D. 173, 174
Latifi, D. 174
Lauf, D.-I. 186, 192
Laufs, J. 134
de Laugier de Beaurecueil, S. 163
Laurent, V. 147
Lausberg, M. 82
Lauwers, J. 10, 21, 22
Lawrence, B. B. 174
Lazari-Pawlowska, I. 186
Leach, E. 192
Lebek, W. D. 80
Le Brun, J. 143
Lecerf, 88
Leclant, J. 10, 64, 88
Le Déaut, R. 125
Ledoyen, H. 10
Lee, E. N. 36
Lee, G. M. 134
Lee, J. Y. 46
Leek, F. F. 62
Leemans, W. F. 32, 33, 70
Leertouwer, L. 27
van Leeuwen, C. 97, 102, 107, 115
Lehfeldt, W. 174
Lehmann, H. 46
Leichty, E. 71
Leivestad, R. 116
di Lella, A. A. 97
Leloir, L. 107
Leininger, M. 46
Lemaire, A. 107, 116, 147
Lemberg, M. 30
Lelong, M. 174
Le Moyne, J. 104
Leonce de Constantinople 129
Lépissier, J. 147
Lerner, R. E. 150
Leroi-Gourhan, A. 34
Leroy, J. 141
Leroy, M. V. 134
Lesky, A. 82
Lesko, L. H. 62
Lemerle, P. 89
Lesnickaja, M. M. 82
Le Tourneau, R. 174
Lévêque, P. 82
Levey, M. 174
Levin, L. 107
Levine, B. A. 104
Levine, L. D. 25, 71
Levinson, N. P. 107
Lévi-Strauss, C. 28
Levtzion, N. 174
Lewcock, R. 174
Lewis, B. 172, 174
Lewis, C. 112
de Liagre Böhl, F. M. Th. 34
Libiszowska, M. 10, 22
Lichtheim, M. 63
Lidin, O. G. 198
Liébaert, J. 134
Lifshitz, B. 116
Ligeti, L. 27
Ligier, L. 124
Li-kouang, L. 192
Lilla, S. R. C. 133, 134
Lin, Li-K. 192
Linage Conde, A. 141
Lindell, K. 198
Ling, T. 184
Lingat, R. 186
Lings, M. 162, 163
Lipiński, E. 57, 97, 98, 116
Little, D. P. 174
Litvak, J. 46
Liu, J. T. C. 198
Livingston, J. W. 160
Loader, J. A. 107
van der Lof, L. J. 147
Lohner, E. 34
Lombard, M. 174
Lombard-Salmon, C. 198
Long, B. O. 98, 116
Löning, H. 124
Lopez, R. M. 49
Lorandi, M. 174
Lörincz, L. 27
Lorton, D. 63
Lossky, B. 82
Losier, M. A. 116
Lot-Falck, E. 25
Lotz, J. B. 192
Louis, A. 174
Loundine, A. G. 153, 154
Louys, D. 107
Loving, R. 47
Lowe, A. D. 98
Lowie, R. H. 35
Loza, J. 98
Lozinskij, M. 147
Lucas, H. 200
Luciani, F. 98
Luck, G. 89
Luckert, K. W. 39
Lüddeckens, E. 32, 63
Ludwig, T. M. 107
Lührmann, D. 124
Lukas, R. 47
Lukesch, A. 47
Lüling, G. 154
Lumbwe Mudindaámbi, NG. W. 47
Lunardi, E. 47
Lundbom, J. R. 98
Luomala, K. 47
Lurker, M. 2
Luschnat, O. 124
Luscombe, D. E. 47
Lust, J. 5, 97, 107
Lyczkowska, K. 71
Lys, D. 98

Maas, F. 95
Maas, P. 34
McCarter, P. K. 57, 71, 107
McCarthy, D. J. 107
McCready, N. 22
McCready, W. 22
McCurdy, J. D. 17
Mac Dermot, V. 57
McDermott, J. M. 147
McDermott, W. C. 82
McDonough, Sh. 175
Maceda, M. N. 49
McEvenue, S. E. 98
Mac Ewen, A. M. 47
McGinn, B. 148
Machalski, F. 10
Machilek, F. 148
Macintosh, A. A. 98
Mack, B. L. 112
McKenny, M. G. 47

McKnight, D. 47
McLeod, W. H. 202
McNeill, W. H. 175
Macomber, W. F. 148
Mac Rae, G. W. 34
Madec, G. 135
Madela, L. 51
Maehler, H. 89
Magnarella, P. J. 175
Magnenant, P. 33
Magnin, J. M. 156
Magnus, B. 20
Mahapatra, M. 186
Mahāraj, B. H. B. 186
Mahdi, M. 160
Maher, J. P. 37
Mähler, M. 141
Maiberger, P. 148
Maier, J. 116
Maier, R. A. 37
Maillard, M. 27
Meillausoux, C. 187
Maillot, A. 139
Mainberger, G. 27
Maisonneuve, H. 148
Majer, H. G. 11
Makarius, L. 47
Makdisi, G. 163, 175
Malaise, M. 63, 86
Malalgoda, K. 192
Malamat, A. 10, 22, 71, 98, 119
Maler, B. 116
Mallet, J. 57
Maloney, G. A. 148
Maloney, R. P. 134
Mancini, I. 112
Mande, P. B. 27
Manferdini, T. 134
Manik, L. 10
Mann, U. 17, 34
Manning, E. 141
Mantero, T. 89
Mantran, R. 175
Manzanares de Cirre, M. 175
Ma^{c}oz, M. 175
Maqbul, A. S. 175
Mara, M. G. 139
Maragioglio, V. 63
Marchetti, P. 82
Marco Polo 10
Marcovich, M. 134
Marcus, D. 117
Mareuil, A. 27
Margueron, J.-C. 71
Margul, T. 11
Marichal, R. 124
Mariner, S. 89
Maringer, J. 37
Mario, F. 47
Marmur, D. 116
Maron, G. 148
Maróth, M. 78
Marotta, E. 135
Marquet, Y. 160
Marshall, H. 124
Marshall, I. H. 116
Marsigli, L. F. 175
Marsot, A. L. al-S. 175
Marston Speight, R. 156, 157
Martimort, A. G. 148
Martin, B. G. 170
Martin, F. D. 27
Martin, G. T. 63
Martin, L. H., Jr. 139
Martin, P. M. 82
Martini, C. M. 6
Marx, A. 103
Marx, E. 175
Masamba, M. M. 47
Masimov, I. S. 38
Mason, H. 175
Mason, Ph. 34
Massao, A. 192
Massé, H. 175
Masson, J. 192
Masumi, M. S. H. 175
Matarasso, M. 22
Maten, E. P. 192
Matilal, B. K. 192
Matkovski, A. 176
Matouš, L. 78
Matsumoto, N. 200
Matthews, J. F. 89
Mattock, J. N. 159, 181
Matuz, J. 11, 176
Mawet, F. 82
Maxwell Stuart, P. G. 82
May, J. 196
Mayer, R. 47
Mayes, A. D. H. 116
Mayrhofer, M. 11, 75
Mazahéri, A. 176
Mazar, A. 57
[Mažuranić, M.] 170
Mazzini, I. 148
Mazzoleni, G. 47
Mbiti, J. S. 26
Means Starr, O. 78
Medina, A. 47
Meeks, D. 63
Mees, M. 125, 135
Meggers, B. J. 47
Meggit, M. J. 47
Méhat, A. 134
Meier, F. 156
Meijering, E. P. 135
Meinardus, O. 28, 141
Meinhold, P. 11
Meissner, B. 2, 3
Meissner, N. N. W. 54
Meissner, W. W. 17
Meletinsky, E. 28
Mellon, C. 125
Memmi, A. 107
Ménage, V. L. 172
Ménard, J. E. 98
Mencucci, V. 148
Mendelssohn, K. 63
Mendenhall, G. E. 117
Mensching, G. 11, 35
Menu, M. 22
Merigoux, J. M. 176
Merkel, H. 125
Merkelbach, R. 89
Merklein, H. 125
Mesch, B. 112
Meslin, M. 11
du Mesnil du Buisson, Comte 86, 89
Mesquita, R. 187
Mette, A. 187, 192
Mettinger, T. N. D. 107
Metuh, E. E. 48
Metz, R. 11
Metzger, B. M. 98
Meyer, G. R. 11
de Meyer, L. 71, 75
Meyer, R. 97
Meyerhof, M. 159
Mian, F. 148
Michalowski, K. 148
Michel, D. 98
Michel, O. 125
Michelat, G. 22
Michon, J. L. 163
Middendorp, Th. 117
Middleton, J. 48
Mieli, A. 176
Mijušković, B. 112
Mikkers, E. 148
Milch, R. J. 106
Milik, J. T. 104
Millar, F. 125
Millard, A. R. 70, 71, 73, 74
Miller, E. K. 48
Miller, J. Lane 2
Miller, M. 2
Miller, R. H. 135
Millward, W. G. 176
Minnerath, R. 125

Mioni, E. 141
Miquel, P. 148
Mishra, V. B. 187
Miskel, J. F. 17
Mitomo, K. 193
Mitros, J. 11
Mitrani, Ph. 48
Mittmann, S. 71
Miyakawa, H. 198
Miyata, N. 200
Mizov, N. 23
Moattar, F. 161
Mode, H. 28
Moeller, W. O. 89
Moereels, L. 11
Moinul Haq, S. 163
Mölle, H. 107
Molnar, A. 148
Molthagen, J. 125
Moneim, M. N. F. 176
Monfouga-Nicolas, J. 176
Monnet Saleh, J. 11
Monnot, G. 89
Monsengwo Pasinya, L. 98
Montanari, F. 82
del Monte, G. F. 77. 78. 79
Montoya, S. J. 48
de Moor, J. C. 78, 117
Moore, R. I. 148
Moorey, P. R. S. 71
Moortgat, A. 2
Moortgat-Correns, U. 71
Moos, G. D. 48
Morag, S. 99
Moraldi, L. 12
Morard, F.-E. 141
Morenz, S. 63
Morgan, F. B. 193
Morgan, G. 82
Morgan, R. 35
Moriarty, F. L. 34, 71
Morin, J. A. 125
Morocho Gayo, G. 82
Morris, R. R. 17
Morrow, F. J., Jr. 104
Mortley, R. 135
Morton, R. 42
Morton-Williams, P. 40
Moskovszky, E. 82
Mottahedeh, R. 176
Mourelatos, A. P. D. 36
Mourlon Beernaert, P. 125
Moursi, M. I. 63
Mueller, D. 61, 139
Mueller, S. A. 17
Muffs, Y. 117
Mugler, C. 28
Muhitdinov, H. Ju. 89
Mühlenberg, E. 112
Mukhtār, ᶜA. al-M. 176
Mulder, D. C. 28
Mulhall, M. M. 108
Müller, G. H. 23
Müller, K. 125
Müller, K. F. 14
Müller, N. 187
Müller, R. 81
Müller, W. 28
Müller, W. W. 12, 153
Müller-Christensen, S. 176
Müller-Schwefe, H. R. 12
Munk, E. 112
Muñoz Jimenez, R. 160
Munro, P. 61
Munters, Q. J. 23
Münzel, M. 48
Muraoka, T. 104
Murdoch, B. 99
Murphy, R. F. 35
Murray, J. 48
Murray, R. 135
Murti, T. R. V. 193
Musgrave Calder III, W. 82
Mushirul-Haq 176
Muslehuddin, M. 176
Muzungu, B. 48
Mylius, K. 187
Myszor, W. 12

Nader, A. 12
Nagel, H. 107
Nagel, P. 12, 89
Nagel, T. 156
Nai Rhee, S. 117
Nakamura, H. 28
Nakhnikian, G. 125
Napoli, G. 156
Nasr, S. H. 160, 163, 176
Naster, P. 71
Naŝturel, P. S. 148
Nath, G. 187
an-Naubahti, al-Ḥ. b. M. 160
Naudon, P. 89
Nautin, P. 135
Naveh, J. 75
Nebe, G. W. 104
Nebel, P. A. 48
Nevada, J. 117
Nedungatt, G. 125
Negretti, N. 108
Neiman, D. 32, 99
Neirynck, F. 12, 125
Nelis, J. T. 100
Nelsen, H. M. 23
Nelson, D. F. 20
Nelson, G. K. 23
Nemeth, J. 176
Nemoy, L. 117, 176
Nenola-Kallio, A. 12
Nersès Šnorhali 148
Nettler, R. L. 160
Neu, F. 78
Neumann, F. J. 48
Neumann, G. 78, 79
Neumann, P. K. D. 99
Neusner, J. 99, 104, 108, 117, 118
Newbery, S. J. 48
Newby, G. D. 156
Newsome, J. D., Jr. 99
Niccacci, A. 63
Nicholson, E. W. 99
Nicolaescu-Plopşor, D. 54
Nicoulitsé, I. T. 54
Niangoran-Bouah, G. 48
Nichols, R. L. 149
Nicholson, E. W. 106
Nickelsburg, G. W. E., Jr. 99, 139
de Nicola, A. 99
Nielsen, E. 99
Nijenhuis, J. 202
Nijland, C. 34
Nikiprovetzky, V. 112
Nimtz, A., Jr. 12
Niyogi, P. 193
Noack, B. 104, 117
Noah, M. M. 117
Nober, P. 12
Noer, D. 176
Noethlichs, K. L. 149
Noggler, A. 48
Noguera, E. 48
Noja, S. 12
di Nola, A. M. 1
Nöldeke, Th. 154
Nolte, B. 65
Noret, J. 149
Norris, H. T. 176
Norris, R. B. 12
North, R. 12, 78, 99
Nosowski. J. 177
Noth, A. 156, 177
Nougayrol, J. 25, 66, 71, 72
Nowaczyk, M. 23
Nowak, E. 149
Nowotny, K. A. 28
Noyes, R., Jr. 82
Numazawa, K. 200
van Nunen, B. O. 48
Nwyia, P. 163

Oakes, R. A. 28
Oberhuber, K. 72
Obeyesekere, G. 193
O'Callaghan, J. 104
Ochoa, L. 48
O'Connell, R. J. 135
Oelsner, J. 12, 57, 66
Offenberg, A. K. 12
O'Flaherty, W. D. 187
Ögel, S. 177
Ogibenin, B. L. 28
Ogiermann, H. 20
Ohana, M. 108
Ohata, K. 117
Ohnuki-Tierney, E. 48, 49
Okechukwu Odita, E. 23
Olan, L. A. 108
Oliver, V. L. 202
Olschak, B. C. 190, 193
Oman, G. 177
Omoyajowo, J. A. 49
Öney, G. 177
Önnerfors, A. 33
Oosten, J. G. 12, 42
Opelt, I. 135
Oppenheim, A. L. 1, 72
Oppermann, M. 54
Orban, M. 83
Orbe, A. 135, 139, 140
Orbell, M. 49
O'Reilly, P. 12
Orlandi, T. 57, 90, 135
Oroz, J. 83
Orozbaev, P. R. 177
Orozz Reta, J. 135
Orr, D. G. 83
Orrieux, C. 117
Orsolić, M. 23
O'Shaughnessy, T. J. 156
Oshima, S. 20
Otten, H. 2, 12, 78, 79
Otterbein, Ch. S. 49
Otterbein, K. F. 49
Otto, E. 2
Otto, S. 132
Otzen, B. 104
Ouellette, J. 99, 107
Outtier, B. 135
Oxtoby, W. G. 12

de Pablo Maroto, D. 125
Padberg, W. 37
Padró, J. 90
Paepe, R. 71
Pagels, E. H. 125
Pairault, C. 28
Palgen, R. 149
Pallis, M. 187
Palokruševa, G. 177
Palomares Ibañez, J. M. 141
Palubicki, W. 63
Pani Ermini, L. 13
Panyagua, E. R. 83
Panoff, M. 28
Pantůčková, E. 177
Pao, K. 193
Papdopoulo, A. 177
Paper, H. H. 99
Parássoglou, G. M. 90
Pardee, D. 104
Paret, R. 13, 156, 160
Park, J. 49
Parpola, A. 10
Parpola, S. 10
Parrett, J. K. 44
Parrinder, G. 41, 46
Parrot, A. 13, 72, 114
Parsons, R. T. 34
Parvulascu, A. 187
Paslick, R. H. 193
Pasternak, B. 198
Pathirana-Wimaladharma, K. 193
Pätsch, G. 26
Paul, H. C. 163
Paul, S. 49
Paul, Sh. M. 108
Pauliny, J. 177
Paulme, D. 34
Pavón Maldonado, B. 177
Payne, W. D. 18
Pearce, R. A. 99
Pecorella, P. E. 76
Pegueroles, J. 135
Peifer, C. 141
Peli, P. 112
Pelikan, J. 149
Pellat, C. 5, 157, 160
Pelli, M. 112, 117
Peñamaria, A. 135
Pennington, B. 34
Perczak, E. 28
Pereira, P. A. H. 49
Pericot, L. 34
Perkins, A. 90
Person, Y. 13
Pesch, R. 126
Peschlow-Bindokat, A. 83
Pestman, P. W. 31
Peter, M. 99
Petersen, D. L. 95
Petersmann, H. 83
Peterson, B. E. J. 63
Peterson, D. L. 108
Petit, P. 13, 85, 136
Petitdemange, G. 112
Petit-Klinkenberg, D. 28
Petitmengin, P. 129, 136
Petolescu, C. 90
Petschow, H. 72
Petschow, H. P. H. 108
Pettinato, G. 72, 73
Petzold, K.-E. 83
Peyraube, A. 198
Pfeifer, G. 1, 13, 107
Pfeil, H. 20
Phaire, B. R. 149
Phillips, A. 108
Philon d'Alexandrie 112
Pichon, J. C. 28
Picken, S. D. B. 20
Pickering, W. S. F. 23
Pigeaud, J. 83
Pighi, G. B. 83
Pigott, S. 54
Piker, S. 193
Pincherle, A. 136
Pingree, D. 160
Piotrovskij, B. B. 79
des Places, E. 87, 115
Plack, A. 49
Plancke, M. 177
Plaskowicka-Rymkiewicz, St. 177
Platvoet, J. G. 49
Plessner, M. 112
Pleuss, P. 49
de Plinval, G. 136
van der Ploeg, J. P. M. 104
Pocock, D. F. 187
Poethke, G. 91
Poirier, M. 136
Polak, A. 166, 177
Poliakov, L. 112
Pollak-Eltz, A. 28, 49, 53
Polo, Marco 10
Polonskaja, L. 13
Pomponio, F. 72
Pontal, O. 149
Poonawala, I. K. 177
Popma, K. J. 136
Popov, I. V. 149
Popova, T. V. 136
Popović, A. 13
Poppe, N. 49
Pöschl, V. 83
Posener, G. 63
Posern-Zielińska, M. 49
Pospelov, G. 23
Postgate, J. N. 72

Potin, J. 108
Potratz, J. A. H. 79
Pötscher, W. 83
Pouillon, J. 49
Poulain, J. 20
Poushinsky, J. M. 49
Poushinsky, N. W. 49
Power, D. 23
Preiss, Th. 138
Presler, H. H. 34
Prete, S. 136
Preuss, H. D. 99
Price, R. 49
Prigent, P. 136
Pritchard, J. B. 34, 90
Proclus Arabus 158
Prozorov, S. M. 160
Prunner, G. 198
Pseudo-Chrysostome 129
Puech, E. 154
Puech, H. Ch. 2
Puin, G. R. 178
Putscher, M. 28
Pye, M. 35

Quacquarelli, A. 136
Quagebeur, J. 92
Quecke, H. 88, 89, 141, 149
Quispel, G. 87, 90
Qitta, H. 37

Raats, P. J. 49
Rabin, C. 99
Rabinovič, E. G. 72
Rabinowitz, I. 104
von Rad, G. 99, 108
Radday, Y. T. 100
Radwan, A. 63
Rafikov, A. Ch. 178
Rahman, M. 163
Rahmani, A. A. 178
Rahmann, R. 49
Rahner, K. 149
Ralston, W. H., Jr. 100
Ramirez, G. 50
Ramsaran, J. A. 29
Ranger, T. 50
Rao, S. R. 38
Rapaport, I. 72
Ras, J. J. 187
Raschid, F. 72
Raschke, V. 17
Rašev, R. 50
Rasheed, Gh. D. 160
Rassadin, V. I. 55
Rathofer, J. 33
Ratschow, C. H. 13
Raum, O. F. 50
Rawson, E. 83
Ray, B. 50
Reboul, O. 20
Recio, A. 149
Reddy, A. M. 187
Redford, D. B. 63, 65, 117
Redjala, M. 178
Reed, W. L. 154
Reekmans, T. 34
Regamey, C. 193
Regnault, L. 141
Reiche, R. 149
Reif, S. C. 110
Reiling, J. 126
Reincke, G. 13
Reiner, E. 1, 72
Reinert, B. 163
Reines, A. J. 112
Reinhardt, W. W. 136
Reinink, G. J. 133
Reisman, D. 72
Rekaya, M. 178
Rempel, L. 164
Remy, J. 23
Renard, M. 90
Renda, G. 178
Renehan, R. 126
Renger, j. 70, 73
Rengstorf, K. H. 6, 35
Reno, St. J. 29
Renou, L. 35
Renoux, C. 136
Resch, A. 35
Resner, G. 44
Resnick, L. 20
Retel-Laurentin, A. 44, 176
Reutterer, R. 126
Revel-Neher, E. 126
Reviv, H. 10
Revunenkova, E. V. 50
Reymond, E. A. E. 63, 64, 149
Reynolds, C. J. 193
Reynolds, D. K. 17
Reynolds, F. 193
Reynolds, F. E. 193
Riad, E. 160
Riaz, M. 90, 178
Ribar, J. W. 108
Richard, J. G. 29
Richard, L. 55
Richard, L. A. 126
Richards, A. 50
Richards, D. S. 172, 178
Richards, J. V. O. 50
Richardson, C. C. 126, 140
Richardson, J. T. 17
Riché, P. 50
Riché, S. 141
Richter, G. M. A. 57
Richter, W. 107
Ricke, H. 64
Rickenbacher, O. 3
Ridenhour, T. E. 100
le Rider, G. 4
Riemschneider, K. 79
Ries, J. 13, 90
van Riet, G. 149
Riga, P. J. 136
Rigby, A. 23
Rijk, C. A. 150
Rikin, W. M. 178
Rinaldi, C. 63
Rinaldi, G. 3, 90
Ringgren, H. 13
von Rintelen, F. J. 20
Riou, A. 150
Ripoli, A. M. 163
Riskin, S. 108
Rist, J. M. 90
Rivière, J. C. 29
Rizvi, S. S. A. 178
Rizvić, M. 178
Robe, S. L. 35
Robert, L. 4, 83
Roberts, J. J. 108
Robichon, C. 64
Robichon, M. 126
Robinson, J. 100
Robinson, J. D. 35
Robinson, J. M. 35, 89
Robson, J. 156
Roché, D. 150
des Rochettes, J. M. 126
van Roey, A. 150
Rogers, J. M. 177, 178
Röhr, H. 29
Röhrborn, K. 178
Rolland, P. 187
Röllig, W. 2, 79
Roloff, J. 126
Rombach, H. 29
Ronart, N. 2
Ronart, S. 2
Róna-Tas, A. 29
Roncaglia, M. 155, 156
Roncoroni, A. 136
Rondeau, M. J. 90
Roques, R. 150
Rordorf, W. 126
Rorty, R. M. 36
Rosen, L. N. 29, 50
Rosenbloom, J. R. 117

Rosenfeld, H. 55
Rosengarten, Y. 72
Rosenkranz, B. 77
Rosenstiehl, J. M. 100
Rosenthal, E. I. J. 31
Rosenthal, F. 178
Rosenthal, R. 53
Rosenwasser, A. 59, 64
Rosenzweig, F. 112
Roshwald, M. 112, 117
Roslon, J. W. 126
de Rossi, I. B. 150
Rost, L. 13
Rotermund, H. O. 200
Roth, S. 112
Rougemont, G. 83
Rougier, L. 126
Roulleau, D. 83
Roquette, J. 13
Roux, J.-P. 2, 178, 179
Roy, A. 23
van Roy, H. 50
Royce, J. 13
Rožanskij, I. D. 85
Ruben, W. 184
Rubin, V. 198
Rubinson, K. S. 76
Rücker, H. 108
Rudberg, S. Y. 13
Rudolph, K. 2, 3, 7, 14, 90, 156, 157
Rudolph, W. 100
Ruegg, D. S. 193
Ruelland, S. 50
Ruiz Figueroa, M. 179
Ruppert, F. 142
Ruster-Werner, Ch. 78
Ryan, J. D. 150
Ryckmans, J. 34, 154

Saake, H. 126
Saake, W. 52
Šabanović, H. 179
Sabattini, P. T. A. 137
Sabattini, T. A. 137
Sabourin, L. 29
Sabugal, S. 137
Sacchi, P. 100
Sacks, J. 112
Sadan, J. 179
Sadek, A.-A. F. 64
Sadat, D. R. 179
Sadjadi, Z. 29
Saeger, R. 17
Safrand, S. 125
Said, S. 160
Ṣāᶜid b. al-Ḥ. 180
Saiyidain, K. G. 156
Saito, Sh. 14
Salditt-Trappmann, R. 57
Saleh, A.-A. 64
al-Salihi, W. 72
Salim, Gh. 179
Salonen, A. 72
Salvieng, de Marseille 137
Salvini, M. 76
Samain, E. 126
Samarin, W. 23
Samb, A. 179
Samir, K. 150
Samson, J. 64
Samuel, A. E. 64
Samuel, D. H. 34
Sánchez-Albornoz, C. 179
Sanders, E. P. 108
Sanders, J. A. 32, 104
Sandesara, B. J. 185
Sandmel, S. 112
San Nicolo, M. 91
Ṣanquer, R. 55, 83
Šanjek, F. 150
Sansterre, J. M. 137
Santer, M. 137
Santiago Simon, E. 179
Santini, C. 83
Santos, A. 150
Sapin, J. 14
Saporetti, C. 5, 73
Sarasvatī, S. 187
Sarestha, B. P. 186
Sarma, E. R. S. 14
Sasson, J. M. 73, 100
Sauget, J. M. 16, 141
Saunders, T. J. 83, 84
Sauneron, S. 14, 64
Sauren, H. 73
de Savignac, J. 126
Savino, E. 84
Savon, R. 132
Sawyer, S. F. A. 100, 108
Sawaguchi, T. 198
Sawyerr, H. A. E. 50
Sbrzesny, H. 50
Scarcia, G. 179
Scazzoso, P. 137
Scerrato, U. 179
Schachermeyr, F. 91
Schacht, J. 159
Schaendlinger, A. C. 179
Schäfer, P. 108
Schaffer, B. 154
Scharbert, J. 107, 108
Schatkin, M. 32, 137
Schäublin, C. 137
Schefold, K. 84
Schefold, R. 50
Schein, B. E. 126
Scheindlin, R. P. 179
Schenke, H. M. 140
Scheuer, J. 2
Schiff F. 84
Schiff Giorgini, M. 64
Schilling, R. 29, 84
Schilling, W. 14
Schiltknecht, H. R. 100
Schimmel, A. 14, 155, 160, 162, 163, 170, 172, 179
Schindler, A. 137
Schindler, H. 50
Schipperges, H. 142, 160
Schippmann, K. 14, 76
Schlanger, J. 113
Schlegel, A. 51
Schlemmer, A. 20
Schlerath, B. 76
Schlette, F. 37
Schlette, H. R. 20
Schlick, J. 11
Schlink, E. 150
Schlosser, K. 51
Schlumberger, D. 76, 91
Schlumberger, E. 55
Schmedding, B. 179
Schmelzer, M. H. 7
Schmid, H. 100
Schmid, H. H. 150
Schmider, B. 14
Schmidt, E. G. 81
Schmidt, H. P. 76, 187
Schmidt, J. M. 118
Schmidt, L. 35
Schmidt, R. 11
Schmidt, S. 51
Schmidt, V. 84
Schmidt, W. 51
von Schmidt, W. A. 29
Schmieschen, P. M. 150
Schmithausen, L. 194
Schmitt, A. 118, 127
Schmitt, R. 14
Schmitz, R. 161
Schmitz-Valckenberg, G. 150
Schmökel, H. 71
Schmöle, K. 137
Schmucker, W. 157
Schneemelcher, W. 150
Schneider, H. D. 64
Schneider, R. 154
Schneider, U. 187
Schnutenhaus, F. 14
Schoedel, W. R. 127

Spencer, P. 51
Sperber, A. 101
Spero, S. 113
Speth, W. W. 35
Speyer, W. 84
Spicq, C. 127
Spies, O. 10, 161, 164, 170, 180, 182
Spieser, J. M. 15
Spilka, B. 18
Spinka, M. 148
Spiridonakis, B. S. 181
Spoer, A. 51
Spranz, B. 51
Springer, J. L. 91
Sprung, M. 35, 194
Spuler, B. 170, 175, 181
Spuler, U. 181
Spuropoulos, A. G. 181
Spycket, A. 73
Srinivasan, D. 30, 188
Staal, J. F. 185
Stalder, K. 138
Stählin, G. 35
Starlowa, K. B. 105
Starr, Ch. G. 38
Staviskii, B. J. 194
Stchoukine, I. 181
Stead, G. C. 138
Steck, O. H. 101
Steenstrup, C. 200
Stehly, R. 103, 136
Steinkellner, E. 188, 194
Steinsalz, A. 118
Steitz, H. 151
Stellway, R. J. 22
Stemberger, G. 109
Stendenbach, F. J. 109
Stephens, K. 194
Stephenson, G. 188
Stepanyants, M. T. 161
Stepniowski, W. 84
Sterly, J. 51
Stern, J. 82
Stettler, M. 30
Stevenson, I. 194
Stewart, C. C. 181
Stewart, D. 20
Stewart, E. K. 181
Stewart, K. 51
Stewart, K. M. 51
Stiehl, R. 31
Stiernon, D. 141, 151
Stillman, Y. K. 30
Stinespring, W. F. 35
Stitskin, L. D. 113
Stjernquist, B. 55
Stöger, A. 127
Stolz, F. 109
Stone, M. E. 101
Störk, L. 64
Straton, G. D. 18
Strauss, D. F. 127
Strayer, J. R. 151
Streng, F. J. 194
de Strijcker, E. 35
Strika, V. 181
Strobel, A. 14, 127
Strohmaier, G. 161, 181
Strömberg, M. 55
Stuart, P. 55
Stuart, S. S., Jr. 101
Stucki, R. 4
Stucky, R. A. 91
Stuhlmueller, C. 117
Stuiber, A. 138
Suhl, A. 151
Sukeo, H. 30
Sundermann, W. 76
Susnik, B. 51
Suzuki, P. T. 52
Swanson, G. E. 52
Swarney, P. R. 91
Swartley, W. M. 138
Swartz, M. 161
Swearer, D. 195
Swearer, D. K. 195
Ṣwerdlow, N. 161
Świderski, S. 52
Swienko, H. 15
Szabó, G. 77, 79
Szczudlowski, M. 63
Szirmai, K. 91

Tacchi Venturi, P. 3
Tadmor, H. 71
Taillandier, M. N. 55
Takasaki, J. 193
Takeuchi, A. 195
Talbi, M. 181
Tamani, G. 15, 118
Tambiah, S. J. 195
Tamer, A. 161
Tang, Chün-i 199
Taniguchi, Y. 55
Tardieu, M. 92
Tarnay, A. 151
Taschkandi, S. E. 180
Taureck, B. 20
Tawfik, S. 64
al-Ṭayālisī 156
Taylor, J. 138
Tealdi, C. J. 20
Tedeschi, S. 181
Teichmann, F. 61
Temming, R. L. 36
Teo, W. K. H. 195
Ternant, P. 127
Testa, P. E. 151
Tetsui, Y. 201
Tetz, M. 138
Thaniel, G. 84
Thausing, G. 64, 92
Théodoridès, A. 65
Theumissen W. P. 151
Thiel, J. F. 15, 62
Thils, G. 15
Thissen, H. J. 32
Thomas, C. F. 113
Thomas, D. 195
Thomas, D. W. 36
Thomas, M. 15
Thomas, R. 151
Thomas, W. 186
Thomov, T. 92
Thompson, G. R. 84
Thomsen, P. 15
Thomson, R. W. 138
Thouless, R. H. 18
Thrower, J. 50
Thümmel, H. G. 127
Tielsch, E. 127
Tibawi, A. L. 180
Tietze, A. 31
Timm, K. 181
Timothy, H. B. 138
Titley, N. 181
Todorov, T. 52
Top, S. 30
Torelli, P. 52
Torres, L. A. 52
Tóth, I. 84
Tournay, R. 101
Towner, W. S. 109
Townson, D. 181
Trager, F. 15
Tran Tam Tinh, V. 92
Trede, J. H. 21
Trégaro, L. 18
Treu, K. 118
Trigger, B. G. 65
Trimingham, J. S. 163
Trocme, E. 127
Tröger, K. W. 92
Tropper, D. 109
Trouillard, J. 92
Trout, J. M. III, 151
Tsering, P. 190
Tsuji, S. G. 151
Tucci, G. 15
Turk, A. 181

Scholem, G. 113
Scholer, D. M. 14
Scholten, R. G. 23
Schoneveld, J. 100, 109
Schoors, A. 100
Schottroff, W. 109
Schramm, W. 73
Schreckenberg, H. 118
Schrey, H. H. 23
Schröder, D. 29
Schub, D. 198
Schubert, J. 190, 192, 194
Schubert, K. 127
Schubert, U. 127
Schuhl, P. M. 91
van Schuler, E. 79
van Schuler-Schömig, I. 51
Schulz, H. 98, 100
Schulz, W. 20
Schulze, B. 151
Schunck, K. D. 100
Schüngel-Straumann, H. 101
Schuon, F. 161
Schuttermayr, G. 101
Schützinger, H. 157, 180
Schwanz, P. 127
Schwarte, K. H. 137
Schwartz, J. 137
Schwartz, S. P. 55
Schwarz, P. 29
Schwarz, W. 91
Schwyzer, H. R. 88
Scobie, C. H. H. 151
Seckinger, D. S. 113
Sed, N. 91, 151
Sedar-Senghor, L. 33
See, Ch. 198
Seebass, H. 101
Séd, N. 109
Segal, J. B. 73, 108
van Segbroeck, F. 12
Ségré, A. 118
Seibert, J. 91
Seifert, J. 11
Seljuq, A. 180
Sellers, J. 24
Sellheim, R. 95
Sellnow, I. 37
van Selms, A. 101, 109
Senarclens de Grancy, R. 22
Sendrail, M. 109
Seneviratne, H. L. 194
Sermonetta, J. B. 113
Serr, J. 137
Servais, E. 23
Sesboüé, B. 137
van Severus, E. 141
Seybold, K. 101, 109
Seydou, C. 14
Seyrig, H. 154
Sezgin, F. 180
Sezgin, U. 180
Sfameni Gasparro, G. 91
Shaban, M. A. 180
Shah, H. 42
Shah, Mir H. 180
Shahid, I. 154
Shāh Walī Allāh 162
Shaked, Sh. 75
Shapiro, S. 29
Sharma, B. N. K. 188
Sharma, U. 188, 194
Sharpe, E. J. 31
Sharpe, J. L. III, 101
Shatzmiller, J. 118
Shaw, S. J. 180
Shea, J. 17
Shehadi, F. A. 159
Sheikh, M. S. 161
Shelton, J. C. 35
Sherwin, B. L. 109
Shih, J. 198
von Sicard, H. 29
Siclari, A. 137
Sidler, N. 24
Sieben, H. J. 137, 138
Sieber, J. H. 91
Siegert, F. 118
Siegler, K. G. 64
Sijpestijn. P. J. 65
Silberg, M. 109
Silver, A. M. 109
Silver, D. J. 118
Simionescu, P. 29
Simon, H. 171
Simon, I. 113
Simon, M. 22, 127
Simon, P. J. 194
Simon, S. J. 84
Simonetti, M. 91
Simpson, C. A. 51
Simpson, W. K. 64, 84
Sims-Silliams, N. 151
Simundson, D. N. 202
Singer, M. 193
Singer, S. A. 109
Singh, S. B. 188
Sinha, N. Ch. 194
Sinnige, T. G. 84
Siraždinov, S. Ch. 180
Siroux, M. 180
Sivaraman, K. 188
von Sivers, P. 180
Sjöberg, Å. W. 73
Skehan, P. W. 105
Skrzypek, M. 14
Skurzak, L. 186
Slanikov, I. 17
Slater, W. J. 85
Şlingerland, H. D. 101
Śliwa, J. 64
Smidt, H. 36
Smith, A. D. 24
Smith, B. L. 194
Smith, C. T. 194
Smith, D. R. 84
Smith, G. R. 174
Smith, H. S. 64
Smith, J. I. 180, 194
Smith, J. L. 27
Smith, J. Z. 15
Smith, P. 30
in der Smitten, W. Th. 76, 101, 118
Smolik, J. 151
Smulders, P. 132
Snaith, N. 109
Snellgrove, D. L. 194
Snesarev, G. P. 76
Sobosan, J. G. 18, 127
von Soden, H. 91
von Soden, W. 2, 3, 15, 57, 70
Soggin, J. A. 118
Sokolowski, F. 84
Sokol'skij, N. I. 84
de Solages, B. 127
Soler, J. 109
Soliman, A. el-S. 180
Sollberger, E. 56, 73
Solodukho, Y. A. 118
Solomon, A. 113
Solomonik, E. I. 91
Sommet, J. 20
Somogyi, A. 151
Sönmez, E. 180
Soper, A. C. 198
Soss, N. M. 113
Souček, V. 79
Sourdel, D. 180
Sourdel-Thomine, J. 180
de Sousberghe, L. 39, 40, 51, 53
Southern, R. W. 180
Soutou, A. 38
Soyez, B. 79
Soymié, M. 15
Soze, A. A. A. K. 180
Spae, J. 200
Spaemann, R. 30
Specker, J. 51
Speight, R. M. 156, 157

Türkdogan, O. 175
Turner, B. S. 23
Turner, C. J. G. 151
Turner, V. 30
Tyloch, W. 32, 105, 138

Ubald, T. P. 52
Uebel, F. 86
Ullmann, M. 181
Ulrich, F. 21
Ünal, R. H. 182
Unger, D. J. 138
van Unnik, W. C. 127, 128
Urbán, A. C. 105
Urvoy, D. 182
Ussishkin, D. 118
Utas, Bo 163
ᶜUthmān b. Fūdī 165
Uysal, A. E. 182

von Vacano, O. W. 54
Vajda, G. 113, 118
Valgiglio, E. 84
van der Valk, M. H. 31
Valloggia, M. 9
Valls, R. M. 85
Vana, L. 188
Vanden Berghe, L. 74, 76
Vandermarck, W. 151
Vandersleyen, C. 65
Vandier d'Abbadie, J. 65
Van't Dack, E. 35
Varona Garcia, M. A. 152
Vasilescu, E. 76
Vattioni, F. 57, 118, 152, 154
de Vaux, R. 101, 105, 118
Vawter, B. 128
Vázquez de Benito, M. de la C. 182
Veenhof, K. R. 73
de Veer, A. C. 15, 138
Veghazi, E. N. 15
Veiga Ferriera, O. 38
te Velde, H. 65
Velimirović, M. 152
van Velzen-Van Wetering, W. Th. 44
Vereno, M. 128
Vergote, J. 65
Verheijen, L. M. J. 138, 141
Vermes, G. 119
Vermes, P. 113
Vernant, J. P. 84
Vernon, G. M. 18
Vernus, P. 65
Verstraelen, E. 52
Veselovsky, N. 161
Vetter, T. E. 195
Vezin, G. 128
Vialelle, M. 143
Vidal de Brandt, M. M. 30
Vidal-Naquet, P. 84, 85
Vidman, L. 88
Vila, A. 65
Vilanova, E. 128
Vilela, A. 138
Villegas, F. 142
Vincent, S. 52
Vink, A. J. 15
Višnevskaja, O. A. 30
Vlastos, G. 36
Vogel, C. 152
Vogels, W. 109
Vogler, P. 52
Vogt, E. Z. 52
Vogt, H. 93
Vogt, H. J. 138
de Vogüé, A. 142
Vööbus, A. 152
Vorbichler, A. 30, 52
Vos, F. 195
Vredenbregt, J. 52
de Vries, G. J. 85
de Vries, S. J. 101

Waardenburg, J. D. J. 16, 30, 182
Wachtel, N. 52
Waddell, N. 195
Waetzoldt, H. 69
Wagner, E. 161, 182
Wagner, F. 33
Wagner, G. 64, 92
Waida, M. 30
Wainwright, W. J. 30
Wakeman, M. K. 102
Waldman, M. R. 175
Waldmann, H. 92
Walker, W. S. 182
Walla, M. 85
van de Walle, B. 11, 63
Wallis, G. 15, 36, 77, 95, 97, 101, 102, 114
van der Walt, B. J. 152
Walter, C. 152
Walters, P. 102
Walters, S. D. 73
Walzer, S. 191
Wangyal, G. Th. 193
Wangyal, Th. 190
Wanke, G. 99
Wankenne, A. 58
Ward, K. 21
Ward, W. A. 57
Warder, A. K. 193, 195
Wathen, A. 142
Warren, M. A. C. 31
Watanabo, H. 52
Waters, K. H. 85
Watt, W. M. 161, 182
Waugh, E. 161
Weaver, M. 113
Weber-Schäfer, P. 199
Wedderburn, A. J. M. 128
von Wedemeyer, I. 53
Wehr, G. 18
Weidkuhn, P. 53
Weidner, E. 2
von Weiher, E. 70
Weil, G. E. 102
Wein, C. 161
Weinberg, J. P. 109, 119
Weinfeld, M. 30, 58, 110
Weinke, K. 21
Weinstein, J. M. 65
Weippert, H. 99, 102, 119
Weippert, M. 119
Weischer, B. M. 163
Weiss, H. F. 110
Weiss, J. F. 137
Weissmahr, B. 152
Wellard, J. 55
Weller, F. 16, 35, 195
Wells, P. 128
Welte, B. 30
Welten, P. 102
Wenig, S. 64
Wente, E. F., Jr. 64
Werblowsky, R. J. Z. 110
Werner, E. 156
Werner, K. 195
Werner, R. 53, 79
Werth, R. N. 152
Wessels, A. 157
Wessetzky, V. 65
Westendorf, W. 61
Westermann, C. 3, 102, 110
Whinfield, E. H. 163
White, H. C. 102
White, P. S. 128
White, W., Jr. 105
Whybray, R. N. 100
Widengren, Geo 2, 57, 76, 161
Wiefeld, W. 125, 126
Wiener, M. S. 109
Wiessner, G. 36
van Wijngaarden, W. D. 65
Wijngaards, J. N. M. 102
Wilber, D. N. 182

Wilbert, J. 53
Wilcke, C. 73, 74
Wild, H. 62
Wildung, D. 65
Wilhelm, G. 74
Wilhelm, H. 195
Will, E. 58
Willaime, J. P. 24
Willemaers, N. 79
Willemen, Ch. 195
Williams, P. V. A. 53
Williams, R. J. 61
Willi-Plein, I. 102
Willis, J. T. 102
Wilms, F. E. 102
Wilson, F. 184, 188
Wilson, H. A. 195
Wilson, J. A. 36, 65
Wilson, R. R. 102
Winnett, F. V. 154
Winter, E. 60, 65
Wirth, G. 91
Wiseman, D. J. 2, 102
Witakowski, W. 119
Wolf, W. 64
Wolfe, H. N. 70
Wolff, H. W. 102
Wolski, W. 54, 92
Wood, Jr. 17
Woodard, W. S. 85
Wortmann, D. 65
van der Woude, A. S. 35, 102
Wright, G. R. H. 92, 154
Wright, R. M. 65
Wucherer-Huldenfeld, A. 18
Wurm, H. 175
Würthwein, E. 102
Wymeersch, P. 53

Xella, P. 74, 79

Yadin, Y. 119
Yalaoui, M. 182
Yalman, N. 182, 195
Yamaori, T. 195
Yamauchi, E. M. 92
Yanuck, M. 183
Yarnold, E. J. 138
Yaron, R. 74
Yaron, Z. 119
Yildiz, H. D. 183
Yocum, G. E. 188
Yoshio, W. 201
Young, D. C. 85
Young, F. M. 128
Young, M. J. L. 169
Yovel, Y. 21
Yoyotte, J. 58
Yu, D. C. 199
Yuyama, A. 196
Yuzbashian, K. N. 152

Zac, S. 113
Zaccagnini, C. 58
Začinović, J. 183
Zafrani, H. 119
Zago, M. 196
Zaidi, S. M. H. 16
Zain-ul-Abedeen 157
Zandee, J. 61, 65, 102
Zaphiris, G. 138
Zauzich, K. Th. 32
Zehrer, F. 128
Zeitlin, S. 119
Zeller, W. 142
Zellweger, S. 85
Zelzer, K. 140
Zerbib, M. 110
Zeron, A. 119
Zevaco, P. 24
Ziegler, A. C. 51
Ziegler, J. 85
Zimmerli, W. 103
Zimmermann, F. 53
Zimmermann, F. W. 161
Zimmermann, G. 53, 142
Zinn, G. Z. 30
Zlotnick, D. 113
Zobel, H. J. 118, 119
Zoberman, N. 107
Zoberman, S. 107
Zoega, G. 16
Zolla, E. 53
Zschietzschmann, W. 53
Zubizarreta, J. L. 72
Zuidema, R. T. 53
Zukovskaja, N. L. 196
Zürcher, E. 199
Zwernemann, J. 53